Love and the Working Class

Love and the Working Class

*The Inner Worlds of
Nineteenth Century Americans*

KAREN LYSTRA

OXFORD
UNIVERSITY PRESS

Oxford University Press is a department of the University of Oxford. It furthers
the University's objective of excellence in research, scholarship, and education
by publishing worldwide. Oxford is a registered trade mark of Oxford University
Press in the UK and certain other countries.

Published in the United States of America by Oxford University Press
198 Madison Avenue, New York, NY 10016, United States of America.

© Oxford University Press 2024

All rights reserved. No part of this publication may be reproduced, stored in
a retrieval system, or transmitted, in any form or by any means, without the
prior permission in writing of Oxford University Press, or as expressly permitted
by law, by license, or under terms agreed with the appropriate reproduction
rights organization. Inquiries concerning reproduction outside the scope of the
above should be sent to the Rights Department, Oxford University Press, at the
address above.

You must not circulate this work in any other form
and you must impose this same condition on any acquirer.

Library of Congress Cataloging-in-Publication Data
Names: Lystra, Karen, author.
Title: Love and the working class : the inner worlds of 19th century Americans / Karen Lystra.
Description: New York, NY : Oxford University Press, [2024] |
Includes bibliographical references and index.
Identifiers: LCCN 2023040351 (print) | LCCN 2023040352 (ebook) |
ISBN 9780197514221 (hardback) | ISBN 9780197514245 (epub)
Subjects: LCSH: Working class—United States—History—19th century. |
Love-letters—United States—History—19th century. |
Literacy—United States—History—19th century.
Classification: LCC HD 8070 .L978 2023 (print) | LCC HD 8070 (ebook) |
DDC 331.0973—dc23/eng/20231130
LC record available at https://lccn.loc.gov/2023040351
LC ebook record available at https://lccn.loc.gov/2023040352

DOI: 10.1093/oso/9780197514221.001.0001

Printed by Sheridan Books, Inc., United States of America

Contents

Introduction: Emotion and History: Working-Class Feeling in an Age of Letters   1

1. "Please Excuse All Mistakes": Letter-Writing, Shame, and Social Connection   22

2. Working-Class Americans Choose a Mate: Nonromantic Courtship and Tribal Intimacy   50

3. The Love Continuum: Understanding Romantic and Nonromantic Attachment   81

4. Sex Talk, Humor, and Fear of Ridicule: Desire and Self-Protection   111

5. Love to All Inquiring Friends: Sustaining Communal Ties in Nonromantic Marriage   133

6. Fighting to Stay Together: Unhappy Spouses and Their Struggles   148

7. Roses Are Red / Violets Are Blue: Emotional History in Rhyme   172

8. Imagining the Eternal Village: Death, Longing, and Loss   198

Epilogue   233

Acknowledgments   241
Appendix A: Writing, Education, and Literacy   247
Appendix B: Literacy and Oral Culture   251
Notes   253
Index   339

Introduction

Emotion and History: Working-class Feeling in an Age of Letters

When I was a child, watching television with wide-eyed enthusiasm, I was engrossed by a police drama that always ended with this line: "There are eight million stories in the naked city; this has been one of them." I still use the line today—albeit slightly modified—when I want to underline a narrative's dramatic power and emotional drive. I hold to the firm conviction that everyone has a story worth telling. *Love and the Working Class* is based on that belief, borne out by endless research in nineteenth-century letters. I have confidence that understanding the lives of ordinary people is essential to capturing the big picture of American culture and behavior. This understanding involves empathetic examination of the social structures they abide, the cultural meanings they absorb, and the economic conditions they struggle to cope with and occasionally surmount. Rather than the naked city, however, their America was mostly rural and still some years away from being an industrial colossus. But even two centuries removed, the TV ending announces my intention to safeguard these nineteenth-century Americans from vanishing into the multitude.

The individual stories presented here are not the usual superstars of best-selling history. You won't find a Lincoln, Grant, Lee, or Roosevelt. Instead you will hear from factory hands, laborers, peddlers, coopers, carpenters, lumbermen, miners, tanners, haulers, tailors, seamstresses, laundresses, domestics, sharecroppers, independent farmers, common soldiers, and wives. The pageant of their lives involved them in the Gold Rush, westward expansion, slavery, the Civil War, the Emancipation Proclamation, and much, much more. But the drama of their everyday existence was also about finding a mate, arguing with a spouse, having sex, raising decent children, dying with dignity and, at the center of it all, receiving community respect and support. Some of their most urgent troubles revolved around the struggle to provide the necessities of life for themselves and their families. What I have collected

Love and the Working Class. Karen Lystra, Oxford University Press. © Oxford University Press 2024.
DOI: 10.1093/oso/9780197514221.003.0001

here are micronarratives, little bits and pieces of a hardscrabble existence that capture their humor, grit, hope, and endurance. I invite you to enter the "anonymous corners" of their lives to understand what they believed and felt about themselves, their kinfolk, and their friends.[1]

As much as possible, I wanted these working-class people living in the nineteenth century to speak in their own words. Since interviews were impossible, the next best thing was letters. Often armed with only a third- or fourth-grade education, these Americans could read but had limited instruction in writing. Yet they sat down to compose a letter, sometimes with no more than a scratchy pen and a phonetic alphabet, because letters were the only way to connect with distant loved ones. Untold numbers of illiterate correspondents also wrote letters through dictation. No one could call, or text, or tweet, or communicate by any other means. In their time letters were literally testaments to life; silence always entailed the possibility of death.

They never called themselves working class, but the term is useful and apt because they worked with their hands, their education was limited, and their income was meager.[2] This meant that they often had to work at a young age. "[O]ur county is hard for the poor class of people," a southern woman wrote, recognizing her lived experience within the local hierarchy.[3] As one historian has said so well, "It is not enough to say, 'There was poverty.' Instead, we need to put a name to the structures that made it so."[4] But naming the structures of opportunity, especially the limitations on their access to wealth and power, cannot encompass all the dimensions of class. In addition we need to recognize the category's broader implications "as an index of social differentiation and consciousness."[5]

Better-educated Americans looked down their noses at the "poor class of people." I discovered this class disdain while writing my first book, *Searching the Heart: Women, Men and Romantic Love in Nineteenth-Century America*. Using the voluminous stacks of love letters the middle classes wrote during courtship, I was able to show how passionately erotic these American Victorians, frequently stereotyped as prudes, were in private correspondence and how obsessively they guarded their sexual expression from public view. I described their concept of romantic love and how that shaped their courtship rituals and led to their marital tensions. They wrote love letters with great pride in their ability to express intimate feelings with passion, creativity, and authenticity. Moreover, they believed their superior expressive skills warranted their higher social standing.[6]

INTRODUCTION 3

Even before I finished my middle-class book, I was curious about working-class beliefs and behaviors regarding love and sex. I was buzzing with many unanswered questions about people *below* the middle class. Did they have the same courtship rituals as their middle-class contemporaries? How did they talk about sex? Were their ideas about love similarly romantic? What about their vocabulary of love and intimacy? What did they think about marriage and how did they relate to spouses? What did they feel most passionately about? In what ways, if any, did they compare themselves to their middle-class peers? I decided to accept the challenge of a study focused on love, courtship, marriage, and sexuality among the working class.

I worried that people below the middle class would not bear witness to their intimate relationships, that I would be forced to fall back on the traces of their lives in birth, death, and marriage records, federal census reports, and military documents. And yes, large data sets can bring the obscure, humble, and unnoticed back to life by charting their patterns of behavior, but the census cannot expose their thoughts and feelings, nor can such records capture their verbal exchanges and emotional interactions with each other.

I was familiar with many excellent studies that accessed these working-class Americans through exceptional circumstances, such as sickness, crime, or vice. "Studying and writing about America's working-class people has never been easy," one historian of courtship observed, "because they so rarely speak to us in their own voices." Like so many other historical specialists, she was "forced to rely heavily on sources produced by non-working-class people."[7] These might include doctors, ministers, lawyers, social workers, or even less sympathetically, police, judges, bosses, vice investigators, and certain reformers. In settings structured by professionally minded public servants, working-class Americans have spoken in legal depositions, courtroom testimony, and pension applications. Their lives have been thoughtfully described and evaluated, sometimes in groundbreaking works, using these sources.[8]

Even so, I remained curious about how ordinary people related to each other outside the purview of middle-class observers and enforcers. I began with the expectation that the letters they sent to each other would best reveal what was on their minds and in their hearts. Civil War historians have a long tradition of listening to and reporting on the letters of common soldiers.[9] A growing body of work also examines soldiers' families, including mothers, wives, and sisters.[10] Western history has a tradition of valuing letters written by pioneers, gold rush Argonauts, and families in the US-Mexico

4 LOVE AND THE WORKING CLASS

borderland.[11] Studies of early factory workers, often focused on women as well as New England mill towns such as Lowell, have effectively utilized letters.[12] Historians have long recognized the value of correspondence. But whether I could find letters that allowed me to study the emotional contours of working-class courtship, love, and marriage was still an open question.[13]

Fearful of the scarcity of sources, I made a critical decision to incorporate not just love letters, but any and all family letters in my search, which soon broadened to include correspondence between friends. Throwing my net far and wide was crucial as I envisioned a study with national scope and sought a large sample for both depth and reliability. I was especially committed to finding letters written by African Americans. I excluded enslaved people because they were forced to negotiate their intimate relationships in an economic, legal, and moral environment that was uniquely malevolent. However, African Americans on both sides of the freedom divide had to cope with an obstructive and inequitable set of constraints on their life choices. Recognizing that race created separation between Americans and distinctive experiences ranged across a spectrum of race, ethnicity, nationality, gender, and more, I sought to investigate the cultural patterns that working-class Americans held in common in their intimate lives. My goal was to understand the shared conceptions and practices of intimacy within a geographically and racially diverse population of free people below the middle class. But I also strove to understand divergent social patterns where they directly affected intimate feelings and behavior. For example, gender imposed very different codes of conduct on mobile young people interested in marriage.

The letters of free Blacks whose status was long-standing as well as recently acquired were an integral part of this study. Black and white Americans voice their thoughts and feelings in every chapter. Additionally, most every region of the country is represented in the book. I excluded, with only a few exceptions, letters by first-generation immigrants because they often wrote in another language and held fast to the customs, assumptions, and rules of their culture of origin. I did not find working-class Latino and Latina letters, though a substantial body of scholarship on colonial New Mexico and Latin America, the Spanish borderlands, as well as histories of California, Texas, and New Mexico utilizes middle-class and elite correspondence.[14] However, for comparative purposes I will occasionally refer to historical analysis of immigrant letters as well as cross-cultural studies of courtship and love.[15]

Finding the nineteenth-century letters of anonymous Americans, beginning roughly in 1830 and ending in 1880, seemed daunting and necessitated

INTRODUCTION 5

a strategic approach. Two requirements were obvious as I began my search for letters: separation from home and motivation to write, especially for the barely literate. I initially targeted three occasions within my time frame that separated loved ones from home: the Civil War, which was the obvious starting point, the Gold Rush, and the many phases of westward expansion. After several years of combing through archives that ranged from the Library of Congress to the Western History Manuscript Collections at the State Historical Society of Missouri to the Southern Historical Manuscript Collections at the University of North Carolina, I discovered an abundance of letters.

Arguably the most important event in nineteenth-century America, the Civil War is also the event that most enabled me to understand the deeper currents of working-class feeling. This war offered an unprecedented opportunity to examine the intimate emotional lives of Americans who were poor, undereducated, and totally obscure. Letters were written in a quantity never before seen in American history.[16] Estimates range as high as almost half a billion letters.[17] I doubt that the illiterate, barely literate, and undereducated soldier and his loved ones put pen to paper at this pace. However, millions of letters were unquestionably sent and received by poor, undereducated men, their families, and friends.

I am certain that the Civil War was the catalyst to correspondence on a massive scale. But volume is only part of the story. Although Americans have been inclined to dispose of "ordinary" family correspondence, they exhibited a bias toward preserving the letters of ancestors who were Civil War soldiers. Tens of thousands of Civil War letters reside in archives across America. And this was one important source of evidence for my study. For the years before and after the Civil War, I depended on habitual savers and family pack rats, bless them, who preserved all kinds of ancestral letters that found their way into archival collections I accessed. I have honestly lost track of the number of letters I read for this book but the figure is well over five thousand.

Working-class Americans corresponded before and after the Civil War, but the conflict was, in many ways, the defining event in their lives.[18] Men were separated from loved ones, in some cases for the first time, and they were strongly motivated to write letters, as were the relatives they left behind. For illiterate soldiers with ready access to willing tutors, the war also presented a rare opportunity to learn to write. Though difficult to measure statistically, a number of soldiers testified to their newly minted writing skills. I was also struck by how many illiterate people found scribes to take dictation before as

6 LOVE AND THE WORKING CLASS

well as during the war. Illiterate correspondents can easily go unnoticed unless they or their scribes identify themselves. Their valuable and sometimes neglected voices join the working-class chorus who speak as individuals and as groups.

The joy of writing this book was in telling the stories of so many hardscrabble Americans who were previously lost to history. This demands an act of historical imagination from both the historian and her readers to bring the past into the present for moments of recognition and reflection. What follows is a brief sampler of some intimate moments from the book.

An illiterate young man learned to write so he could thank his young female gift-giver in his own hand. "Lookover anll mastackes," Marcellus Mitchell entreated her in the first letter he ever wrote, "and when I lern better I will do beter."[19]

The wife of a Union soldier had Midwestern neighbors who did not cut and haul her wood, a common courtesy given to spouses in small towns. Her illiterate husband's scribe was puzzled by this unpatriotic violation of community norms in her small Ohio town. "[S]omething is the mater," he announced in one of her husband's letters. He knew nothing about Sarah's Native American ancestry, which may have been the cause.[20]

The son of Sojourner Truth, working on a whaling vessel far from his New York home in the early 1840s, sent a letter to his mother with a popular song lyric about a homesick Native American boy whose pleas to leave his eastern school were ignored. Feeling trapped, the boy wanted to return to his home in the West and demanded, "white man, let me go!"[21] Truth's son identified with the defiant protest in this verse. He is one of many African American correspondents whose voices helped reveal the shared patterns of working-class culture within the often taxing, frequently onerous circumstances surrounding Black lives in the nineteenth century.

Brothers and sisters as well as parents gave advice and acted as courtship go-betweens. In 1850 a Black Virginian instructed his son, who was in the navy, to ignore the "pretty Spanish girls" and find a mate by letting "your old song Be true," drawing on the last lines from "Carry Me Back to Ole Virginny."[22] White Iowan Elizabeth Rawlings pressed her brother in the late 1850s: "Robert I want you to Come home and that as soon as possible donte wait to get you awife we have aplenty of girls heare I will speake for one for you so come along."[23] Black and white working-class Americans often oriented their emotional lives toward collective relationships that were associated with place—neighborhoods, villages, small towns, or, less commonly, states. However geographically defined, their boundaries of belonging included an almost universally accepted and taken-for-granted racial subtext. Working-class courtship was embedded in a sense of community that was tacitly understood to be racially homogeneous.

A young soldier from Maine exhibited a geographical allegiance that stretched from the local maidens to the local prostitutes. "They are hard old biddies and a good style is hard to be found in New Orleans" was his comment on the city's hookers. He was proud of his home-state prostitutes. "Give me a Maine girl for all the Louisianans."[24] The loyalties of young men to the hometown girls could even be extended to prostitutes.

One anxious suitor drew a young woman's name from a Valentine's Day lottery created by a group of Confederate soldiers in the Georgia Eighth Regiment. The awkward swain opened his valentine letter with this memorable line: "Miss O. Espy this is the first of my undertaking efforts to Exspress my entire ignorance to you."[25]

A male cousin joked with his female counterpart about their friend Dick [William] Wood's erection. "I was Completely Captivate with some of the girls of that County I am sure that you Could of seen that if you had of tried & as for Dicks part it stuck out about afeet or 2."[26] Young men often laughed about sex with each other but also shared sexual humor with young women. Sex talk was almost never serious and exposed a fear of ridicule and group shame that plainly demonstrated both the fun and the anxiety of belonging.

In a very rare disclosure, a Lowell mill girl confided to her brother the details of a sexual assault by her mill boss. This man invited her up to his room, surreptitiously locked the door, and was in the process of raping her when he was interrupted by a knock on the door. "[H]e said as he got cheated out of his object this time he would call and see me some time when I was alone at home," she wrote to her brother. His threat terrified Eliza. She told her brother but swore him to secrecy and warned her sister away but did not reveal the real reason, even when this sexual predator became her sister's boss.[27]

After marriage, husbands and wives argued about jealousy, adultery, money, and emotional rejection. Hearing tales of her husband's drinking, gambling, and whoring, Jennie Spencer threatened to run off with a theater troupe. Her husband, an upstate New York textile factory worker who enlisted in the Union army, actively solicited the help of a friend who worked in the freight department of the New York City Railroad in Rochester. "Now Barney for Gods sake if you can try and persuade her to give up the Idea

8 LOVE AND THE WORKING CLASS

of going. and I will send evry cent I get to her. and try and do better." The source of Jennie's anger was her husband's lack of financial support, slyly fueled by friend Barney's rumor mill. However, both husband and wife temporarily united against Barney after he accused Jennie of fooling around with other men.[28]

Love and death came together in the letter of a captured Confederate soldier. He was one of the prisoners of war who was picked in a random lottery to die in reprisal for the execution of seven Union prisoners of war taken at Pilot Knob. In a dramatic dispatch on the eve of his death he wrote: "My dear wife, don't grieve after me. I am going to rest, I want you to meet me in Heaven." He told her to take care of his dear children and to kiss them for him. "I send you my best love and respects in the hour of my death."[29]

On the Union side, Tillman Valentine, a sergeant in the Third US Colored Troops, composed a poem to honor his wife's father:

> Your aged father is gont to rest
> We his face weal no mor see
> but when we meete in hevens streetes
> O we shall hapy be

The central theme of Valentine's poem is the belief that family and friends will meet "in heaven's streets" where they will be reunited with loved ones.[30] A real location for most working-class Americans, heaven reflected a yearning for permanent attachments without loss or change. This utopian vision was an almost universal conviction that was shared across the color line.

Another young man left the girls in Lawrence County, Missouri, for the California gold fields in 1850.[31] Two years later he was thinking of returning home to marry. "You must Choose one for me," he told his sister and brother-in-law, "and tell her all the fine storys you can think of and try to keep her single until I return then I will try my luck and sea if it is better than it is in the mines." He ended with one of the most memorable phrases in all working-class correspondence. "Keep wonder for me and I believe I can shine."[32]

In creating the narratives of obscure and humble people, it was not hard to keep wonder. Discerning their intimate lives has been both an exciting and demanding quest. Individuals with more to say appear in several chapters. But the prevalence of short runs of letters sometimes made it difficult to tell an illuminating story or find a clarifying benchmark. By identifying cultural patterns in large numbers of geographically diverse letters, however, I was able to provide context that allowed interpretation of otherwise opaque content. Important help also came from census, demographic, and military records. With help from such records, a single surviving letter written by a widow during the Civil War revealed an older woman's passion and desire for Daniel Turner, a neighbor ten years her junior. This impoverished woman wrote that she would rather see Turner than eat. That is as intense and evocative a statement of desire as I have read in sophisticated love letters written by the literati. Saved only by a whim, the widow's stand-alone letter illustrates how even one document can tell us much about lived experience.[33]

Contemporary readers, who live comfortably in a world of texts—print and digital—have a challenge to meet in this book. They can apply the judgments of a schoolmaster. Or they can leave deeply ingrained standards of grammar and diction and spelling behind and enter a more fluid and innovative environment where sound is more immediate and written expression is oral in its rhythms and its phrasing.

This requires some patience because these correspondents did not necessarily write standard English. Though the rules of composition might have been a mystery, they knew how to talk. Consequently they sounded out written words as they spoke them, and so can we. The great surprise and joy of these letters is hearing them speak by decoding their writing. This requires a willingness to listen to the voices embedded in the phonetically spelled words of their letters. "Pnau many" is an apparent stumper, but say it out loud and it is clearly an accented version of "pneumonia."[34] "Pearch" is not a fish but rather a sound-alike version of "perish" in southern dialect.[35] "Cimpersise" is an easy-to-recognize rendering of sympathize.[36] "You nedente to send me any nore invrops" echoes the pronunciation of the black-smith telling his wife he does not need envelopes.[37]

Many working-class correspondents demonstrated their ability to evoke the written word through sound. Their spelling actually mixed the oral and written in unpredictable, and yet communicative ways. "We ar Bilding up a town," one unidentified friend wrote another, "we have mail calog and fee mail cimonary."[38] He was referring to a male college and a female seminary. The line between oral and written culture was blurred for many undereducated Americans. They often spelled words as they would have pronounced them in conversation. "i Am destitut of nus," John Fuller wrote Miss Frances after running away from his Alabama home to join the Confederate army. "[T]hu Army is Anoop in [a napping] we expect A fight in A few Das Al tho tha solgrs ses tha Dnt think we will have mush fitn hier."[39] A patient reader can literally hear the writer speaking.

It is easy to laugh, and I welcome a sense of humor in my readers, but it is also worthwhile to consider seriously the emotions embedded in the phonetic sounds of their fractured spelling. Nonetheless, in order to ease the flow of reading and the comprehension of a text, I have occasionally translated passages into standard English, putting the original in a note. This is indicated by an asterisk (*) before a translated quotation or series of quotations from the same letter. I have also inserted bracketed standard English when I did not think the entire passage needed to be converted.

Writing just as one would talk had other components, among them a freewheeling use of colloquial language. In trying to describe to his mother what it felt like to be on picket duty all night in the rain, Henry Richardson, a New Englander with the more proficient writing skills characteristic of his region, relied upon a very earthy image to convey his discomfort. Ankle deep in mud and prohibited from lighting a fire during the night, with no place to sit, much less lie down, he wrote his mother, "there we stood . . . from five at night till daylight next morning (about fourteen hours) very much in the position of a Boy who has pissed his Breeches."[40] While this is a delightfully irreverent image to the modern reader, Henry's language would have raised middle-class eyebrows two centuries ago.

Many studies of working-class Americans in Henry's era focus on some aspect of work: transitions from preindustrial to industrial work habits, union organizing, labor leaders, rank and file activists, employment laws and labor strikes, to name a few.[41] Class was inscribed and measured by other physical manifestations in the nineteenth century, however, including property, possessions, dress, and general standard of living. But less material class boundaries such as language skills and the ability to express oneself in speech and writing were also important. These language skills were a prominent marker of class standing in the nineteenth century.

My earlier research on better-educated Americans has taught me about these class markers and has given me a crucial advantage. In identifying middle-class patterns of courtship and marriage before I attempted to unravel working-class experiences of intimacy, I could better distinguish the two. Because I was able to recognize the similarities and the differences, I could sort out the separate patterns of attachment as well as the overlap.

It was a long journey of discovery. Though many historians had valuable insights, I had no template to follow and few clues about what I would find.

INTRODUCTION 11

Including letters to family and friends as well as to spouses and eligible mates was crucial to my understanding. It was the only way I found a key element of working-class courtship ritual: the use of intermediaries to communicate feelings and to establish mutual interest in marriage. Only a minority wrote love letters during courtship. I found that some working-class couples were susceptible to romantic influences. However, the majority radically diverged from a romantic concept of love. Finding an effective vocabulary to describe their experience was daunting.

This was especially difficult because love has been intensely saturated with romantic meaning in the context of coupling. So much so that to associate a type of love that was *not* romantic with courtship and marriage is, to contemporary Americans, alien territory. When love appears in the vocabulary of a nonromantic working-class courtship, it is easy to impose a romantic intention that was not theirs. Grasping what the nonromantic concept of love might mean in a relationship that leads to marriage is one of the chief topics of this book.

The larger experience and worldview of working-class Americans was expressed in a courtship practice that was so foreign I struggled to grasp what was occurring, much less why. Eventually I realized that their sense of intimacy was expressed, for the most part, through group relationships. Towns and villages across America provided the setting for collective courtship patterns defined by geographical and racial boundaries. Relationships with the opposite sex were performed collectively as "tribal" affinities embedded in a sense of place and tacitly understood as racially homogenous.[42] Marriage usually followed within months of a public coupling. Even though they married as individuals, the community bracketed the individual in collective bonds of affection, giving them a sense of relationship founded in group loyalty often identified with place.

In romantic relationships, love was the lingua franca of intimacy. Not so in a majority of working-class marriages. What was surprising and puzzling was that love was withheld from a wife or husband in the same letter that it was sent to children, parents, siblings, friends, and neighbors. In many cases, correspondents felt free to direct love to practically everyone *but* their spouse. I explored the unstated cultural logic of this practice in nonromantic marriage. Although they used the word differently than their middle-class peers, working-class Americans did not abandon love in their language of everyday life. The vocabulary of love spanned the social divide, despite the fact that the meaning, emotional intent, and norms of usage often changed dramatically.

12   LOVE AND THE WORKING CLASS

I had many more surprises on my journey. Writers placed a relatively low value on privacy, even in intimate exchanges between married or unmarried couples, and the practice of sharing intimate letters was widespread. The boundaries of privacy were often blurred in nonromantic courtship and marriage, which did not mandate the same kind of confidentiality as romantic intimacy. I probed why and how this fit with the larger experiences and worldview of working-class Americans.

This relates to another surprise. While sexual desire was constantly expressed during middle-class courtship as part of the language of love, erotic feelings were seldom verbalized in working-class letters. The lack of privacy played a role. American Victorians obsessively guarded their sexuality from public view and luxuriated in the erotic in private. Ironically this protective shield fed the myth of Victorian prudery that still pervades the popular (and sometimes academic) imagination. Middle-class Americans were much more sensual on paper than their working-class peers, who could be bawdy when they discussed sex, but most often made a joke. I believe humor reflected their matter-of-fact approach to physical coupling and was a pivotal antidote to their fear of public ridicule.

Another revelation was their confidence in poetry; not just any kind of poetry, however, but what is often called doggerel today. This would be the "Roses are red / Violets are blue" kind of rhyme that I designate a vernacular poem. Though the middle class disparaged these rhymes as childish expressions of love, I intentionally approach this verse with respect, recognizing that it carried legitimate feeling that the sender and receiver might not easily express in their own words.

Besides their emotional value, vernacular poems had other virtues for working-class writers. They were easy to remember and came to the point quickly and clearly. Significantly, their favored rhymes were created within a folk tradition that was accessible to and shared by whole communities. In that sense well-known rhymes connected the sender and receiver to a larger collective practice that was popular in the oral culture of both Black and white communities. These poems were also contained in letters written for an identifiable audience in a specific historical situation. Working-class correspondents sometimes added commentary and context. Vernacular rhymes in letters are thus a rare record of the actual historical "performance" of literature by many barely literate Americans.[43]

The most popular rhyme in working-class letters was some version of "When this you see / remember me / tho many a mile / a part we be."

"Americans have not always been able to leave home with ease," one historian, studying homesickness, has concluded about nineteenth-century migration.[44] Fear of being forgotten outside the interactions of their face-to-face communities was intense for working-class Americans, and being remembered confirmed a past identity as part of a group along with the possibility of a future homecoming. In 1830, where this study begins, 91 percent of Americans lived in places with populations of less than twenty-five hundred. Fifty years later, when the study ends, more than 70 percent were still living in communities with fewer than twenty-five hundred people.[45] Though the industrial system was expanding, small towns or villages still dominated the American landscape both physically and, I believe, emotionally as well.

If the working-class majority understood love in relationship to their tribal identity, they understood death in communal terms as well. They intended to rejoin family and friends in what I call an eternal village. Poor, undereducated Americans, along with their middle-class counterparts, expressed their human needs in the yearning for an afterlife without loss. The deepest emotional satisfactions of working-class relationships, however, were defined as collective and were not yet fully individuated. This included the positive aftermath of dying, which was the joy, satisfaction, and deep pleasure of rejoining a community of friends and family. The goal that defined peace and happiness—and heavenly bliss—was to become a permanent member of a group.

Working-class Americans, at least until 1880, did not believe in progress. They repeatedly identified change with pain and sorrow. Indeed nineteenth-century America was often a troubled place for its poorer citizens. They sought stability and permanence in relationships and believed this was attainable only in heaven. While much has been made of Americans' belief in the "good death," this was often achievable only when a person had a slow demise from illness or old age. In infant mortality and sudden adult death, emotional comfort was most often taken from the idea of a family's and friends' reunion in the afterlife.[46]

Human mortality was part of the fabric of everyday life and was integrated into its flow in ways that jar contemporary sensibilities. Death hovered in people's minds throughout the nineteenth century, but was intensified during the Civil War. However, the Civil War was an important subject in this book for reasons other than death. This war initiated a surge of letter-writing by poor, undereducated folks the likes of which had never been seen before.

14 LOVE AND THE WORKING CLASS

One historian has claimed that "Military service [in the Civil War] helped forge privates and noncommissioned officers into a working class."[47] This is an intriguing idea that has multiple levels of interpretation.[48] Still, those privates and noncoms were, at the very least, aware of their relative position in the social hierarchy before they enlisted. Besides their modest means, I found that their lack of education was a key to their understanding of class. Insecure about their learning deficiencies, they continually expressed shame over their lack of writing skills. In modern parlance, poor, undereducated Americans had internalized a sense of inferiority fostered by the judgments of middle-class authorities even before the Civil War began. This class shame, especially built on their self-conscious sense of educational inadequacies, turned *some* of their response to social power into self-blame.

As I worked on my research over the years, more and more letters came online. I began with extended on-site visits to archives around the country, including the Library of Congress, the Southern Historical Collection at the University of North Carolina, Western Historical Manuscripts Collection at the University of Missouri in Columbia, Duke University Manuscript Collections, the Newberry Library in Chicago, the Huntington Library in California, the Minnesota Historical Society, the Indiana State Library, and several other state archives. I also made cyber visits to digitized collections at the Library of Philadelphia, Virginia Tech Library Special Collections, Missouri Digital Heritage, St. Louis Civil War Project, University of Pittsburgh, the American Antiquarian Society, South Caroliniana Library, the Auburn Digital Library, University of Washington Digital Collection, Iowa Digital Library, the Gilder Lehrman Institute of American History, the Newton Gresham Library, Sam Houston State University, Civil War Manuscripts Project of the Connecticut Historical Society, the Ohio Memory Collection, the University of New Mexico Digital Collections, and four other outstanding primary source archives on the web: Documents of the American South, the University of Virginia's "Valley of the Shadow," University of Massachusetts Lowell Libraries "Lowell Mill Girl Letters," and the Civil War Archive's "Letters Home from the Civil War."

This study was not done through indexes or even the summary reports in manuscript collections. After I eliminated military officers and anyone with a professional career, for example, minister, lawyer, doctor, I still had to lay my hands on paper or stare at the scanned letters in digitized collections to evaluate, first of all, the correspondent's education. This could be accomplished with relative efficiency. Establishing occupations and comparative prosperity required a closer reading of the documents. Farmers, the largest occupational category in the nineteenth century, were sometimes tricky. Their writing—spelling, grammar, punctuation, and diction—were not definitive in establishing social class but provided an important point of departure.

I spent a great deal of time trying to track individuals in the federal census, state marriage and death records, and military documents. Ancestry.com is an unparalleled tool for searching large databases. This amazing gateway to online historical records made it possible to search for disparate individuals located across the United States. There were borderline calls that I judged on a case-by-case basis: I eliminated the well-educated Lowell factory girl who hoped to go to college. But I kept the country schoolteacher whose father was a well-off farmer. She looked down her nose at the local hoi polloi. I learned through the census, however, that with no better prospects she eventually married a widower with one child and a farm one-fourth the value of her father's.[49]

As the great historian of the English working class, E. P. Thompson, insisted: "Class is defined by men [and women] as they live their own history, and, in the end, this is its only definition."[50] Lived and felt experience, interpersonal relationships, and the active participation of individuals in creating meaningful lives are what this book is about. And it is through this lens of personal relationships that poor, unschooled Americans show us how they practiced courtship and marriage and created meaningful attachments in their uncertain lives.

They were most often group oriented, and their intimate lives were characterized by a tribal identity deeply shaped by small communities. In a culture that has been described as individualistic, working-class Americans still sought a supportive community and the sustaining practice of place-related rituals. When they left home, they used letters to promote a sense of continuity with the people they left behind.

Letter-writing was as important to working-class Americans as it was to their middle-class compatriots. Outside certain fields of research, this has not been well understood. The assumption that their lack of education or even their illiteracy kept them from taking up their pens is incorrect. Given the will or need, correspondents repeatedly demonstrated that they could overcome their writing deficiencies. They made do in surprisingly effective ways, communicating the most complex feelings with the most rudimentary skills.

Their writing is not always easy to read. But the reward for this effort is a compassionate understanding of the structures of feeling that opened up as well as limited their ability to relate to each other. Expression was an act of social division, but it was also an act of belonging. In exchanges with their family and friends, working-class Americans often expressed a profound emotional yearning for stable attachments, structured by their need for collective identification and continuity with the past. The experience they sought, such as courtship and marriage, were often tightly woven into their long-standing social networks. They had little faith in progress. War, sickness, economic dislocation, and death were challenges that they frequently endured with stoic acceptance. Their utopian vision was otherworldly: an afterlife where delayed gratification in this world was rewarded by the capacity to give and receive love without fear of loss.

INTRODUCTION 17

A cooper proudly poses with one of his barrels in a daguerreotype taken sometime in the twenty years before the Civil War. He is in work clothes and displays a hand adze and a hoop driver.
Library of Congress DAG 1196 LC Control # 2004664286.

18   LOVE AND THE WORKING CLASS

Two sisters pose with their weaving shuttles and scissors in this 1859 ambrotype. They wear blouses with lace collars and decoration, but their functional skirts have pockets and also tabs where their scissors hang.
Library of Congress LC-DIG-36964.

These two chimney sweeps were photographed with some of their equipment, including drop cloths, belts, and a long brush. They seem to be sitting for this picture at the end of a hard workday.
Library of Congress LC-DIG 10990 Call # LOT 14022, no. 66.

20 LOVE AND THE WORKING CLASS

A carpenter holds up a hammer and a nail, his most basic tools. In this daguerreotype, additional tools sit beside him on another chair. Many working-class men, like him, wore hats for occupational portraits done in the nineteenth century.
Library of Congress LC-DIG-USZ6-2045.

INTRODUCTION 21

A blacksmith in work clothes clasps a hammer in one hand and pliers holding a horseshoe in the other. He is ready for a job in this daguerreotype from the 1850s.
Library of Congress DAG 1192 LC control # 2004664282.

1

"Please Excuse All Mistakes"

Letter-Writing, Shame, and Social Connection

Letter-writing was a crucial form of labor in nineteenth-century America. And like other forms of labor, it divided people by social class. Those with little education who performed physical work with meager or uncertain compensation, mostly working-class Americans, often wrote for very different reasons than their better-educated, wealthier, professionally oriented peers. Excluding their business or government letters, working-class writers were often motivated by a profound need to maintain community attachments; middle-class Americans, by contrast, were often motivated by a need to define themselves, writing for self-exploration, self-expression, and greater understanding of their personal distinctiveness.[1]

Working-class letter writers were not nearly as concerned with their individuality. They wrote for reassurance that they were still connected, at least by memory, to the family and community they left behind. In a time when letters were almost the only way to communicate across a spatial divide, letter-writing was frequently a familial and communal affirmation that answered a deep need to be part of a larger collective. The web of face-to-face relationships they so valued was constantly endangered by the disruptions of migration and war. Letters became opportunities to maintain group cohesion and share feelings in absentia.

"Remember me" was the sometimes confident, sometimes plaintive, demand of these ordinary Americans. To be forgotten by people with whom one had shared an intimacy of place was a painful erasure of identity. Virgil Pomrhon immigrated to Liberia after being freed in 1841. He sent a letter to his former master asking to be remembered to "all my colard friend my Brothers and ant and ther children Sip and Philip old Ben Parks Ben umstard Danel matson and his family." Virgil singled out thirteen more African Americans by name and added two more white men to his inventory. He continued: "I cold call 100 Moor nams [I could call 100 more names] but Tell Them all howday for me."[2] Like Virgil, most working-class correspondents

Love and the Working Class. Karen Lystra, Oxford University Press. © Oxford University Press 2024.
DOI: 10.1093/oso/9780197514221.003.0002

were intent on being recalled by those who had once been entangled in their daily lives.[3]

Seventeen years later, Joseph Cross, an African American Union soldier from the Northeast, sent his love to sixteen family and friends by name, including news or commentary about another eleven. He also wanted "to know what has become of that Black Dog that I left home have you Got him now."[4] Cross was part of a tight-knit community in Griswold, Connecticut, 630 miles north of Pomrhon's North Carolina neighborhood.[5] Cross owned at least one acre of land, but worked as a day laborer before and a farmhand after the war.[6]

"When I first com to Texas I Wrote to ov Forty now I hav only got Ten," white Minnesotan William Johnson complained in 1869, "and expet to hav about 5 When my tim is out."[7] A soldier in Company B of the Tenth Infantry Regiment stationed in Corpus Christi, he had written forty letters but received only ten replies.[8] Pessimist or realist, he expected only five correspondents would continue to respond faithfully. For Johnson, the depth of community ties was defined by the mutual exchange of letters.

In spite of her self-conscious feelings of inadequacy as a writer, one mother nonetheless enthusiastically affirmed, "for what is done by letters is my comfort or a big share of it, tobesur."[9] Though most working-class correspondents would have agreed, they missed the opportunity to talk with family, neighbors, and friends. "it makes me real home sick to see aney body from the <u>vicinity</u> of home," Amy Galusha confessed to her parents, "so that I donot care about seeing them unless they can stay long enough to see me and tell me about . . . things." Amy was working in the mills in Lowell, Massachusetts, in 1851 and missed her small-town community in Berkshire, Vermont.[10] Both men and women recognized that they could talk better than they could use their pens. John Garriott confessed to his sister: "Well to tell you the fact it is hard work for me to write a letter at any time and I believe I am gitting poorer or wers to rite every day."[11]

Working-class correspondents were often embarrassed by their poor writing skills. They were extremely self-conscious about their deficiencies, even in letters to loved ones. "Ann I think this will try your peations [patience] I hope you can make it all out," Elizabeth Sterling worried aloud to her sister. "I am sutch a poor riter and bad speller that I am a shaimed to rite any one that can rite so much better than I can please excuse all mistakes and rite to us soon."[12] Elizabeth Sterling's sense of shame was widely shared, but her forthright self-appraisal was unusually candid. Most undereducated

24   LOVE AND THE WORKING CLASS

letter writers were more defensive: "iges it is time for me to quit scridling as iam in ahury and my pen is por," Elizabeth's father, Isaac Osmond, wrote. "Idont belive iever rote so poor be fore in my life iam almost ashamed to sent it."[13]

Problems with "scridling" were often blamed on pens, paper, and ink. "Excuse all mistakes and bad writing," Polly Lanphear, on the brink of quitting her factory job, wrote her sister, "for my pen is so poor I cannot hardly make a work with it."[14] Her brother George characterized one of his letters in an alliterative postscript: "poor paper poor pen poor writing Amen."[15] John Christy, an African American who was farming in Pennsylvania, apologized to his brother-in-law: "pleas to excuse My riting the paper is bad."[16] Inferior ink was also blamed for their epistolary faults. "[Y]oumust excuse my bad riting," one wag concluded a letter, "for my pen is bad and my ink is pale so I must quit or I will faile."[17] Another poetic scribbler added this postscript to his letter: "my pen is bad my ink is pale / I hope my love will never fail / its badly roat you may know / with out looking any more."[18]

Working-class correspondents offered a litany of excuses owing to their shame and embarrassment over what they called their bad writing. Sometimes they openly identified their feelings. "Let no one see this for I am truly ashamed of my part," a female cousin confided to another.[19] Anxiety about the negative judgment of others, including peers, was widespread among working-class correspondents. "You must excuse my Bad righting," a candid Georgia man confessed apologetically to his "uncle and ant," "for I am in a hury and cant do mutch better nohow."[20] One young African American wife apologized to her husband: "ples to excus the bed riting for I am in ahar."[21] Lack of time was a common defense against their deficiencies with the pen.

Some adults accepted their deficiencies without complaint. "[E]xcuse my bad riting and spelling," a brother requested of his sibling, who was a shoemaker, "as it is th best I can do."[22] An elderly woman said simply, "I am oute of pratchtis."[23] A poor soldier had a reasonable solution for his "bad way of righten." "I want you to doo tha best you can," he advised his wife, "and I will do the best I can."[24] Matter-of-fact scribes were the exception, however. Most felt compelled to "explain away" their blunders. Working-class correspondents routinely expressed anxiety, defensiveness, and shame over their "bad writing."[25]

A few correspondents, embarrassed by their writing skills, were able to joke about their blunders. "Please excuse this poorly writing letter and do not publish," quipped one lighthearted wag.[26] On the topic of bad writing, however, undereducated scribes seldom saw any humor. They were more often afraid that they would become the butt of a joke. One young man, writing to his cousin in Indiana, pleaded at the bottom of his last page: "this is my first doint laf et it."[27]

Loved ones did laugh in spite of such heartfelt appeals. "[W]ell Jennie Deer I do hope you will pray for all of us," eighteen-year-old Frank Flint wrote his girlfriend, "hoping youl overlook all mistakes & write soon for I look for yor letters a good eal more anxious than I do for the Pay Master & that's saying a good eal."[28] His plea notwithstanding, Jennie found it impossible to ignore some mistakes. "Now Miss Jennie youv got to stop laughing at my letters I don't write leters to be laughed at," he scolded. "You say I called you a Deer well you are so hard to catch that I think I was warented in calling you that."[29] Finding himself the butt of her humor, Frank cleverly turned his mistake into a joke. But he was obviously self-conscious about his blooper. "I have writen three letters before this since I heard from my little Dear or (deer)."[30] He had learned his lesson in homonyms the hard way.

Showing that almost anything can be used as a metaphor for love, John Shumway phrased his yearning for his wife in terms of spelling. "You know when I was with you," he wrote, "I always looked to you to tell me when I was right O how often I have wished that I could ask you if this or that was spelt right. And I long for the time to come when I can once more."[31] Shumway's romantic thoughts of spelling were exceptional. Most correspondents lived in dread of their mistakes.

For undereducated correspondents in the nineteenth century, poor spelling was a source of shame. Silas Browning, a piano maker, confessed to his wife that it kept him from writing friends. "I am glad that my Girls are good spelers," he told his daughter Clara, "for I am asshame to write becous I spell so may words rong." Loving his daughters, Silas made a special allowance. "You say that my girls read my letters," he wrote his wife, "woll you can sett them to correcting the spelling & bad Grammer and if there is a word left out they can supply it so you can make sence of my letters & it will learn them to write correctly."[32] In spite of his fear of ridicule, Silas was willing to be a source of instruction for his children. Letter-writing was an act of courage for many unschooled correspondents who braved the laughter and derision of peers and loved ones, as well as the scorn of their more educated countrymen.

26 LOVE AND THE WORKING CLASS

While they recognized the existence of expectations for proper English usage, undereducated correspondents frequently relied on the sound of the spoken word as much as the spatial or visual technology of writing. This often indicated that they read little and, with the exception of the Bible, had scant familiarity with published texts.[33] Though most could read and a majority had basic writing skills, they still relied heavily upon the oral culture of their face-to-face communities.

Long before Mark Twain perfected readable literary dialect, ordinary Americans were writing just as they talked. "Dr Peassn is docteren hour for the pean in hur liver [Dr. Pearson is doctoring her for the pain in her liver]" is alive with the speech of Pennsylvanian Isaac Osmond, a cooper, farmer, and occasional peddler.[34] "We are all hir nomerd with the living an receiving areasble posion of health," Mississippian William Littlejohn drawled in pen and ink to his Uncle. He hoped that his relatives were "ingoing of good health an all the comfort and blesing that is alowd for us por wonrean soles hir in this low worle of cin [enjoying good health and all the comfort and blessing that is allowed for us poor wandering souls here in this low world of sin]."[35] African American Hansel Roberts dictated these words to his more literate brother Ransom: "I will send your money in a letter if you seasoe the letter that I sent you word that I had not got I got it at northamton cort Souse [I will send your money in a letter if you say so. The letter that I sent you word that I had not got, I got it at Northampton courthouse]."[36]

Words they did not know they sounded out. The majority of working-class correspondents converted the spoken word into writing through their spelling. This process reflected the world of speech, not the rules of middle-class literacy. In spellings such as "youmer" (humor), "loins" (lines), "apparet" (appeared), "isen teny" (isn't any), "muth besseer" (much busier), and "cuind wehess" (kind wishes), the writers translated the sound they would make in speech to the spelling of the word.[37] Their pronunciation was inscribed on the page. In this sense, the world of writing was still aural, still a world of sound for many undereducated Americans.[38]

As many literary critics have argued, the theoretical opposition between oral and written culture is often unworkable in actual historical circumstances.[39] Working-class letters point to a complex and intriguing overlap between the two forms of communication. Writing transforms the spoken word into a coded inscription according to literary rules and images. But for many hardscrabble writers, this conversion was incomplete. Words were formed on paper as the writer pronounced them in actual conversation.

"PLEASE EXCUSE ALL MISTAKES" 27

Thus they spelled words as they heard them, creating phonetic dialect that brought the sounds of their language to the page. "I did knt in Joie mye self as Well as I did ovr thare with you all," D. A. Carey told Joshua Lipscomb, "forTha aulacte like a town se rotehit To deth With Bam Boo brirs." Repeat the last part of the sentence out loud and it will eventually make sense. Translation: "for they all act like a town serrated to death with bamboo briars."[40]

The line between oral and written culture was blurred for many nineteenth-century Americans. Even those who never learned to write, and mostly lived in a world of speech within their small communities, had to negotiate that line.[41] Property transfers as well as wills required written documentation. Voluntary or involuntary mobility forced oral communicators to reckon with correspondence in their personal relationships. They needed people with writing skills to inscribe their speech into alphabetic symbols that could be sent across space and comprehended by their family and friends. In that sense, and many others, even illiterate people straddled the boundaries between oral and written culture.

After receiving news of her daughter's death, Sarah Barksdale dictated a letter to her son-in-law. "I condole with you apon the loss of your companion and a dear childe," she wrote William Holman through a third party. "[U] rest assuard that my affetion is till with you and my confidence the I am as it were wile my childe lived I wish I was near to you so I cold assist you with the children," she said sympathetically, asking him to come for a visit in the spring and to stay until fall.[42] She even urged her son-in-law to marry again. Sarah showed no sign that she was inhibited by her need to communicate through a scribe. Whether they were literate or illiterate, working-class correspondents found a way to express themselves in writing when they were motivated.

Nineteenth-century Americans were part of an oral culture that did not disappear with the spread of writing literacy.[43] Elizabeth Fuller could write, but she had a haphazard orientation to the numerical calendar, dating her letter "the 3 sebeth I donot no the day of the Month I do not no when the month come in."[44] Her lack of knowledge of the formal month and day is indicative of her immersion in a nonindustrial cycle of seasons. She had been living in an oral culture that did not always require the use of calendar dates.[45] Her next letter, however, was correctly dated. A compelling need to correspond with her husband, who was no longer available in a shared space, had reoriented her to the numerical calendar.

28 LOVE AND THE WORKING CLASS

Abby Cross, a free Black woman living in Connecticut, was reminded by her husband, "Now remember that this is the last day in the weeak last day in the month & last day in 1864." He was a soldier in the Twenty-Ninth Connecticut Volunteer Infantry (Colored), writing his wife a letter on December 31, 1864. Though she was not literate, he felt the need to make certain she was oriented to the numerical calendar.[46] Letters written as well as received impelled a more specific awareness of the shared abstractions of calendar time. A heightened self-consciousness about personal chronology, especially numbers and dates, was an important part of the reorientation to time that the Civil War imposed on some uneducated, task-oriented Americans still remote from the demands of an industrial culture.[47]

The need to write to their absent husbands pressed on the unschooled wives left at home. A Confederate soldier from southeastern Alabama responded to his wife's question: "you wanted to no whether I could read your letter or not I can read it I have to read a heepe of mity bald riteing," he reassured her in a backhanded way. Apparently he read letters from home to illiterate soldiers in his company (Thirty-Third Alabama Infantry, Company G). "I was proud to think that you would try to rite your self rite me one ever week and that will improve your riteing and ma bee once and a while I will git one of them."[48] His prediction proved correct. "I am glad to see that you have improved in righting," he praised her close to six months later. "I can read yours very easy and am all wais pleased to git them."[49]

Perhaps even more unexpectedly, the totally illiterate were sometimes regular correspondents, importuning relatives, friends, and even comparative strangers to chronicle their reality. Fifty-four letters that George Deal dictated in the twenty-one months he served in the Ohio Twentieth Infantry during the Civil War were saved by his wife, Sarah, and their children.[50] "[I]f i could rite my self i would rite oftener to you," George patiently explained to his complaining wife, "but i hafto git others to write to you and so i hafto wait for others to rite for me." Mailing four letters and receiving none in return, Sarah asked if he "thout any thing of my family." George responded earnestly: "i do as well as ever i did nor i never forgot to rite nor i never forgot my family." George's wife did not see his deficiency as a legitimate excuse because she also used a scribe: "the nex time any one rite fur you," he prompted her in early April 1863, "youstate who he is and his name."[51]

But Sarah began to work on her writing skills. George's short aside four months later revealed his wife's newly acquired competence. "[Y]ou wanted to no if i could read that letter i got," George repeated Sarah's question: "i can purti well *so rite away* i can reede them."[52] His response was a double surprise: Sarah had learned to write a letter and George, unless he was referring to his scribe, knew how to read them. He seemed little interested, however, in acquiring his own writing skills.

George managed to recruit a variety of comrades-in-arms to take dictation for him. This may have weakened his motivation to learn to write. Some of his scribes were silent collaborators; one identified himself discreetly; and one, H. J. Souder, actively commented on Deal's interactions with Sarah.[53] A reciprocal exchange of labor formed the basis of Souder's transcription service for his messmate. "I ama cooking for a mess and George he is ina the mess," Henry Souder explained, "and he is a good fellow to help me when I git in a pinch and lotets to do."[54] Souder was a popular scribe, writing letters for at least two other men in one day, "and I haint tird yet," he boasted.[55]

Souder empowered Deal to speak his mind and reveal his feelings outside of direct interactions with his wife. But the scribe also engaged in his own dialogue with Deal's wife, and that is revealing for different reasons. Souder functioned almost like a Greek chorus, commenting on the inner workings of the Deal's marriage as well as the solid, frayed, or broken connections to their community.

This active scribe interjected himself into Deal's letters without compunction. When Deal's wife reported that basic services such as chopping wood, a common courtesy given to the wife of a soldier, were missing at home, Souder wrote, "I pity any man that has a family at home, but I do think the nabor is good to my family I get all my wood halled [hauled] and chopped for nothing there is good union men there left to take car of my family." Souder wondered whether there were any good union men where she lived in Ohio, then announced, "something is the mater I hope they will do beter for you and try and help you."[56]

When Souder puzzled over Sarah's lack of support from her neighbors, he did not grasp the possibility that an unspoken prejudice was the cause. Twentieth-century family lore has it that one of Sarah's grandparents was Native American.[57] George never mentioned her heritage. Nonetheless, Sarah may have been the victim of an insidious ethnic bias that left her isolated and bereft of community support when her husband was gone.

Finding a willing scribe may have been difficult under the circumstances and helped motivate Sarah's quest for literacy. She was writing her own letters by the end of July 1863, according to her husband, who died a year later, yet she (or her children) told the 1870 census taker that she could neither read

30 LOVE AND THE WORKING CLASS

nor write.[58] George was clearly unable to write, but the 1850 and 1860 federal census-takers took no notice; both failed to record this fact.[59] Obviously large population data sets tell only part of the story.[60] Whatever their flaws, however, aggregate records are frequently invaluable tools in identifying humble nineteenth-century correspondents. Take for example a single surviving letter written by a widow during the Civil War. This letter was saved by a man named Will Cobb, who sent it to his educated cousin Bettie Herring, along with a stalactite he collected in a local cave. Calling the letter "a literary curiosity," he considered them equivalent oddities.

> September
> Dear sir iseate my self to lete you no that
> iam well and truly hope when these few lines
> cums to hand they may find you well and
> doing well and go throu the war and cum hom
> e safe to my hand safe and then you will
> be mine ifyou are wil in inever wanted to
> sea eny body as bad as idoyou ihad rather
> sea you than to eate whe iam hungry i don't
> no whether you ever think of ne ornt
> when i am asleape iam areaming about yu whe i
> am a wake i sea no peac [she interjects two poems] iwant
> you to send me your likerse so ican hav it
> ot [to] sea if icant sea you this fron the widow Peebles to
> Daniel Turner
>
> > fail not to rite to me
> > when this you sea rmember
> > tho fare a pre webe[61]

Not unexpectedly, the widow's love letter contained very little contextual information. She included only the month, September, and not the year; she included only her last name, Peebles, preceded by the honorific, widow. She named her addressee in full but mentioned no other defining characteristics. With her letter alone, no definite identification could be made.[62]

Luckily the widow's envelope was preserved. It was addressed by her to "2 regemet N C in care of the captain to Daniel turner." Someone else turned the envelope forty-five degrees and inserted the full date, "Sept. 17, [1864]" and "Summerfield, NC." Summerfield is a small town in northwest Guilford

September

Deare sir i reade my self to lete you no that
i am well and Truly hope when there few lines
cums to hand they may find you well and
doing well and go throu the war and cum hom
e safe to my hand safe and then you will
bi mine if you are wilin i never wabnted to
sed eny body as bad as idoyou ihad rather
sed you than to eate whe idm hungry iaont
no whether you ever think of ne ornt when
i am arleape iam areaming aboutyu whe i
am a wake i sed no peac the sworld is wide

they sed is deadpe in your arms i long
to sleape ohe rose is red the wilent is blue
shugar is swete but not like you iwant
you to send me your l ikese so ican hav it
ob sed if icant sea you this from the
widow Peebles to
Daniel Turner

fail not to rite to me
when this you sea rmember
me to tho fare a pre webe

The widow Peebles wrote this love letter to Daniel Turner, a much younger man, in September 1864. She had sexual feelings for Turner and hoped to marry him. He was illiterate and had to have her letter read to him.

Wright and Herring Family Papers, University of North Carolina, Chapel Hill.

County, part of the Piedmont region of North Carolina. This clue proved to be a critical piece of information. However, her record was seriously complicated by a census taker's mistake. After sorting out the mixup, I provisionally identified her as Sallie A. Peebles, twenty-five years old in 1860 and living in North Division, Guilford, North Carolina, the county where she was born. A woman who had four children eight years old and younger, she was

32   LOVE AND THE WORKING CLASS

married at the time to Albert Peebles, age thirty-one, also born in Guilford County.[63]

Persistent trial and error and the algorithms of genealogical software, combined with the all-important location on the envelope, led to the 1860 census and a tentative identification of the sender and her family. Her oldest boy was attending school. Her husband was a laborer who owned no land. His sister, Menerva Halbrook, and her child were living with the Peebles family in 1860.[64] The family's total personal estate was valued at $75. This Sallie had a husband who was alive in August 1860 when the census taker inventoried their household. If she was in fact the woman who wrote the love letter to Daniel Turner, her husband would have died sometime after August 1860, when the census taker called, but before September 17, 1864, the date on the envelope.[65] His death between those dates had to be confirmed in order to ensure a correct identification. Several Albert Peebles appeared in census, marriage, and cemetery records, but most were alive and none had died in the critical time period. The mystery was solved when I discovered that Albert's last name was spelled *Peoples* in his military records.[66] They showed that he died on November 16, 1863, possibly as a result of the battle of Kelly's Ford, Virginia, which was the Second Regiment's last fight before his passing.[67] Finding this Albert confirmed the identity of the widow Peebles.

So eleven months after her husband died, Sallie was pursuing a replacement. This poor southern widow was impatient to find a husband, no doubt motivated by her economic need. Following her letter's conventional beginning, Peebles rushed headlong into her longed-for future: "And go throu the war and cum home safe to my hand safe," she boldly envisioned, "and then you will be mine." Almost immediately uncertain of her confident declaration, she added: "ifyou are wilin."[68] Apparently the widow was not sure if Daniel Turner was "willin" to marry her. She had not waited for him to take the initiative.

Her push to marry Turner was driven by more than economic need, however. Obviously smitten and anxious to wed, she made an extraordinarily open declaration of emotional and physical yearning: "ihad rather sea you than to eate whe iam hungry." The audacity of this statement was again followed by the ambiguity surrounding her actual relationship to Turner: "idont no whether you ever think of ne ornt [me or not]." Peebles was, of course, testing Turner, but she also seemed unfamiliar with his thoughts and feelings. This was not unusual in working-class courtship.

So who was the man she hoped would be her new husband? Sorting a blizzard of Daniel Turners was daunting. Once again location was a key. The 1850 census identified a Daniel Turner, age five, living in Guilford with his parents, Henry and Margaret, and six siblings. He was still living in Guilford in 1860 with his mother and five siblings. His father had just been killed.[69]

From the envelope, we know that Daniel Turner served in the Second North Carolina Infantry. William Cobb's note to his cousin specified that Turner was in Company E, known as Guilford's Guards.[70] A North Carolina troop roster confirmed that he was serving in the same company as Sallie's husband.[71] Friends and neighbors enlisted together, so the two men almost certainly knew each other.[72] Daniel was part of Sallie and Albert's community. The three of them shared an intimacy of place.

His service record indicated that he was ten years younger than Sallie, but she was clearly undaunted by their age difference. "[W]en i am asleape iam areaming about yu whe i am a wake i sea no peac," she announced. His youth likely added to his physical attraction. In modern vernacular, she had the "hots" for Turner. According to the observations of a Confederate nurse, marrying a younger man was becoming more frequent as the war progressed.[73]

He survived the war, but did Sallie A. Peebles become his wife? Tracing Turner after the war was a challenge, especially because his was a common name and his postwar location was not a given. Knowing his parents' names and birthplaces proved to be the decisive factor in discovering whom he married. A North Carolina marriage certificate that included the name of his father and mother allowed for an unambiguous identification of Turner's bride as Mary S. Humphries. She was also a widow.[74] They married on September 23, 1869, in Person, North Carolina. The following year's federal census revealed that Mary S. Turner was around twenty years older than her husband.[75] The widow Peebles's unconcern about their ten-year age gap was borne out by Turner's marriage to an even older woman. In 1870 he was farming a modest plot of land. Daniel's choice to marry a much older widow did not appear to be influenced by her assets, which were minimal.[76] However, she did own an ox, which would have been a big asset to a poor farmer plowing his field alone. In 1870, Sallie was still without a husband.[77] David, her eldest child, was supporting them by working on a farm.

The 1870 census also clarified the reason Will Cobb possessed Sallie Peebles's love letter. Daniel Turner could neither read nor write. Will Cobb graduated from the University of Pennsylvania's medical school before enlisting as a private in the Confederate army. By the time Turner received

34 LOVE AND THE WORKING CLASS

his letter from the widow Peebles, Cobb was the assistant surgeon for the Second North Carolina Regiment.[78] Perhaps Turner gave him the letter to read. However he acquired it, Cobb sent the letter to his cousin as a specimen to be examined and enjoyed. "The style is decidedly novel," he remarked sarcastically. Twice calling it a "literary curiosity," the widow Peebles's letter served the function of confirming the superiority of its middle-class readers.[79]

What educated, middle-class Americans could not see then (and perhaps even now) was that without grammar, punctuation, or spelling, the widow Peebles still managed to convey her feelings for Daniel Turner with power and economy. "I had rather see you than to eat when I am hungry" is a potent evocation of her feelings of need, yearning, emotional hunger, and loneliness. Nonetheless, writing proficiency was an important class boundary, and undereducated Americans recognized their own inability to cross it.

Though basic reading literacy was widely available to white children of all classes by the mid-nineteenth century, the development of writing skills, including the use of proper grammar, was clearly tied to parental wealth.[80] The economic status of nineteenth-century parents controlled the continuation of their children's schooling and thus many of the options available to the young.[81] Even in the nineteenth century, length of education was a critical variable in achieving middle-class standing and occupational status. Affluent children, ages fifteen to nineteen, were twice as likely to be in school as their poorer counterparts. This pattern applied to both urban and rural families.

As important as formal schooling was to the acquisition of writing skills, one often overlooked accelerant of literacy was the Civil War. While the middle classes continued their prolific correspondence, the working class experienced unprecedented opportunity and encouragement to write. Some of this was situational: being away from home for the first time provided a reason to write. Knowing that one's life might be cut short by a bullet was a powerful incentive to take pen in hand.

The Civil War provided a context of support for letter-writing that was unprecedented in American history.[82] "I have to write a great many letters for men in our company who cannot write," Samuel Potter, first sergeant in the 140th Pennsylvania Volunteers explained. "I have concluded it would be cheaper to teach them to write their own letters. I have several scholars."[83] Teaching one Union soldier to write had unusual results. Oliver Coolidge of Massachusetts wryly observed that James Holehouse of Fall River "is alive

During the Civil War, thousands of letters passed through this tent post office at the headquarters of the Army of the Potomac in Culpeper, Virginia.
Library of Congress LC-DIG-12834.

and full of fun all the time he has been learning to write that is the reason why there are so many places with his name in them."[84] Holehouse might be viewed as a nineteenth-century graffiti tag.

After Marcellus Mitchell, a poor illiterate soldier, sent his friend Rebecca a thank you note (for a needle case) written by someone else, he vowed that the next letter she received from him would be in his own hand. "[N]ow Rebeca I will tell you how I come to not right sooner," he explained one year later. "I could not right and I awlways sed that that I nast right it my selph so it went on and I now took a notion that I could right plane anoofe foe you could under stande ne. maby I got me abible and reed it and I feele very comfted and I hope I hav not muc more that I can say miss you must ecuse bad righting and Lookover anll mastackes and when I lern better I will do beter so here my thanks and cuind wehess to you and all friends to the soldiers."[85] Mitchell came into the Civil War unable to write. He had probably never been away from home. Face-to-face interactions had always sufficed. But now he was motivated to write by a need to communicate that speech could not satisfy.

36 LOVE AND THE WORKING CLASS

Perhaps he was self-tutored, but he more likely took informal instruction from someone like Samuel Potter.

Alabamian Sydney Fuller learned to write after he joined the Confederate army in the summer of 1862. "[P]ap iwhant to se you the worst kind andiwode beglad if you wood git atrans fur her sowe cod bea to gether," he pleaded with his father, who had joined the army as a paid substitute out of desperation to make some money. "[Y]ou must ex cuse my bad riting," Sydney wrote, "for ihav Just lurnt to right sense ihav bin incamps."[86]

Black soldiers serving in the army also benefited from opportunities to learn to write during the war. The opportunity for education was routinely denied to those in bondage. But free Black literacy was rising before the Civil War. In 1850, 63.8 percent of free Blacks aged twenty to twenty-nine were literate; the corresponding rate in 1860 was 70.9 percent.[87] Clearly, a majority of young Black soldiers free before the Civil War were literate, but soldiers who enlisted straight out of bondage were apt to be illiterate. Kentuckian Edward Francis, likely a bondsman until he joined the US Colored Infantry in June 1864, gleefully told his wife: "I am learning to write myself & I can scratch right smart."[88]

Corporal Chump Pugh, serving in Company G of the Third US Infantry, a Black unit, wrote his white teacher Esther Hawks from Jacksonville Florida in June 1864: "and I think you Mis Hawkes for lern me," Pugh told her. "I learn me very much in deed and I hope the Lord will be with you wher ev you go and I hope I will see you agane in this wirld and give my love to each one of the should [school] and it is a pruty plas and I gate along very well in deed and I dont know an thang more to write to you Mis Esther H hawkes at thes time."[89] Pugh was sounding out the words as he inscribed them. In transition from oral to written culture, he could think of little content to share, but he was very grateful for the skill.

African American soldiers were very anxious to learn to write and would send their own letters to family and friends almost as soon as they took up the pen. "The soldiers had made wonderful progress in their writing, of which, of course, they were very proud," another white teacher, Elizabeth Botume, observed. "Each letter was an improvement upon the one before. Most of these were written by the soldiers themselves."[90] A congressional report of the Committee on Freedmen's Affairs concluded that "regiments of colored soldiers have nearly all made improvement in learning."[91]

Material aid for letter-writing came from organizations such as the United States Christian Commission, which provided services and supplies to Union soldiers during the Civil War. "Paper costs ranged between one and seven cents per sheet, and ink prices varied even more," two historians of everyday life in New England report; "a bottle might run from four to twelve cents, and if of quality ink, from twenty-five cents to thirty-seven and a half cents."[92] This was more than pocket change for the nineteenth-century working poor. "I am now writeing in the Commissinar room," Union soldier James Lockwood wrote on US Christian Commission stationery. "[T]hay have 2 long tabels for soldiers to write on they furnish them with ink pen and paper and thay can sit dow and write about 70 at a time thay give them a bible or testamen and him book and if thay doant have mone to pay postage thay will pay it for them."[93] Though southern churches created no equivalent support structure, one Confederate soldier told his wife, "Nay I can get as many stamps her as a mule could pull so you need not send ay to me."[94] An African American soldier in the Massachusetts Fifty-Fourth had the opposite experience: "i Was so glad that you Cent me som poas stamps," he told his wife, "fer i had got mi likens taken and i had nun to poot on the letter."[95]

Teaching illiterate men to write and improving the skills of the barely literate were two unintended consequences of the Civil War. Another was the public mail calls for soldiers that allowed peers to observe who received letters (and how many) from home. Peer pressure motivated men to write and to urge those at home to do likewise. A member of the Second Minnesota Light Artillery Battery, Frank Flint monitored a comrade who "got two letters today but I don't know who they are from." He clearly expected to find out. Another friend of Flints cursed the postmaster after receiving no letters. "I told him that his wife had gone and married somone els," Frank teased.[96] His humor was based on a widely shared assumption that the act of writing a letter demonstrated feelings of caring and connection, no matter the actual expression within.

Besides encouraging letter-writing, Civil War camp life intensified the common working-class practice of sharing letters. The force of peer pressure was especially on display when soldiers were harassed to share their letters from home. Oliver Coolidge, a working-class Union soldier, described one memorable mail call of about two thousand letters, books, and parcels. "If you could have seen the excitement after receiveing them you would have laughed," he told his father and sister. "[W]ell those who had none would not be satisfied until we lucky ones read to them the news which were contained in those we received." But the unlucky ones were still not appeased. "We gave

A group of Union soldiers read letters and papers and play cards while resting from drills in Petersburg, Virginia. Matthew Brady took the photograph in 1864.
National Archives Identifier 524639 Local ID-111-B-220.

all our papers out to the men who got nothing from friends to keep them quiet while we could take the sense of our letters."[97]

Letters, as well as papers and books, were viewed as community property by foot soldiers in the Twenty-Fourth Massachusetts Volunteers. "Papers, books, old letters & evry thing has been overhauled for reading matter to amuse us," Oliver revealed on another long rainy day in North Carolina. Cooped up in their tent and trying to stay dry, they had "some sport over some that have been sent to one of our fellows by the name of Jennings from the town of South Adams."[98] Reading personal letters aloud was common among working-class soldiers. A Confederate soldier from North Carolina, writing from a camp near Winchester, Virginia, remarked, "I hant got but one girle to write to me yet I wish you cood see some of the leters that is past to an from."[99] Working-class camaraderie often included a tribal etiquette of sharing letters that was completely antithetical to romantic standards of privacy. Minnesotan Frank Flint not only read the letters written by his friend's wife, but sent summaries and critiques to his girlfriend. "I dont exactly like some of <u>her</u> ways her letters for instance," he complained about his friend's wife, "she always is taking on so about him is afraid he will be killed . . .as if she was the only one that would suffer."[100]

Group reading of letters from girlfriends and spouses as well as relatives, friends, and community members was also practiced among Black soldiers. "[T]hey want to read my letters I get from you and I wount let them do it," an African American member of the Massachusetts Fifty-Fourth Volunteers, George Delavar, apprised his former teacher. "I am one that dont want any one to know any more about my busness than what I am mind to tell them and that is not much because sometimes it is not vise."[101] Though Delavar resisted his comrades' pressure, reading a letter was sometimes seen as a communal exercise, and it was expected that soldiers would share their letters.

Civilians shared letters as well. Women in Mary Caplinger's village of Marion, Illinois, read their husbands' letters out loud for news of the local soldiers: "sarah got a letter from bill yesterday & I heard it read which informed us that you was all below vixburg & had been skirmishing to days." Mary feared that it would be an "awful place" and that many men would die "away from their family and friends." While she wanted to hear "how you all come out," she told her husband she was "afraid to hear for fear you or some of the rest will be killed." Mary carefully tracked the letters received by wives of the soldiers serving with her husband: "the letter that sarah got yesterday was the first letter which had come from the 31st scince the 5th of this month and that has been the longest time since any of you has been gone." She reported that in the past two weeks she had the "uneasyest time that I have ever saw," clearly indicating that letters from his comrades functioned as surrogates for her husband's correspondence. The practice of publicly reading letters from relatives and friends was common in Marion and was part of the social ritual in other working-class communities in America both before and during the Civil War.[102] The fear of humiliation was softened when it came to reading an intimate letter out loud, probably because mistakes could be disguised and lines could be censored, while still maintaining an ethic of tribal loyalty.

While mistakes in grammar, spelling, and punctuation were the source of considerable embarrassment and shame, poor, undereducated Americans did not have the same anxiety about sharing the content of personal letters as their middle-class contemporaries. One reason for their more open attitude was the working-class conception of correspondence as external news. "Now Jennie I wish I could write something worth while," Frank Flint explained, "but I cannot for thare hant any body got killed or married here that I know of."[103] For working-class Americans, reporting external events was the main purpose of all letter-writing. Lowell mill girl Louisa Sawyer admonished her cousin to "write all the news you can think of."[104] Edward Francis, a Black soldier serving in Brownsville, Texas, in early 1866, sent a short letter to his wife, explaining, "I have nothing that is interesting to tell you [so] I will close my letter by begging you to write soon to me."[105] "I believe I have told you all the news," Ellen Everingham told a cousin. "I would like to fill the page but I cannot so Farewell."[106] The problem of having nothing to write was ubiquitous among working-class correspondents. There were some prolific pens, but they were the exceptions, not the rule.

Some letter writers held an even narrower definition of news. "Arthur I don't know hardly what to write being as nothing Strange has ocured lately," one man informed his brother-in-law.[107] "I have not got enny thing strang to rite to you," a brother wrote his sibling from Mississippi, "oly I have stop hir to make acrop this yare I ame to go wess nex foul if nothing happen."[108] One Confederate soldier repeated the negative lament: "ihant nothing very strang to rite to you at present."[109] Blacksmith Riley Luther echoed these sentiments: "I have nothing strange to write to you any more than we have bin on another march."[110] A union soldier shared the same sentiments about the contents of letters: "I was glad to hear from you once more I have nothing verry strange to write at the present time."[111]

These correspondents saw everyday life as too uneventful to write about. They assumed that the receiver was primarily interested in hearing about "special" circumstances, especially those that were exotic or different. Personal reactions to ordinary life were often considered substandard epistolary content. This presents a striking contrast to middle-class letter writers who obsessively examined their individual responses to daily existence.

Even when working-class correspondents were surrounded by new and unusual circumstances, they sometimes had difficulty finding something to write about. Joseph Aid was drafted on May 12, 1864, and had an array of new experiences during his first two weeks in the army, but after noting that he had seen "some of the prettyest Country & Scenery that I ever saw in my life," he admitted, "I don't know anything more to write to you."[112] Their conception of what was newsworthy was part of the problem, but it was not the only reason that working-class writers had difficulty figuring out what to write about.

Even if they had "news" to tell, correspondents sometimes found they had little to say. Their skill level was obviously an obstacle but not an insurmountable barrier. The real source of their difficulty was not their technical deficiencies of grammar, spelling, and punctuation. What they had not mastered was the skill of self-reflexive thought. Individual thoughts or interior feelings were not generally included in the working-class definition of "news."

Two New England sisters had relocated with their husbands to Mobile, Alabama, and experienced much that was new. One sister found nothing to write about, while the other corresponded regularly. The letter-writing sister explained the silence of her sibling: "she wants to see you all but it dont do her any good to set down and write that she is well and hopes you are and the Children are well, and hopes yours are, and she says that is all she can ever think of to write she has no news only she wants to go home and that is not news to any of you, so She has nothing to write there you have it just as she said it one day."[113] This sister had a common excuse for not writing: she could think of nothing to say. This was not so much a matter of writing skills, or even noteworthy experience, but rather of valuing self-knowledge, which is often the ability to identify a variety of personal reactions to life experience that can then be reported to the outside world.

Though their correspondence began conventionally with the usual emphasis on news, the possibility of writing as more intimate conversation eventually dawned on a farmhand and his girlfriend. "I do not know of any more news," Louisa Russ declared in her first letter to John Shumway. "I have wrote more now than you did."[114] Almost eight months later Louisa was still troubled by the absence of news. "Now John I don't think of any more to write," Louisa confessed, "for I cant write so well as I can talk, for I have hard you say that the Brown's could talk and I am half Brown."[115]

But Louisa made an important discovery in the intervening twenty-two months. "You said you wrote just as you would tak to me, that is whet I like," John cheered. 'I almost seem to be with you O! I hall be so glad when you are with me here and all well. I shal enjoy myself then yes yes!" Now John had his own epiphany. "I an going to write to you just as I would talkit if I was with you."[116] The irony is that poor, uneducated correspondents often penned words on paper exactly as they voiced them, but this did not necessarily translate into an understanding that writing could be just as you would "talkit." This had to be discovered by correspondents like Louisa and John.

Articulate and prolific correspondents, though poorly educated, demonstrate that schooling is not the only way to acquire linguistic and conceptual tools. Nonetheless, formal education had a strong influence on cognitive

42 LOVE AND THE WORKING CLASS

processes. Some important affinity between thinking and writing can be learned in the classroom. One soldier in the 131st Illinois Volunteers made a forceful connection between education and writing. "Father do send him to School eevery day if you please for my sake and as my last request," Joseph urged on behalf of his brother Jimmie. "I would not take one thousand dollars for the use of the pen it is more comfort."[117] The use of the pen was sometimes less comfort and more adversity for the undereducated writer of the nineteenth century.

The problem for working-class writers was not so much overcoming their technical deficiencies, but rather valuing and then deciphering their own thoughts and feelings. Nebulous, indistinct, and perhaps even confused, their interior reactions to life could not become part of their shared experience until they were named or conceptualized. But first they had to value the effort. Feelings and thoughts in an inchoate state are not available to communicate. One female shoe binder, trying to write in her diary, complained: "[W]hen I sit down to write, my toughts will wonder of. I try to keep them together, but they will not stay."[118] John Garriott figured out why letter-writing was such hard work: "I cant put any thing to gether any more."[119]

"Pa is yet teaching School he has the scholars to write compositions on different subject," one adolescent wrote her girlfriend in 1870. "They could not think of much to write about the subjects which he gave them," she observed, so "he promised to take a walk with us some fine afternoon over the green hills which surround the town, for the purpose of strengthening their minds and to draw out their thoughts to get them to express in words or to write with a pen what they thought and I wrote one too."[120] Apparently she took instruction from her father, who found his students lacking in cognitive skills. While teaching composition, he saw that he must also train them in the value of self-awareness and the art of self-expression.

Whatever the state of their self-awareness, poor, undereducated letter writers had little guidance in the value of self-creation. But they understood the worth of education. A. D. Buck, who hailed from upstate New York, urged his brother Marco to educate himself at home. "Now is the time for you to improve," he pushed. "[T]ake a sheet of paper and write—practice writing or write letters; you can write me what you are doing from one week to another." After suggesting mathematical and reading homework, Buck concluded: "I see am writing a regular lecture. . . . But I want you to succeed and you will not unless you are educated."[121]

"You must prevail on Nora to go to school this sumer," Orra Bailey wrote his wife: "tell her its her last chance as she is getting to be of that age in which youing ladies think they are to old to go to school but I think we are never to old to learn," the concerned father added. The problem, perhaps typical, was that his daughter's age did not match her grade level. "[I]ts not much we can give our children but let that little be in an education that no one can take from them we both of us never went to school much and now we see the need of a good education."[122] Education was highly valued by Americans who felt inferior because of their lack of formal schooling.

Carter Page, trying to learn the jewelry trade, was well aware of the difficulties of life for those without an education. Noting that his mother wanted her children to "make something of them Selvs," Page counseled her not to despair, "for we are all young yet yow know we have to fight at a disadvantage for wee have no Education and when one goes out in the world he sees the need of it."[123] Flint, Buck, Bailey, Page, and others clearly placed a value on education, even if they had little formal schooling themselves. They also accepted a class hierarchy that placed the better educated above them, not only economically but also culturally.

Nineteenth-century schooling did more than teach reading, writing, and arithmetic. It helped to transmit a value system that associated education with intelligence, refinement, social status, and gentility. It also helped to inculcate the values of self-awareness and self-expression. And expressive competence was expected to differentiate individuals along class lines. Verbal skill had class meanings. Writing to his mother and sister, Charles Henry Richardson commented on the issue with working-class tongue-in-cheek: "you must be careful how you write to me in the future for you know I am now an Officer in the U.S.A. and they are a class that don't take much slang from anyone— but I guess I shouldn't hurt anyone I know."[124] "Well as I am writing to an Oficer I must be verry cautious," his mother replied, "but we aint frightened, we had a good laughf when we read your letter." Mother and son poked fun at a class system embedded in the linguistic skills acquired through formal education. "But ho stop I am writing to an Oficer I am afraid the slang will show in this letter."[125] The basis of their sarcasm was a widely held belief among all ranks of American society that to be inept with language was to demonstrate one's lower social standing.[126] Though many correspondents did not openly identify the class implications of their language skills, they recognized their social disabilities in making excuses for their mistakes while simultaneously defending their social honor. Anxiously describing her letter

44 LOVE AND THE WORKING CLASS

as "poorly done," one woman asked her daughter "not to escpose them or any I send."[127] Her feeling of exposure underlined the vulnerability that working-class Americans felt about their educational deficiencies.

In spite of their fear, anxiety, and sense of inferiority as writers, letter-writing was mandatory in nineteenth-century working-class culture. Bare literacy, even illiteracy, was no excuse. Letters were a demonstrable measure of family loyalty, caring, and communal attachments in working-class culture. The common expectation was that letters would be reciprocated up and down the class hierarchy.[128] Nevertheless, to break the chain of epistolary response was potentially more hurtful to correspondents with modest levels of technical proficiency.

"Joseph we would Like to Write to you every month," his sister-in-law confessed, "but we would fail to entertain you with News of enough kind the times is so dull in this Country but we will write to you as Long as you . . . will write to us."[129] Sally Kesterson expressed the common belief that her monthly letters would lack the requisite "news" because "the times is so dull," but she was willing to risk what she saw as a deficiency in content on condition that she received letters in return. This is an unambiguous statement of the rule of reciprocity. The mutual exchange of letters gave value to what she had to say and, by implication, also reassured her about her worth to her husband's family.

A barely literate correspondent, Isaac Osmond wrote to his far-flung family every Sunday because "I think it a grat plesher to hea from my folks wether the doe from me or know so I have lots of them to blot and scribbl." Isaac wrote with the common expectation that his letters would be reciprocated. One especially long interval between letters created a suspicion that his son "thot so little of us that you dedent think worth wilel to right to us." His sense of devaluation and indifference was explicit. But after the long-awaited letter from his son had arrived, all was forgiven. "We was over regoist day befor yesterday wen we receved a welcm viset ter," Isaac waxed beneficently. "[Y]our worm welkum letter it guiv us a greadel of pleasher to hear of your good helth and worldly prosppects." That the decidedly un-middle-class barrel-maker saw family letters as welcome visitors is a sign of the high value working-class Americans attached to personal writing. A letter was always a concrete demonstration that the sender valued the receiver. They were a crucial emblem of caring in poorer families.[130]

"[T]hat preshes leter Com wen I was taken care of the sick," Isaac's daughter Ann informed her sister-in-law. "O wat a comfort they ware to me you little no how often they have ben read and them deer picters have been luked at I all most think that I could of visited with you." A poor writer by her own estimate, Ann could sometimes feel less isolated by taking up her pen. By writing a letter, "I would have a visit," she told her sister-in-law.[131]

"I have to rite if I ever here from any of my foalks," another Osmond daughter plainly stated.[132] Even though she hated to write, Elizabeth was

Two young working-class women intently read letters. In this ambrotype, one woman rests her arm on the shoulder of the other, which may indicate that they are sisters. Certainly they are friends who may well have read each other's letters.
Library of Congress AMB/TIN 2075 LC-DIG-36461.

46 LOVE AND THE WORKING CLASS

motivated by a reciprocity rule that applied to letter-writing up and down the social ladder. Working-class correspondents with the scantiest of writing skills, or none at all, were still expected to observe the normal sequence: letter received followed by a written reply. To break the rule of reciprocity was read as a sign of indifference and a lack of love. After writing several letters to her family and receiving no response, Mary Walker concluded, "I cannot accunt for it unless they huve fogoten me."[133] Matthew Marvin was very upset when he discovered that no family member had written his sister in three or four months. "If some of you don't write to her regularly," he threatened, you will have "to answer to me."[134]

A dearth of correspondence was a sign of disrespect. What was worse, it might be interpreted as an erasure of identity within a family or community. To go unremembered at the post office was a special affliction for mobile Americans. "My delay in writing is not because you are forgoten," Grandpa Hillman reassured his son's family. "[N]ot a day passes over my head but you are remembered and while I live I trust you will be." Hillman's letter, sent the previous year, had never reached its destination. He was trying to repair the broken link of family attachment.[135]

Offering no word of gratitude for the present her children sent, one mother brazenly asked for a cash gift on the next occasion. After this gaffe in May, she looked in vain for a letter of reply. Reading the epistolary tea leaves, she finally tried to heal the rift by writing again in early October, closing with a conciliatory postscript: "I thank you for the present you sent me."[136] Hurt feelings based on the reciprocity rule were clearly reflected by the next correspondent, who had not written to one of his brothers for three or four years. He intended to try one more time, "and then if he don't write he may go I have never done him any harm," he told another brother, "and I don't see that he is any better than I am."[137]

An African American soldier, George Delavar, waited long months for a letter from his white teacher. He took an aggressive stance toward her silence. "I feel so sorry to have it to say that yur are truly for gotten me Mrs Hawkes what have I done to you So great that I am So little noticed by you whom I love you so well," he began his January 13, 1864, letter. Esther broke the reciprocity rule and this deeply insulted Delavar. "[W]hat do you mean by that not sending me any thing," he demanded.[138] Receiving a letter in response, he proudly waved it in front of his peers, but refused to share its contents.

A young Iowa farmer, drafted into the Iowa Thirteenth, felt seriously devalued by the absence of correspondence from his family and friends. "I

"PLEASE EXCUSE ALL MISTAKES"   47

have not Read a line from you since I have been in the service and you both promised to write. but I suppose that you are like the rest of them up there think I am not worth writing to."[139] Jesse was offended, not just by individual neglect, but by "the rest of them up there," referring to the people where he lived in Hamburg, Iowa.

The reciprocity rule had wide application in working-class culture and was relevant not just to individuals and families but to groups.[140] Working-class correspondents—both Black and white—constantly asked to be remembered to their "inquiring friends." They recognized an oral culture of remembrance alongside a written one. One African American soldier from Pennsylvania instructed his sister "give my love to all the inquireing friends."[141] Another Black soldier from New York told his wife: "give my love to all enquiring friends, especially to Julia, Mary and mother and the baby."[142] Another from the South directed his wife: "Give my Love to all inquiring fried."[143] This phrase was repeated over and over again in working-class letters. "I send my best love to all of my nabers that requires [inquires] after me," one Confederate soldier wrote.[144] A New England farmer and peddler, off to make his fortune in the West, asked his wife to "give my love to all that inquire fore me."[145] One brother from a small town in upstate New York told his sister, "give my love to all inquiring friends."[146] "Give my best wishes to Dennis, Shelly, Haenry, Johnny, G.W. Silas & Bird & all others who may inquire after me," one Kentuckian living in Indiana requested of his friend back home.[147] A Lowell mill girl wrote simply, "Remember me to friends."[148] Another mill girl used the standard phrase: "give my love to all inquiring friends."[149] This common request recognized the web of connections in their face-to-face communities. It also recognized the limits of writing. Individuals could not possibly correspond with all their friends, yet they felt the need to acknowledge the relationships that had bound them together in a specific locality.

Love to all inquiring friends contained the hope of being remembered by one's tribe but also a deep-seated fear of being forgotten. What if there were no inquiring friends? Some people made their fear explicit by adding, "if there be any."[150] One young woman bluntly expressed her insecurity: "Give my love to all my friends if I have any."[151] Another northern mill girl elaborated: "give my love to all my inquiring friends acquaintance and School mates if they Should happen to be any."[152] "[G]ive my love and respects to your self and family and all enquiring friends if any there be," one southern sharecropper wrote his neighbor, "if not return it to the one from whence it come."[153] The

48 LOVE AND THE WORKING CLASS

disruption of community created insecurity about past relationships and an unsettling awareness of collective loss. But the generic decree of "love to all inquiring friends" was a way to counteract this loss by assuming a continuation of relationships that defined communal intimacy.[154]

Some letters contained demands to be remembered to long lists of relatives and friends, with anxious appeals for correspondence. Indeed, writers sometimes gave specific instructions to recipients about whom to contact and what to read them. On occasion, letters or notes meant for different people were composed on the same sheets of paper, creating a communal experience in the plural format of their text. However, the shared reading of a letter, especially letters from intimates, was the most dramatic illustration of the gulf that separated working-class from middle-class sensibilities. When love letters were involved, middle-class Americans found this lack of privacy almost sacrilegious.[155] Working-class Americans often saw no harm.[156]

Reams of paper and untold quantities of ink have been spent on theorizing social class, but a neglected dynamic of class creation was embedded in these working-class letters: shame. "So I will wright next Sunday if I can," William Dunlap told his sister in anticipation of his own death, "& So that is all at present excuse bad wrighting and spelling So Good By for now and for ever." Dunlap offered no hope of an afterlife, just the finality of absence in his last goodbye. He thought he might die at Harpers Ferry, but even in the face of imminent death, he apologized for his bad writing. He survived the war and was a practicing blacksmith in 1870.[157]

This is a dramatic demonstration of how self-conscious and ashamed Americans were about their educational deficiencies. Working-class letter writers constantly expressed embarrassment about their bad writing in general and their spelling in particular.[158] They openly expressed fears that their writing would provoke the ridicule and laughter of their peers and of their better-educated compatriots. And this fear of social dishonor was rooted in shame, which can be seen, as one clinical psychologist aptly observed, "as a result of the internalization of a contemptuous voice."[159] Nineteenth-century working-class Americans did *not* exhibit a "crippling self-hatred," but they did articulate feelings of shame.[160] For many people the negative appraisal of the self that followed helped solidify nineteenth-century social hierarchies.

Such "class shame" had a partial antidote in community care, respect, and recognition. Collective unity and closeness most certainly provided support and security in their often difficult life course. Thus the disruption of social networks was especially threatening to the working-class American.

Less firmly rooted in the advancing culture of individualism, poorer, under-educated Americans felt intensely the loss of their face-to-face community. Unlike their middle-class compatriots, they usually did not believe the romantic notion that one person could act as their emotional refuge in a hostile world.[161] Exchanging letters with family and friends supported their need for a safe haven within a larger group.

"Remember me / When this you see / Tho many a mile / a part we be," the most-often recited poem in their letters, reflected a pervasive anxiety that physical absence might mean an erasure of mutual attachments.[162] Correspondents urged memory and connection with this poem, hoping that letters would provide a means to circumvent the forgetfulness and loss of familiar relationships that they feared. This fear had special meaning in a culture with high death rates and high rates of geographical mobility spurred by ambition, poverty, and war. Letter-writing helped organize the experience of loss by connecting people to their past relationships in meaningful ways. Letter-writing also worked to maintain community attachments in situations of temporary absence, anticipated homecomings, and unfulfilled longings for permanent connections.

2

Working-Class Americans Choose a Mate

Nonromantic Courtship and Tribal Intimacy

In 1830, only 8.8 percent of the US population was living in an urban place, defined by the census as any population over twenty-five hundred. Fifty years later, that number had more than tripled, to 28.2 percent.[1] Even so, in 1880 more than 70 percent of Americans were still living in places with populations of fewer than twenty-five hundred people. One of the reasons was that most permanent interstate migration in the nineteenth century was not to cities but to rural areas.[2] In the mid-nineteenth century nine out of ten migrants settled permanently in rural locations, followed by a slow increase in the American preference for urban destinations.[3] The foundational fact is that most of the country—whether old or new migrants—inhabited face-to-face communities marked by webs of interlocking relationships.[4]

For working-class Americans, these small communities had a special meaning. The geographical boundaries of towns and villages were often treated as a form of nuptial commitment. And until marriage was imminent, they often remained emotionally attached to the pool of eligible mates defined by their community. In larger cities, smaller neighborhoods, districts, or work environments could define a class-based community.[5] Intimate relationships belonged to groups in working-class culture and were steadied and calmed by the geographical spaces they inhabited.

What was tacitly assumed, and almost never mentioned, was the racial homogeneity that was expected in marriage. Most Black and white Americans saw courtship as racially exclusive. This was such a covert and deeply held conviction that it was never stated.[6] The assumption of racial uniformity was almost always taken for granted when nineteenth-century Americans referred to their potential mates.

A communal ethos prevailed in working-class courtship. Small-town culture continued to provide the laboring class with a deeply satisfying group bond that regularly carried emotional priority over individual aspiration.[7] One expression of this group bond was the strong emotional pull of

Love and the Working Class. Karen Lystra, Oxford University Press. © Oxford University Press 2024.
DOI: 10.1093/oso/9780197514221.003.0003

community in courtship and marriage. Working-class courtship persistently embodied a commitment to home and a need to belong to a community. The intimate connections to place, together with racial exclusivity, formed a circle of "we" that defined marital choice and the meaning of love.

The phenomenon of homesickness was widespread in antebellum America and received particular attention during the Civil War, when Union doctors diagnosed some five thousand soldiers with the disease, claiming seventy-four died of acute trauma from being away from home.[8] Far from being rugged individualists, working-class Americans were attached to their local community during most of the nineteenth century. They organized their mate selection rituals around group membership and anchored their choices in the shared assumptions of belonging. Only when they could not return home did young singles reorient to a new community, sometimes reluctantly and sometimes appreciatively, and then set about choosing a mate.

"I wish I could see the Girls about home if I could come to old Chatham I would hug them as hard as ever I did," North Carolinian James Beavers wrote his brother, "for when I was down there before I hughed them and they hughed so good I want to hug them again."[9] James Beavers imagines himself hugging "them"—a group of girls at home—based on his memory that "they" hugged "so good." His description of this "group hug" is a graphic testament to a radically different mode of courtship than his middle-class countrymen were practicing at the time. While their courtship rituals were romantic, private, and dedicated to uniting two unique individuals, his was collective, public, and focused on a local pool of eligible mates. Romantic love was neither required nor expected within the dominant pattern of working-class courtship in nineteenth-century America.

When Nancy Glen inquired about the tribe at home in her small community (perhaps Ava), located within Noble County, Ohio, she singled out her girlfriend by saying, "who goes with you" but then added "and the rest of the girls." She followed by asking, "who does the boys go with."[10] Both Beavers and Glen saw the geographically bound pool of eligible, unmarried men and women as a "home team." Their emotional commitment was widely shared by nineteenth-century working-class men and women whose expectation—whether actualized or not—was to marry a member of their local community or "tribe."

The expectation of in-group marriage was the foundation of a distinctively nonromantic style of courtship commonly practiced by working-class Americans. This nonromantic approach to courtship can be roughly divided

52 LOVE AND THE WORKING CLASS

into three stages. In the first stage, the local marriage pool functioned as a collective sweetheart. Developing a courting relationship with someone in the community was part of belonging to the tribe. "Tell the girls that am comeing back," white Tennessean Charles Smith directed his relatives in the spring of 1851, "and when I get back I am agowing to pop the question."[11] Whether or not Charles had anyone in mind, he directed his future marital intentions to all "the girls." He was still in a compound relationship to the unmarried white women in his hometown tribe. The local "girls" and "boys" were expected (though this expectation could be thwarted) to define a person's marital future. Charles returned to marry Tamar Patterson, a girl from his local tribe in Overton County, Tennessee.[12]

One young Iowa soldier asked his sister to get a group photograph of four single white girls. "I will send my likenes to you and I want you girls to get your likeness you Mary McKingrie Amanda Comden Sara Crawford and Amanda Allen to get yours taken together and send then to me and I will pay fore it."[13] His request for the group photo was unusual and graphically demonstrated this local boy's attraction to the "girls" at home in Crawfordsville, Iowa (population 249).[14] Civil War soldiers from around the country were committed to the hometown girls. Confederate soldier J. M. Watson wrote his friend and neighbor J. B. O. Barkely, a shoemaker: "i Wish i could get home and fly round the girls with you bub."[15] His home was in Anderson district, South Carolina. Ansel Safford, a Union soldier, informed his parents and siblings, "I am learning to ceep house very well." He requested that they "tell some nice girl to wate untill I come home & we will make a link."[16] Home was the small town of Kirtland in northeast Ohio.

The Civil War did not establish, nor perhaps even strengthen, this courtship pattern. Giving first priority to location in thinking about courtship was common. Mobile men most often expressed a desire to return to a place they considered home to find a mate, even if that goal did not always translate into actual behavior. This intention was characteristic of the first stage of working-class mate selection.

Young men repeatedly expressed the desire and intention to marry one of the hometown girls. "I am not mared yet but I have Great hopes," J. W. Estes informed his parents, "I want you to tellall the Girls if I should chance not to get a wife That I will be with them After a while And they will have to stand abought."[17] Estes, who had been moving around Kentucky and Tennessee in the 1830s, thought of the white girls back home in East Tennessee as a secure marital pool. Another young man, Franklin Bell, had left the girls in

Lawrence County, Missouri, for the California gold fields in 1850.[18] Two years later he was living in Placerville and hoping to be the cook in his own boarding house. "You seem to think that Jasper and I had better come home and get marred," Franklin told his mother and siblings in the summer of 1852. "I think so to give me your hand on that you may tell the girls that I am comeing home some of these times when they will not be looking for me and they may prepare them selves for a foot race fite or a wedding for I am bound to marry as soon as I come."[19]

The first stage of nonromantic working-class courtship was often characterized by an explicit identification with a pool of eligible mates living in a particular place. "There is several of the boys that will come with me," Franklin continued, "and they are all cean to marry So if there is any girls that wishes to marry they shall not be disappointed when we come."[20] Men took the geographical pool of eligible singles seriously. They responded competitively, anticipating a successful match with the hometown girls, and fearful of ending up with an unsavory choice only if they stayed away too long.

Normally references to "the girls" at home were prideful and characterized by an intense geographical loyalty. However, it was not uncommon to criticize the "visiting team," that is, women in other locations. Charles Watson, a Minnesotan stationed in Helena, Arkansas, during the Civil War, conceived of the girls in Arkansas in the typical terms of working-class racial and regional boundaries. "There is no white Girls here scarcely none anyhow that are very good looking," he observed: "they look like the last rows of sumer."[21] This evocative rural metaphor of desiccated corn stalks effectively discredited the women of another geographical tribe.

Henry Clay Russell compared the girls of Memphis, Tennessee, very unfavorably to the Iowa maidens he left behind. "I must cofess that I do not like the southern girls as well as I do the Northern. they begin to paint down here as soon as they get out of the cradle." Henry was referring to cosmetics such as powder and rouge, "and by the time they get to the eighteenth or twenty they look like a fish all scaly. that is the old scales of paint begin to drop off. they ar not all as bad as this there ar some of them that hav not spoild themselves."[22] His image of some white southern women as scaly fish was strikingly unattractive, but it conformed to the practice of criticizing potential mates who were outside the hometown tribe.

Women operated within similar assumptions of tribal courtship. Hailing from Vermont, Polly Lanphear worked in a factory in Rosco, Illinois, where she socialized with the boys from New England. "They say that we seem some

54 LOVE AND THE WORKING CLASS

like their own folks, because we came from the east," she observed of the New Hampshire men, "they don't like the western folks verry well and I don't either."[23] Lanphear's expressed loyalty to her region was in sync with the boys'.

If a girl moved away from her hometown, however, she reacted differently than her male contemporaries. Unlike the young men who often remained loyal to the local girls, young women were almost always forced to switch home teams. The difficulty of moving around as a single woman was usually an overwhelming obstacle to reconnecting with the old tribe.[24] Unmarried women's geographical relocation usually resulted in a reconstituted set of tribal loyalties.

After moving from Vermont to Minnesota, Polly's sister, Mary, quickly adopted another pool of eligible men. "[T]here is more beaux here than you could shake a stick at in a year," Mary exulted to the folks at home. "Tell Abby Rogers if she wants to get married she better come out here for she would not be here a week before she would have a dozen offers."[25]

This was not the case with her brother and many other unmarried men, who expected and desired to return home to pick a mate. "How be the Girls their in Hartland," George Lanphear inquired about his Vermont village, "all fast as the Devil for getting married if so just let me know it and I will pitch in and see what I can do in the shape of relieving them." Though George was socializing in his newly adopted state of Minnesota, the collective pool of hometown girls in Vermont still claimed his loyalty.[26] Contrast this to his sister Mary, who rather quickly oriented herself toward marriage with one of the new tribe of young white men. Single women, whatever their wishes, had to relate to a new male collective.

"[Y]ou say that you kick the young men sometimes," a young white woman wrote her friend Margaret Dunlap, who was a hired servant, but "you must not kick them to hard you say that you cant kick the right one I cant tell you now to do about that I have not got any baus now I left two or three over the mountain the one i loved best is married and i dont care one cent about the rest." Her relationship with the boy she "loved best" was not highly individuated or emotionally intense, as she dismissed him along with the rest of the eligible men she left behind. "[I] have not got acquainted with any of the pasture boys yet," she observed expectantly.[27] Moving from "over the mountain" to the "pasture" in Craigsville, Virginia, this young woman had been forced to shift her focus to the boys in close proximity. Women of marriageable age were expected to reconstitute their tribal commitment to a new community when they relocated.

Not everyone was enamored of the place they left behind. Sarah Rice, for example, was happy to leave her hometown. Setting out at seventeen from her home in Somerset, Vermont, she found work as a "hired girl" for a family of seven in Union Village, New York. Almost nineteen at the close of 1839, she was confident in her judgments and full of self-righteous condemnation of her hometown. "No one knows how much I suffered the ten weeks that I was at home," she wrote her parents. "I never can be happy there in among so many mountains." Rice was full of disdain for her Vermont village. She bragged that her place in New York was "a good deal better than I can have there." One of her critiques was religious. "If I go home I can not have the privelage of going to meting [church] nor eny thing else." She vowed: "and as for mayyring and settling in that wilderness I wont."[28]

Supporting herself as hired help in another state, she indignantly announced that she would not be returning to "earn nothing" on a rocky farm with only two or three cows and no cash crop to sell. "It surely would be cheper for you to hire a girl that can do your work one that would be contented to stay in the desert than for me to come home and live in trouble all the time." She bristled at the very thought of returning to work on her parents' farm and marrying a hometown boy. For her, the local tribe was "a profane Sabbath breaking set." While she asserted, "I cannot bare the thoughts of going there . . . to live," she acknowledged that she had a "good father & Mother."

Surprisingly, the rebellious teenager closed her letter with a nod to parental authority: "I want you should write me an answer directly and let me know my fate." Clearly she believed her parents could command her presence at home. Her covert campaign for parental approval might explain the vehemence of her letter. "Do come away," she exhorted her long-suffering parents. "Dont lay your bones in that place I beg you."

After rejecting not only the people but the geography of her hometown, Sarah was still single and considerably more tolerant and good-humored six years later. "I want to see you all and proberbly shall in the course of a month or two," she wrote her father in 1845. "I want you should write immediately and tell all the news you can think of."[29] Though she felt a few pangs of nostalgia for the folks in Dover, Sarah made good on her promise never to marry in that "wilderness." She tied the knot in Massachusetts in 1847 after working there as a live-in domestic and briefly as a weaver in a textile mill.[30] She lived in the Bay State for the rest of her life.[31] Sarah Rice was very unusual in her self-conscious rejection of the tribe back home. Nevertheless, she was similar

56 LOVE AND THE WORKING CLASS

to many young women in her eagerness to connect to a new community of eligible men.

Working-class cultural assumptions surrounding mobility were clearly gendered. If the boys moved around, it was assumed that they would return home to marry a girl from the hometown tribe. The assumption was common, even if the local boy never reappeared. Single women had much less mobility than single men, and girls remained committed to the hometown boys from a stationary position within their village or town. "Robert I want you to Come home and that as soon as possible donte wait to get you awife," Elizabeth Rawlings admonished her brother, "we have aplenty of girls heare I will speake for one for you so come along."[32] Speaking on behalf of the girls' team, Elizabeth urged her brother to return home, implying that a number of hometown girls were ready to marry him. She illustrated the dilemma of the girls left behind: the more mobile boys had to return home to participate in a working-class courtship ritual that was local and face-to-face.[33]

The New England manufacturing town of Lynn, Massachusetts, is a textbook case of tribal reconstitution. More than 80 percent of female migrants from other parts of New England married men they met in Lynn and stayed there until they died.[34] Young women seeking temporary employment in another center of factory production in New England, Lowell, Massachusetts, were more mixed in their response. Hannah was working in the textile mills in Lowell in April 1836 when she suggested that her friend Mary return to work in Lowell, but more importantly, come back to "court" a "pretty fellow" who might be looking for a wife.[35] She and Hannah had grown up together in Pomfret, Vermont. Hannah was orphaned at sixteen and, following her own advice, did not bother to return home, marrying a New Hampshire lad in Dracut, another mill town just north of Lowell.[36] After moving away from her hometown, Hannah quickly reoriented herself to the new tribe of men in the Lowell mills. Mary, unlike Hannah, returned home to find a mate in their small town of 1,774.[37] Under certain conditions, including safe, reasonable transportation and geographical proximity, women too might return home with the intention to marry a local boy.

One sample of New Hampshire women who worked in the Lowell mills illustrates the risks and rewards of going home to find a mate. More than 24 percent returned to their hometown to marry and remained until they died. By contrast, 33 percent lived in Massachusetts cities for the remainder of their life (about 20 percent married in Lowell). Most of the rest lived in New Hampshire towns where they had not been raised. Evidently a majority

Many marriageable-age factory workers gathered together for this group photograph in a nineteenth-century Dover, New Hampshire, textile mill. Some of these young women were undoubtedly looking for mates among the men in Dover.
Courtesy of the Dover Public Library.

of women from the Granite State reconstituted their tribal loyalties and married eligible men from around New England whom they met in Lowell.[38]

Marcia Cole was one of those New Hampshire lasses who related to a new male collective, adopting the pool of eligible white men in Lowell where she went to work in the mills. She hated the "absolute confinement" and the lack of "pure light" or "the benefit of good . . . air." But one aspect of her experience was positive. Men as well as women might widen their mate selection pool when they worked in places where mobile young people gathered in significant numbers. She and her future husband, Charles Wardwell, met in the Lowell mills and married outside their local tribes. Rejecting any thought of resuming her work in a Lowell mill, she actually returned to her hometown in New Hampshire before their wedding. But she had taken herself out of the local pool and married Charles, a Maine native, within six months of her homecoming.[39]

58 LOVE AND THE WORKING CLASS

The danger of rejecting the pool of eligible young men after women relocated to a new location, even for temporary employment, is dramatized by the Lowell example. Rural New Hampshire women were, on average, twenty-three when they married and settled in Lowell.[40] If they worked in the mills and waited to marry until they returned home, their marriage age skyrocketed to thirty.[41] To leave the hometown eligibility pool at a marriageable age and return home to find a mate was, for women, to risk not just being the last chosen but never chosen. Forty-six percent of New Hampshire women who worked in Lowell returned home and never married. Of course these women would want the support of their family and their tribe (and an unknown number may have deliberately avoided marriage). But almost twice the proportion of unmarried female millhands from New Hampshire was living in their hometown when they died compared with their married peers.[42] This suggests, alongside other influences, that young women had good reason to reorient themselves to the immediately accessible tribe of eligible men when they moved.

While unmarried women who left their hometown (whether for paid work or not) generally conformed to the gender assumptions around a reconstituted courtship pool, young men most often expressed their intention to return home to get a bride. "I am single but I am keeping house," one bachelor wrote his friend Josh Liscomb. He explained that he was living with his hired hand along with the married blacksmith and his wife so that she could keep house for the men. "[S]o you no I must need a wife vary Bad," he confessed. "Josh I have But one thing a gainc Texas and that is Girls is to scarce and they are not so worthey as the girls is in that country all tho the scarity makes them valuale." Though he had relocated to a place near Waco, Texas, from Calhoun, Alabama, this man remained loyal to the hometown girls.[43]

But he assumed that the hometown girls, if they relocated, would switch their allegiance to the new tribe of boys. "Josh tell all the girls to come to texas if they wish to marry," he wrote in the fall of 1858, "for this is the plac for girls to marry." Loyalty to the hometown team still predominated on the boys' side, however. "[T]ell July Kirby that John Webster is talking about coming back after her," he wrote his friend Josh about another Texas émigré, "and tell her that he is a splendid fellow and I wood come to But I don't know who I could get I don't know of any girl thare that I could get."[44] The letter writer is himself probing whether any eligible white girls in his hometown might be interested in marrying him. He hints broadly that if Josh could identify which girls on the home team might say yes to a proposal, he would return home to wed. It is not so much that one particular girl was desired, but rather that a girl from the tribe was wanted for marriage. But he was not willing to risk public rejection and humiliation, not to mention the cost of returning home, without some reassurance.

This man had significant insecurity about his own looks and attraction. But his work as a cooper and wheelwright was prospering.[45] "[W]hen I first came hear," he revealed, "you no I must have had quite an onerly apperance and I were hardly countinenc by any But time has chang thing vary muc of late I have ben driving a fine horse and buggy and it is getting to Be Mr. Green."[46] Though the technology was different, this type of personal enhancement through transportation sounds very contemporary.

One father urged a regional loyalty that was more expansive than hometown allegiance but functioned similarly to define his son's pool of eligible mates. Black Virginian William J. Walker instructed his son in early February 1850 to stay true to his roots: "get you a wife from old Virginia old Virginia Shore—John for the sake of your happyness here after take the advice which I gave." John was in the navy and his father warned him not to fall for one of the "pretty Spanish girls," but to remember "let your old song Be true."[47] He was almost certainly referring to the earliest version of "Carry me Back to Ole Virginny," introduced in late 1847 or early 1848 by the Christy Minstrels.[48] The second stanza relates the cautionary tale of a rover who worked on a fishing scow and never settled down with a "Virginny" girl.

> If I was only young again,
> I'd lead a different life;
> I'd save my money and buy a farm,
> And take Dinah for my wife.
> But now old age, he holds me tight,
> My limbs, dey are growing sore;
> So take me back to Old Virginny,
> To Old Virginny's shore.[49]

The song's advice is to marry according to the demands of local affinity.[50] Race and geography were combined in Walker's sense of an ideal mate. Under certain conditions, a local attachment could be redefined to encompass loyalty to a broader region or even state. However, collective identification was usually anchored in a face-to-face community, which elicited expressions of loyalty and emotional bonding.

60 LOVE AND THE WORKING CLASS

This good-looking young man was photographed in work clothes. Would he take his father's advice about choosing a mate? His gaze is direct, determined, and world-weary.
Library of Congress LC-DIG-11060 Call # LOT 14022, no. 101.

At some point, both young men and women began the process of winnowing the eligible mates in their tribe. This was the second stage of working-class courtship. Friends and family were crucial to this sorting-out process, but hopeful singles still controlled their final choice. Although community members observed the mating rituals of young people with curiosity, interest, or dismay, there is little evidence of parental restrictions. Fathers like William Walker might give advice, but parental approval was not required by custom or law. Freedom was the watchword in working-class mate selection.[51]

Still, community vigilance was constant.[52] The local tribe monitored the activities of its members and created collective judgments that could be used to assess the disposition and abilities of a future husband or wife.[53] Community gossip provided feedback on the activities of local men and women, communicating important information about prospective partners. Though parents did not determine whom their children married, the tribe that surrounded young adults had an outsized influence on their choice of mate.

Since young and old alike were free to choose their spouse, it is important to discover how they differentiated one marriageable person from another. The working-class focus on a local community or tribe was a very useful starting point, as this practice dramatically narrowed the field of choice. Working within their local eligibility pool, singles gravitated to external appearance and everyday skills, with looks predominating as the number one criterion for both men and women. The high value placed on qualities of appearance harmonized with a practical attitude to mate selection that had little or nothing to do with emotional identification.

"I found me a might pretty sweet heart while I was down there," one female cousin wrote to another in Georgia, "he is fair complectod & blue eyed & red hair & he is smart as well as pretty."[54] Working-class women often singled out good looks when they discussed their "sweet hearts."[55] One young widow had a photograph taken with her boyfriend and flaunted his looks to Ella Buck, her Hoosier cousin: "we are going to have some more taken and then I will send you one to let you see how good looking my fellow is."[56] "I have one of the deares fellows in the world, and he is handsom," Mary Kesterson bragged to her Missouri cousin. "He is very tall 6 feet or more has blue eyes and light mushtash and black hair. you know he is good looking," she crowed. "I want you to promice to come up here Christmas and you will get to see him for he is coming then."[57]

Young men were at least as concerned with physical appearance as their female peers. Among working-class suitors, qualities of the inner self were most often subsumed in judgments of appearance. Time and again they expressed to brothers, sisters, friends, and parents an almost obsessive interest in courting a pretty woman above all else. *"I have been to two parties since I have been here and I haven't seen but one pretty girl yet, and she was from Missouri," a brother living in Texas told his sister. "Jack Barnes claims

62   LOVE AND THE WORKING CLASS

her and I claim her and I don't know how many go to see her. She is the best looking girl in Texas."[58] This young man most likely hailed from Missouri and was partial to a woman from his state.[59]

Male competition for the prettiest woman was a central component of working-class mate selection. "You musent brag to soon about your weoman," Matthew Marvin warned his brother George, even though "she may be all you represent her to be for I never saw her but once & did not see her then." Marvin probably meant that he did not know she was his brother's girlfriend, so he did not pay much attention to her. "I hope she is as good as you say," he acknowledged. "But I will lay you all in the shade for I will hunt this wide world all over & in to an other Ill go but what Ill beat you."[60] Born in New York, Marvin was living in the small town of Batavia, Kane County, Illinois (pop. 1,621), when he enlisted in the early months of the Civil War.[61] Though he bragged that he was willing to hunt "all over" for a woman who was more appealing than his brother's sweetheart, he selected his wife from the local pool in Kane County two years after the war ended.[62]

To attract a physically desirable woman was a sign of standing in the male community and directly correlated with male self-esteem. "I am five foot six inches pretty good looking fellow you know especially with such a heavy beard and mostach as you can judge I have got it would make that Miss Libby look out of her eye corners if she seen me," the harnessmaker Charles Watson wrote competitively. "I am afraid she would not think much of that other fellow ... and I think I will stand a pretty good show to get a pretty good one if I should be spared to get out of the army all right."[63] Watson's description of his future marriage partner—"a pretty good one"—said it all.

Though physical appearance was the quality most frequently mentioned by young working-class men looking for a mate, practical abilities could be important as well. Other than good looks, working-class men mentioned domestic skills more than any other qualification for mate selection. *"There is some nice looking girls here in old Virginia," Thomas Gaither admitted to his brother, "but most of them cannot get a meal's victuals [or] spin a roll. [They have] never seen a bur of cotton and they do not suit a North Carolina boy. I would not give a good North Carolina girl for a half dozen of them. I do not think [much] of Virginia [girls] nohow."[64] Thomas was yearning for the tribe of hometown girls. "[T]ell all Girls to be pretty Girls and write to me,"[65] he instructed his mother and sister. This was an ambiguous command. But it seems as if he meant that any local girl who wrote to him would look pretty to

WORKING-CLASS AMERICANS CHOOSE A MATE 63

Three young Union soldiers strike the pose of buddies who are used to having fun. They would certainly expect to court the girls back home.
Library of Congress LC-DIG-27116.

a soldier far from home. Good looks were an explicit priority but not an exclusive one. He clearly wanted a wife who had domestic skills.

Similarly, J. R. Littlejohn, writing for himself and his friend William Wood, insisted: *"I am going to marry between now [September 1856] and spring if I can get the right kind of girl. I want a girl that knows something about domestic affairs. That is just the sort of girl that I want for a wife. And Dick says that is the only sort of girl that he will marry." These men prioritized domestic skills over good looks in their search for the "Right kind of a girl." Both agreed that their cousins' pool of single women in Benton County, Alabama, was preferable to theirs in Spartanburg, South Carolina. They had decided to marry and settle down "before long" with an undetermined female member of their cousins' tribe.[66] The boundary of place was a necessary parameter in the working-class process of choosing a mate, even when they surrendered loyalty to their hometown voluntarily.[67]

In this intermediate or second stage of nonromantic courtship, connubial sifting was almost never done alone. Friends and family were expected to act as go-betweens to help establish a mutual interest in marriage. In order to save face in the group and avoid potentially embarrassing face-to-face rejection, couples might not even communicate directly until they had established clear intentions. The lack of unguarded communication was certainly an impediment in James Brewer's search for a wife. "I have got one of the prettyest likeneses Ever you saw and She is my Intended wheather I Ever get her or not," the unmarried Brewer, a seasoned cavalry soldier in the Twenty-Eighth Illinois Regiment, informed his sister Margaret. "I have knew her for about 15 years She is a Snorter I tell you for fun I have had more Social Glee with her than any other girl I Ever was with."[68] James put a high value on "social glee," a memorable phrase that implies a fun-loving person with a good sense of humor. Having known her for fifteen years, he had the experience to make his choice from among the women of his tribe without much worry or anxiety.[69] His only doubt was whether she wanted to marry him. He does not know because neither one has revealed their feelings to the other. For that, he needed an intermediary. His married sister Margaret did not volunteer, perhaps because she lived in another state.

Though George Lanphear had a special interest in one girl back home in Hartland, Vermont, after moving to the Midwest with a bunch of his siblings he never contacted her directly. Unlike a middle-class swain, who would have immediately begun a correspondence, Lanphear used an intermediary instead. Teasing his sister and brother-in-law about sending train tickets so that they could attend a dance with him, George added: "I want you should let Elen Shattuck see the card and tell her to be shure and come for I know she could lick the hul crowd a dancing."[70]

Little more than a year later, he asked where Ellen Shattuck was spending the winter. "Give my best respects to her," he directed his sister, "and tell her

I would like to see her very much I beleve that I shall have to write her a few lines one of thes dayes I promised her that I would write to her when I first come west but have not written yet."[71] He confirms a common pattern by asking his sister to act as an intermediary. But George saw no contradiction in socializing with the young women where he was currently living. "I am agoing to the singing school after supper," this transplanted New Englander informed his sister and brother-in-law, "and if nothing happens I shall go home with a darnt poaty Girl that I have got aquainted with for it is something that I have done a god many times since I have bin hear."[72] A frequent opportunity to meet prospective mates was provided by the nineteenth-century singing school, run in two- to four-week sessions by an itinerant musician who collected a small fee from each participant. Though music was a part of each evening's activities, singing schools were mostly a place for socializing with the opposite sex.[73]

They were also an opportunity for group kissing. In early March 1864, one North Carolina girl attended a singing school and observed that the participants turned it into a night of "play," by which she meant a kissing party. "You Just ought to have bin there to seen Miss Mollie Forenin and your little Clemmy play you could have Jot a many a sweet Kiss from her lips and if you had have bin there you would have Jot them to," she concluded.[74] Turning the singing school into a kissing party did not seem unusual to young people who were playing the field. Popular kissing-game rhymes inculcated and reinforced their mate-selection values. For example, after a boy and girl had been chosen to stand in the center of a ring, the circle would chant:

> Row the boat! Row the boat!
> Let the boat stand!
> I think —— —— is a handsome young man;
> I think —— —— is as handsome as he,
> And they shall be married, if they can agree.[75]

This game rhyme promoted physical attraction and endorsed marriage as a practical arrangement. Another popular kissing round had multiple regional variations:

> Had I as many eyes as the stars in the skies
> And were I as old as Adam
> I'd fall on my knees, and kiss whom I please,
> Your humble servant, madam.[76]

66 LOVE AND THE WORKING CLASS

Group activities included dances and parties celebrating various holidays and anniversaries.[77] After spending time with his brothers and sisters on New Year's Eve, 1855, Lanphear wrote an absent sister that he went "to a kissing party that evening ant staid till 12 aclock and then my self and to other chapes got up a team and went to the town of Rockton to a new years Ball ant ther we staid till morning I think that was a spending new Years party haperly."[78] George was doing odd jobs, such as chopping wood. His real devotion, however, was to having fun with the girls, a devotion he shared with his peers.[79]

After establishing a homestead in Minnesota the following year, Lanphear once again turned to his sister for advice and perhaps some third-party persuasion. "After I get my farm well under way so that I can live," he wrote, "I wouldent wonder if you should see me back their to Hartland a prowling round after me a little woman; if I can find one that would come west with me, but I doant know as I could, what do you think about it, do you think I could or not."[80] George Lanphear counted on his sister to act as his intermediary, communicating his feelings, indicating his intentions, and establishing a mutual interest in pairing off. Most likely his sister discovered that Ellen Shattuck was not interested, for George never mentioned her again.[81]

Mary Vanhorn gave her brother Joseph Hall some unfortunate news about his girlfriend back home in Ohio. "Mary i am Very glad that you hav informed me of What is going on i Will Send her picture to her and the same time send for my Ring," he announced, "tell Mother that I hate her that is [T]ill Baldwin [his girlfriend] i mean Worse than a Snake." He is hurt but refuses to admit it. "I don't Want you to think that I care a snap of my finger for her," he boasted to his sister, "there is Girls in the South here that She is not fit to black there Shoes that I could git if I Wanted them But I am in no hurry."[82]

Joseph outlined the procedure for breaking up in nineteenth-century poor man's style. First, stop talking about her: "I don't want you to mention Till Baldwin to me any more for She is plaid out." Second, return rings and pictures: "all that I want of he is the Ring that she had got of mine I am Independent of any of the Baldwin family I will send her picture to her and send for my Ring Mary." Third, get a sibling, parent, or friend to find you another girl: "Mary have me a nice Girl picked out a gainst I get home." Fourth, make fun of your ex: Mary should pick "one that wont play out like the one that has got Such Big feet ha ha ha."[83] His sister was the ultimate go-between, causing the breakup by reporting on his girlfriend's inappropriate behavior and, at his suggestion, singling out another "nice girl" for him when he returns home.

"What do you think of my Case," Jaspar Bell asked his sister and new brother-in-law, "do you believe I could marry if I was to come back you must recollect that I am prettyneer a bachelor." He is likely referring to his age. "You must Choose one for me," he wrote, "and tell her all the fine storys you can think of and try to keep her single until I return then I will try my luck and sea if it is better than it is in the mines." He ends with one of the most memorable phrases in all working-class correspondence: "Keep wonder for me and I believe I can shine."[84]

Cousins were also prime candidates for the role of go-between. "Tell Melly hendricke to hold on I will be back before it gets much longer," H. C. Hunt, a hired hand working in a brickyard in Washington State, wrote his cousin in 1882, "if I don't take a notion to take the school marm that is here."[85] Hunt had yet to write Melly Hendricke and was communicating through a family member. Some couples exchanged letters, but the majority chose to connect through a third party. This is one reason why their courtship letters were scarce.

The information that passed through intermediaries was sometimes casual. One married woman who ran a boarding house in Rosco, Illinois, told a young lodger that "their was a young fellow over in Vermont that wanted to get him a wife by the name of Hiram Mott." This upbeat landlady was volunteering to play the go-between with one of the three female factory workers renting her rooms. While an unlikely scenario given their geographical separation, the young boarder was not put off. "She said she should like to see him I think they would be a handsome cupple don't you." Naming him was an indication that the landlady's intentions were not completely frivolous. "I should like to tuck them up the first night," was her hopeful benediction.[86]

Third-party transmission allowed one to claim misunderstanding if an overture was rejected. Cover could even take the form of a "joking" claim in instances where there was sufficient ambiguity. "I went to singing School and got see the Girls," George Deen told his sister. "Margaret there is some of the pretiest girls here in the world well I must ask you something about whether that old mans Girl is maried that keeps tavern in Lineville if she is not tell her to wait for me."[87] Deen was curious enough about the tavern girl's feelings to send out a feeler. If he was rejected, however, the "bravado" of his command

68   LOVE AND THE WORKING CLASS

could be interpreted as a joke. There is a clear level of self-protection operating here and in other examples.

Ned directed his friend David to act as an intermediary with a hometown girl. "David tell Sarah S to not get married till I get home," Ned instructed. "I am going to bring hur a little Reble he is a nise little fellow," he joked, then requested "give this ring to Sarah S."[88] Serious enough to give Sarah S. a ring, Ned still spoke through a male friend.

Predictably, parents offered advice and also served as go-betweens of sorts. The parents of Russell Ferguson wanted him to come home to Missouri. Hoping to motivate him to leave California, they hinted at the shrinking pool of local maidens. "Russel perhaps if you are a gone to come here to get a wife you had beter com soon."[89] The following year, Russell's parents were even more specific. "Misses Roth and Miss Ann Bolin sends there best, lov to you. Ann is yet single," they hinted openly. "The ould lady says you was her choice of all my sons."[90]

"Please beare with mee I don't know how you are sittuated," one father cautioned his widowed son, "but it seems to mee if you could find som one to suit you it would best for you to get A companion but don't go to the world to hunt for one but to the church." This father told his son to ask God to guide him but then provided his own advice. "There might be A chance heare for you aftor A while Duncella Musich who married fred Lee lost hur husband last winter about 6 months ago she has one Child and will have another is good looking A Mithodist and has some money."[91] His selection criteria included religion and economic assets, but he positioned good looks first in his inventory of her assets. She was a young widow, an age factor that his father also considered.

Mothers as well as fathers performed their role as intermediaries with alacrity. An unmarried Confederate soldier addressed his "dear friend" Margaret in a letter he was writing to his mother. "I recived Afew linds from you and was glad to hear from you," he noted plainly. "I send you A brespen and finger Ring for your kindness to me and I Want you to Ware them and Remember me and I Want you to rite to me and I Will rite to you as often as I can." This young Alabamian singled Margaret out from the local tribe of girls in a short note contained within his mother's letter. Following his note to Margaret, he quickly affirmed his attachment to the larger pool. "[T]ell the garild [girls] All houddy for me and tell not to Marry tell the War ends," he instructed his mother, "for I may Want to Marry my Self When I get back."[92] There is self-protection in maintaining an attachment to the tribe of girls. Using the intermediary services of his mother, Elizabeth Fuller, was also a shield.

Margaret also preferred to communicate through his mother. Elizabeth Fuller told her son that Margaret did not expect a gift from him for the "trifling present" she sent him. "[Y]ou was mour then welcom to what she dun for yu and wish it was in ther pow er to do mouer," Elizabeth Fuller dutifully reported, "but shee returnes you many thanks for your pressents you sent her." Clearly Margaret was comfortable employing his mother as a liaison, even using her as a mouthpiece to flirt: "she ses you must send her word hoo she must keep frorm marring so as shee ma taulk to them," Elizabeth cheerfully repeated. She obviously approved of Margaret's interest in her son: "you mus write to her and let her no how you are," she urged.[93]

Rufus Wright, a soldier in the First US Colored Troops, instructed his wife to tell Miss Emerline that "John Skinner is well & sends much love to her."[94] African American soldier David Demus, a member of the Massachusetts Fifty-Fourth who lived in Pennsylvania before the war, asked his wife to pass along some information to Ginney. "[G]ive mi love to giny gater and tell giny that i heave a nice youn man fer her and if se Want to rite to him Wiy let me now in the nex letter fer he Wod lik to rit to som yon lady verry much."[95] David asked his wife to find out if Ginney Gator wanted to begin a correspondence with someone "nice," presumably within her community of eligible men. David's brother-in-law, Samuel Christy, upped the ante by identifying himself as the eager swain: "tell Miss Gator if she is still a bout that i Wont hur to Write to me," he instructed his sister.[96]

Simeon Anderson Tierce, an African American soldier from The Hills community in Westchester County, New York, informed his wife, "There is a young man coming home with me when i come—i don't know when that will be—by the name of Mr. Johnson. Tell Mary to have her cap set for him when i come home as he is the handsomest man on the ground."[97] Tierce was a sergeant in the Fourteenth Rhode Island Heavy Artillery (Colored) and was writing from their training camp on Dutch Island. Mary was the sister of a close friend and neighbor. The Hills was a Black community with around 190 residents, resulting in a very small pool of eligible marriage partners. Mary had likely complained about the scarcity of marriageable men. Tierce was expanding that pool by bringing Mr. Johnson home to meet his friend and neighbor. "[T]ell Mary for me that there is a plenty of young men down here," he responded in another letter, "for there is a plenty."[98]

70 LOVE AND THE WORKING CLASS

Many rural Black communities in the North experienced the problem of very small pools of eligible mates. Nineteen-year-old Aaron Freeman was an African American who lived in Hinesburgh, Vermont, and worked as a farm laborer for the Robinsons, a white Quaker family. Twenty-two-year-old George Robinson, his employer's son, was in Savannah, Georgia, in 1847 on business when he directed his older brother Thomas back in Vermont: "Tell Aaron I could get him a very nice wife here, either a little black, a good deal black, or as black as tar, as we have all varieties." George was hypersensitive to skin color as befits someone who was described by one authority as expressing "a sort of rank-and-file racism." Clearly race was an agreed-upon boundary in local mate selection. George was responding to the scarcity of Aaron's pool of eligible mates by suggesting that he expand his geographical reach. However, Aaron waited ten years to marry an African American woman where he lived.[99] In a state where the total number of Black Americans was 718 in 1850, and only around 15 percent of them lived in Aaron's county, such allegiance to his local community is striking.[100]

Unmarried men and women who grew up in the same community formed a racially uniform pool of eligible mates defined by region and town. They established mutual interest through the mediation of go-betweens and the context of group gossip and support. Working through an intermediary provided a buffer against losing face in a situation where privacy was minimal. The instructions to go-betweens reveal that for many there was little emotional disclosure in face-to-face interactions or in letters until a marriage was imminent.[101]

Tribal intimacy eventually narrowed into an individual, or third, stage of nonromantic courtship. But what was, in effect, an act of pairing off played out somewhat differently for young women than young men. For the men, a woman was singled out from among the tribe with the help of a go-between who established her willingness to be courted. One New England cousin described it as "stepping up to a girl," an apt description of how courtship worked for men. This female cousin added, "and we think it will be a match."[102] Men would "step up" to a woman who agreed to be courted by stepping out of the eligibility pool.

In the third phase of nonromantic courtship, a decision to marry required a readiness to leave the eligibility pool and pair off with the opposite sex. A man signaled his choice of a mate to the entire community by calling on a single woman at her residence. Their continued interaction as a couple apart from the group was public confirmation of her willingness to marry him.[103]

WORKING-CLASS AMERICANS CHOOSE A MATE 71

A young woman of marriageable age is dressed for a formal studio portrait in 1861. She may have intended to give this photograph to her family or to a special friend.
Library of Congress AMB/TIN 5309 LC-DIG-11074.

72 LOVE AND THE WORKING CLASS

"Well I heard of another wedding going to be next Sunday week I was surprised when I heard it," Mollie D. Gaither admitted, reflecting the watchful eye of the community, "for I never knowd of any person going to se her."[104] Normally when an unmarried man paid a call on an unmarried woman, the community was watching. Mollie was surprised because the couple kept their intentions secret by avoiding pairing off in public—a ritual act of commitment that involved separation from the tribe. Of course, relationships could be broken off before the wedding, but this was not common. Working-class couples were motivated to avoid such public "failure."[105]

When a working-class man regularly sought the company of a specific woman at or around her house and she reciprocated, the presumption was that they would soon be married. In other words, to "keep company" with a specific person on a consistent basis was the nonromantic equivalent to being engaged. This American understanding of keeping company was also common in working-class England.[106]

Once the man stepped up to the woman and she stepped out of the eligibility pool, marriage usually followed within months.[107] "He proposed to two other girls before he did to Roanna to his certain knowledge & how many more he don't know," as one man reported the gossip from Dakota County, Minnesota, where he was homesteading, "and after *2 weeks* acquaintance with Roanna, married her." What was the local verdict? "He has turned out to be the smartest carpenter in town, & altogether is a pretty clever fellow, he is building a house for himself this winter so that I think Roanna will have a good comfortable home & a husband that will take care of her."[108] Two weeks was short, even by working-class standards. Nonetheless this marriage was approved on the basis of its practical results. The bystander gave little thought to its emotional foundations.

According to her brother, Mary Lanphear went to more than thirty dances in Minneapolis and attracted many prospective suitors.[109] But one was finally the "write one." "I never saw a Girl courted any harder then she is at the prsent time," Mary's brother told their sister Eliza: "to day she & Mr Cummings have gon to take a ride up to Hutchinson about 17 miles from hear but how things will terminate is more then I can tell."[110] Mary and Frank Cummings were married in less than two months. Marriage most often followed a public pairing off within three to nine months.[111]

Though circumstances and motives varied, working-class suitors generally saw individuated courtship as *following* a generalized decision to marry. Middle-class suitors thought courtship overall was an essential process *preceding* a decision to marry. Eighteen-year-old Frank Flint, the son of a farmer, shared the middle-class interpretation of courtship. Consequently he had a jaundiced view of the marriages of his peers, based on their rush to the altar. "There would be a great many more happy matches," Flint contended, "if people would not be in quite so much of a hurry about getting married."[112] Though he was definite, short courtships did not necessarily correlate with unhappy marriages, because they were the last stage in a process deeply embedded in tribal boundaries, local knowledge, and the mediation of family and friends.

One important gender difference permeated the dynamics of choice in stage three. Young women might express their preferences through intermediaries as well as directly, but they still had to wait for the man to single them out from the tribe. "I dremp the other night that you and Mary Dodson was to be married," one single woman teased her male friend. "I thought I herd you ask her to have you and she sed she would have you if you would be for southern rits."[113] The two Kentuckians supported the Union but had family and friends on the other side of the Civil War. In this dream, the young man asked Mary Dodson "to have" him, followed by her conditional acceptance of his offer. Young women had the power to reject overtures or set conditions for acceptance, but their social mores did not give them permission to "step up" first. If they were observing their culture's constraints, women could encourage, reject, or hold back, but they could not initiate the decisive pairing off.

Charles H. Smith apprised his family that on his travels to Missouri he found his "old sweetheart in health and well to doo tho she aint maried yet." Almost as soon as she saw him, "she said as how She would like to now my mind," he reported, "and I told her I guest she would now it by waiting."[114] His response to her forceful inquiry might have been tactful, but it was also mocking. In spite of her frank approach and her clear desire to marry him, she could do nothing but wait until he decided to make his intentions public.

"They hant any of the girls about here that have got smart enough to catch Mr Goodal Lovina," one unmarried woman informed another, "and Laura Shippy and Emily Dosworth went over and made him an after noon visit and they did have a jolly time they never got home until it was almos dark."[115] The women of this Minnesota community might flirt, but however much they wanted to "catch Mr. Goodal Lovina," they could not initiate a pairing off of their own volition.

A country schoolteacher, Justina Woods, found most of the available men in her community beneath contempt. In reviewing potential candidates with her sister, she evaluated each with a cold, critical eye, reckoning his merits and demerits in terms of physical appearance. "He is tolerably good looking," she informed her sister, "he has hair just like Marlow Teasis only it is about the color of mine but I think his eyes are two close together for me."[116] Though she disdained most of the men who paid court, Justina was not indifferent to finding a marriage partner. Writing to her sister Zelia, she declared her intention to marry before spring. Helping the process along, Justina wore a dress so tight that, she said, "it had like to kill me when ever I put it on." She wore it two days "because there were beaux about." The result was that she "could not draw a long breath or hardly turn my self in bed for a week."[117]

In spite of her intention to marry, the critical Justina was still single four years later. She was aware that teaching in several rural communities expanded her pool of eligible mates beyond her hometown of Belleview, Missouri, with its eighteen hundred inhabitants.[118] What she did not understand was why this multiple community exposure failed to yield a husband. "It is a wonder that I cant nab some body when I go into strange places," she confessed to her sister eight years before the Civil War stripped the countryside of men. "I recon I could if I would be content to take a whole family There is no young men down here, that I would give shucks for, and not many of any sort, but lots of girls."[119] She is a reminder that the intention to marry did not always lead to the church or courthouse. Justina's problem was likely exacerbated by her schooling and her farm family's land wealth. Her ambiguous class position heightened her negative attitude toward the poorer, undereducated men in her tribe. Nevertheless her highly critical stance toward the single men of her acquaintance, including her claim to have shunned single fathers, though no doubt sincere, was also a defensive maneuver in the face of masculine indifference to her expressed desire to marry.

Judging by her own criteria, Justina was forced to lower her standards in order to get married. At age thirty she wed a widower who was sixteen years her elder. When they married, her husband's farm was one-quarter the value of her father's and located in a township in Missouri that was one-quarter the size of her natal home.[120] Justina was able to avoid the burden of caring for someone else's large family, however, as her husband had only one child, a girl who was ten years old. When the pool of eligible single mates shrinks beyond a certain point, as Justina discovered, widows or widowers were often the only recourse. She got pregnant almost as soon as she was married and had four children before she died in 1869.[121]

Working-class men and women might find carefree fun and visible enjoyment in all three stages of nonromantic courtship, but they could also experience anxiety, pain, and doubt. Fear lurked just beneath the surface for those who did not find easy acceptance in their tribe. Their anxiety and distress had to do with the expectation and reality of an ever-shrinking geographical pool of single men and women. "We are all well and all the girls is well," Julia Sutton told her friend Russell Ferguson, "and if you don't come back pretty soon you won't get a wife in this neighborhood unless you take the last." The geographical limits of tribal courtship were clearly reflected in her warning: "if A.B. does marry there will be but four girls left on this side of the river."[122] Being the last chosen if you were a woman or taking the last woman if you were a man was a worrisome prospect.

Defining courtship as a group relationship removed the private pain of middle-class couples in romantic love but created more opportunity for public rejection and humiliation. Choosing sides for a youthful sporting match would be a modern analogy. In drawing from a pool of players and picking them off one by one, the undesirability of the last chosen is palpably demonstrated. So too in nineteenth-century working-class courtship: to remain in the pool too long was shameful and potentially disastrous.

After almost a decade-long sojourn in Northern California, F. L. Bell admitted that he probably "could not get any of the young ones in that country," meaning his Missouri home, "so I think that this is a better place for me to get a wife than that."[123] Bell abandoned his hometown tribe only when he thought the available pool of women back home had shrunk to "old maids" and older widows. In working-class culture, unmarried women who remained in the eligibility pool were, by a certain age, presumed to be undesirable "picks."

Women of all classes were long vulnerable to the derisive, shaming power of the term "old maid." "I want you to fetch me a Virginia wife out here Some hansom and clever girl. Tell Betsy young girls are ready sale here but old maids rate at 25 Cents a hundred," William Meeter joked about frontier Missouri (Callaway County) to his cousin who lived in Greenville, Virginia.[124] Harriet Buck had a more optimistic message. "The old maids don't get married of very fast over their," she observed about her home state of Vermont. "[T]ell them to come out here," referring to Minnesota, "if they want a fellow rich and poor all visit together out here they don't feel so proud as they do their."[125] She and her husband were farming in Minnesota, and her reference to old maids is couched in terms of a more egalitarian and inclusive system of social interaction that, by implication, provided a larger pool of single men. She resented the hierarchical class system she left behind in Vermont.

Mollie Houser was aware of the limited pool of unmarried men still at home in Virginia. She wrote: "we have a good many [weddings] here young ladies marry old Bachelors I dont no how we will do when they are all [married]." Most of the eligible young men were in the Confederate army, and Mary disdained the young women's rush to the altar as the pool of eligible men shrank. "I think I will marry for riches & marry an old Bachelor," she joked. Then she stated her true intentions. "I believe I would sooner marry a yong man with nothing in hand than for to marry an Old man with a thousand tracts of land."[126] At twenty years old, Mollie was young enough to bide her time until the soldiers returned from the war.

"Don't you think Aunt Harriets oldest son is married you would never guess who is the honored person," Manchester, New Hampshire, millhand Anna Mason gossiped with her mother. "[N]o other than *Ellen Stevens* Laura Sails oldest girl Perhaps she thought it was her last chance." The mismatch was obvious to Anna. "She has taken her *Piano* carpets and all her accomplishments into the woods."[127] The clear message is that the pool of eligible men had shrunk to the point where Ellen had few choices left.

More than 75 percent of never-married women who were once employed as domestics and later in life transitioned (between 1850 and 1885) to the Boston Home for Aged Women, migrated from small New England towns when they were twenty-six or older. The average marriage age across the country for white females in the period 1850 to 1880 wavered between 22.8 and 23.4. (In the New England census region the marriage age was around 1.5 years older.) This suggests that many unmarried women migrated to the big city only when the local eligibility pool had shrunk to the point where they no longer believed marriage was a realistic possibility. One of the major benefactors of the Home for Aged Women, a lifelong single woman herself, explained that she wanted to shelter older women like her "from the 'world's dread laugh.' "[128]

Women were vulnerable to the fear that no man would want them for a wife, but men were also afraid of being rejected as husbands. The image of the "old bachelor" as someone who could not get a wife was powerful.[129] Mollie D. informed her boyfriend Burgess that their cousin was married. "He said he was determind that he would not keep bachlars hall I do not blame him for maring if he wanted to," she wrote, never mentioning his bride.[130] Her cousin's decision to marry overrode the specific person he chose to wed in Mollie D.'s revealing omission. These personal decisions were themselves shaped by the group, for as the pool of eligible mates shrunk, there was greater urgency to get out of the pool and not be the last choosing or chosen. Scarcity in the collective pool of eligible mates was usually viewed with some alarm by both sexes.

John Garriott, a bachelor farmer, mocked the negative stereotype to his family: "The old Bathler wount hurt any buddy if he ant good looking he is a batchler and every expects to be . . . it is seldom he thinks of the girls onley his friends an connction." But Garriott knew how misleading the image could be. If he returned home from the war, "it would be the best thing to get me a wife," he confided to his family, "if I could git any boddy to have the old curley hed this I know." At thirty-one, he was deeply insecure about his looks and his age.[131]

His sister, acting as a go-between, suggested a "nise girl worth any boddys attention" by the name of Mary Hill. John agreed with his sister's judgment but was disheartened. "But what is that to the old Batchler in the war. She Woud not Look at me hardley if I was there and no buddy else would sutch an old fellow as I am." John opened up to his sister. "Do you think that I wanto Marrey: Shaw what could I do with a woman: But if I was surtin that I could git Mary Hill I would Desurt and come and Marrey her."[132] John was in the Mississippi delta with the Eighteenth Missouri Infantry Volunteers.

His low self-esteem was based upon his physical appearance: the courtship criteria that he believed most disqualified him. "I don't keer if you don't show it to any boddy else," Garriott responded to his sister, who did not like the photograph that he sent her, "for I know that it is not good lookin Neather Can there Be a good one takin from my face if I was not so miserabel ugley I would have it taken agin an send it to you."[133]

Seven months later, Garriott had changed his tune. Two women were pursuing him. One was Mary Hill, the old friend his sister Nancy had recommended, and the other was a widow who wrote "some mighty good and awful loving letters to me: you ought to se them. If I was there I would sho them to you: she wants me," he preened happily: "oh that you could see the letters that she writes to me: they are most to mellow for me."[134] It was sacrilegious in middle-class courtship to share love letters, but the public boundary of working-class "intimacy" was much wider and more inclusive.

John was conflicted about the widow. "I exspect that shes a good women," he told his sister. "I still write to her but I do not know what to think of hur." Garriott asked his sister to make some discreet inquiries.[135] The widow, Permelia Meadors, failed to pass muster because a year later he was writing confidently about "my girl Mary."[136] But Garriott's confidence was misplaced, because Mary Hill married William Turner in December 1864 before he returned from the war.[137] Men could also be thwarted in their choice of mates.

Born in Indiana, Garriott moved with his family to Iowa and then Missouri. John was farming with his brother-in-law and sister in Medicine,

78 LOVE AND THE WORKING CLASS

Mercer County, Missouri, before joining the Union side in the Civil War. After the war he married a woman seventeen years his junior and had seven children, relocating to Kansas in the early 1880s.[138] The death toll of the war worked to older men's advantage in finding a younger wife.

In nonromantic working-class mate selection the decision to marry was given primacy over the unique individual as long as the tribe offered a range of choice. This meant that the geographically defined pool of eligible mates had not shrunk to what participants considered unacceptable limits. If a range of choice was available, prospective brides and grooms were reassured that they would find someone willing to fill the role of husband or wife within the tribe. Thus the collective carried more weight than the individual even though marriage itself was not communal. Choice was an important part of the tribal mate selection process, but it operated more along the lines of "the best available person willing to marry me" than the romantic "You are the only one for me."

James Beavers longed for a group hug with the single women of Chatham County, North Carolina, after he enlisted in the Confederate infantry.[139] He exemplified the tribal affinities of stage one in nonromantic courtship, while his younger brother George had already entered the intermediate stage of winnowing the local pool.[140] Although his choice was provisional and ex-ploratory, George had already picked out a woman of interest named Mildred Yates. "I was glad to here from Miss mildred Yates that she was getting on fine with boys," he wrote his brother-in-law. "Tell Miss Mildred that I would be glad to here from her at any time it would giv me Joy." Typically, Beavers thought nothing of sending messages to Yates through a go-between. "I ad-vise hir not to lov none of them till pece is acomplished," George instructed his brother-in-law, "an all of the solders return home to there intended an most sirley respected." Though he hinted at his interest in marrying Mildred, his actual promise was not personal but collective: he included himself in the group of local soldiers who would return home with the intention to marry some woman from their tribe.[141]

Nonetheless his letter to his brother-in-law contained a singular expres-sion of feeling for Mildred Yates in the form of a love poem.

To Miss M Yates

Miss I pray that the winds that blow
Over the tops of the trees may cary

My love to my native land an
My hapy home an so to my
Entended, never forgot.[142]

Beavers's charming poem is not in formulaic rhyme, which was the common idiom of working-class poetry. Probably an original expression, it underlines the primacy of place in the emotional world of working-class intimacy. Beavers sends his love on a journey, first, to his "native land," meaning North Carolina; second, to his "happy home," meaning Chatham County, his local community; and, third, to the potential mate he identified with home.

The fact that Beavers thought nothing of including a love poem at the bottom of a letter to his brother-in-law dramatically demonstrates the gap between middle- and working-class sensibilities. Nineteenth-century Victorians would have scoffed at the very idea of using intermediaries during courtship to express their love. Privacy was almost a religious vow. Within the working-class ethos, however, privacy was neither required nor expected.

In the middle-class world, the use of the word "entended" might indicate that the couple had made a formal arrangement, such as an engagement, or that they had some understanding about a future together. In the working-class world it often indicated something more basic and less developed. Beavers's use of the word "entended" was a signal that Mildred Yates was a "woman of interest." This meant he had tentatively singled her out from the group. Though he had the prerogative to take the lead, she must reciprocate or the relationship would not go forward.

Four months later, he told his brother John that he "ant hird from Miss Mildred in so long I recon she has forgoten me but I hant forgoten her yet. Giv hir my best love an respect."[143] Beavers was still communicating with his "entended" through an intermediary. His ambiguous references in that same letter to a collective sweetheart—"I don't want them to get mared till I come back home"—and nonspecific yearnings for "a grile [girl] to fly around aboat once a week"—indicate that he was still attached to the eligible girls back home as a way to hedge against rejection but also as an expression of his own uncertainty.[144] Whether or not Mildred Yates was on his mind, Beavers clearly intended to have a relationship with a local girl. "[T]hat is what I like here in this troebleson world," he declared. Mildred exercised her prerogative to deny him, as far as his letters reveal, by simply being unresponsive to the cues provided by his go-between. She married another soldier from North Carolina more than a year before George returned home.[145]

80 LOVE AND THE WORKING CLASS

For most of the nineteenth century, tribal courtship was the dominant path to marriage for working-class Americans. George had passed beyond his attraction to a group of local girls and had entered another stage of courtship by expressing his interest in Mildred Yates. But he was stopped from moving forward by Mildred's rejection of his overtures. Even before George was clear about Mildred's intentions, he remarked "I hant forgoten her yet." By adding "yet" to his assertion, he signaled that he could put Mildred out of his mind, perhaps anticipating that she did not reciprocate his preference for her. Like many single men, he believed that he would be able to find a wife from among the eligible women in his tribe. After he was mustered out, George arrived at the last stage of courtship by deciding to marry and then pairing off with a Chatham County girl named Caroline H. Williams who, unlike Mildred, agreed to step out of the local eligibility pool with him.[146] George and Caroline joined the majority of working-class Americans who were content to marry an acceptable member of their tribe who was willing to marry them.

3

The Love Continuum

Understanding Romantic and Nonromantic Attachment

Frank Flint, a Civil War soldier from Minnesota, scrutinized the courtship behavior of his comrades-in-arms and friends at home. "No couple ought to get married at first sight nor the second," he insisted; "thay ought to know each other perfectly and be sure that thay love each other." Unlike many of his working-class peers, Flint believed in romantic love: "a great many make themselves unhapy by marrying before they know whether they love each other or not, they think they do but after a while it turnes out to be nothing but fancy or admiration of a pretty face and when the fancied thing is gone their love is gone also."[1] The kind of love Frank valued was a private, inward-looking emotional experience based on mutual trust and understanding. He believed that couples should demand a high level of personal awareness and self-disclosure before they married. In his words, they ought "to know each other perfectly."

Frank realized that his pals did not probe their inner feelings or those of the women they courted. He may or may not have recognized that a different group of Americans was aiming to live up to his courtship ideals. Better educated and certainly more affluent than Frank's peers, these middle-class Americans believed in romantic love and conducted their courtships with an intense focus on getting to know each other. Frank believed that this kind of mutual self-knowledge was the true definition of love. He was part of a minority of working-class couples who sought to cultivate the feelings of romantic love in their intimate relationships. By contrast, his working-class friends and acquaintances approached marriage as a practical matter of choice, often centered on the good looks of eligible mates in their local community.

The language of their letters suggests that the working-class experience of love is best described on a continuum. Those like Frank Flint, who shared their sense of love with middle-class romantics, congregate at one end of this emotional continuum, while the large majority of working-class Americans

Love and the Working Class. Karen Lystra, Oxford University Press. © Oxford University Press 2024.
DOI: 10.1093/oso/9780197514221.003.0004

were located on the nonromantic side. Some couples were situated in the middle and seemed to mix and match romantic love with elements of nonromantic attachment.[2]

Young men and women (as well as widows and widowers) alert to the possibilities of marriage were especially attuned to the meaning of love. Those who practiced nonromantic courtship were willing to pair off with the best available member of their tribe. They experienced love as an intentional, place-driven set of feelings dependent on their identification with a group.[3] Group associations created boundaries that helped people define their marital futures by regulating their choice of mate and channeling their expression of love. "I expect to marry some respectable Ladie when I get home," Delos Lake, a white Union soldier whose family lived in Michigan, told his mother, "and I want to write to them all."[4] In his next letter, he instructed his brother: "Give my love to all of the young Ladies there."[5] Expressions of love in the first stage of tribal courtship were collective, as demonstrated by Lake's offer of love to all the young ladies at home. But this seeming inclusivity was deeply rooted in an unspoken assumption of racial homogeneity.

Another soldier, born a free person of color, addressed his sister: "give my love to all the inquireing friends an like wise to yourself and to all the girls." Writing at the end of May 1865, Jacob Christy had survived the Civil War in the Massachusetts Fifty-Fourth, and he proudly anticipated not only his homecoming parade but also his reentry into the local community of Mercersburg, Pennsylvania, with access to the pool of eligible African American women.[6] Once again structural and emotional commitments overlapped in his expression of love. Communal intimacy was primary.

Ten months earlier his brother Samuel sent his "love to Father and to Elizabeth And to all the rest of the Frends. . . . Give my love to Ant mary and unkel Solomon," he wrote his sister, "and to all the ladys and tell them to take Good Care of them sels for i think i Will Be Home to Sea them Before long."[7] Like his brother, Samuel directed love to the collective "ladys" at home through an intermediary. They were both focused on a local pool of eligible mates defined by race and place.

Rufus Wright served in the First Colored Infantry, which saw duty in Norfolk, Portsmouth, and Yorktown, Virginia. A bondsman in North Carolina before the Civil War, Wright married a Portsmouth girl in 1863 who was also a former slave.[8] He acted as an intermediary for his fellow soldiers, writing to his wife about the marriageable girls in Portsmouth: "all the Boys sends there love [to] them."[9] The young men's loyalty was attached to a place,

A Union soldier is caught alone and in a contemplative mood, perhaps thinking about the friends and family he left behind.
Library of Congress LC-DIG-11206; LOT 14022, no. 174.

84 LOVE AND THE WORKING CLASS

Portsmouth, where they had served as a regiment. Like his white peers, Wright took for granted that "the girls" collective would be the same race as "the boys." And he anchored the men's marital prospects to a specific community where they had worked together as a group.

Another correspondent wanted to marry but had no particular woman in mind. He was *not* looking for a romantic bond with one special woman but "A wife," which is a role that could be filled by many women. *"I want to come home worse than I ever did in life," white South Carolinian D. Ellis confided to his brother in 1852. "I am not satisfied at all and can't be without I can get a wife. I think I shall come home and look out for one before long."[10] His role orientation was common among working-class men who were thinking of marriage. He had no attachment to or for a special individual in his Darlington, South Carolina, community. His expressed intention was to marry one of the girls in his tribe. Thus he told his brother to "giv my Lov to all pertickly the garls." In the initial stage of tribal courtship, working-class Americans seem most comfortable with a "love" relationship to a collective or group.

Young women rarely sent messages of love to the hometown boys as a group because they were not oriented to, and had much less experience with, temporary mobility. If they moved, young women were expected to quickly reconstitute their tribal loyalties in a new location. Naturally, some men and women defied expectations but waiting to find a husband until returning home risked an ever shrinking eligibility pool for women who, unlike men, were not often able to expand their prospects by marrying a much younger mate. Women of marriageable age did not usually go away to war, relocate to make their fortune, or wander around in search of new experiences. Unlike men, who most often hoped to return home, young women were usually expected to stay home or relocate permanently. Nevertheless, the pressure to find a husband did not mean that young women were passive recipients of men's affections. They actively participated in attracting the attention of individual men. One young woman who moved from the mountains to the pasture in Craigsville, Virginia, immediately shifted her attention to the new boys she encountered. "One he came home with me from preaching the other sunday he is a nicey nice little fellow and rich at that but i dont care for any of them." Even though she claimed indifference, she was cultivating the little fellow's interest in her by spending time with him.[11]

The transition from collective expressions of love to individual relationships defined the second phase of nonromantic courtship. Nineteen-year-old William Amos, visiting relatives in Ayersville, North Carolina, four years after the Confederate surrender at Appomattox, illustrates the feelings and thought processes constituting love in stage two of tribal courtship.[12] He was interested in courting a girl back home in Indiana. Eager for some positive response, but unsure of himself, Amos kept practice drafts of his letters, either for future correspondence or as a record of those he had mailed.[13] In one draft letter, dated May 30, 1869, Amos expressed exasperation with MB and delivered this ultimatum: "I have written to you over and again but never have received any answer I will write this time and if I don't receive an answer I am done fare well sweet MB."[14]

The rest of his draft is a classic example of the thinking that animates nonromantic love. He requests news of the crops, the weather, the health of friends, and "wether all the young ladys is married or not an wether they want ter marry or not." This query is a standard convention of tribal courtship. Amos continued: "you may be married for what I now but I hope not eny how I will write and see for my self if you are married don't get mad with mee for sending this letter but pick out me asweat heart in that country some where and tell here to write for I intend to get married to some of you SC girls if I can get you." Amos ended his letter with a profession of love: "So nomore at this time only I am in love with you of the pureest kind of love farewell for this time Wm H. Amos.[15] While he declared that he loved MB "of the pureest kind of love," he saw no incongruity in simultaneously asking her to pick out a sweetheart for him if she was already married.

How does this make sense? The key is how the local girls functioned as a collective sweetheart (before pairing off) in the first stage of working-class courtship. The young women in Shelby County, Indiana, served as William Amos's initial attachment.[16] Asserting his attraction to MB was his declaration of (nonromantic) love. If she was married and thus had already withdrawn from the local pool of eligible mates, he took for granted that his love for her would be nullified. At that point, he reverted to his initial commitment to the local community of unmarried women. Amos would be comfortable if MB were to act as an intermediary to find him someone else to love within the remaining set of eligible women.

In his working-class conception, love did not mean, as it would in romantic relationships, a shared understanding based on reciprocal feelings and mutual identification. At the time he knew almost nothing about MB's feelings, much less whether she was single or married. Even more perplexing by a middle-class standard, Amos was pledging to her that "only I am in love with you of the purest kind of love" little more than five weeks *after* he wrote Nancy that "I have been in love with you for along time." This was a two-faced betrayal by romantic standards. Within the norms of nonromantic

86 LOVE AND THE WORKING CLASS

courtship, however, Amos could love both women "of the purest kind of love" as long as neither had consented to be courted by him. As a consequence, they remained attached to the tribe as far as he was concerned and eligible for mate selection.

His sense of love deviates emphatically from romantic love as it was widely accepted by middle-class Americans in the nineteenth century. For them, love was a gift of one's entire self, reciprocally offered and received. It was a strong attachment to a unique combination of specific qualities that the loved one possessed. In the ethos of nonromantic courtship, Amos could love both women because, while he would be willing to separate from the tribe with either one, no one was receptive to his offer. Thus he was still in a love relationship with a place-based, unmarried collective.

Love was fungible in nonromantic courtship. One acceptable woman or man could be substituted for another. A person's preference was usually based on external judgments and role expectations, not mutual self-knowledge through intensive communication. Love was an "offer" of coupling, not deep devotion to a unique combination of specific qualities that the loved one possessed. Amos could love one woman or another without any emotional taint or betrayal (he called it pure) as long as neither had agreed to leave her local eligibility pool.

The question of who was willing to marry whom was sorted out, most often, by intermediaries. The process involved shifting preferences and changing parameters as eligible singles married, left the pool, and could no longer be considered. Lack of success with MB and Nancy may have motivated Amos to seek out the help of intermediaries after he returned home. Even from five hundred miles away, he was asking MB to "pick out me asweat heart in that country some where." William Amos finally found his mate when Eliza Miller agreed to marry him in 1873.[17]

In spite of the safety provided by go-betweens, some young women (and young men like Amos) initiated their own probes in the "sorting out" that defined stage two. Olivia Espy was someone who sought more than normal control of her marital fate. She was an Alabama maiden who had captured the hearts of many a boy soldiering for Dixie.[18] Half a dozen soldiers wrote letters trying to gain her favor. But Espy was dissatisfied with all of them. She was interested in Richard Hays, a man who was *not* in the long line of supplicants for her attention.

After waiting in vain for a response to the bouquet she sent Hays, a highly unusual gesture, Olivia wrote him a gently prodding note. His response was polite but lukewarm. Excusing himself because of sickness, he thanked her, telling her he would be glad "to Receiv a line from your hand," and then closed his letter with an inclusive address. "I can say to you that I often think of my friends in Cherokee Especially you and all those young Ladies that take so great an Interest for the soldiers . . . give my Best Respects to all the neighbor girls & friends accept my respects and Best wishes for yourself."[19] This was hardly the response that Miss Olivia wanted to encourage.

Hays grouped her with the young ladies and neighbor girls who "take so great an Interest for the soldiers," seemingly determined to keep her part of the collective pool of eligible mates in Cherokee County, Alabama, even as she was trying to elicit a more individualized response.[20] She married her cousin who lived in Georgia and was a wagon maker a little more than six months after the Civil War officially ended, rejecting the lion's share of her hometown suitors. In her case, kinship trumped the bonds of place, though a hometown boy appeared to be her first choice. Based on her letter to Hayes, it seems as if she did not trust the local intermediaries. However her disdain for nearly all her hometown suitors may indicate she had some romantic inclinations and wanted a more intense emotional experience. She was certainly not content to wed the "best available" man in her community.

One male suitor expressed the more customary, less specific approach of nonromantic love. "Mate I want you to give my love to Evaline Tish and tell her to wait patiently for the war is not a going to last long," Jerome Farnsworth, a soldier in the First Minnesota Volunteer Infantry, wrote his sister. "I don't expect that it will be of any use to give her my love for Walt is ahead."[21] Jerome was still willing to have his sister put in a plug for him. A northerner, Jerome teased his sister about marrying a southerner, but he clearly intended to mate within his geographical tribe in Le Sueur County, Minnesota.[22] In 1860 there were 175 white women and 196 white men between fifteen and nineteen in Le Sueur County.[23] Jerome gave his love to Evaline, knowing that "Walt is ahead," presumably judging by some evidence of her preference. Yet he was not threatened or upset because the love he sent was not exclusively attached to her. She had not reciprocated, so his love was not binding. For him, young women were clearly substitutable within limits.

Writing from Knobnoster, Missouri, one young suitor sent a message of love to both a group of girls and an individual. "I want you to speak a good word to the girles for me," B. A. Campbell wrote to Sarah Kesterson in 1870, "tell then what a ugly boy I am and how no count I am so they will know me when they see me I want you to tell them I fell in love with some of them while I was down their especially that one next doore to you but you nead not tell her so she might think that I was flatering her but I mean what I say no flatery about it but it is the truth every word of it."[24] Campbell joked about his appearance and character, but he was probably not kidding when he referred to falling in love "with some of them . . . especially the one next doore." He demonstrated his seriousness by inserting "I mean what I say" about her. As long as public pairing off had not occurred, loving one or many was acceptable. He was vacillating between the security of group love and the attraction of an individual relationship.

Like midwesterner William Amos, southerner Balus King Draper saw no problem in loving several women simultaneously. Though their letters were separated by eighteen years, they shared the same working-class understanding of love. After attending a wedding in Jefferson County, Alabama, about fifteen miles from his home, Draper informed his female cousin: *"The wedding is over at last. . . . We had a great deal of fun there, played until three o'clock in the night." The next day he attended a dinner reception at the local inn where he scrutinized the ladies' attire. "There were about eight hundred dollars' worth of jewelry there; that is besides what the gentlemen had. One lady by the [name] of Miss Elizabeth Trus had one hundred and fifty seven dollars' worth of jewelry. She was one of the waiters." His valuation of Miss Elizabeth's jewelry is comical in its exactitude but he seems to be sincere. The cost of the jewelry worn at this 1851 wedding intrigued him.[25]

"Miss Frances Hague Wood [was] another waiter. She had one hundred dollars' worth of jewelry. She is one of my beaus," Draper bragged. "She is as pretty as a pink and I love her so hard, it almost makes my heart sink. Oh what pretty black eyes she had got, what rosy cheeks; too pretty to ride a poor horse. I had the pleasure of conversing with her at the wedding." Balus made a positive assessment of her looks and the value of her jewelry, but a negative evaluation of her horse.[26]

Declaring love for one young woman did not dissuade him from sending love to another girl. "Give Altimirah my best love and respect and tell her that I haven't forgotten her yet and don't intend to. Tell her to write to me and write as quick as you can."[27] Balus (spelled Baylis in official documents) declared his love for two young ladies: Frances Hague Wood and Altimirah Woodruff. Clearly his feelings were driven by physical appearance and personal wealth, not self-revelation, self-discovery, or shared understanding. And he used an intermediary to convey his love to Altimirah.

Draper flirted with prospective brides in several locations, but seven months later he wed a hometown girl.[28] By 1870 they had five children and were poor farmers still living in Jefferson County, Alabama. At a time when the average American farm, as reported by the 1870 census, was worth

$2,799, his was valued at $900.[29] Moreover, the family's personal property was worth a meager $200. His wife did not bring expensive jewelry or other personal wealth into their marriage.

"[G]iv my love to all the girls," an Iowa soldier instructed his sister. Though engaged, Henry remained focused on the group of hometown girls: "tell mary McKinnie Howdy for me," was the only nod he gave to his fiancée. The pull of the collective was strong in spite of his "engagement." Clearly he was not betrothed in the romantic sense of the term. "You say or ask if I am looseing interest in Eliza," he wrote, repeating his sister's question about a woman other than McKinnie, and then answered, "I am not but you know that still water runs deapest (and it is getting to run deaper)."[30] He had been "engaged" to Mary McKinnie for a year, albeit most of the time he was not at home. His commitment was minimal and in all likelihood so was hers. He was still playing the field, while affirming a continuing interest in Eliza.

His sister, who undoubtedly typified his small community, accepted and even encouraged his simultaneous interest in two young women. At the same time, he remained open to considering other girls in his hometown pool. "[W]rite at once and tell me all about the girls and boys," he directed his sister, "and tell me what they kiss each other for." The war had ended and "all boys are at home," and Henry worried "that some of them will go where they ought not to go."[31] He was likely referring to some kind of sexual relationship with the girls, Mary McKinnie included. Unsurprisingly, he married neither Mary nor Eliza, waiting three more years to tie the knot and settle down to farming in his hometown of Crawfordsville, Iowa.[32]

Lucy Smith was a young woman of marriageable age who worked as a domestic in several locations in Massachusetts and Vermont. Like most women, she was interested in attracting the attention of individual men in her tribe, the key component of stage two. She was not a person to put herself forward in any obvious way, however. And since she worked in several places away from home, reconstituting a place-based eligibility pool and accessing the local intermediaries who might have helped her was challenging.[33] She was surprised, therefore, when a letter arrived from Luther Richardson, whom she knew from a previous position.

Lucy and Luther shared a special bond of antipathy for a family they had worked for one summer, probably 1859.[34] Coping with this family's demands—she as a servant and he as a hired hand—was a shared experience that had brought them closer. "I have often thought of you," Lucy admitted, "and wished you well but had given up all hopes of hearing from you." It was likely two years since they had seen each other at their former employer. "[I]f I were you I never would go again," Lucy responded, "they don't know how to treat folks deacent there they tried as hard as they could to kill us both but they did not do it." Nonetheless, she complained, "they are trying to kill me here this summer but they wont come it." After stating the obvious, "I am still alive and to work," she confided, "but my health is not very good I have to take the whole care of the work and do a bout all of it there is four of us in a family and five cows there is two Children a girl and a boy the girl is sixteen and the boy twelve they go to school."[35] Lucy was working for an old family friend when she replied to Luther's unexpected letter.

Though she was carefully guarded, her interest in Luther may have been more than a casual one. Now in the employ of a widower, Lucy felt the need to defend her honor against the common presumption of female sexual misconduct. "[L]et them talk if they want to I care not what they say I shall live for all what peapel say perhaps you will laughf when I tell you I am to work for a Widower." Lucy challenged the common village gossip and the sexual jokes she knew circulated about young female servants and their older widowed employers: "but you need not think any worse of me for that for I have always worked in his family more or less ever since I was big enoughf to work he is a good man respected by all who know him." Lucy wanted Luther to know that she was not setting her sights on marrying the widower. "I shall be happy to hear from you again when you see fit to pen me a line but I will close by bidding you good Night From your true friend."[36] There is no evidence that they ever communicated again. Lucy gently encouraged Luther's interest after he contacted her, presenting herself as an available mate, but he did not pursue her. Following the common courtship pattern of young women who looked for a husband where they relocated, she married a man she had met in Shelburne, Massachusetts, while working there as a domestic in the summer of 1860.[37] Her husband was a member of a higher social class, but perhaps his search for a mate was not as class-conditioned as usual because his father had been living in an insane asylum for at least ten years.[38]

Luther Richardson had a bevy of female admirers and so did his brother Charles Henry, who often went by his middle name. Unlike Lucy Smith, Orie McCoy did not wait for Luther to write her. She may have felt emboldened by her widowed father's recent marriage to one of Luther's widowed sisters. "I wors all most supprised this morning by receveing a letter from you," Luther admitted, "and will show my thanks by righting to you the first thing." He made many excuses as to why he had not written earlier, which probably meant he had promised to correspond before he left to enlist in the Union cause.

She was only sixteen, but she was already trying to attract individual male attention within her tribe. Anxious to elicit some flattery and affirmation of her appeal to the opposite sex, she told Luther she was thinking of "keeping Old Maids Hall." He responded in a generic way telling her, "I think you had better wate a little while before you set up on your own hook."[39] His genial reassurance was not the amorous comeback she was hoping for.

Several months later, with her sights on another Richardson boy, Orie asked Henry for a "date," anticipating when he would be home on a furlough. "A great Exhibition at the Town Hall two weeks from next Tuesday evening. 'Tickets fifteen cents,' I shall be very happy to have you call for me, Don't want you to think strange of it." Orie was obviously uncomfortable with her boldness but justified her offer on several grounds. She reminded him that he said he would have accepted her invitation to an earlier exhibition. The exhibitions she referred to were amateur recitations, speeches, and dialogues held in schools or town halls. This being a leap year, she also asserted her "right" to ask him out on the extra day in February 1864. "[C]ome with out fail," she continued. "I shall get ready in good season by (5) five o'clock if El is fair,, I will be glad to wait upon you,, and will pay all cost,, ha ahem ha ha, enough of this."[40]

Orie's approach was direct and assertive. She appears to be impatient to gain the individual attention of young men from the tribe in Lowell, Massachusetts. If her flirtations with the Richardson brothers were any indication, she seemed to crave the approval of eligible males whom she was willing to prod to take an interest in her.[41] This might be an attempt to elicit the start of a romantic relationship that could grow emotionally over time. It is more likely, however that she was attempting to exert some control over the winnowing process involved in nonromantic courtship. Since her early efforts faltered, she may have eventually relied on intermediaries to help her find a mate. Orie waited five more years before she was invited to become a wife.[42]

Direct contact was appealing to Orie and to the Richardson boys, but it could lead to great confusion. Henry described a courtship mash-up in 1865 of hurt feelings, mixed signals, and serious misunderstanding: "as near as I can find out it was a kind of a mixed up mess between Mrs. Barker—who thought I was a Courting Susie, and Susie who thought I wasn't courting her—and Ed Peasler who wanted to court her—and Abby Graves who wanted to

92 LOVE AND THE WORKING CLASS

A young working-class woman wearing two rings is arm in arm with a young soldier. Was he her boyfriend, husband, or even her brother? Whatever their relationship, they are sitting close together and her attitude is possessive.
Library of Congress LC-DIG-36871.

court me according to what I have heard Susie was the only one of the lot that showed any sense in the matter."[43] Their confusion may have been created by Henry, who was trying to abide by the privacy required in a romantic courtship while holding on to familiar nonromantic rituals that functioned through group sharing. This blending illustrates the hold of nonromantic courtship practices even when couples began to favor less public disclosure. With so much potential for misunderstanding and uncertainty, little wonder that many working-class couples clung to intermediaries and stayed within the boundaries of their customary rituals.

When men and women agreed to love the best available mate in the local pool, they entered the third stage of tribal courtship. This pool was not static, and as it shrank, eligible residents who had never been married, especially if they were young, felt an urgency to close the deal. If intermediaries had done their job, men offered and women accepted with few surprises. The decision to marry preceded individual courtship and choice was based on a sliding scale that was often determined by the practical limits of a place-based pool of eligible mates. Working-class Americans were not looking for the "only one for me" or the "love of my life," but rather someone they liked who liked them well enough to marry.

"Jim if you want a wife I have been corresponding with a young lady for some time & she wants to marry," Virginian Mary Houser informed her cousin Jim.[44] As expected, Cousin Jim asked Mary to describe the young lady. Mary responded by giving her cousin some unsolicited advice: "well Jimy you requested me to tell you how that Lady would suit you from the discription I think she will do very well alwais Marry For love & make beauty & riches no objection And try to get a wife of industry & good principle is my best advice."[45] Mary's advice to "always Marry For love" was clearly *not* a romantic recommendation as she described Jimmy's potential mate as someone who would suit him and "do very well." From Mary's perspective, she was the best available woman in the pool.

Although this emotional logic was widespread in working-class courtship, it is rare to witness a young man's proposal of marriage and even rarer to observe a young woman articulate the thinking behind her decision to marry him. "Dearest one I am at a loss what to wright but I recon I will have to answr your request," Mollie D. Gaither responded uneasily to her cousin, Burgess Gaither. "[Y]ou said you hoped that I would except of you offer your offer," she summarized, then answered candidly, "your offer is exceptable with me if it is with you for I love you better than any other Jentleman." Her comparative approach to his "offer" of marriage in the phrasing "better than any other" is noteworthy. Her statement reveals the emotional state that led her to say yes and further unlocks the meaning of nonromantic love in working-class courtship. While perhaps the most honest and accurate way to assess many feelings of affection, "I love you better than any other gentleman" would not be acceptable in a romantic declaration of love. As if to reinforce her stance, she repeats her comparative "best available" approach to her emotions. "but

94 LOVE AND THE WORKING CLASS

I hope it will not be long untill I will se you for I want to se you worse than I do any boddy that is in the army."[46] They both lived in Iredell, North Carolina, but he was soldiering for the Confederacy at the time he proposed.

Not completely satisfied with her response, in a subsequent letter Burgess pressed Mollie D. for a stronger commitment to marriage. She carefully articulated her emotional logic in an important and rarely verbalized account of the feelings behind a young woman's choice of mate. Mollie's thoughtful self-examination highlights the emotional reckoning that often undergirded marital choice. "Dearest one you said you wanted me to let you no if what you wrote to me stood as a prommus," she began. "[Y]ou said if I was willing you was and if I did all was wright it is all right then for I think more of you than any other Jentleman and I recon you are the one as you say you are willing."[47] The first and necessary condition for marriage had been met: Mollie thought more of this man than any other in the pool of eligible men in Iredell County, North Carolina. Her choice was clearly defined by and limited to her tribe. The sufficient condition had also been met: he wanted to marry her. "I recon you are the one as you say you are willing" was not starry-eyed idealism. Her acceptance was practical, grounded, and matter-of-fact.

Mollie's stated reasons for accepting his offer of marriage were nonromantic. She told him, in effect, that she had done the side-by-side comparison and he was the best available man in her tribe. His proposal—"you said if I was willing you was"—was every bit as nonromantic as her acceptance. On both the male and female sides, the language of romantic love was missing. Mollie D. had made her choice. "You may be shure that I will remember you in my prayers for you are one that I esteem higher than any other Jentleman," she concluded. Tellingly she did not directly express her feelings of love. She was very circumspect, especially about the word "love" itself, using it only in the lyrics of a love song she sent him.[48]

Concern for privacy was one element that came to the fore after their engagement. Burgess warned his sister not to tell "Paw nor Maw nor no boddy els." He asked his sister not to "let on like you now it for I told hur I would not tell it." Burgess violated the privacy that he recognized he should be protecting and was uneasy about his behavior. He warned at the close of the letter: "so do not tell anyperson what ever let no won see this letter nor read it."[49] The working-class reasons for privacy were more practical than their middle-class counterparts. Mollie heard that one of the girls was planning to run away to get married. She was reluctant to reveal her identity to Burgess because "if any thing was to happin that they would not marry then they would not like it."[50] The push for privacy in working-class relationships often involved the fear of public humiliation and shame, not rules of intimacy that protected shared romantic feelings.

In small, tight-knit working-class communities, courtship almost inevitably took place in public view. Mollie D. continued to observe closely the potential swains who visited Burgess's sister whose first name was also Molly (spelled this way to distinguish her from his girlfriend, Mollie or Mollie D). "[Y]ou wanted me to tell you how the old Court ship was coming on," she wrote. "I tell you there is so many old widowers wants Molly [his sister] that I do not no which will gain the day Uncle E Gaith and Mr Andrew and Mr Albea and I don't know how many more." Mollie D. heard through the grapevine that Mr. Albea went to church with Burgess's sister last Sunday, and she regretted that she "missed the sight."[51] Privacy was difficult to come by in small communities, and gossip was rampant.

It was a strain for working-class couples such as Mollie and Burgess to withdraw from the pool of eligibles without being able to marry because he was away fighting. The pull of tribal courtship made the exclusive commitment to one person difficult to sustain over a long period of time.[52] After accepting his offer of marriage, Mollie continued to participate in the collective rituals of young singles. "[S]chool was out yestourday and we all went fishing in the evening," she informed Burgess. Mollie had a sense of humor and a keen eye for the pairing-off process. "I tell you we caught 4 fish but some of them caught drie [dry] land fish." One of Mollie's girlfriends told her that she was not going to "ketch water fish" but hoped to hook a boyfriend. Mollie made it clear to Burgess that she did not pair off with any of the boys, noting emphatically, "for there was enouf girls for the boys with out me and more than enouf."[53] By deliberately removing herself from the boy-girl pairing of this group outing, Mollie confirmed her commitment to Burgess in a public manner.

Conversely, Burgess signaled less commitment to Mollie D. by asking his sister to assess his choice of mate *after* his marriage proposal was accepted. "I want to now what you think of hur any how tell just what you think let it bee good or bad."[54] The use of his sister as an intermediary would have been common in the second stage of nonromantic courtship. In stage three, however, after his proposal has been accepted by Mollie D., it suggests that Burgess was uncertain about his choice and open to changing his mind. He continued to feel the lure of the tribe.

96   LOVE AND THE WORKING CLASS

The difficulty of their delayed marriage is reflected in the rituals of direct emotional testing they exhibited. Though they had already agreed to marry, their courtship testing was sometimes fiercest around the subject of rival sweethearts. Burgess encouraged a jealous reaction from Mollie D. by asking her about Lina, a young woman in their tribe. "I cant tell you how Miss Lina is but you no more about her than I do she is your sweet heart," Mollie responded bluntly.[55] She may have heard rumors that Burgess was partial to another young woman at home. This would have been normal behavior *before* his proposal had been accepted, but it was aberrant after.

Perhaps motivated by the immediate possibility of dying in the war, Burgess seems to have asked Mollie to marry him before he was ready. "[T]ell hur howdy for me," Burgess instructed his sister regarding the young woman named Lina, "an also tell hur if she Please to excuse me for not write to hur for I have not had the chance." Burgess continued to use his sister as an intermediary: "I will write to hur soon Mol [his sister] giv hur [Lina] my lov and best wrespects tell hur to writ for it will be gladly received for I lov to hear from all friends."[56] Burgess used the word "love" to communicate his friendly regards. He did not mean romantic love, as he demonstrated by quickly subsuming her with "all friends."

While Mollie D. was irritated by his attention to Miss Lina, her real fear was that Burgess would die in the war. She did not hide her dread. "Oh my dear friend I want you to have your type takin," she told him, "and send it to me for if you never was to Jet back it would do me good to have it to look at."[57] Burgess himself was aware of his vulnerability. "[P]ray for me to get home safe," he closed a letter to his sister on July 20, 1864.[58] Those prayers were not answered as he died at the end of July on a ship in Charleston Harbor, nursed by his cousin and his shipmates.[59]

This working-class couple blended a few elements of romantic courtship into their premarital camaraderie. Typical of romantic courtship, Burgess asked Mollie to reveal her feelings directly to him, without the services of an intermediary, and he agreed to practice a romantic version of secrecy. However, he violated his promise, telling his sister he was engaged and asking her for a frank evaluation of Mollie D. His request was normal in a nonromantic courtship, but his timing was unusual. He did even more to violate the normal stages of nonromantic courtship by asking his sister to encourage Miss Lina, another young woman in the tribe, to write him. Sending his love to Lina after he was engaged was a sign that Burgess was ambiguous about his commitment to Mollie. He was acting as if he could still consider another woman from the field of eligible mates (stage two), even though he and Mollie D. had stepped out of that pool by agreeing to marry (stage three). This was a noteworthy confusion of tribal courtship practice.

In romantic courtship, lovers routinely tested the depth and strength of inner feelings of love through emotional dramas enacted directly between them. This testing involved the creation of major or minor crises in a courting relationship. Often participants used the life materials at hand—debt, illness, other men and women, religious differences, character flaws—to set obstacles in the pathway of love, which they had to overcome, usually through either actions or words of reassurance. Middle-class couples were involved in private testing rituals that allayed their doubts and fears, strengthened (or occasionally shattered) their emotional bonds, and reassured them about the correctness of a major life decision.[60]

The working class, by contrast, tested nonromantic love by a person's willingness to separate from the group. And their tests were commonly made through intermediaries. The point is easily blurred and thus worth repeating. They tested a willingness to be loved—defined behaviorally by the act of pairing off from the group—not inner feelings of love. These tests were done by intercessors who were supposed to ascertain this crucial information and report back. Working-class courtship rituals were communal and involved public support and group-related approval. The point was to avoid public shame and embarrassment.

Burgess apparently bypassed such group appraisals before he asked Mollie to marry him. This left him confused and uncertain about his decision to step out of the eligibility pool at home. His ambiguous attempt to make Mollie jealous by asking her about Miss Lina, but also requesting that his sister invite Lina to write him, was not romantic testing because he was not assessing Mollie's love for him, but his for Mollie. Thus *her* jealousy could not reassure him of *his* love. And he knew that she had publically affirmed her pledge by withdrawing from the pairing off that went with youthful activities at home. It was Burgess who had doubts, not Mollie. He asked his sister to confirm his choice, a nonromantic test that addressed his uncertainty. On the love continuum, this couple was located nearer the nonromantic style of courtship.

The situation of an African American, James le Renisan, presents another rarely documented proposal of marriage that included a description of his emotional state. "[Y]ou told me that there was a chance for me i wuld like to no what it means to gain or to lose," he asked Lucia Knotts, living in Round Top, Texas, more than twenty years after the end of the Civil War. In spite of

98 LOVE AND THE WORKING CLASS

his uncertainty, the question applied to his feelings, not hers. Unfortunately for James, Lucia had already rejected him. "[Y]ou says that you ony regards me as a frin," he admitted. Fayette County had a Black population of 8,763 in 1880, so the pool of eligible mates was substantial.[61] Nonetheless, he was unwilling to accept her feelings as final, as he demonstrated by ignoring Lucia's kind but pointed brushoff. "[D]ear i am unable to lay open To you the present state of my feelings to wart you is stronger than those of friendship." James acknowledged that he did not have much capacity to describe his emotions, but he emphasized that his feelings went beyond friendship. "[I]f your love is very hard my love is so hard that i cant hardly rest saterfide studer bout [rest satisfied studying about] you."[62] This sounds like a version of romantic love.

He proposed marriage: "dont rite nothing that you dont mean if you love me enofe to marry let me no." Even if his feelings were romantic, James seems to be asking her for a practical, willful, best available choice of mate: the nonromantic "love me enofe" not the romantic "love of my life." But he also recognized that his chances were slim to nonexistent. "I dont want [to] do lack you did be so wrong The next time i may be rong but i will . . ." He broke off here, unable to complete his thought. He seems to be accusing her of misleading him, then he stopped abruptly in mid-sentence, perhaps unsure what he would do the next time. Their class difference was one obstacle that he could not overcome. She was a middle-class African American schoolteacher who was being courted by Calvin Rhone, another middle-class teacher living in Texas. Le Renisan was a poorly educated farmer.

Still James held out hope. "If there be a chance for me please let me no dear." Though his language skills were not highly developed, he did *not* convey the heartbreak of romantic love.[63] His high opinion of himself may have blunted even the most forceful rejection. It seems likely that he had approached her directly and refused to hear her negative response, which may have been oblique at first and intended to spare him pain. Even if he felt the stirrings of romantic love, his relationship with Lucia was not based on physical and emotional intimacy. James did not know how to conduct a romantic courtship. Thus his proposal was steeped in the precepts of nonromantic love. Two months after he wrote this letter, Lucia married Calvin Rhone.

Love was not any more romantic the second time around for most working-class men and women who had lost a spouse. "I had all most forgot the little widow," Shelton F. Martin, a widower serving in the Fourth Illinois Cavalry, wrote his sister-in-law: "if she is pretty and you have Recomended me as well as you have her I shall not nead to spark her Before the union takes place." "Sparking" was a term for courtship that included verbal as well as physical endearments. "I would like to spark her a little after I get her and it seames that, that would be all that is necessary But you neither told me whether She was hansom or what her name was or any thing a Bout it," the widower worried aloud before he set down an ultimatum. "But if She is not prety I shall not have nothing to do with her for I cannot love nothing But a prety woman and if She don't Behave I cant love her long then."[64]

Shelton was willing to marry almost any woman his sister-in-law recommended, as long as she was pretty. He cared almost nothing about her non-physical assets, talents, or unique attributes, though he had some vague behavioral requirements that were probably moral. Personal qualities other than appearance were secondary. It is clear that he had little or no interest in his future wife's personality or interior self. Getting to know her was unnecessary, so he did not need to court her until after their union, and then he thought only "a little" was necessary. If she was physically attractive and an intermediary he trusted had endorsed her, he was willing to love her and become her husband. This was not romantic love in the understanding or practice of middle-class Americans.

Another widower, Frank Beavers, was also looking for a wife through an intermediary. "[T]ell Miss Anleza Jinkins that I love her as a sister an I wish to be loved by her as a brother," Beavers wrote his own sister, "and would cross the wide ocean for her if she is not maried." The qualifier is significant, for it indicates another kind of relationship was on his mind. "[A]n if she is not maried tell her to write to me and let me no what she is doing an what she is going to do." Frank was "tending to a farm for a man at $25 per month," he informed his brother-in-law. "I have worked hard as a negre ever sense I left that old cuntry I am living a lowsom [lonesome] life . . . I am the only white person on the place I am confine here day an knight."[65] Beavers was employed as an overseer in Tennessee.[66] He was lonesome and thinking of his "two little motherless children" in North Carolina and a possible remarriage to a hometown girl. Not knowing whether Miss Jinkins was still single, he played it safe, sending her brotherly love while waiting for his sister to find out if she was willing to be his mate. He was not that picky. His choice was motivated by an urgent need to find a woman to care for his children, a spousal role that he was willing to fill from the single maidens who were left at home. Marrying for romantic love had never occurred to Shelton or Frank.

In contrast to their peers, some working-class men and women were willing to be led to the altar by their romantic feelings. These couples deviated from the

100 LOVE AND THE WORKING CLASS

dominant nonromantic mate selection practices in their community. Perhaps they had greater exposure to middle-class values and more familiarity with the practice of romance. Perhaps they were more affected by the disruption in their face-to-face community necessitated by war or the push-pull features of economic relocation. For some, distance provided an opportunity for early separation from their tribe and the freedom to initiate or deepen one-on-one emotional involvement. For most working-class men and women, however, distance was not sufficient. The men vowed to return to their home to marry and the women reconstituted their tribal loyalty in a new face-to-face community.

Whatever set them apart, some couples engaged in romantic courtships, using the word "love" to mean their willingness to share themselves. They focused on one person of the opposite sex and engaged in a courtship ritual that involved them in escalating self-scrutiny and self-revelation. These more romantically inclined suitors wrote courtship letters and were expected to keep up their end of the correspondence. They were a minority; nevertheless they demonstrate the inroads that romantic love was already making in working-class mate selection. The love letters of one suitor illustrate the challenges of conducting a romantic courtship in communities that still privileged the values and practices of nonromantic love.

"I am sorry I got a Fourlough for I wanto Be With you all The Tim," William Johnson wrote longingly, "—oh how I long for my Time so that I can call you my wif and Have you with me all The Time The Tim wont be long Sliping away."[67] Johnson was typically obsessed with thoughts of his beloved. "As to day is Sunday I have Bin Thinking of you all day for it was always my day to be With you," he reminded her, "and it was our last day to geather before Parting And I Will always think of that day till I am with you again and I know you think of thois days as well as Myself."[68] Waxing elegiac about their Sunday strolls a little over two months later, he remembered "those Plesant Walks" and then how "the old Lady [came] down after us Wouldent It be nice." He mused nostalgically about trysts with his Maggie.[69]

In addition to his obsessive thoughts, Johnson displayed another response characteristic of romantic love: effort to please the loved one.[70] "Maggie, I hav don Something That Will Please you I know," William reported proudly. "I hav quit Smoking and drinking I have not Smoked nor drank anything since I left St Paul and I Am not agonto do those any more you may beleave it tho I am telling the Truth."[71] He was succeeding with Maggie, but not with her mother. "Also you say your Mother wants you to give me up an I am glad to hear of you holding out so true to the one you love so well," William offered encouragingly, "and Maggie you wont be Sorry for it Wont be long tell I will be with you then Whe will always be happy."[72] Maggie's mother tried her best to keep her daughter away from William. Being in love, the daughter was not easily swayed by her mother's objections. But she continued to be bothered by rumors of William's philandering.

As was typical of tribal courtship, many eyes were watching him. "Someone told your mother that I Was In St Paul on Wendsday With Cap steward and that I Was drunk—And that Steward brought me home and put me in the Guard House," William announced to Maggie. "Now you Can see how Some one Is trying to git you or your Folks down on me for I can prove that I was not down town on Wendsday by the Whole company," he wrote defiantly, "for I whent to St Paul on Monday eavning to a party and git back on Tuesday morning and put In the guard house for going away without leave." He was hopeful that once he told Maggie's folks, "then they can see how things Is."[73] But being thrown in the guardhouse for going AWOL the day before his alleged indiscretion was scarcely the defense he imagined.

"Maggie I hope that you have no hard Feelings against me," William wrote defensively. "For I think I have gave you no cause for I think I have Treated you as a Gentleman ever Since I knew you." Lacking confidence, however, he felt compelled to test Maggie's commitment: "Well I Must bring My letter to a close as It Is getting late I thot that I would write a good long letter as posibly this will be the last one tho I hope not and I hope that whe will Meet again and often and take miney walks together how I should like to hav you ancer this letter as soon as you get this."[74] William was looking for an affirmation of his capacity for good behavior and reassurance about Maggie's feelings for him.

Though Maggie did not end her relationship with William, which was a behavioral affirmation of her affection for him, she continued to be uneasy about the rumors of his carousing. "Maggie I hav got one favor to ask you and that is this you have herd so menny Stories About me Since I have got acquainted with you probly you begin to beleave them tho I hope not So I thot I would Ask you weather you are Willing to keep my compny as a friend." William explained his motives. "I have bin thinking latley that something was not right and that you wanted to Say Something to me and did not like to. But Maggie If there is any thing you wish to Say I hope you will Tell me.—Tho I Should feel verry sorry If any thing Should Stop me to See you."[75] Significantly, he asked her to reveal her doubts and fears to him. William was willing to risk full self-disclosure, and he encouraged even her unpleasant revelations, a valuable experience in the typical romantic courtship.

He also initiated a series of courtship tests.[76] For example, irritated at one point by the long intervals between letters, William went on a testing "offensive." He presented Maggie with an obstacle to their relationship that she had to remove. "What you say If I should Stop her [stay here] till Spring only two month longer that not long tho Should only be two more letters for me." This was a threat. "I know you would give you consent to my staying as long as I Wanted to and another thing I like Texas so Well and don't like [to] lev."[77] He was serving with the military forces occupying Corpus Christi, Texas, during Reconstruction. His courtship testing was meant to elicit some reassurance that Maggie wanted to see him as soon as possible.

William not only tested Maggie's commitment; he also had an insightful strategy to counter the rumors of his misbehavior. And he used his trump card with skill, playing it at a crucial moment to undermine Maggie's confidence in gossip of all kinds. "When I First got acquainted with you I was told by Some of your best friends at least you think So that I would get fooled If I Whent with you for as long as I got you preasants I would Be all right."[78] As soon as his gifts stopped, according to this poisonous rumormonger, Maggie would leave him. William's clever use of the gossip about her worked beautifully to undermine the legitimacy of the gossip about him. Their community was an important influence, even as they tried to conduct a romantic courtship that emphasized their unique emotional and physical intimacy.

Three months later, however, William was in trouble again. "Your intended had Some Company from St Paul last Sunday," J. H. Benson, William's best male friend, informed him. "They had a hot time of it Mrs Mayall told Mag that you was always fond of flirting & Corisponding & that she was personaly acquainted with three Girls in St Paul that you were engaged to & one in particular and you was writing to then Regularly." Benson was acting as a go-between, a standard feature of nonromantic courtship. William's nonexclusive flirtations with the single girls back home was another ordinary stage in nonromantic courtship. "Mag said nothing but let them talk on untill they left & then The tears fell quick & fast," Benson reported. "My Folks had to take her Down to the house to try & keep her from Crying her Eyes out I never saw anyone Change So much as She did Since." Benson offered his interpretation and suggestions. "She feels offal Bad over it," he told his friend. "She Don't know what to Say wither you are Guilty or not but She things you are not. I Don't think She will write untill She hears further."[79] Maggie's reaction demonstrates how difficult it was to conduct a private romantic relationship within the expectations and customs of tribal courtship. Whether the charges were true or false, William convinced a receptive Maggie to continue their relationship. "I send you a good sweet <u>Kiss</u> In return for The one you sent me," he cooed.[80] Four months after this exchange, on April 17, 1870, Johnson and Maggie (Margaret) were married. They lived in the Mendota area until at least 1875.

"Love recognizes no barriers," the writer Maya Angelou observed in the next century. "It jumps hurdles, leaps fences, penetrates walls to arrive at its destination full of hope."[81] So it was for Eunice Richardson Stone, a poor white widow who did domestic work for hire. Romantic love helped her jump the racial divide. But it did not alter the unspoken but powerful community assumption of racial homogeneity in marriage that she defied. After her courtship and marriage to William Connolly, a Black sea captain, she pondered and described, with clarity and grace, the emotional power of romantic love in overcoming *her* racial prejudice. "When I was trying to see if I could bear to tear myself from him,—I believe he is firm in his attachment and faithful in his love for me. I have sometimes thought when I have seen Ira [her brother-in-law] devote himself to Harriet [her sister] so lovingly that If I should get a Husband that would love me so much and try to make me happy as he did her I would be satisfied. But I am satisfied now. I would not change Husbands with her, if hers has got a white skin."[82] With Connolly's love and support, which tapped her deep need for economic and emotional sustenance, she challenged the racial norms of courtship and marriage in her working-class community.

Eunice Richardson Stone said goodbye to her mother in November 1869 and married William Connolly.[83] It was a second marriage for both, and they moved to the Grand Cayman Island in the British West Indies with her two children. After her move, Eunice urgently tried to reconnect with her family and friends. "Mother I want you to tell me if you want to come out here and live with me. I can not say much now for not having heard any thing from you I do not know how your mind is toards me and mine." Eunice was both defensive and defiant. "I have a Happy home and an indulgent loving Husband," she reported. "I have a plenty to eat drink & eat and do not have to sit up nights sewing by Lamp light making and trimming dresses to get it either."[84] Emphasizing that she had an abundance of food and drink was one sign of her past economic desperation as a widow with two children. Marriage to Connolly relieved her of what to her (and to others) was the onerous work of laundress and live-in domestic. This unquestionable economic advantage was not lost in her decision-making process.

104 LOVE AND THE WORKING CLASS

If this photograph was taken in 1863, as the note on the back indicates with a question mark, Eunice Richardson Stone would have been around thirty-two years old. Her first husband died early that year fighting for the Confederacy. She married her second husband, William Connelly, in November 1869.
Lois Wright Richardson Davis Family Papers, Rubenstein Library, Duke University.

While economic motivations played their part, she openly avowed the romantic love that propelled her action. Eunice was eloquent about her feelings for William.

> But much as I love you and cherish the memory of other dear friends I could not go from him for the sake of seeing all. From the time I first began to be

acquainted with him I had respect for him, and that grew into love which his gentle affection has increased till I am most devotedly attached to him, And it is all his kind ways and thoughtful acts prompted by love and respect which he has for me that makes it so, he holds me to him with a strong cord you see, He told you he would do everything he could to make me happy. And I may say he devotes himself to that and I feel sure it is the pleasure of his life to see me enjoy myself. And I am determined he shall not do more for me that way than I do for him so far as I know how to do to make him happy. So while there is a mutual desire and each one takes pleasure in making the life of the other pleasant and happy there is nothing to fear, As I told you in America.[85]

Eunice was very cognizant of what romantic love meant in his behavior and in hers toward him.

She was also cognizant of the racial challenge that her courtship presented to her community. "I often think of you and always see you as you looked the day I bade you Farewell," she wrote her mother,

striving as I well knew to be brave, not a tear in your eye. But with a face blanched to whitness itself, and a yearning look in your eye that I never can forget as if you was even then trying to pierce the misty future which was just opening before me. I saw it all but my own heart even then felt the cord of love and affection drawing me away from you. And I knew I could with[draw] and go from you my mother easier than I could give him up even though public opinion was against him and against me on his account.[86]

Racial prejudice deeply embedded in working-class courtship practice drove "public opinion" against their marriage. Her word choice clearly indicates the collective nature of the opposition. Most often observed without acknowledgment or comment, when the unspoken rule was breached, community censure could be swift and merciless.

A woman who may have been her mother's friend or neighbor attacked Eunice over her choice of a Black husband, so much so that she confessed: "I cannot quite get over some of her slurs." Eunice's mother also argued long and hard against marriage to the sea captain. "He still pets me feeds me as he used to do in America," Eunice wrote her mother. "You used to laugh about it and say 'when he got me fast and in his own home he would forget all such things.' But he remembers them to even more. For he is in his own home now and feels at liberty to act all the love he feels for me without fear of disturbing anyone."[87] Eunice was responding to warnings from her mother about how William's courting behavior would change for the worse once they were married and far away from her watchful community. Eunice was anxious to refute her mother's critical voice. She recognized that her decision to leave the United States was almost as controversial as marrying across the color line.

Eunice's family delivered their judgment on her violation of working-class norms by isolating her. For more than two years, no one in her extended family communicated with her.[88] After posting a few letters, her mother stopped writing altogether and only sister Ellen corresponded fitfully before she stopped as well. "Mrs. Connolly begs you to let her know how you are getting along now in your old days," William entreated his mother-in-law. "[W]e regret that you are so far from us so that we cannot help you now when we should." Perhaps trying to motivate some familial response, he reminded her relatives of their relationship to his young daughter: "Tell them my little Louie is always talking about her Yankee Aunties & her Mammy Yankee."[89]

Thirteen months later Eunice again begged her mother to communicate, if only by sending newspapers, "or some thing that way—it will make me see that you have not forgotten me, or thrown me away altogether." Her brother Henry's silence was especially hurtful since they were once so close. She sent her love and good wishes "to all that will accept it. For Brother Henry and wife I do not know what to say for whenever I have heard from home I have never heard from them or even heard they so much as sent to be remembered by me."[90] Eunice's marriage to a Black man apparently rankled Henry deeply, and the family collectively did what Eunice feared they would: "thrown me away altogather." She closed her letter: "I can not write long letters now untill I hear from some of you so with much love I am your faithful." It appears that no one responded. After years of silence, one of the sisters, Ellen, was motivated to inquire about Eunice and her family out of interest in a possible inheritance. She discovered there was none, and that Eunice had died at sea with her husband in a hurricane off the Mosquito Coast of South America.[91]

Eunice paid a cost in crossing a racial boundary to marry outside her community norms. The price was isolation and rejection by family and friends. Was it worth what she gave up? She told her mother that as long as he loved her, "I shall never regret linking my life with his."[92] Several years later, Eunice admitted she was homesick and that her husband would go to live in America if he "knew what he could do" to make a living.[93] We will never know what she thought in the minutes or hours before the storm ended her life. But her marriage to the Black sea captain demonstrates that the unspoken demand

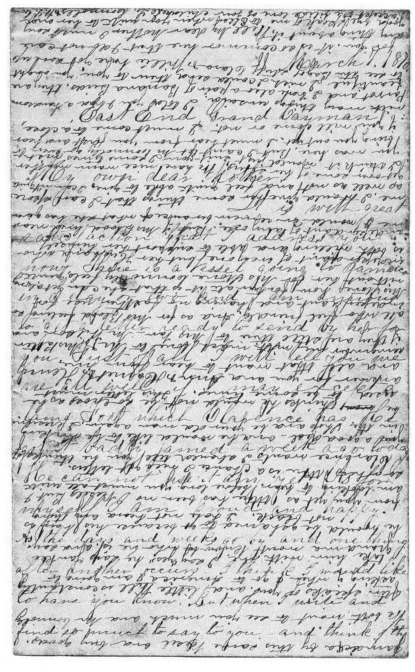

Eunice Richardson Stone Connelly had been married four months when she wrote a letter on March 7, 1870, to her mother, Lois Richardson Davis, about the racial prejudice she encountered from friends and family when she decided to marry a Black sea captain. Letters can be hard to read for many reasons; when she ran out of room, Eunice turned her letter upside down and wrote in the space between her original lines.

Lois Wright Richardson Davis Family Papers, Rubenstein Library, Duke University.

Continued

for racial uniformity in working-class courtship was a compelling force. Her love led to her communal exile. No one wrote her—a symbolic testimony to her banishment from the collective attachments of her tribe. Romantic love broke down the racial barriers between two individuals but could not touch the group hostility to interracial marriage. Mrs. Connolly was set apart by silence.

While the white working class shared large swaths of culture with their Black peers, white prejudice against African Americans ran deep. This is hardly news. Communities of attachment were the bedrock of working-class intimacy, and they were most often segregated. The working-class sense of tribalism—structured by connection to local communities—created a homegrown identification defined by geography but also by race. The very culture that Black and white Americans shared in the nineteenth century ended up sharply dividing them.

In African American usage, "the people" were groups of Black people.[94] In white usage, the hometown was a white community (even if that was demographically untrue) entirely embedded in a specific place. There was no pay her expences from the vessel that carried her. to her Grandmother. You never saw such a time as there was with her and Willie. They both set up such a crying- it was quite amusing to see the thing go of. She told her father that if he was going to send her to America he might just as well take her right out and drown her at once for she had got to be away from her Father & Mother. she had rather be in the bottom of the sea than any where else. And Willie kept saying he should never see Clara again. he could only stand by me with his arm about my neck crying and say that. she can not be made to say she wants to go since that. and she does not seem to think of it. The other Boys are well and hearty. So much for them. Now a few words concerning my Husband & myself. and I am most close. I dont know whether he will feel like writing a few lines tonight or not. For he is a busy body always doing something- He is neither an idle or a lazy man – And now at this time he finds plenty to do I'll assure you. He is having his Boots filled and between that and his land. and his work about home he does not find much playtime. The New House is not yet made. But we

Continued

ethos of cosmopolitanism to dilute the localism that focused on the tribe. The group that gave one a stable identity was racially separate. Romantic love could detach two individuals from the group and support the primacy of the self over collective feeling. But nonromantic attachments were often defined by group identity and heavily mediated by group support. The collectivity often claimed as much or more feeling than the conjugal pair. Though interracial couples were important exceptions, intimate group identification worked against overcoming racial prejudice.[95]

Love is a dangerous word, because people can—without noticing—mean different things. Middle-class Americans thought that the right way to love a mate was romantic, while working-class Americans did not give it much thought, unless they were, like Frank Flint, a nonconformist. For most of the nineteenth century, the working class felt secure in the meanings and expectations of nonromantic love. Rooted in geographical and communal traditions, they accepted the benefits of their "home team" courtship and local marriage. Love was, on the continuum where the majority resided, an agreement to leave the local eligibility pool and become a couple. Thinking better of one man or woman in your tribe was the nonromantic basis of loving that person. Economic resources might be scarce, but living in a place where you knew the people gave you the possibility to love them and to find someone among them to love. And that knowledge kept you committed to your tribe.

4

Sex Talk, Humor, and Fear of Ridicule

Desire and Self-Protection

Members of the working class, when they wrote about their sexual experiences, most often laughed at themselves and others. J. R. Littlejohn joked with at least one female cousin, Caroline Lipscomb, about their friend Dick [William] Wood. "I was Completely Captivate with some of the girls of that County I am sure that you Could of seen that if you had of tried & as for Dicks part it stuck out about afeet or 2 that was his whole topic all the way coming home."[1] This working-class man felt comfortable joking with a single woman about erections.[2] Sex was certainly a subject of group gossip, but sincere premarital sex talk in pen and ink was rare.

The laboring folk did not exchange intimate erotic feelings or express their passionate desires in letters. The atypical couple conducting or attempting to conduct a romantic courtship was one exception. Young men who bragged about their sexual conquests were another. Other than kisses and embraces, however, the majority did not describe or comment seriously on their amatory behavior.

Middle-class couples took pleasure in verbalizing their sexual experiences and desires, which added to the erotic intensity of extended courtships.[3] But they had the protection of a deeply held ethic of privacy that was lacking in working-class culture. The laboring folk, by contrast, had a porous sense of privacy, reflected in the common practice of sharing letters of all types, including correspondence between married and unmarried couples. Given the truncated value they placed on privacy, and their more relaxed attitude toward disclosing the intimate details of their lives, what was noticeably absent from working-class letters was any earnest erotic content. When they discussed sex, it was most often treated humorously. This attitude extended from exchanges between men of any age, male and female friends of marriageable age, married couples, and even parents and adult children. The unwillingness of laboring folk to discuss erotic feelings seriously in front of their tribe, when they were willing to

Love and the Working Class. Karen Lystra, Oxford University Press. © Oxford University Press 2024.
DOI: 10.1093/oso/9780197514221.003.0005

112 LOVE AND THE WORKING CLASS

talk about so much else, is worth probing. Did certain anxieties provoke this unspoken reserve about sex?

Fear of ridicule is a common feeling, not limited to one class or one historical period. In small, tight-knit communities, people are especially vulnerable to the disapproval of their peers. Unsurprisingly, working-class correspondents were sensitive to the negative judgments of family, friends, and neighbors. Their vulnerability was apparent in the inferiority and shame they expressed about their writing skills. Hyperaware of their error-prone letters, they often offered their readers an apology in advance. They appear quite vulnerable to the external judgments of others, anticipating that their inadequacy might expose them to ridicule.

Their anxiety about ridicule for a nonsexual matter such as writing helps to explain their reluctance to consider sexual behavior (other than boasts) with any seriousness. Though they did not openly acknowledge their concern, the absence of earnest sexual exchange indicates a discomfort with public exposure of physical intimacy. Working-class correspondents understood the constant potential for group ridicule in writing letters that were shared with others. In the face of that risk, they were usually careful to avoid deeply personal expressions of sexual desire. Lacking the middle-class culture of privacy in intimate relationships, they were vulnerable to public disrespect and mockery.[4] Their sex talk was almost all comical or entertaining. Young men bragged and joked about sex with each other, and single women also joined the fun. Their humor looks like a form of self-protection within the communal ethos of group sharing.

The issue of public exposure was addressed directly by Jennie Russell, who expressed concern over public-private boundaries as her relationship with Frank Flint grew more romantic. "You say you think sometimes that you could write me a real love letter," Frank summarized her feelings, "but if you seys any body should see it it would look so silly." Jennie feared being seen as stupid or ridiculous in front of her peers. Other people's observation made her fear of failure more intense and her sense of inadequacy more acute. This was the double-edged sword of community support. Tribal solidarity could create a sense of security that tamped down people's anxiety, but it could also create deep apprehension.

Jennie knew that Frank might let others in his company read her letters. The public-private boundary in working-class culture was most often permeable and ambiguous. "Well, I don't know as it would [look silly] but you may hav no fears about any one seeing it after it gets to me for no one reads any of my letters," Frank reassured her, "so if you want to write a real love letter its at yur own option."[5] The fear of being laughed at, in effect, the fear of being shamed in a group, was what primarily drove Jennie's concerns with sharing intimate sexual feelings.

Men and women in some relationships, especially those that were closer to the romantic end of the spectrum, felt their letters required a special protectiveness. Flint was unhappy to hear that his sister Susan had read letters he had left in his trunk on a visit home to Langola, Minnesota.[6] Reading those letters was well within the range of normal behavior for working-class Americans, yet Frank felt uncomfortable about it. Spurred by his romantic attachment to Jennie, he sought more privacy and confidentiality than many of his peers required.

Many pitfalls existed around personal letters exchanged between single men and women in a working-class environment. Before he enlisted in the Twenty-Fourth Massachusetts Volunteers, Oliver Coolidge was a wood turner or carver who lived with his sister and father in Cambridgeport, one of three distinct districts that formed the town of Cambridge, Massachusetts.[7] Around a dozen men in Oliver's company came from the town.[8] Until the last two decades of the nineteenth century, the geography of American life was anchored in small towns and rural villages. Perhaps nothing is more illustrative of this fact than in 1860 Cambridge, with a population of little more than twenty-six thousand, ranked as the thirty-third largest city in America.[9] Although it was a large city by American standards in 1860, young single women and men still felt a strong local identification. This happened because divisions within the larger city created tribal enclaves that might be identified with neighborhoods, districts, or urban villages.[10]

Trying to amuse themselves one rainy day in May 1862, Oliver Coolidge and his tent mates passed around their personal letters.[11] Exchanging letters from their wives, single and married friends, relatives, and neighbors apparently caused no concern, perhaps because of the emphasis on "news" in most working-class correspondence. But a man named Jennings, obviously seeing little that was exceptional in his courtship letters, shared them with his compatriots. Coolidge hand-copied one of these "billy ducks," as he mockingly called them, in a letter he sent to his sister and father.[12]

deer bill
    I F yew git my letterS arnser soon I F yew git hit or killed git shubil Snow to write to me soon as It happens so I will no all abowt it at onst if you send

me your munny I can take care of it Better than your mother can if You Love me as i hope you do you will do As i Say and not mind what she says about me there is Lots of the fellers heer who want me if you Dont So rite and let me no soon as I cant wate much longer remember when on the battlefield a dyin a long way from me

Hattie S Sewell

Clinton Mass

Coolidge and his working-class buddies mocked Hattie's naive expressions of affection as well as her presumptuous attitude and bossy directions. One central ingredient in the joke was the correspondent's age, which contrasted with her haughty self-image. At thirty-one, Miss Sewell was getting long in the tooth for a first marriage.[13] In 1860, 71.7 percent of white women in the New England census region were married by age twenty-nine. The average marriage age of white females across the country was 22.8 years.[14]

After copying the courtship letter for his sister, Coolidge recalled the reaction of the hapless recipient: "We told Bill to send for her," he chuckled, "& we would try and see if some of us could not comfort her in case he was killed." Bill was not amused. "He said it was just like some darned fools they could not read a fellers letter without letting all the world know it." The gullible Bill had failed to predict that he would become the object of scorn. "So we thought we would stop & goto bed and dream of Hattie," Coolidge teased.[15] This situation illustrates the constant potential for group ridicule inside the closed tribal boundaries of working-class culture. Modern research confirms that ridicule can create conformity and fear of failure in bystanders.[16] Every soldier in that tent and in untold numbers of camps across the Union and Confederate armies learned or relearned the lesson: beware of serious courtship letters, especially those with content that might be mocked or ridiculed. This included anything that went beyond the normal boundaries of acceptable behavior in one's tribe.

But if these Massachusetts soldiers amused themselves by making fun of certain letters they received from home in May, the hometown girls were infuriated when the news reached them in December. Coolidge's sister reported that the girls had been urged to write directly to "the boys," bypassing the usual intermediaries. "I was into Mrs. Jones, Emma and some other girls were as mad as they could be," Oliver's sister wrote, and "they guessed when they wrote to the soldiers again twould do them good. It seems the boys when they go away begs the girls to write to them and they have just found out that

SEX TALK, HUMOR, AND FEAR OF RIDICULE 115

Soldiers of the Twenty-Second New York Volunteer Infantry relax in camp; one of them holds a letter. Did they pester him to let them read his letter? Working-class soldiers often read each other's mail to entertain themselves.
National Archives Identifier: 524568, Local ID: 111-B-149.

their letters are all read to each other in camp."[17] She then made an unladylike wish: "Godam their head hope they have a good time over them."[18] The girls were furious for being ridiculed by the very boys who asked them to write letters in the first place.

"The laugh denotes what you can laugh about, who can provoke laughter, and who can laugh along,—and with what outcomes," an astute social psychologist concluded in her study of bullying and humor.[19] What can you laugh about? Oliver Coolidge and his tent mates felt free to use the girls' letters as entertainment, though only Hattie Sewell's letter to Bill Jennings was singled out by Coolidge for extended commentary. At thirty-one, her age was funny because she claimed so many suitors while still being single many years beyond the female marital norm. The men also laughed at Hattie's keen interest in controlling Bill and his money.

Who can provoke laughter? Bill was mocked for considering her a potential mate. Her bossy, presumptive style crossed some boundary of masculine

116 LOVE AND THE WORKING CLASS

power and dominance. The group used humor to disparage her self-assertion and perhaps that of other female correspondents. Oliver joked that he would go to bed and dream of Hattie. And if Bill died, he promised, he and his tent mates would be happy to "comfort" her. These allusions to sexual relations were meant to mock Hattie and bait her suitor.

Who can laugh along? Bill did not join in the fun, and neither did the girls at home. Taking offense, they became an even more attractive target of ridicule. Perhaps Bill had some genuine feelings for or connection to Hattie. Or perhaps he was simply awkward and flat-footed in the competitive male sport of repartee. Coolidge himself called their humor at Bill's expense a "sport."[20] Whatever Bill did as a result of his ribbing, group norms of sexual attraction, including masculine authority and feminine deference, were hammered home to every participant by humor.

When the single Cambridge women found out their letters were being used for entertainment, their fear of public shaming came to the fore.[21] This interpretation is supported by Oliver's sister's mocking phrase: "hope they have a good time over them." Being denigrated publicly, above all being laughed at for some inadequacy, was a dominant working-class anxiety. Witnessing ridicule leads observers to avoid engaging in behavior that could make them a target of derision.[22] The fear of revealing sexual feelings that might be mocked shaped the content of letters subjected to public scrutiny by one's tribe.

Working-class sex talk was overwhelmingly humorous, itself a form of self-protection. Sex was presented as a public topic of fun and self-aggrandizement. "Frank tels me that you cane around a mong the girls with your ears pricked up like a mice in a bag of pumkinseeds," Jaspar Barritt kidded his brother William. "I cant say that I blame you for that for I should like to see some of the loving creatures my self."[23] This was the sort of friendly teasing that was not meant to belittle the subject. Jaspar openly identified with his brother's obsessive attention to the girls.

Unmarried men not only joked with each other about sex, but also joked with unmarried women and, more surprisingly, with their parents. "O what a joyful day it would be to hear the Cry of pease once more," a young soldier from Illinois, Joseph Fardell, wrote his parents during the Civil War. "I think I would Come home and take me a sweet little pease and setle down ether come home and get her or bring her home with me."[24] According to the *Dictionary of American Slang*, "piece" was used to mean "piece of ass" by 1785, and the word evolved into vernacular American speech for a person

SEX TALK, HUMOR, AND FEAR OF RIDICULE   117

regarded as a sex object. Fardell felt no compunction about sharing this sexual pun with his mother.

Similarly, another Civil War soldier reported that his camp was full of drunks and "sum of the men in my company has the horns."[25] The horns is nineteenth-century slang for an erect penis, or more generally, for sexual excitement. The son's use of this slang term in a letter to his father and mother indicates, as do other letters, that working-class mothers were not shielded by a boundary of gentility as were their middle-class peers. This may be because sons witnessed their mothers' less-than-refined sense of humor about sex.

Mary Mellish told her son about an incident in early 1865 on a train somewhere between Woodstock and Boston.

> [A] would be nice young lady came into the car & just at that time a soldier somewhat dirty and the worse for the wear; was leaving, the lady wanted to know where that dirty fellow sat! No one answered; she asked the question again; no one spoke. At length an Irish woman spoke: with some emphasis 'He sat on his A__s & when he went out he took it with him.' The lady looked blue! There was a general shout—and an old gentleman sat near the Irish woman he took out his purse and gave her a five dollar bill, saying she had earned it! that is the best of the season.[26]

The complexities of class were laid bare in this story as the "lady" was bested by a person below her station who demonstrated more patriotism and humanity than her social superior. Everyone in the car acknowledged the Irish woman's moral preeminence with the "shout" and one man rewarded her with a monetary gift. She must have looked humble enough to prompt his largesse. Though Mary does not spell out the word "ass," it is perfectly clear she approves of the Irish woman's retort and disapproves of the "lady."

Lois Richardson advised her son Luther to "be careful and not have children." He told her that while some soldiers might leave offspring in New Orleans, "I gess I shall not be trubled with any."[27] She tacitly accepted her son's sexual activities as long as he was careful not to father a child. Lois might have wondered, however, why her son only guessed at his possible paternity. Perhaps he was deliberately teasing her.

If young men were willing to joke about sex with their parents, it is no surprise that they used even raunchier language with each other. "The girls in this Country is as wild as two year old stud Colts, are not brid [l] ewise so wild I cant get my hand on them," William Meeter joked. "They are so

118 LOVE AND THE WORKING CLASS

wild I [can't] get Close enough To Shake Salt on their [Ass]. I want you go give me some information on the Subject. Tare this off and let nobody See it," he instructed a male friend in 1827.[28] Knowing his letter would normally be read by members of his tribe, he insisted on privacy. Why did he ask for confidentiality? Was his feeling of vulnerability situated in the comical comparison of local women to wild "stud colts," or his use of a crude phrase to describe their standoffishness? Perhaps. But the writer's Achilles heel may also be found in his plea for information about how to handle the girls. That request, an admission of inexperience and uncertainty, might hold him up for ridicule among his young male friends.

Another young man, Joseph Sewell, was full of confidence in his ability to handle the girls. His swagger, however, seems exaggerated. "[Y]ou ought to see I and Burgess. desevil the girls," he bragged to a male friend, "they never look upon us with desdain and our drabs are scarce uphere." "Drabs" was slang for whores. He seems to be telling his male friend that girls who were not prostitutes had accepted his sexual advances. "I guess our shines never look on us dolorous our stolid girls are scarce." Translation: their girlfriends, or shines, were not "stolid," meaning they were not impassive, or incapable of being excited.[29]

"[S]o far as to apple rines and to Miss Mollies piec," he continued, "I have got so I can quit eating those things that are for children." His reference to apple rines was probably to breasts and "eating those things that are for children" may have meant oral sex, which he disparaged as sexual activity for those who were not as mature as he was. "Thomas I think you said to come farther than Miss Bs some time." Miss Brown was slang for a woman's external genital organs, specifically the vulva. "[B]ut you was speaking of Mollie saying that if I got hungry and would get upon a stump she would administer apiece you tell mollie that I have got so when I whisper it is not asking those sort of gifts at all, but one that you can do with out yourteeth to bite."[30] Joseph was bragging that he had gone beyond oral sex and now expected or demanded intercourse. Did he intend for his friend's sister Mollie to be included in the joke about fellatio? Or was this a comical dare? Young working-class women joked with young men about sex, so it is credible to suppose that he meant for Mollie to participate in his verbal play.

Joseph closed with a double entendre that referred to bush, which was identical in meaning to contemporary slang: "I went from bad to worse so no more this time come up sure and bring a cart load of those Iredell girls to the party tell Mollie not to wear out her face too bad with the cedar bushes good night Thomas."[31] This sexual talk between two unmarried working-class men likely contained as much imaginative wish fulfillment and image manipulation as actual sexual experience. What is most noteworthy, however, is his inclusion of his friend's sister in the bawdy dialogue. Joseph could anticipate that his letter would be shared with young men in his North Carolina tribe. His references to Mollie may have been intended to tease her brother, but perhaps Joseph also expected to involve Mollie, and other girls, in the sexual repartee.

"I want you to keep the Girls strate," William Crawford wrote his brother in a letter addressed to his parents, "and wright to me and Let me now what Girl you are sparking."[32] A member of the first Missouri Cavalry Company, William became raunchier in a letter written to his brother. "We have A Dance every night or to," William bragged. "[T]here is Some of our boys marying. . . . But As for myself I hav No use for Sutch Stock As the peple in the South West. . . . I want you to Keep the rabet ride stalk in good Humer If posable but Be Indipendent with them As for the saf stock I supose the will never mary."[33] In mid-nineteenth-century slang, a "rabbit" could refer to a harlot and "ride" to copulation. "Rabbit ride" was probably a colloquialism for intercourse with "loose" woman. William divided the hometown girls into "rabbit ride" stock, women of dubious moral character, and the "saf stock," who he jokingly supposed would never marry. Even in his comic taxonomy, he conveyed loyalty to the women of his tribe as opposed to females in another region of the country.

The next soldier, James Mansfield, was much more direct about the opportunities for prostitution in his camp in Baltimore. "The [w]hores are as thick as the delve around here," he bragged to his friend Horace Dresser, "now fucking on evry corner of the camp ground 50 cts a go Cheep for Cash."[34] Seth Eastman, another pal of Horace Dresser, boasted about his noncommercial conquests. "I formed acuatance with the Widow McKeen I went up to Stoneham before I left home an a Damn good time with her. She is a good peace I tell you god never made a prettier bum than she had got hung to her I took her before I lift home." Seth Eastman was referring to intercourse with the widow before he enlisted as a private in the Twelfth Maine Infantry. "I started from home Sunday morning and stopd with her until Monday night—then I wint home and had a rist I then went up to Browns and took Susan and took her over to abe Grahams an thare I gave her Hel but she can't come up to the widow."[35] Seth's narrative was meant to enhance his image among the young males of his tribe. He was completely comfortable detailing his sexual conquests, even naming both women to authenticate his "achievements." This was serious sex talk but without any personal empathy or emotional intimacy. Seth portrayed himself as a conqueror who had intercourse with two women for his own pleasure and ego gratification. No emotional vulnerability peeked through his boastful narrative.

A brickmaker before he enlisted, Seth enjoyed his role as a sexual storyteller. Reporting on his life in occupied New Orleans, he told Horace: "I have been into as many as a dozen hoar houses and I hant seen but two good stile in the hole lot, but a dirtier damn set of cases you never see. We boys go in evenings and see them dance but have not touched a woman since I have been in the place." As it turns out, the reason was not hygienic. "A man has got to have money. They ask all of the way from three to five and 7 Dollars. We have not been Payed off yet and we are all straped we are going to paid off next week and then we can have some fun."[36] Their fun resulted in seventy-five cases of syphilis and gonorrhea.[37]

The tribal loyalties of young men to their hometown girls could be extended in some surprising directions. Seth's geographical allegiance stretched from the local maidens to the local prostitutes. "They are hard old biddies and a good style is hard to be found in New Orleans. Give me a Maine girl for all the Louisianans."[38] Another friend of Horace Dresser also highly recommended the homegrown hookers of Portland, Maine. He bragged that he paid one of them three dollars, "put it to her three times in an hour," and "told her I would call some other day."[39]

Working-class men employed a language of sexual objectification about women they considered "loose," not just in letters but in other settings. One character witness called to give courtroom testimony in an 1872 bastardy case reported that he had felt the plaintiff's "titties and monkey," likely referring to her external genitalia. Another testified that he overheard two men discussing the plaintiff, and one said, "I have screwed her as often as I have fingers and toes, and the other man replied, "she don't know more than a hog whose child it is." In a different case, one male neighbor testified that another told him: "A stiff prick knows no conscience." The public nature of this testimony in an Illinois courtroom, with judge, jury, and large crowds of both men and women from the local community in attendance, demanded the self-protection of sexual humor and boasting. Significantly, the men were reporting on dialogue they had heard in regular male sociability outside the courthouse.[40]

SEX TALK, HUMOR, AND FEAR OF RIDICULE   121

Around the same time, a man in California was joking about same-sex encounters in his journal, which was likely written with an audience in mind. Nahum Wood, a Southern California sheepherder, wrote in an 1871 journal entry: "Pard is in high glee; was seen on the high road to Debt- to Anaheim with a Biped,- if I mistake not it will turn to a quadruped before morning." Wood predicted that his male friend would be having sex with someone in the "quadruped" position before dawn.[41] His pard's bedmate was likely a man. Why they walked to Anaheim is unclear; though even with a small population, the place no doubt had a bar and a chance to gamble, thus the reference to debt.[42] "I expect to see himself in Crinoline soon, he is learning to dance on the off side." Crinoline is a hooped petticoat worn under a skirt to give it a rounded contour. Wood was not literally expecting his partner to become a cross-dresser; he was joking about his friend's willingness to play the role of a woman in his sexual encounters. Saying he is learning "to dance on the off side" strengthens this interpretation. In the West, "off-side" can refer to mounting the wrong side of the horse, which was sometimes labeled, with intentional disrespect, the "squaw" side. Nahum seems to be joking about his coworker's gender inversion, a term employed at the time to refer to men who dressed, walked, talked (and so forth) like women and women who presented themselves like men.[43] Nahum expressed no moral qualms or negative judgment about his partner's male bedmate. What he seemed to be mocking was his gender presentation; he saw no issue with his homosexual desire or the same-sex pairing itself.

Wood's own role in same-sex encounters appears to follow nineteenth-century masculine gender conventions.[44] Two days earlier he quipped: "Today has been observed partly as the Lord,s Day and partly as the devil's—for I hung an ax today."[45] Nahum's reference to "hung an ax" is a logger's term for "put a handle in it." Sexual contact between men in logging camps was quite common.[46] Nahum could be using camp slang for an act of sexual penetration with a man. Wood jokes that this is the "devil's" side of Sunday. But he appears confident in his masculine role, offering no humor about his own sexuality. In the cultural lexicon of his era, same-sex relationships were no threat to his masculinity as long as he conformed in appearance and behavior to the standard male role of his time.[47] Wood's laughter was reserved for the gender inversion of his friend.

In the same entry Wood commented: "Pardr went bumming last night you know what Bum I mean, howevr he returned at 3 today."[48] While Nahum

122 LOVE AND THE WORKING CLASS

does not clearly delineate the gender of the "Bum," he was likely referring to a same-sex encounter. Nahum added, "you know what Bum I mean," indicating that he was expecting someone to read his comments. Humor was a working-class style of discussing sex within a communal ethic of group sharing. Nahum's journal entries seem to be written for an audience who could share the jokes embedded in his ambiguous gender references, an audience who might also share the camaraderie of same-sex male desire. Nahum Wood never married; he died in San Diego at age ninety-four.[49]

Unmarried men employed a range of sexual boasts, but some took a gentler approach to sexual experience. "Tell Mr Barkley that I havent got old abes coat buttons yet but some of his men lack to of got mine," Confederate soldier William Turner teased his single male friend. "I would lack to see you when you get able go over and see your little boy I hear that they had named it af ter you," he quipped. "[Y]ou musent git mad at my Joke but if I could see you I could tell you more than I could write in a week."[50] The joke about fathering a child out of wedlock was common among single men.

An illiterate day laborer until he enlisted in the Twentieth Ohio Infantry, George Deal wrote letters to his wife by dictating to willing scribes. In one letter to his spouse, he directly addressed a young woman, Permelia Jane, who had been asking his advice about prospective mates. George responded negatively to the mention of one young man in particular. Then he teased, "he sed his furlow was out I think he had better keep it in his britches or he mite git the end of it frostbite and then he would be in a pretty fix wouldent he." George was comfortable joking about a prospective suitor's penis with his young female relative.[51] Turning avuncular, he scolded facetiously, "I don't want to hear tell of you staying with any of them males or I will box your ears or give you a good Spanking when I come home."[52]

Unmarried women might also initiate sexual humor with young men and with other women, though neither was as common as men with men.[53] "I suppose old Smith and Betty Parish will make the wiggle soon," Justina Woods wrote her sister, employing another graphic bit of local color—"make the wiggle"—to gossip about a neighborhood courtship. "He goes to see her twice a day, I have under stood; they are both so nice that I am afraid when they get together the cant say beans."[54] Women could express amusement over the sexual follies and foibles of their tribe.

In rare instances, the talk of physicality turned grave and upsetting. Eliza Bixby, writing to her brother in 1852, described a sexual assault by her Lowell mill boss, whom she referred to as Mr. H. "I went to Nashua [New Hampshire] with him to get my bonnet reformed and trimmed," she recalled.[55] Her boss was "very sociable" until they came to a secluded portion of the road with woods on both sides. After looking "behind and before us" then listening "to be shure no one saw us he put his arm around my waist and asked me if he might kiss me." Successfully rebuffing his first advance, Eliza reported: "I told him no and if he did not keep his hands off me I would pull the horse by one rein and tip him over and break his neck." She related tongue-in-cheek that he chose "to guide his own horse," and his conduct was civil for the rest of the trip.

After arriving at their destination, Eliza began to shop alone but was soon joined by Mr. H., who went into another shop and "when he returned he had a ring on his little finger." Finishing her errands, she went back to the tavern with her boss, who invited her up to his room. She was impressed by the "handsomely furnished room," and at his invitation she took a seat on the sofa while he sat in the rocking chair. "[H]e becond to me to come and sit on his knee I refused," she related firmly. He wanted to show her his ring, "but I would not be enticed by him." When he got up, Eliza did not recognize the danger she was in. He quickly locked the door and "then seated himself by my side and took that ring off his finger and put it on mine and said it was mine I told him I did not want it and I offered it to him he would not take it I laid it on his arm he took it and put it on my finger."

Mr. H. seemed to take his gesture, commonly associated with marriage vows, as a signal to escalate his assault. Eliza described what happened next: "he put his arm around me clinching both of my wrists put his face over my nose so I could not breathe through it and the same time sucking my breath from my mouth until I became so exasted I was obliged to lean my head on his shoulder then he commenced to lay me down on the sofa." At that point someone knocked and Mr. H. opened the door, announcing to the concerned caller that the lady had fainted and needed water. Though she did not mention the reason for her rescue, the sounds of her distress almost certainly drew someone's attention to the room.

Mr. H was clearly a serial sexual predator.[56] "[H]e said as he got cheated out of his object this time he would call and see me some time when I was alone at home." His threat terrified Eliza, who explained to her brother that "this was reason I would not stay alone if Mother does laugh and call me her baby." After his sexual assault and verbal intimidation, Eliza was unwilling to be left by herself, even when her unwitting mother scoffed at her timidity. Her plea to her brother not to "expose" her to the family revealed

124   LOVE AND THE WORKING CLASS

the considerable shame she felt over what had happened. Moreover, she did not tell her sister Lydia about the assault, even after her sister went to work for Mr. H. Though she warned her sister away, Eliza did not reveal the real reason for her counsel.[57] Likewise, female operatives in English textile mills in the late nineteenth century did not normally challenge abusers directly or individually. They would change jobs and warn other women about the mistreatment of their previous supervisors.[58]

It was extremely rare for an unmarried nineteenth-century working-class woman to pen a firsthand account of sexual harassment and assault. Eliza Bixby's report revealed her anger, shame, fear, and disgust with her textile mill supervisor. It also contained a paradoxical evaluation of her attacker as "a man of good qualities." She was not referring to his character, however, calling him "one of the greatest villains I ever got acquainted with without exceptions," an "artful rogue," and a man who attempted to "seduce every innocent girl that was in his power." Her reference to "good qualities" was about his social class, which likely included his dress, education, and language. She was not expecting such villainy from a man who appeared to be so well bred.

The feeling that motivated Eliza's silence was shame at the thought of public exposure. She was afraid of being blamed or perhaps laughed at for her naiveté. Eliza was willing to share her terrifying experience only with her brother. Sisters and brothers had a special relationship and shared intimacies with each other that they might not disclose to others. "[H]ow I wish you was whare I could see you once in a while," another single textile mill girl wrote, "for none have a larger share of my love than my brother."[59]

Most exchanges between siblings that involved sexual attitudes and behavior were more lighthearted than serious. William Simons, an African American, was a northerner stationed in Louisiana during the Civil War. He wrote his sister in June 1864 that it was not a healthy place, noting the "mer ceters [mosquitoes] ar very thick out we cant hard[ly] live" (a prescient observation, for he died in August of malaria at Fort Jackson, Louisiana). He remarks that fruit is plenty *"but oranges have ripened to about [the size] of the Hazard girls. You ought to see the women out here that have tits as large as a cow." Apparently the size of the Louisiana oranges reminds William of the noteworthy endowment of the seven Hazard girls back home in Griswold, Connecticut. But some Louisiana women who "have tits as large as a cow" surpass the hometown girls in his regard.[60] William thought his sister would appreciate the funny side of large breasts.

SEX TALK, HUMOR, AND FEAR OF RIDICULE   125

Sisters also expected brothers would appreciate their humor. "I dident tele you the message that wm dale sent me," Jestena Webb, a white widow, wrote her brother about a prospective suitor. "He said that he had bout him a fine suit of cloths to come to see me in and he wanted me to understand that he dident need no sait [suit] at tall."[61] Though his comment might be taken literally, as a reference to casual clothes, it seems likely that "no sait [suit] at tall" was a joke about nudity. Working-class women were comfortable with mischievous sexual innuendos.

York County, Pennsylvania, is where Sallie Seeper Scott lived in 1865 when she wrote Robert James Barnett, who worked in a carpentry shop in Washington, DC. Besides informing him that there was plenty of work on the canal, which ran from York to the Susquehanna River, Sallie was anxious to share the local gossip.[62] She attended the wedding of William Moor to Mary Hickman Sunday at Pine Grove Church, which prompted this teasing innuendo. "I don't know what gussie will Do know when wil moor as she Calls him is gone unless you Come up + hold her once a Week but if that dont pleas You + I exspect if you ware to come Home you could get into a job Of sleeping with Mary Jane Snyder for I exspect she has to sleep by her self since John went to the Army."[63] Sallie's relaxed sexual banter was a working-class style.

While middle-class Victorians of the same era could also joke and laugh about sex, they imbued the physical with a different set of meanings. Both groups appreciated the sensate experience of physical coupling, but only Victorian lovers described their physical sensations in detail. The better-educated correspondent had a facility with language that was a factor, but it was not necessarily determinative. Privacy, a sacred trust in middle-class love letters, removed the fear of embarrassment, fear of being laughed at, and fear of feeling inadequate.

However important privacy was in encouraging Victorian sex talk, something else was also at stake. In nonromantic relationships, sex was a physical attraction, a bodily need, an act of procreation, a self-centered gratification of lust, an expression of affection, or even a statement of dominance or submission. But sex was *not* seen as an expression of an individual's inner self. In the romantic ethos, however, making love was the ultimate act of the individual personality: the revelation of an "authentic" self, part of the hidden essence of the individual, an expression of one's real and truest identity. Giving one's body was giving one's self in romantic love.[64]

126 LOVE AND THE WORKING CLASS

Working-class Americans in nonromantic relationships did not invest sex with the meanings of selfhood or individual authenticity. What is more, they did not view sex as spiritual. Their middle-class contemporaries embedded the erotic in a complex transmutation of Christian imagery, structure, and belief. Passion was a form of worship in many romantic relationships. Kisses were "holy," marriage beds "sacred"; romantic love was "salvation," and sex was a sacramental act.[65] Working-class lovers, whether single or married, did not appropriate Christian symbols in speaking of sex (unless they were in a romantic relationship). Sex had no spiritual dimensions in nonromantic coupling. This was one of the most distinguishing contrasts or differences between romantic and nonromantic love. Unmoored from its spiritual symbolism, sex in nonromantic relationships was most often viewed irreverently, even after marriage.

"[Y]ou can prepare to cook orsters fur me when I git home," George Deal joked about the notorious aphrodisiac with his wife.[66] He also joked about babies: "but waite till I git home there will be a nother one to name."[67] Deal was illiterate and dictated all his letters, so he was talking to another man when he acknowledged, after bragging about his health and vigor, "and what more could I want yet there is something lacken I will tell you what it is when I git home then you can judge for you self but I think it will all be rite when we kill our hogs." The male pig, according to animal experts, is "capable of a great number of copulations before exhaustion occurs." So George's reference to hogs was likely his way of saying that he would be making up for what was "lacken" in his sex life when he returned to his farm. And perhaps he too would not easily be stopped. "[Y]ou must excuse me," he continued, "for I think it is better to laugh than to cry."[68] His humor, couched in the language of the farm, was intentionally raunchy.

African American soldier Joseph Cross was literate, but his wife had to have her letters read by someone else, perhaps the "local postmaster or pastor's wife." Like George Deal, Joseph felt comfortable joking with his wife about sex. "I did not suppose that Lemuel lester could make a raise he has had it so long but here is good luck to him." Cross is likely referring to Lester's ability to have an erection and father children. Lester was around forty, so the joke involves his virility in middle age. "[I]t is war times now and Some Body has got to do some thing For their Country." Cross was making fun of Lester's home front "service" compared to his own military sacrifice. "I am Glad that I aint their so he cant Blame me for it."[69] Cross's joke had a disapproving edge: Lester was at home making babies while he was in the Union army serving his country.

In this portrait, the photographer has captured expressions of amusement in the looks of the three adults. Smiles and laughter, however common in daily life, are rarely displayed in nineteenth-century photographs, perhaps because the long exposure time required sitters to remain very still.
Library of Congress 2010650825.

Simeon Tierce was identified as the father of a newborn child while he was serving in the Fourteenth Rhode Island Heavy Artillery Regiment (Colored) in Louisiana. Apparently the mother, while she was in labor, told the midwife that he was the baby's father. Simeon's wife seemed to believe the charge. "It made my heart ache when I heard that you cursed and swore," Tierce responded piously to what he considered her blasphemy. But his general reaction was tempered with humor. "She had no business to name that child before I came home for I never put in for it, and the next one she names after me I want to be there." He dismissed the accusation with what was an adept sexual pun: "I never put in for it." Like Cross, he joked about not being physically able to impregnate a local woman until he returned home. In the same letter, he teased his wife about kisses. "I send you my best respects and my love, 1 oxcart load and 1 barrel, 1 hogshead, 2 wheelbarrow loads, and a wagon body full of kisses."[70] Sadly, Simeon never returned home, dying in Louisiana of typhoid on July 8, 1864.[71]

Adultery, though commonly represented through sexual jokes about married men fathering children out of wedlock, was rarely viewed in terms of a wife's indiscretion. Consequently Ann Stevens's letter to a lover provides an unusual glimpse into a woman's motive for an extramarital affair. Her fear of public exposure went beyond the ordinary for good reason. Stevens wanted to get rid of her husband so she could have uninhibited coitus with a younger man. She was living in Woodside, a small Northern California town in 1882, while she was plotting to persuade her husband to go to Colorado. Sensitive to the lack of privacy in her working-class community, she wrote her letters in code, an extreme measure meant to guarantee concealment. She told her young lover: "once [he] goes I will take good care he never comes back." Her motivation was unambiguously sexual. "[T]hen there would be some tall diddling done and a little hugging thrown in. . . . And when I see you again, perhaps I might find the way up your trowsers leg." Coding her letters was like hiding in plain sight, and she responded by openly expressing her sexual desires to Walter Knight, her young lover.[72]

In another letter to Walter, she voiced her desire in uncensored colloquial speech: "I wish you was here tonight . . . I suppose we should do some tall fucking." Believing she was protected from the scrutiny of her husband and her tribe, Ann openly yearned for extramarital sex with Walter. She thought her lusty self-disclosure, written in code, was safe from the prying eyes of her working-class community. In spite of her careful planning, however, Ann's safeguards crumbled. Somehow her husband came into possession of these letters, decoded them, and used them as evidence in a divorce suit he brought against her for adultery.[73] It appears that Ann never cohabited with or married her lover, who was close to fifteen years younger and a stage driver at the time of their liaison.[74]

Another kind of sex talk, rarely captured in letters, took place many years earlier among women. Mary Samms, the loquacious narrator, was a

Quaker who was active in her local meeting.[75] In a letter to her daughter, she described an exchange in early 1846 with several married women in her community. When the women's gossip during a New Year's Day party turned to pregnancy and childbirth, N. P. announced that a friend had just given birth to a baby boy. Mary said she warned N. P. that she too would soon be pregnant if she did not do something about her "common luck."[76]

Samms took it upon herself to give some specific birth control advice to N. P. in the presence of the assembled women. "I toutched plain on the subject and she did not deny it," Mary informed her married daughter. "I told her . . . of thy recommending Uncle Lam's [or Sam's] lether pocket." This was a type of condom made from the skin of animals, more affordable than the highly prized and priced condoms made from animal intestines.[77] The specific brand name appears to indicate a commercial product (perhaps made locally), not a homemade device. "[S]he thought that good enough says she will try it soon and firace says she will soon as the next Sunday." At least two women seemed confident they could easily obtain the recommended contraceptive.[78] One woman was very open about trying the leather pocket as "soon as the next Sunday." She casually acknowledged the frequency of intercourse in her marriage while indicating the product's ready availability.

Condoms were part of this community's store of local knowledge, which was promptly shared by both men and women. One brother "talks strong of it and I urged it all," Mary wrote. Her daughter also strongly advocated for the use of condoms. "[B]ut be patient yet," Mary advised her, "I think they all intend it."[79] This is a valuable glimpse into the conversation of one group of married woman about family limitation and birth control. The discussion was not private but community based and involved an ethos of shared advice on marital sex. In all likelihood, this was not an experience unique to these Quaker women. Whatever methods they might have used in addition to condoms, Quakers were the first group to lower their birth rate.[80]

One historian has suggested that working-class English women, at least in the late nineteenth century, were able to obtain necessary birth control advice from friends, neighbors, and coworkers and that this information was available to almost any woman who was involved in her local community.[81] "They all intend it" raises the possibility that women arrived at some contraceptive decisions in American working-class communities through group support and collective decision-making. Community involvement in the intimate lives of working-class Americans meant that sex information, possibly

130 LOVE AND THE WORKING CLASS

including birth control advice, was passed along in groups of women as well as men.[82]

What is clear is that working-class American communities were sites of sexual banter through which the uninitiated might learn not only biological facts but cultural attitudes. One woman wrote her family in 1857 about a neighbor's likely abortion, asking her relatives not to repeat her reasoning: "Her poor health was caused by gitting rid of a child as I suppose. Alphens [her husband] did not feel able to maintain another one." Eliza followed her serious commentary with a sly reflection: "She was very large when she came here and in a short time she slunk to her usual size. Perhaps it was the dropsy."[83] Dropsy is an old term for edema or water retention. Eliza was joking. She would not have suggested abortion if she had actually believed that expelling water caused the woman's abrupt "shrinkage."

While working-class letter writers joked about some violations of sexual norms, such as adultery, other deviant sexual behaviors were avoided. Women rarely referred—either seriously or jokingly—to their lack of sexual agency. One exception was the attempted rape of a Lowell mill worker by her supervisor. This young woman must bear witness to the use of force in other sexual encounters where the victim was ignored or remained silent.[84] Lowell was the largest industrial city in America in 1850.[85] Men had more freedom to harass, molest, and abuse women in urban settings, where they acted more independently and had fewer external restraints. But enslaved women were vulnerable everywhere.

Lack of privacy provided some protection, imperfect as it may have been, for young women in smaller communities. Most often conducted within the bounds of the residential setting, working-class courtship was monitored by parents, friends, neighbors, and other young people in the eligibility pool. The public nature of tribal courtship helped to keep young men (and young women) in line. Gossip, according to a discerning nineteenth-century historian, was central to community experience "because it was a primary means of circulating information and also because it regulated moral behavior."[86] Local familiarity as well as vigilance offered young women at least some protection from sexual predators.

In small towns and villages, gossip exerted considerable social control because people cared about their reputations. One staid northern soldier worried about what the girls back home in Monroe, Wisconsin, might think of his cursing. "I hope you have not told any one of it," he warned his male friend, "in particular the girls as I do not want the folks in Monroe to think

SEX TALK, HUMOR, AND FEAR OF RIDICULE   131

I am a heathen because I belong to the U.S. Army."[87] His concern was for his reputation in the local tribe. He wanted to keep from damaging his image with the collective pool of eligible white women in Monroe, population 937.[88] The exposed nature of tribal courtship, which occurred with minimal expectations of privacy, was one potential counter (though opportunity was never closed off) to sexual predation.

Lack of privacy also created a group environment for sexual expression that encouraged joking as opposed to serious eroticism. The working class kidded about sex before and after marriage. They favored slang and often used it to comical effect. Sex jokes were frequently focused on the male body, especially the penis. Women's sexual organs were not ridiculed as much as men's, though large breasts, backsides, and external genitalia sometimes prompted crude comments meant to elicit laughter.

Working-class men did not think prostitutes were criminals, but they also did not think of them as eligible mates. Still, they were not embarrassed to talk with other men about their experiences with hookers and presented their need to use such services as normal, not as deviant.[89] However, prostitution was one topic that seemed to be off-limits with women of their tribe. Prostitution became, according to one historian, more "associated with economic necessity, poverty, and ultimately the lower classes" in the early nineteenth century. Perhaps as a result, working-class men were ill at ease bragging or joking with women about purchasing intercourse from females who were not too different in social class from their wives and sweethearts.[90] Also the fear of slipping into sex work due to circumstances beyond their control may have sobered and soured poor women's attitudes toward prostitutes. Nonetheless, there was very little explicit moralizing among and between men and women about sex. Young men in the laboring class shared ribald sexual comments with their mothers, demonstrating the widespread cultural acceptance of sex talk between men and women of all ages.

If the middle class associated profligate sexuality with the lower sort, the common people had no such view of themselves.[91] Young people as well as parents treated sex as a matter-of-fact experience. "[A] little screw don't hurt nobody," one young man informed a young Midwestern woman.[92] Though the statement proved to be misleading, it illustrates a pragmatic view of sex as natural, harmless, and ordinary. Overactive impulses were sources of brags or laughter. Men's adultery was consistently presented in terms of jokes about illegitimate children and warming married women's beds in the absence of their spouse. However, female adultery was sometimes overlooked, albeit married women were in those beds. A vital sexual appetite was embraced by and for men as well as women.[93] There were limits, however, which the community monitored through the powerful mechanism of ridicule. One's tribe still determined the boundaries of acceptable sexual behavior by enabling its members to feel worthy or by fostering a sense of unworthiness. Sexual humor constructed camaraderie, in the sense that when everyone shared an understanding of acceptable sexual norms, laughing became a unifying affect. But sexual humor also created alienation, by exposing the outlier to embarrassment and shame.[94]

5

Love to All Inquiring Friends

Sustaining Communal Ties in Nonromantic Marriage

If the purpose of working-class courtship was to wed the best available person within one's tribe, the challenge was to set up a separate household without breaking communal bonds. If the purpose of middle-class courtship was to nurture and develop romantic love, the challenge was to adjust the subjective and volatile romantic bond to the compulsory social obligations of nineteenth-century marriage.[1] Middle-class couples, marrying for romantic love, were committed to the primacy of the self. In the grip of romantic love, they were happy to separate themselves from others through barriers of space and walls of privacy. Working-class couples, however, who married for nonromantic love, were committed to the primacy of the group. They were wary of conjugal attachments that necessitated retreat from the bonds of community. Spouses involved their tribe in many everyday activities. They deliberately or perhaps more often customarily kept the boundaries between their marriage and community porous and diffuse.

Working-class husbands and wives did not ordinarily use the vocabulary of romantic love. This bothered First Sergeant Samuel Potter, who read and wrote letters for many uneducated northern men during the Civil War. He had a reputation as an expert in composing love letters, and the unlettered flocked to him for epistolary aid. Potter was in a position to assess the relationships of these poor, undereducated men and their wives. "Sophie, when I read complaining letters from wives to their husbands, letters without one word of love or encouragement, I think of the contrast there must be between their homes and mine." He looked at working-class marriage through a middle-class lens, marveling at the "difference between the letters they get, and yours to me."[2]

Though Potter, a soldier in the 140th Regiment of Pennsylvania volunteers, correctly reported that wives grumbled—"their letters are all complaints and murmerings without one cheering word of love"—he was tone deaf to their emotional attachments.[3] Expecting "cheering word[s] of love," he did not

---

Love and the Working Class. Karen Lystra, Oxford University Press. © Oxford University Press 2024.
DOI: 10.1093/oso/9780197514221.003.0006

134 LOVE AND THE WORKING CLASS

understand the basis of working-class marriage nor appreciate the nuances of their connections.

The majority of correspondents did not express their affection in the vocabulary of romantic love. Still, they did not necessarily neglect their spouses as a consequence. Their feelings were often symbolized in prospective acts of kindness. This included wishing for the material possessions that would make life easier or better. Food was one of the most common symbols of women's affection in a working-class marriage: "i am glad that you have as good to eat as you have," Susan Jones wrote her husband, "i wish you had some of the nice butter that i make and some of the nice letuace and onions and redishes and i think you could do very well." She relied on a concrete, everyday calculus of vegetables to convey her feelings.[4]

Likewise Mary Caplinger expressed her affection in the symbolic vocabulary of food. "I am sory to hear that you was so unwell & that you cant get any thing that is good to eat," she wrote in early June 1863. "I never set down to eat but what I think of you & often wish you had something which I now [know] you love & that is good buiscuits milk and Butter & fried Chicken O if you could only get that I know you would like it better than what you have to eat."[5] Mary conveyed deep feelings of attachment for her husband without employing the vocabulary of romantic love. She shared her nonromantic love by imagining the food she would cook for him, a wifely duty that she embraced.

Concrete behaviors were signifiers of feelings in working-class marriage. "I want you to send me some of all of your Hare and have your likeneses taken," another barely literate husband wrote, instructing his wife on how to seat his family for the photograph (likely a tintype) and what each should wear.[6] "[W]hen I go to my Breakfast I feel lik you ort to Be there and eat with me to eat it makes me feel lonesome," he revealed.[7] His wife would have cooked his breakfast each morning, and he missed the love she conveyed in preparing and sharing the meal that began his day.

Working-class husbands frequently demonstrated their love by sending money home during their absence. This concrete behavior fulfilled the obligation of a husband while at the same time signaling his affection or concern. It was a tangible sign of marital commitment. During the Civil War, common soldiers often sent money home to needy wives. Hillory Shifflet, a private in the First Regiment, Ohio Volunteers, Company C, was determined that his family not be deprived. "I want you and the children to hav all you can git for I no that I want you to do well and liv well." When his wife failed to receive one of his payments, he was "mity sorry . . . for hit will put be back

LOVE TO ALL INQUIRING FRIENDS   135

a good deal," but he planned to send her all he could next payday.[8] Leonard Caplinger, another Union soldier, felt the same commitment: "i Want you to git any thing that you need go and git it."[9] Nonromantic love was conveyed by fulfilling his husbandly duty to provide a wife's needs.

Sending money in letters was normal during the Civil War, but the risk of theft or interception by the enemy was ever present. "[T]ha was two hundred and fifty thousand dollars on the train that day," Shifflet wrote, "and the dam suns of biches got hit all."[10] One of his letters with ten dollars folded inside was on that train, and he cursed the Confederate raiders, showing no compunction about using such language with his wife. He calculated that he had sent thirty-three dollars home in letters that were lost and he vowed in frustration that he "never will start enny more in letters." He quickly broke his pledge, however, and mailed two dollars in his next letter.[11] Not yet cognizant of his change of heart, Jemima was upset by his vow to stop sending money. "[S]orry to her that your feelings was hert with me," he apologized softly, "I dident aim to hert your feelings a tall all that I was mad a bout my money that I started to you and the sesesh got hit I intend to send you all the money that I can."[12] Wives not only depended on the money for economic survival but also saw it as a sign of emotional connection. Jemima told him not that she was in financial distress, but that her feelings were hurt. Sending money home fulfilled the husband's sex-role demands in his wife's eyes and at the same time conveyed love. Failing in that husbandly obligation created serious emotional tension in working-class marriage.

In defining a good marriage, kindness was one of the primary values that wives affirmed in the decades before the Civil War. Kindness was about a positive attitude in performing tasks, but it was also about going beyond the expected spousal roles to display consideration of and extra helpfulness to a mate. "[A]nd after all that has bin said," one married woman mused, "I have got one of the bet men that this world afords he is as kind to me is a man can bee to his wife and if I am sick he tries to do all that he can for me to make me well."[13] Her married sister agreed, but added something else to the equation: "you hope I am contented yes mother I am contented I have a kind afectionate Husband and a bright eyed pratling boy to make me happy in my new home."[14] (Taking care of her baby boy did not keep Ellen from attending a party given by the No. 7 Manchester mill boys. "I danced all night," she bragged, "and it broke up my cold.")[15]

Responding to a question about how she liked the married state, newlywed Olive Brown told her girlfriend: "I never enjoyed myself so well in my life as

I have since I have been married. I have one of the kindest husbands that ever a woman had and that is to be preferred before riches."[16] Kindness and help that went beyond a husband's basic obligations were at the top of wives' inventory of praiseworthy behavior. Men valued the same characteristics in their wives. William Scott drew attention to the qualities he admired about his new mate. "She is kind and Affectionate and lovley," he told his sister and brother-in-law. "She the light haird Blue Eid girl that I was to have."[17] This newlywed husband mentioned his wife's kindness before he described her physical appearance.

A good-looking Union soldier sits next to a woman who stands with her arm casually draped over his shoulder. She is likely his wife and may be pregnant.
Library of Congress AMB/TIN 2052, LC-DIG-36905.

Though Samuel Potter failed to understand the mindset of working-class spouses, he accurately observed the absence of "cheering words of love." One of the striking characteristics of letters exchanged between working-class husbands and wives is how sparingly they used the word with each other. Affection was most often expressed as a form of action—either in fact or imagination—involving physical objects and behaviors that were meant to improve a spouse's quality of life. Couples conveyed nonromantic love by performing expected gender roles: women by preparing food and clothing; men by sending money home to provide necessities for their family. The vocabulary of romantic love was missing from the majority of nineteenth-century working-class marriages, whatever the level of care between partners.

Like many poor soldiers on both sides of the Civil War, receiving a box from home was a huge morale boost and an affirmation of wifely affection. Hillory Shifflet was especially proud of his wife's cakes and shared them with his captain and lieutenant as well as other friends. "Amos eat some of your cakes and sends has best love to you," he wrote. This seemingly innocuous communication stood out because Hillory never expressed love directly to his wife. Other than the phrase "dear wife," he did not articulate loving feelings in his letters. Nonetheless, he almost casually passed on the "best love" of his friend Amos.[18]

Many working-class couples seem to be keeping some unstated agreement that actually prohibited the open expression of love. Only a minority of husbands and wives identified themselves as loving their spouse, especially when bringing their letters to a close.[19] There was something off-limits for the majority about sending love to spouses. The strength of the prohibition was especially striking when correspondents directed love to their children, friends, neighbors, or even an entire village while avoiding any mention of love for their husband or wife. Married couples never took any overt notice of this obvious disparity in their emotional expression. Sending love to everyone but their wife or husband was a deep-seated and taken-for-granted behavior that is left for the historian to puzzle out.[20]

In one sense no explanation is needed. Concrete behavior was the lingua franca of working-class love. Nonromantic love did not call for a verbal affirmation of the inner self; it required unspoken conduct or commitment to future care. Couples conveyed deep feelings of attachment without needing to employ the language of love. By contrast, romantic love was an interior condition, known only to the individual, and thus necessitated the verbalization of the innermost feelings of affection. Putting nonromantic love into

138   LOVE AND THE WORKING CLASS

words was about expressing intended or completed actions, not revealing the inner self. It follows that the working-class spouse preferred the phrase "yours until death" to "love." They wanted to convey an intention to act, not just an emotional state. The preposition "until" marked the duration of "yours," a pronoun that indicated a steadfast personal relationship. Giving preference to "yours until death" as a letter sign-off suggests an implicit hierarchy of feeling that favored steady lifelong commitment over the immediate bonds of sentiment.[21] That is why "yours until death" was, in many cases, a more satisfying closing than "love." The former actually said more about the rationale of a majority of working-class marriages than the latter. Commitment to a spouse, demonstrated by adequately performing one's gender role, was love as they understood it.

Riley Luther, a North Carolina blacksmith, began a correspondence with his wife in May 1862. He was imprisoned in the Confederate guardhouse for an unnamed offense. Throughout the month, he seemed more interested in the pigs, land, and crops at home than in his wife or his children. Letters from Riley were always very practical and directive: pay this, buy that, send soap and food but not "invrops [envelopes]."[22] "[W]rite often as you Can for it is all the satisfaction I Can See is to hear from you and the Children" is about as affectionate as Riley became in his letters.[23] But neither his writing skill nor his vocabulary prevented more elaborate emotional expression.

Riley's correspondence reflected the behavior and attitude of a man who commanded and directed at home. He gave his wife little discretionary power, sending cash home only as she requested it. Near the end of the war, he dispatched $100, keeping back another $400 that he intended to mail only if she could purchase grain.[24] He was someone who spent little time considering the feelings of others or his own for that matter. "Please or thank you" were not in his emotional repertoire—nor was love. Throughout the war he never penned a term of endearment or a word of tenderness to his wife. She was more demonstrative, closing her only surviving letter with the ritualistic, though emotionally charged: "I Remain your afectionate Wife untill death."[25] Riley did not allow himself this degree of sentiment.

He went so far as to reiterate that he wanted to come home and see his wife and children, and in one letter he was especially frantic. "[Y]ou donte now how bad I wante to see you and the little Children so you muste do the best yo Can and write son."[26] Riley was homesick and expressed a strong familial connection that was grounded in his role as husband and father. But prolonged absence and the threat of death did not grow or change him into someone who expressed more feelings for his spouse. Riley is at the far end of the nonromantic relationship spectrum.

"My Dear companion it is with pleasur that i take my pen to informe you of our hel the [health] wich is good at presant," John Boley began a short letter to his wife Lucinda in early 1860, "and hope that thease lines may find you and the children all Engoing the Saim Blessing." John was heading for Fort Kearney in Nebraska Territory and wrote about his journey west, closing with these lines: "Ciss Lucinda and Sammantha for me Rubans Russells are all well you all hav my Best Respect Remember me at a throne of grace when it is wel with you." Sending his wife "Best respects" as part of a family group was not the most intimate way to close his letter. He expressed more physical affection for his children than for his wife. Though she was his "dear companion," he was another working-class husband who did not use the language of love to express his feelings.[27]

Even when couples shared empathy and emotional connection, expressions of love were neither automatic nor habitual in their relationships. Rhoda and Rowland were poor tenant farmers who lived in Pendleton, South Carolina.[28] Rowland had left home to join the Confederate cause at the end of 1861. "Roda I hope I will git a letter from you before this reaches you if I dont I shall feel very uneasy," Rowland confessed to his wife. "I am verry lonesome to might this time last Sunday night I was at home with you all now I am away here and no wife nor children to comfort me." Rowland was deeply homesick: "oh how I wish I knew whot you was all a doing tonight I set and think of you tell it seemes to me I can allmost see you I can allmost hear <u>Keeper</u> bark and can hear you all talking about milking and feeding and making fires but alass will I ever see or hear these things again."[29] This poor tenant farmer was sensitive not only to visual images but to sounds. He was missing the routine noises of his family at home, including his dog. He expressed affection for his wife in concrete longings rather than in the abstract language of love. Nonetheless, he was comfortable sending love to his friends and to "Dady and Mother," while he omitted love to his wife, closing with "good by boys, good by Roda / may god bless you all." This was not an accidental oversight. In his next letter he sent love to "Dady and his boys" and "to evry body else who may ask about me."[30] By contrast he closed with this line to his wife: "receive to yourself the affections of Rowland / so fare will dear Rhoda." He plainly avoided posting love to his wife.

Fingering a lock of hair that Rhoda included in a letter, Rowland recalled a time of great intimacy. "I was delighted to get it," he told her, "oh how well I remember the time I cut your hair on the Island." But the same letter brought devastating news: her cow had died. "<u>Hun</u> I would almost as leave be dead as to suffer in mind as I have since I got that newse but I will have to try and bear it." A dead cow, likely their only one, meant an essential loss of milk, cream, and butter. Survival would be more difficult, and his family's quality of life would be diminished. He was empathetic to his family's loss and his wife's predicament, closing warmly: "Hun may God bless you fare well / your affectionate Rowland."[31]

Rhoda expressed her affection with equal intensity, favoring the emotionally charged but conventional closing of the common folk. "Hun I dayly neel and try to ask God to remember Rowland and to spare your life and myne that we may live together again and live peaceable and happy O how often have I tried to pray for this one thing Good by dear/I remain your true Rhoda till death."[32] Absent the vocabulary of romantic love, she still expressed her deep attachment for Rowland. Her closing, most often preferred in working-class letters, captured the intense feeling of life's impermanency combined with the high value placed upon loyalty and constancy. In the lives of people like Rhoda and Rowland, change was often for the worse.

Although Rhoda did not send him love in words, she performed love by preparing a box for her husband that contained food, homemade clothes including underwear, thread, and tobacco. The scratchy underwear worried her the most and she tried to justify her choice of cloth. "<u>Hun</u> I dont know that the clothes will sut you the drawers are very coarse I did make it for that but I thout it would be very warm and would last alittle while I intend to make you some more clothes just as soon as I can <u>Hun</u> I aimed for you to ware the drawers rong side out."[33] They both understood that the content of the box was a concrete expression of her love for him.[34] This understanding was widespread; in fact the boxes from home became something of a competition among the married soldiers—a way to measure and compare the affection and regard of their wives. Several men had received boxes, and Rowland admitted, "I wanted to let them know that my wife thought as mutch of me as their wives thought of them."[35]

In the last extant letter of their correspondence, Rowland created a vividly romantic image of home. He was a wordsmith, however unschooled. "I am setting by a window in my <u>little shanti</u> right where I can look out & see the moon and I fancy to myself that you are at this moment setting in the doore and thinking of your absent Rowland O what a lovely night this is and how I wish I was with you we would take a walk down towards the Rail Road or out towards the Big Road." He evoked an intensely romantic image of looking at the moon and thinking of her simultaneously thinking of him. Continuing to concretize their emotional connection, he visualized a walk together, something they had likely done repeatedly on warm, moonlit evenings. While calling her "my darling little Gal" and "my beloved Rhoda," two intimate terms of affection, what he emphasized was loyalty and constancy, signing off and underlining "<u>as ever</u> Rowland."[36] He and Rhoda were deeply attached, and they had certain romantic proclivities, but both withheld direct expression of love for their spouse.

Orra Bailey closed almost all his letters to his wife Sophia with "yours Truly."[37] Yet Bailey urged his wife to "not go without the least thing" and advised her to let her boarders go if she was unable to do the work.[38] He was expressing his affection in the money he sent and in his belief that she would spend it wisely. "You need not borrow any trouble about what I shall think about how you spend the money I send you," Bailey reassured his wife. "If I hadent confidence in your judgement its not likely I should send it to you I believe I have always told you to use the money for what you wanted not to go without things yourself nor let the children as long as you have any I don't see as I can say any more upon that point."[39] His concern for his wife's welfare seemed equal to the care of men who openly avowed their love, yet Bailey never used the word "love" in his letters to her. This was very deliberate because in writing her he would send love to other people, closing one letter with "My love to all," while in the next breath singling her out with a formal "Yours truly."[40] Bailey was a private in the Seventh Connecticut Volunteers, lived in Hartford, and worked in a silk mill after the war.[41] As with so many others, he took pains to sustain his emotional connections to his tribe.

Rufus Wright, a North Carolina freedman who had joined the First US Colored Infantry in July 1863, wrote his wife from near Hampton, Virginia, that he hoped she was "Enjoying good health as it now fines me at Prisent." He immediately asked her to "give my Love to all my friend." Pleasantries aside, Wright had bad news to report. "I met witch a Bad mich-fochens [I met with a bad misfortune] I ben [S]ad of I Lost my money." Saying no more on the subject may indicate that Rufus was the responsible party. His wife, a freed person herself, lived close enough to visit his camp and he urged her to "com to see me." He asked her to "Give my Love to mother and Molley," and also to "give my Love to all inquiring fried." Then he closed definitively with "No more to Say Still Remain you Husband untall Death."[42] Sending love to everyone but his wife, Rufus adhered to the common code of behavior in

142 LOVE AND THE WORKING CLASS

nonromantic marriage. He repeated the practice in another letter he wrote in haste before a battle in late May, sending love "to all & to my sisters," and telling his wife to "give my love to Miss Missenger" but including no love for his wife. He closed with "No more from your Husband."[43] Directing love to a spouse was as unwarranted in some portion of the Black working-class community as it was in the white. Likewise, Black and white spouses shared a determination to nurture community attachments.

This practice of withholding direct expression of love for a spouse continued into the early 1880s. One white Virginian, writing her husband in May 1883, sent "love to all" but none to him specifically, closing her letter with "good bye my Dearest from your homesick wife." She obviously felt considerable affection for her husband, admonishing Willie to "take good care of your Dear little self I wont stay away any longer than I possibly can help." But she followed the long-standing pattern of avoiding love in addressing her spouse.[44]

Looking back at courtship, young men used love freely to refer to their tribal attachments. Sending love to the group of eligible girls in their local community was a common practice. (Young women remained at home or reconstituted their tribe in a new location.) Singling out a particular girl or boy for love in a personal courtship letter was not expected. Usually mate selection was mediated by friends and family who established a mutual interest in marriage based on practical, concrete, and external criteria such as physical appearance and survival skills. This pattern of external judgment continued into marriage, where conscientiously doing the conventional work assigned to husbands and wives by their tribe was the bedrock of marital satisfaction.

But if failing to verbalize love for a spouse might be seen as a consequence of the working-class preference for behavioral signs of affection, what are we to make of the continual use of love to endorse relationships with family, friends, and even whole communities? Matrimony was a primary goal met by almost all Americans, but in working-class culture marital commitment was in tension with collective loyalty. This tension was expressed in letters by the relegation of spousal attachment to second, third, or even fourth place behind family, friends, and tribe. The community had an emotional priority in working-class feelings that appears to be threatened or at least tested after marriage. Spouses signaled concern about collective ties and expressed anxiety about community connections by sending love to specific friends, family members, and children, as well as groups of neighbors, villagers, and well-wishers, while never mentioning love for their spouse.

LOVE TO ALL INQUIRING FRIENDS   143

"[I] Reman your Dear husband" and "i remember you day by day" were as openly affectionate as Union soldier Lewis Strayer ever became with his wife.[45] Yet he was willing to "give my Best love . . . to all my frends."[46] He directed his wife, in another letter, to "give my love to all my neighbors."[47] He ended another with "give my love to All that inquire after me."[48] Each of these letters was sent without any expression of love for his wife. Strayer included his wife in a familial group when he wrote, "I give my Love to you all and may god bless you all is my prayer." Still he did not single his wife out, obviously feeling more comfortable imparting love to a collective "you all."[49] With the exception of his children, all the love he acknowledged was group love.[50] Strayer favored his community attachments, seemingly anxious to communicate his continued loyalty to the tribe.

Pennsylvanian David Demus was a free person of color who enlisted in the Massachusetts Fifty-Fourth in May 1863. David and his wife, Mary Jane, who worked as a live-in domestic and seamstress, blended romantic and nonromantic feelings in the letters they exchanged throughout the remainder of the war.[51] In his first year of army life, however, Demus eschewed any declaration of love to his spouse. He sent love to "all the frends" or "his love to everbody" and even passed along love to his wife from several friends in his company but he did not send his own love to her. He also directed his love to Aunt Mary and Uncle Saul Harrison and later to Jenny and Aunt Mary Harrison.[52] He closed one letter, *"Give my love to Father and Elizabeth and to Aunt Mary and to Uncle Solomon Harrison and Cousin George and Cousin Rachel and to all the friends. Nothing more at present but remain your dear husband until death, your friend."[53] His most affectionate closing in the first year of separation from his wife was some version of "but still remae yor dear hus bean."[54] This fit the dominant working-class pattern.

Seriously wounded in the assault on Fort Wagner, Demus anticipated a furlough, expecting that his local doctor would plug the hole in his head with a piece of silver.[55] Anxiously awaiting a leave, David continually promised to be home soon. In early November he offered to buy his wife a shawl on his way home, telling her that he would *"fetch you one home if [you] send me word what kind you want."[56] Mary Jane replied in early December that she wanted a dove-colored or a red, green, and white patterned double shawl.[57] Her husband was expressing his feelings in a material way. She openly and more directly conveyed her feelings while waiting for his return: "for if dont com this tim I will be varry much disponed."[58]

A handsome family is dressed up for a photograph during the Civil War. This portrait of a Union soldier with his wife and daughters was found in Cecil, Maryland.
Library of Congress AMB/TIN 5001, LC-DIG-36454.

Their separation took a toll on Mary Jane. She was not happy to hear he would be returned to combat, and she was worried they would never see each other again. "[I] tre to keep mi seff in harte but it wis a hard things." She can only "put ar trut in god for he the only one wee cane look too." She instructed him to "give love to the rest gorge and the boys" and then she sent her "best" to him; love is implied but never openly expressed. Her letter closes with "good night pece be with you."[59] At times she self-consciously revealed her inner feelings, telling her husband she was troubled and depressed by his absence. She made it clear that her emotions were not based on her economic need. She had few complaints about her work as a seamstress and reassured him that she "get alongs very well."[60] Her romantic inclination to share her inner self seemed to be inhibited by the nonromantic conventions of working-class culture.

More than four months after he promised to buy her a shawl on his way home, and still waiting for his return, she explained: *"When you wrote the other time you were coming, I sat up every night looking for you until ten o'clock. Then I would give you up and go to bed and lay and listen. I could not sleep half [the night] for I was so sure you would come. Father would say, 'He won't come tonight.' O but I do wish you could come." She again expressed deep anxiety about his physical well-being and took solace in the typical working-class hope of reunion in an afterlife. Mary Jane wrote that her "father send his love to you all." She also passed along the love of Uncle Solomon and Aunt Mary, but sent no love of her own, closing with "pece be with you all."[61] In spite of yearning for his company and revealing her deep affection, she avoided a direct expression of love.

John Wilson was a husband who was not romantically inclined and gave emotional primacy to the collective. Wilson had been a peddler and farmer in Vermont before he went west to seek his fortune in 1859.[62] At first he transported vegetables to San Francisco from a nearby ranch, but by the next year he had become a bartender in Virginia City. Having caught the silver fever, he was investing almost all his earnings in mining claims.[63] He missed his wife but grouped her with the rest of his folks at home: "thaer is not ome hower [one hour] in a Day but what i think of you and all the rest off my foalks. i think of Father and Mother a thousand times in a dy I hope you are thar at home with them fore i no they must bee very lonesome."[64] His concern for his parents' feelings seemed paramount. And while he asked his wife to "give my love to all that inquire fore me," he settled for "So good knight once more" in closing his letter to her.[65] In another letter he was willing to send his love to four specific relatives and friends whom he named, but not his wife, closing with "God By deer Mary."[66]

In another missive, he instructed his wife to "Give my love to every body Farther and Mother in perticular." But he sent no love to her.[67] He was willing to send her a kiss with a drawing of two hearts, however, and he reported a dream of them together at a dance "and when I wake I was mad to think I was hear."[68] He told her explicitly that he missed her "you cannot think how mutch I think of you and how I want to see you and the baby but I cannot bare the thought of coming home poore." He had a dream: "I want to stay till I can bee able to build a hous off oure drem and ride in our own Carige and bee as independent as the rest of then."[69]

By May 1861 John had decided he needed five years in Virginia City to realize his dream. He began lobbying his wife and child to join him: "this sitty

146 LOVE AND THE WORKING CLASS

is incorporated now and we have regular sitty laws thare has bin no one killed her fore the last six months Men are sending for their famileys from all parts of the world when I came here thare was no wimen here but now the meating Hous is ful every Sunday." Leaving his Vermont community was more difficult than John acknowledged, however, and after extolling Virginia City and urging his wife to relocate, he instructed her to tell his brother, "fore Gods sake never to leave his (Wife) fore Gould or silver God noes if I ever live to see you once more I never will leave you again." John missed his family and his community, asking questions or commenting on fourteen different people in his local village. He even asked about a pet: "is my Old Dog Argos alive." But he never sent love to his wife.[70]

As it turned out, bartending in Virginia City was a dangerous occupation. A friend was stabbed five times for refusing to "let a rowdy have Whiskey on Credet," Wilson wrote his wife. "[H]e fell and died in five minutes." Wilson met a similar fate, shot in anger over trifles by the drunken owner of the saloon where he worked.[71] His wife was cheated out of her interest in his mining claims, which probably totaled about $3,000, and she ended up with nothing but his back pay.[72]

Time and again, married men and women imparted love to the group rather than a spouse. They obviously felt an intense need to reinforce their relationships with the community. Without much thought, J. C. Owens closed a letter to his wife: "So fare well ford while but I hope not all ways." To his neighbors he wrote: "I send my best love to all of my nabers that requires [inquires] after me."[73] Tribal identification was strongly inculcated in working-class culture, and married couples sought to remain connected to their tribe. This connection meant that the boundaries between the married couple and their community were not closed off the way they were in middle-class romantic relationships.

Consequently, the circle of marital intimacy was much more inclusive and collective in the working-class marriage than its middle-class counterpart. Isham Upchurch wrote a letter to his wife that he mailed to John W. Beavers, his brother-in-law, with these instructions: "coppy this letter John W. Beavers and rectify Mistakes *tell Defia* [Isham's wife] *I began to want to see her*."[74] Isham expected his brother-in-law to edit a draft letter meant for Isham's wife and, most remarkably, compose some terms of endearment in the rewritten note. That Isham assumed his feelings for his wife could be articulated by his brother-in-law illustrates the permeability of their marriage boundary. This porous border destroys any notion of amorous privacy or exclusivity.

LOVE TO ALL INQUIRING FRIENDS   147

A letter from Simeon Tierce, an African American, also displayed the fluid boundary that existed between the married couple and their community of friends. "Tell Sarah to tell Prescilla to forward this letter to William, in the name of the lord, as he is all the time 'grumbling.'" The letter, written in a Civil War army camp in Rhode Island to his wife Sarah in the Hills, a hamlet in Westchester County, New York, included ten thousand kisses and twelve lines of love poetry. But this did not faze Simeon, who directed that his entire letter be shared with William and his wife Priscilla.[75]

Hillory Shifflet, the white Union soldier introduced above, also asked his wife to share a letter. He was "in low spirits," he revealed to Jemima, but added thoughtfully, "I donte want you to greve your self a bout hit." He directed her to write immediately "all the good nuse you no," apparently believing that positive news from home was an antidote to depression.[76] Shifflet suddenly interrupted his letter, addressing a few lines to his friend Sam and instructing Jemima to "let Sam see this letter."[77] Neither Tierce nor Shifflet acted as if their spousal relationship required privacy.[78]

Matrimony, however, did necessitate a certain distance from the tribe. The dominant nuclear structure of American households—husband, wife, and children under one roof—created a potential barrier between the couple and those on the outside.[79] Spouses in working-class marriages often tried to overcome this separation by affirming and reaffirming their communal ties. Love to all or love to all inquiring friends was an assertion of tribal membership and group allegiance. This practice seems intended to break down the potential isolation of the married pair and to reinforce community attachments.

Group solidarity was compromised by a couple who differentiated themselves too sharply from the rest of their community. Working-class spouses took considerable pains to remain available to their tribe. Maintaining shared commitments may have been an emotional as well as economic priority, because their community, more than their marriage, gave plain folk the promise of reliable shelter from the confusion of their uncertain lives.

6

Fighting to Stay Together

Unhappy Spouses and Their Struggles

Several working-class couples disclose a great deal about the dynamics of community and marriage. They often reveal the various points of tension and contestation between the group and one another. Married couples, in many instances, maintained permeable boundaries with their tribe. Those weak boundaries affected good as well as bad marriages. But troubled relationships were especially vulnerable to community pressures. These relationships vividly demonstrate the active role that intermediaries played in marital conflicts. They also display the most common source of marital disputes: the adequacy of a husband's contribution to the household economy.

A full-blown marital argument between Solon and Elisabeth Fuller, poor farmers living in Alabama, comes vividly to life 150 years after it occurred. It is a rare glimpse into the married life of nineteenth-century Americans with minimal education and a hardscrabble existence. Elizabeth and Solon Fuller expect neighborly help and support, specifically in their childrearing crisis, but they also expose the reality of community indifference and destructive gossip. The Fullers' marital arguments played out in uncensored letters that open a detailed view of marital tensions and group dynamics. (Elizabeth was married for the second time and may have been bolder and less submissive as a consequence.) Most significantly, both spouses left a record of their point of view in an individual voice that is conversational and unguarded. Satisfactory spousal role performance was a point of contention for both husband and wife. This is a rare opportunity to eavesdrop on the common man and woman's marital arguments and exchanges.[1]

Solon and Elizabeth Fuller each had children from a previous match. Solon's son, John, and Elizabeth's granddaughter, Caledonia, were living with them at the time that Solon plunged their marriage into crisis by joining the Confederacy as a paid substitute for a Mr. Johnson. "O my Dear husband," Elizabeth began, "I take up my willing pen to in form you of the times here thar are bad anuff for I have bin seck ever ence you left which you wose aware

Love and the Working Class. Karen Lystra, Oxford University Press. © Oxford University Press 2024.
DOI: 10.1093/oso/9780197514221.003.0007

of when you left home for you new that john would not do enny thing unless I wos after him he has left me." Her stepson John had run off, over her strenuous objections, to take a job driving a chicken wagon for fifteen cents a day. But after two days his employer sent him home. She scolded John, telling him she was not going to put up "with such do ins go off when you please and come whene."[2]

Trying to reason with him was fruitless. So she threatened another form of discipline: to bind him out as an apprentice until he was twenty-one, with a legal obligation to work for the contract holder. This threat had no effect. According to Elizabeth, he "would strole about and hunt and stay in the negro hous ef and dance shoeless." His unshod feet especially galled her, but predictably her objections fell on deaf ears. Even though she tried to restrain him, she reported, "it all don no good." After being gone a week, John returned for his clothes and told her he was living better away from home where "he was goin to work for his selfe." He was well aware that if his father came home, "he could not get to go no whare."

Elizabeth not only had to deal with a rebellious, smart- alecky stepson, but also hurt her back and consequently had to pay someone to get her wood, dig her potatoes, and harvest the corn. Two things really stuck in her craw. First was the way her husband handled their finances. He took the partial cash payment he received as a substitute into the army with him. He even kept Johnson's note for the balance that was due in nineteen months. Elizabeth questioned his motives. Did he think she was dishonest, she wondered?

Her stepson's tattletales, based on a supposed conversation with his father, also angered her. The stakes of the argument had become intensely personal. "[H]he told me that you intend taken him out of hell for you wos tiard of living in hell well Mr I marred you to live whot few days I had to live with you but if it was your choises to in jure [endure] the hardheps of the ware to get out of hell tho if you wished to get away from me you could uv stayed her and took care of john for I much feare that he will come to some bad end."

Elizabeth was stung by her stepson's taunts and gave them some credence. *"I do not ever expect to lay eyes on you again," she admitted in a postscript. "You promised me that you would get a furlough and come home. I suppose you did not want to come." She feared the community gossip was correct. "Johnson said that if you did not get in you might get home the least [longest] way you could. Cludy Ware heard him say so and you know that he was a mean man."[3] She listened to the tribe and was at least partially convinced that her husband was planning to abandon her.

150 LOVE AND THE WORKING CLASS

"You know that if I had cared no more for you and John than you both care for me," she reminded her husband, "I could go to my children, where I could have lived well. No, I stayed here and tried to do all I could to [make] my home agreeable."[4] Grown children in second marriages provided wives with some power to leave an unhappy situation. This in itself contributed to a more fluid marriage boundary. Declaring her option to exit the marriage, Elizabeth pointedly contrasted her loyalty and commitment with her husband's. "I did not turn you and John loose in the world to perish." Still her situation was precarious. Without an infusion of cash, she had no money to buy salt, which was necessary to preserve meat, and without feed, she reminded him, "my cows will go dry." She wondered aloud why Solon spent $100 of his substitute money on a mare who was a big eater while she was starving and went barefoot. She threatened to leave but continued to work to get his wheat (two bushels) hauled to market. While Elizabeth criticized her husband's inadequacy as a provider, she was more offended by the gossip that he left because he thought it was hell to live with her.[5]

In his next letter, Solon vigorously rejected the motives attributed to him by his son and neighbors. "[M]ey dare you Donte think that I was tird of livenge with you for god nose that it is not the case bute I wanted to gite of poverty an if god spares my life I think thate when I gite oute of the armey," he wrote hopefully, "I will to liv better [than] we hav bin living." He sent some money home to test the safety of the mails and assured her that he would send more if the first installment arrived safely. He closed, "carey Dear I hop I have Don for the best so fare you well at presante I remain yuer a fectionate hus ban until Deth."[6]

Meanwhile Elizabeth had not been placated, and her emotional bruises were still tender. "I have hope that this letter will find you in good health and well satisfied," she responded on November 24, "for it has been about 9 months since you have appeared to satisfied where I was." She wanted Solon to own up to the predicament he had left her in. "I have not got 1 grain of salt since you left. I am a living upon parch meal coffee and bread without salt. I have got no shoes yet and my feet are on the cold frosty ground," she complained. "I have not spent 1 dime of your money, only to pay the expense of your mare for I did not know whether you wished me to live off of it or not as John has left." Elizabeth was testing her husband's love and commitment by playing up her suffering.[7] Unshod feet "on the cold frosty ground" was meant to shame him into giving her money.

The argument was not yet resolved in Elizabeth's mind, for she returned to the sore spot and reiterated her grievances. "Mr. Fuller, you said that you thought I had cast you off, which was very far from me; for I did not go off but I tried to stay with you. But you were determined to leave for if you did not get into the army you intended to leave here. For in my presence you [said that you] had rather go in the army and be shot than stay here and perish."[8] No doubt Solon did tell her that he would rather be shot in the war than stay where he was. But what were his reasons for leaving?

Trying to understand his motives and to weigh the odds of his return against the chorus of naysayers, Elizabeth inventoried her role for faults and missteps. "While I live Mr. Fuller sleep is a stranger to my eyes, for when I lie down at night I lie there thinking what was the cause of [you] leaving; for I never did one thing nor said nothing to you that I ought not to [have] said."[9] She was half persuaded that he would never return. "It is all right," she noted mockingly, "I will bear it like I ought and hope I shall not be long in your way. For if peace was made tomorrow, I never expect to see you again. For that was what you left here for: to get shut of me. So I dare not hope ever to see you again."[10] By repeatedly testing her husband's intentions, she indicated that she had not given up hope in his commitment to their marriage.

This extraordinary marital argument, captured on paper, continued in the next letter as Solon responded to his wife's anger. "[I]t gave mee pain hare that you was un well and thate John had left you and the way thate the nabers has treted you I hope thate you will git better for ite gives mee sore to hear thate you ar sick you have senchared mee aboughte leving hom and I Donte noe how I cold a Don enney better in the Surcemstances that I was plaste in ate that time for I cood make nothing thar and times wa so hard that I did note mow whate to doo."[11] Solon defends himself by arguing that hiring out as a Confederate army substitute was the only way he knew to fulfill his husbandly role as a provider.

Now came the apology. *"Betsy, if I have done wrong, I am sorry for it. For I could not have made two hundred dollars there in two years and I have made fifteen hundred, and if I die or get killed, you and Johnny will have it." He presented his reasons for leaving as purely economic, and his financial calculus seems believable. He thought she would pity him if she knew how anxious he was to see her, his son, and step-granddaughter. Fearing that something bad might happen to his son, he offered John a twenty-dollar bribe "if he will come back and do well." Authorizing his wife to spend all the available cash, Solon was now striving to overachieve as a provider.[12]

In this November 24, 1862, letter, Elizabeth (Betsey) Fuller rebukes her husband Solon for leaving her suddenly to join the Confederate army as a paid substitute. He has left her no money, she is short on food, and she can find no one to help her with their farm in Alabama.

Solon L. Fuller Papers, Rubenstein Library, Duke University.

Solon Fuller wrote to his wife on November 30, 1862, responding guiltily to her accusations of abandonment. He defends his decision to leave home as a last-ditch attempt to provide for his family.

Solon L. Fuller Papers, Rubenstein Library, Duke University.

154 LOVE AND THE WORKING CLASS

Desperate economic circumstances seem to be his principal motive for leaving Elizabeth even though she suspected otherwise. "[W]hen I took the notion to come in the army," he added a postscript, "[I] could see no other way to live for there was no way to make money and I did not believe that war would last long and neither do I now." He predicted that the Civil War would end in March 1863, and "if it does, I have made a good winters work if my mind could be contented but it is not."[13]

Salving his guilty conscience, Solon made amends in his next letter for leaving his wife to "perrish," in her words. "[Y]ou [were] right that I left you to starve," he responded honestly. "I could see nothing but starvation when I left home and [didn't know] how I could have got money to buy corn or salt." He contrasted the bleak situation he left at home with his ability to give her money now, almost bragging about what he had sent to make her comfortable. Reassuring her that his thought "is all the time night and day about you and the rest of them," he vowed that if God let him return home, he would never leave again. He added that he had sent her some salt but someone will have to pick it up, "and that is all the way I know how to do."[14]

He continued to be very worried about his son, asking his friend and neighbor, Mr. Ware, to take "control of him until I come home." He told Ware to make his son stay with his stepmother and if he refused, to make him work for Ware; and if he ran away "to bring [him] back and whip him severely for I am determined that he shall not be a strutting about the country."[15] Teenage rebellion and a worried parent are still common, but giving complete responsibility for a son to a neighbor is grounded in the bonds of nineteenth-century working-class community.

On Christmas Day, after finally receiving his earlier letters, Elizabeth openly embraced him. "You speak of coming home. I can't flatter myself that I [will] ever see you again for that happy day is too far ahead for me ever to [say]. So if you can get home, make haste and let me see if I shall live to see that happy day." She closed with "fare well my love."[16] Two things had changed her tune: he made clear that he intended to return home after the war, and he authorized her to spend whatever money was on hand to improve her quality of life.

"We are absent in distance many a mile but my mind is with you continually," he wrote tenderly, "I want to come home very much but I can't come home now for the smallpox is raging here and they won't let a soldier leave the camp now."[17] After these words to his wife he turned his attention to his son and addressed him directly in the same letter: "Johnny, O my son, why won't you do as I wanted you to do? Then I should be happy. But as it is, I can't but be miserable. Johnny, my son, do be a good boy and do as Ma wants you to do."[18] After more admonitions, Solon offered his son two bribes: "a hansom present" and the first colt of the mare he bought with his bounty money. And if he is killed, he told his son, "If you are a good boy, all that I have shall be yours."[19] However, in trying to bribe his son with the ultimate promise of all that he had, Solon failed to take into account what effect this would have on his wife.

Just as she resolved her feelings of abandonment, and they moved toward a rapprochement, another misunderstanding took shape. Several letters had crossed in the mail or been delayed, and on January 1 Solon responded testily to his wife's complaint that she waited empty-handed while Bill Ware received two letters.[20] "I received your letter and you were kind enough to tell me that you would not write any letters until you got one from me," he scoffed. "If it is against your will to write to me, don't write any more for there has not been a week but I have written [you] a letter and some weeks I have written two." Solon theorized that his son had stolen his letters from the post office box, so he made plans to thwart him. Feeling increasingly lonely, "for I don't feel as though I had one friend in the world," and worried sick about his son, Solon described his mind as "tore to pecis."[21] Ironically, given the crux of their misunderstanding, he closed the letter with a desperate hope "that I shall get a chance to come home before long so farewell my dear wife and may God bless you."

On January 20 Elizabeth took up the gauntlet he had thrown down on January 1, informing him first that she had received all his letters: "John did not take them out. It was some mismanagement [by] the postmaster. I heard from John: he is well and living with a man in Oxford by the name of Taylor and gets 25 [cents] a day and that is all I know about him." She was an adept practitioner of the old adage that the best defense is a good offense. "You said if I did not wish to write I need not do it. It was a plain case to me that if you could write to Ware that you could write to me. I thought that you cared not for me for you said that John was to have all you had when you died. I have children that will support me if I will go to them."[22]

In the meantime Solon confessed that he was "out ov all hart," having received only three letters from her in two months. "I think that I will be able to live in a better state than when I was home before for I could see nothing but desperation for I had made nothing to eat nor nothing to wear. But now I shall have something to live on so do right as soon as you get this letter and

156 LOVE AND THE WORKING CLASS

let me know how times are there . . . if you knew how bad I want to hear from you, you would write immediately, but out of sight, out of mind."[23] Solon got in a dig that also tested her commitment to him.

Elizabeth responded to his complaints about the infrequency of her letters with "Mr. Fuller, you need not think hard of me for not writing for I answer all of your letters as soon as I can. When the weather is cold, I can't write at all for my hand is so numb." After taking care of some business dealings, she continued: "I must come to a close for you see I can hardly write at all. I could fill the sheet but my hand is in such a fix. You must write soon for if I can't see you, I am glad to hear from you." She closed her letter with unambiguous affection reminiscent of middle-class romantic symbolism: "my love you must kiss these lines for the wont of the purson as I have to do so fare well my deare."[24]

On the eve of his first battle, Solon decided to entrust the rest of his money to his wife. What this meant was the note he held for the balance of the $1,500 that he "earned" as a paid substitute in the war. Solon thought he might die and he told her to put it out on interest, but then he gave her complete control, admitting, "you know better what to do with it than I do for I have got no more [than] ten minutes."[25] He was feeling very vulnerable and waxed philosophical. Feeling sorry for Caledonia, his step-granddaughter, he suggested that his wife cheer her up as much as possible, "for [the] girl she sees hard times. But I hope that she will see many happy days to make up for these bad ones." Cheerleading himself as much as his step-granddaughter and wife, he instructed them to keep up good courage and not to give up. "It is a hard world to live in," he opined, "but if it was not for [the] hopes of all beings we would be the most miserable but God knows what is best for us all."[26] Still in a philosophical mood six days later, he mused that if the Almighty was willing, he would return home and "we will enjoy [our]selves better than we ever have done." Solon held a common working-class belief that the world was a troublesome place with "but verrey lettle plesher in it." He went further and said that he sometimes felt willing to die, but then he quickly added, "the lord will be done."[27]

Betsey was full of sympathy and concern in her next letter. "I was most distracted for fear you was killed. Mr. Fuller, you don't know how uneasy I am about you for I never go to bed but I think and pity you living on the cold ground and not a pillow to put under your poor old head and I do not know whether you have any [blanket] to cover with or not." She admonished him not to expose himself to the elements, "for my dear I feel that if it please

God to spare your life and you get home again it don't matter how poor we are [for] I could be happy."[28] Solon's woes went beyond uncomfortable living conditions, however, and his wife expressed heartfelt sympathy for his intimate physical affliction. "I am very sorry to hear that you have got the itch for I am as afraid of it as I am the smallpox. . . . Mr. Fuller you don't know how bad I want you to come home: worse than tongue can tell or pen can describe."[29] The tenderness in Betsy's response to his sleeping arrangements in camp and to his "itch" discloses a nonromantic love relationship of compassion and affection that was broken but then restored by Solon's willingness to give her control of his bounty money. In her eyes he had fulfilled his duty as her husband.

In his last extant letter, dated March 23, Solon wrote his friend Mr. Ware, asking him to collect the remaining money on Mr. Johnson's note the minute it came due, April 13. If Johnson could not fulfill the substitute contract, Solon intended to leave camp immediately.[30]

Elizabeth gave some credence to neighborhood gossip (as well as her stepson's claim) that her husband might never return home because he considered their marriage a living hell.[31] She also jealously compared the number of letters she received from her husband to the number he wrote to their neighbor Mr. Ware. Solon recruited Ware to deal with his financial affairs and his son's unruly behavior. He even asked Ware to convey his desire to see his wife "verey mutch."[32] However, neither Solon nor Elizabeth asked him to act as a mediator. Though intermediaries did not directly intercede in the Fullers' marriage, Solon and Elizabeth were typically enmeshed in tribal loyalties.

Couples like the Fullers, in nonromantic love, can demand specific behaviors as a way to repair their marital rifts. This only works, however, if both spouses remain committed to their marriage. In spite of their feelings of anguish, sorrow, and frustration, the Fullers broke their cycle of hurt—being hurt by a willingness to continue communicating through the mails. Though both made veiled threats to leave the marriage, they continued writing letters that conveyed their point of view and justified their feelings. Solon broke the emotional logjam when he explained why he had to leave in order to get the resources they both desperately needed to eat and thus survive. Elizabeth believed him when he gave her permission to use the money he had earned as a military substitute to buy the necessities of survival. They both learned the value of their relationship by continuing a dialogue that was not always supportive or pleasant, but eventually allowed them to recognize that they would rather live poor together than apart.

158 LOVE AND THE WORKING CLASS

Though romantic marriage was an infrequent experience in working-class culture, some couples put the middle-class ideas and emotions of romantic love into practice. Their coupling was often more difficult than they expected. In the marriage of Edward Spencer, an upstate New York textile factory worker who enlisted in the Union army, and Jennie Spencer, an aspiring actress, working-class standards of marital behavior were mixed with a romantic notion of love that transcended all spousal role obligations.

Though Edward married his wife Jennie for romantic love, he did not practice the confidentiality that usually accompanied romantic middle-class relationships. Rather, he actively solicited the help of an intermediary in negotiating his marital problems. In nonromantic marriage, relatives, neighbors, and friends were often drawn into the couple's personal conflicts. The Spencers' romantic relationship should have exhibited strong reactions against outside interference and public exposure. Though their feelings were romantic, they did not guard their marriage from public scrutiny. Instead, the Spencers blended romantic and nonromantic conventions in a marriage that had significant strains.

Hearing tales of her husband's drinking and gambling, Jennie threatened to run off with a theater troop. "I suppose Jennie thinks I am like the most of Soldiers spending my money for Whiskey and in Gambling," Edward confided to his friend Barney, who worked in the freight department of the New York City Railroad in Rochester. "And perhaps she thinks I am after Women in evry Town we go in. but I am willing to take an oath Barney that I have had nothing to do in any way with a Woman since I have been away from Home."[33] Jennie was living with Barney and his family, and her husband's old pal was the obvious choice to play the go-between.

"Now Barney for Gods sake if you can try and persuade her to give up the Idea of going. and I will send evry cent I get to her. And try and do better. She has often talked of such a thing but if she was to go then I don't care what becomes of me. For she is my all on this earth and I don't think I should ever see Her again." However farfetched Jennie's threat to join a traveling theater company appears, Eddie took her seriously. He expected Barney to present his case for continuing their marriage rather like a defense attorney representing his client. To keep his wife from leaving him, he even admitted he was at fault: "she has good reasons for it for I have not sent Home as much money as I ought to." But he also offered the excuse that he had to buy food "and a Thousand different things" to survive.[34] Well aware that his letter might routinely be reread or passed around, Eddie asked Barney to "burn it up as soon as you read it," and at the top of the first page Eddie wrote in double underline: "don't read this to any One be sure." His admonition reflected the working-class expectation that letters would be shared.

Yet in spite of his apparent concern for privacy, Eddie asked Barney to be an intermediary in a very intimate marital fight. Moreover, Eddie had no compunction including this postscript to Jennie in an earlier letter to Barney: "Ninnie take good care of Health $450,000 worth of Kisses at a penny a piece for my Ninnie from Eddie."[35] Although their marriage was based on romantic love, this couple continued to observe some important components of working-class intimacy, especially the use of intermediaries.

Friend Barney's persuasions initially quieted Jennie's anger. "I hope and pray that we may long be spared to enjoy the love that now exists between us. and Jennie dear why should it be any other way," a more confident Eddie asked her two weeks later. "[H]ave we not always loved each other from the moment we became acquainted and for my part it has grown stronger and stronger from day to day till I think love is a poor name for it," he acknowledged. "[F]or if ever a Husband worshiped a Wife it is me. And since you have given up the Idea of going away with the old Theatre how much more do I think of my Jennie. If you had went it is not likely I should ever seen my Pet any more." Eddie professed a common miscalculation among the foot soldiers of the Civil War. "[B]ut I think this war will soon be settled and then I can come Home to my loving wife never to part again. Why if I had thought I was going to be gone from you so long as I have been. Thousands of Dollars would have been no temptation to me."[36] Regarding their last argument, Eddie was willing to concede defeat. "You say I seem to know that I am a little in the rong. I know I am a great deal so but I have your forgiveness and I am satisfied now and I will try and never give you reason to complain of your 'Eddie' again."[37]

Predictably, Jennie found reason to complain little more than four months later. He replied, "Jennie you say that you do not get the letters that I send that has any money in but you do all the rest." His wife suspected that Eddie was lying about sending money home. "Now Jennie I can prove I have sent you $40 since I have been here evry time I send you any I put it down in My Diary the last I sent by Express and I will send it all so in the future so If it is lost I can send you the bill of it."[38] Their quarrel about money would soon recede, however, as they united against a common foe—their go-between.

Both Spencers turned on Barney after he accused Jennie of fooling around with other men. Jennie now doubted the veracity of his earlier insinuations about Eddie. She told her husband that Barney was sorry for his accusations against her. But Eddie was unwilling to accept Barney's apology, and he conveyed these feelings through his wife. "[W]ell he has got to write and say he wrote me a lot of lies," Eddie insisted, "or I never shall forgive him <u>and I don't want you to go there under any Consideration</u>."[39] The role of a marital go-between was tricky. Jennie moved out of Barney's household and took up residence with her cousin Rose, who also lived in Rochester.[40]

Unfortunately for Eddie, Barney continued to pass unflattering reports of his conduct to Jennie. Expressing her dismay by addressing him as Mr. Spencer, Eddie responded in kind by addressing her as "Mrs. St. J Spencer." Eddie's clever insertion of St. (Saint) was dripping with sarcasm. Deliberately stirring up trouble, Barney told Jennie that Eddie spent his last month's civilian pay in "Whoreing and drinking Whiskey." Tellingly, Eddie only denied one of the two charges. "I can say before God or man that I have stayed with no Whore nor any Woman since I had the pleasure of marrying you." He tacitly admits to having sex with prostitutes before he married and to drinking as charged. But he vowed to reform. "You say when I get yours you suppose I will go and get drunk Well now it is 'played out' whatever may happen to me I will never be drunk again."[41]

This couple quarreled most often over money. "You say you asked me for $25 Dollars, and I have the extreme Impudence to send you 15. You say $11 for a pair of Boots. Jennie did I ever tell you I had to pay so much for them. I sent you by Express the 15 . . . I paid $8 for my Boots, and the rest I kept for my Tobacco. That is the way in which it went . . . [his ellipses] but if you see fit to still call such a <u>Damned</u> Loafer a Husband you shall have $25 the next time and evry pay day after." He seemed to be conceding her point but then mounted another defense, once again role-playing her side of the argument as well as his own. "You say you thought Soldiers were supplied with Clothing. So they are such as they are, but Ed (<u>the Son of a Bitch</u>) must put on just so many airs. the government furnishes nothing but cowhide shoes and a man cant stand it very well in this Country without Boots."[42] Eddie fought back with sarcasm and irony, but also relied on his charm and shrewdness to win her over.

At the end of the letter he became conciliatory. "You say you have stood it as long as you are going to. I don't blame you any but if you are a mind too I should like to try it again for a few months that I have got to stay." He was, as he said, "hoping you will judge favorably of this I bid you good Bye." He was only emboldened in a postscript to send 450,000 kisses "if you

FIGHTING TO STAY TOGETHER   161

will accept them."[43] In a more confident mood, Eddie once sent her "400, 000,000,000,000,000,000, 000, Kisses," so he has taken a more cautious approach to conveying amorous wishes after their latest squabble.[44]

Jennie accepted his smaller bundle of kisses and relieved Eddie of his worst fears. "I had made up my mind you had got _mad_ at me and would keep so some time. But _Nin_ is not so very hard hearted as _some_ might think but my Baby if you knew the feelings and the sorrow you cause me when you write such letters I think you would not do it any more." Not only was the Spencer marriage less than stable, both husband and wife had dubious reputations to live down. Jennie continued to test Eddie's trust in her virtue. "You say I speak as though I thought you were guilty of what Barker said about you, now you know what I think of him, and as for my believing that you would do anything wrong it is all nonsense, and _you know it_ too. Now Baby own the truth don't you _know_ I put all the confidence in the World in you, and think you will not do anything wrong."[45] Barney Barker, their intermediary, was once again a villain. In one letter, Eddie even called him "my most bitter Enemy."[46]

But the Spencers' reaction to Barney was as changeable as their tempers— one month he was their enemy and the next their friend. Eddie conceded: "I see no reason why you should not get along well with Barneys whole Family I could." He continued in this vein: "You say you all get along without any trouble and that Barney says he never had any hard feelings against me and I am shure I have not against Barney." Eddie predicted a bright future for all of them with an important caveat: "I think as he does if I live to get in Rochester we will have a good time yet."[47] All was quickly forgiven. Jennie moved back in with Barney and his family in December 1862.

When Eddie was discharged from the army in 1863, he was rehired at the textile factory in Auburn, New York. Jennie remained in Rochester with Barney's family. "Nin why cant you come down and stay here as long as I do," Eddie asked politely. "You can do it as well as stay there. They was asking me last night when I expected you down and seemed surprised when I told them I did not know."[48] The inquiring "they" were his tribe of family, friends, and coworkers. Eddie explained to Jennie that he was not yet strong enough to work in the shop in Rochester. Still she did not come.

More than a month passed and Eddie finally asked her point blank: "now when are you coming or are you fully determined not to come at all if so I want you to say so one way or the other and relieve me of the suspence in which I am thrown by your silence."[49] Eddie explained his vulnerability: "the

162 LOVE AND THE WORKING CLASS

minute I get away from the Shop I don't know what to do with myself and I don't want to go down there evry night. to pass away the time so what shall I do unless you come down to see me."[50] In Eddie's mind the choice to continue their marriage was Jennie's, and she must have voted with her feet to stay with him. Seventeen years later, the Spencers were living together in a village south of Auburn. Apparently childless, they were residents of a working-class boarding house along with two carpenters and an artist.[51]

Eddie and Jennie, he a factory machinist and she a young wife at sixteen, formed a marriage that blended the conventions of both romantic and nonromantic love. The Spencers' use of an intermediary to communicate intimate feelings was a working-class practice that was helpful to them, even when the go-between was gleefully reporting damaging information about one spouse to the other. They united at times against their common foe, seeming to heal their hurt in the process. But they also utilized another key benefit of nonromantic unions. Working-class couples could demand the dutiful performance of spousal roles as the path to repair nonromantic love. By contrast, romantic love is not repairable on demand because it is *not* thought, felt, seen, or given as an act of will. The Spencers seemed to agree that meeting the common community expectations of a husband and wife would solve their marital conflict. Though their commitment was stressed when they quarreled, neither husband nor wife gave up on their marriage. They did not get overwhelmed by appraisals of their feelings of romantic love, nor did they demand that their spouse love them more, an emotional bind that was often impossible to unknot. Their conflict revolved, at least in part, around whether Eddie's behavior satisfied his responsibilities as a husband. Jennie had to accept his conduct as adequate for their marital rapprochement to succeed.

In the nineteenth century separation was a common form of dealing with a troubled marriage.[52] In response to the pull of marital tensions and the push of economic privation, the husband in the Fuller marriage and the wife in the Spencer marriage initiated a temporary separation. But in each case, some accord was reached; physical and emotional separation did not become permanent; and the marriage was preserved.

On the other hand, permanent separation or desertion accompanied by illegal remarriage (bigamy) was not that rare.[53] This practice was confirmed by claims that were filed under the 1890 Civil War Pension law, which made money available to widows of Civil War veterans who demonstrated financial need regardless of how their husbands had died. In order to qualify, women

FIGHTING TO STAY TOGETHER   163

had to prove that they were dependent on their own labor, were earning less than $96 per year, and had little or no savings or property. The government assigned examiners to investigate contested claims (possibly one out every thirty applications), which were often characterized by a tangle of multiple identities based on geographical relocation and personal reinvention that included the use of aliases or, even more often, an opportune revision of the past that expunged a still legally binding marriage. Though legal divorce was rare, these working-class claimants demonstrated that permanent separation or desertion was not unique.[54] Demands for improved behavior are beside the point if one spouse abandons the other.

Luther Richardson left his wife Lois for another woman. Their correspondence is a rare look inside a working-class marriage that began with separation, quickly transitioned to bigamy, and eventually ended in divorce. It is an extraordinary record of the couple's thoughts, emotional responses, and interactions with their community. Lois eventually remarried a man who turned out to be a penny-pincher and threatened to leave her when their differences intensified. Her response was to withdraw her wifely services, including meal preparation. Once again the behavioral expectations of husbands and wives were at issue. Lois and Luther as well as a Greek chorus of parents, neighbors, and friends speak about the couple's motives, feelings, and experience.

"In the still of night on my bed alone in solitude," Lois Richardson wrote what was probably a journal entry, "have I mourned over my unhappy fate why is it that I must be left to mourn in silence alone," she asked plaintively. "[W]hy is it that a dear and once loved husband must be led the downward dissipated road to licenciousness and to compleet the work of distruction on himself and family to take to himself a fallen prostitute and have the sin of Bigamy upon his head." She explained that when "cares increased and providence frowned and clouds gathered then the Loved one sought the darks haunts of vice."[55]

But Luther, her husband, did more than visit the "haunts of vice." He abandoned his family. Desertion was much easier for husbands than wives, although such negligence announced a husband's ultimate failure to carry out his spousal duties.[56] Moving from Massachusetts to West Winchester, New Hampshire, Luther found work in a sawmill.[57] He also illegally married, or openly cohabited with, another woman, probably in the spring of 1851.[58] His legal wife understood that his act of bigamy left her "tenfold worse than widowed." She had two little boys to support somehow and a recently deceased daughter to add to her burden. "Then comes reflection," she self-consciously mused. "[Y]ou have a stuborn heart to be subdued you are proud and haughty this must all be subdued or you can never enter the gates of heaven."[59] Her immediate solution was humble submission to God and her fate.

Lois continued to write to her father- and mother-in-law, inquiring about their son, her bigamist husband. "[W]e shall always be glad to hear from you," her mother-in-law Polly informed her in late January 1853, "we have no hardness towards you nor do I believe what has been said." Polly placed responsibility directly on her son's head. "When I think what L[uther] has been and what he is now it is astonish to m[e] that he should leave the wife of his youth and leave such a great family of children those that were near & dear to him I am ready to say how can it be I think you must feel verry lonely." Polly did not understand the actions of her son, but she sympathized with her daughter-in-law.[60] One of Luther's adult daughters was more certain about the cause of her father's betrayal. She blamed "strong drink," lamenting that it had caused the "shipwreck" to their "once happy family."[61]

Waiting close to four years for Luther to return home, Lois finally gave up hope, perhaps spurred by suitors and the prospect of a second marriage.[62] "I should bee very happy to hav you to take a ride up to London and see my resideing plase," Alexander Moody wrote Lois, "and see how you wood like and I will a wait on you to the best of my a bilits."[63] Receiving no answer to his invitation, Moody tried again, this time offering a less subtle advance. "I don't now but wat you think I em a roge but proveing the pudding is eating the bag and if you and I ware both suted I should like to make a wife of you and if you git this letter I want you to right to mee your most true and afechnated friend."[64] This rare glimpse of a working-class marriage proposal was devoid of romance and romantic imagery. Marriage was presented as a pragmatic choice defined by constancy, compatibility, and behavior, that is, "proveing the pudding is eating the bag."

In February 1855 the wayward husband weighed in. It is likely that the senior Luther heard rumors that Alexander Moody was paying court to his wife. "[P]rehaps you can start that justice writ now," Luther sneers: "you & C[o.] may drive your team as hard as you please I defy you to do the furst thing more than you have done." Daring Lois to divorce him, Luther was not only unrepentant: he blamed his wife for their problems. "[Y]ou have lied about me to hide your own gilt it is a shame for a man & woman to live in the

FIGHTING TO STAY TOGETHER   165

shape you have lived."[65] He closed with a taunting postscript: "Yours in haste if you have any conscience it must torment you dreadfully."

Luther was a sawmill worker when he wrote his defiant letter to Lois, who may have already divorced him. His prideful arrogance was challenged by Lois's sister, Martha, who had heard a "bad report" from friends. Martha was living in Northfield, Massachusetts, and Luther was situated just across the border in New Hampshire about seven miles away.[66] "I have not seen him he works for Mr Ball in Winchester the woman he lived with when you was here is dead she was confined and lived some five or 6 weeks & died in a shocking condition being so filthy & decomposed that it was most impossible to move her." Her description of the very sick postpartum woman living in a poor, unsanitary, and disorganized household seems plausible. Apparently the newborn was then informally adopted. "Mrs Lyman of Winchester Mr Murdocks Sister has taken the child the other woman left they feel very much atached to it & want to keep it as their own, say it is the picture of Luther."[67]

"He was married again in a few weeks to one of the same family & live in the same filthy way," Lois's sister sneered. Luther's cohabitation with a relative of his deceased wife is credible. But was the sister's account of the rest of Luther's household believable? "[T]he children go to bed with their cloths all on & wear them untill they drop of." Among Massachusetts factory workers, the failure to dress well or maintain clothing was regarded as a serious disgrace. Families would sacrifice food and housing to appear well dressed.[68] This gossip about the children reflected the high value some working-class families gave to their attire. Interestingly, Martha did not want Lois to reveal her source of information. "If you write to him you must not let him know that I told you these things." Martha's motives were unspoken, but perhaps she simply wanted to keep her distance from a volatile situation. She felt the need to protect herself as well as her informants.[69]

Possibly due to his self-proclaimed reputation as a rogue, Lois rejected Alexander Moody, her first suitor, in favor of another, Mr. Davis, who was a shoemaker with at least two of his own children.[70] They married sometime in the spring 1855 and apparently lived harmoniously in the first several years. But Davis had a volatile temper and by 1862 the relationship degenerated into a series of threats and counterthreats. Davis moved his shoe business from the house into a shop in the spring of 1862. Lois was pleased. "I have the room in the house where he used to work," she told her son. "[T]he water is good here and evry thing is pleasant and I have more room which I needed verry much." The reason she needed more room was clear in her next quip. "I have had boarders since I moved hear so you see I get enough to eat."[71] Her husband was stingy and tightfisted with his money, one source of their marital tension. Once again the husband was judged inadequate in his role as a provider.

Lois's sons were even less fond of their stepfather than their mother was of her husband. After Davis warned his wife that "he was going to break up keeping house" and was planning to "let you take care of yourself," his stepson Charles wrote in disgust, "good riddance to bad rubbish."[72] Charles, a corporal in the Twenty-Sixth Massachusetts Infantry Regiment, offered more than rhetorical support. "[W]e are expecting to get four Months pay in a day or two you wlll get eighty dollars then I guess that you can get long without any of his help." Charles openly expressed contempt in his next letter. "[H]ow does S.C.D. Esq prosper. Give him the most <u>worshipful regards of his most</u> affectionate Son C.H. R," he wrote mockingly.[73]

Though Lois was still living with Davis, she accorded him little respect, deliberately nurturing her son's contempt. "Well Davis has waked and has had one of his terrible dreams lost his wallet and somebody stole his hat and he had a hard time. Can you tell what maks him always have such ugly dreams I can hear you say yes it is be[c]uase well you may tell the rest."[74] Charles reacted strongly in a later letter: "You wrote in your last that the old man was going to leave you again for Gods sake don't hinder him let him go if he will and good riddance to him I think you would be better of without him."[75]

Wives in second marriages were sometimes more assertive and less willing to take guff from their husbands than their counterparts in a first marriage. Such contrast in women's behavior might be related to age and experience, but the structural reality of older children who could provide crucial economic support was paramount. Lois's power as a second wife came from her own ability to keep boarders and her sons' willingness to send her money and emotional validation.

Mother and son were united against her second husband. "You say Davis is bound to leave the first of April he may go to that place where they buy brimstone by the wholesale if he wants to," Charles quipped. His pen was dripping with sarcasm about his stepfather. "I am almost dieing to hear from our dear 'Papa' I take it that he still remains with you . . . how is it does he still continue to be as good natured as he used to be? is his temper still as mild, even and amiable as of yore? Give him a kiss (or kick) from me."[76] "You wished to know about Mr Davis," Lois responded to her son, "he is here he boards himselfe lives on crackers he has made a fool of himself he still talks of going off."[77]

The stages of Lois Richardson Davis's marital life—marriage, household formation, children, her husband's departure and subsequent bigamy, divorce, remarriage, and possible abandonment by her second husband—reflect the volatility of working-class relationships. Her biography reinforces what one historian has dubbed, referring primarily to broken relationships, the "fluid marriage."[78] Certainly geographical separation was symbolic of marital rejection. But the mutability of working-class marriage had an even broader application. Even in stable relationships, the permeable boundaries between the couple and the group that surrounded them might qualify their marriage as fluid.

After Luther left her, Lois waited several years hoping he might return. At least initially she was sympathetic, believing that financial stress and economic setbacks had pushed her husband over the edge. However, his ability to get work in another community indicates that his difficulties did not originate in job skills. His one letter was angry and accusatory, blaming Lois's infidelity for their breakup. But this seems to be a classic case of projection. He accepted no responsibility for abandoning his wife and family, but in fleeing his community he suggests the burden of their negative judgment weighed heavily on him. One daughter was certain that her father's abuse of alcohol was the cause of his bad behavior. Alcohol seems a likely candidate in assessing his removal to another community where the chorus of condemnation was likely less vociferous. While there is no evidence that either husband or wife sought a go-between to heal their rift, the tribe was ever-present in its observation and judgment of their marital troubles. Working-class couples had weak fences around their relationships. This was a two-sided condition: community support in time of need, but also community criticisms and censure.

George Deal and his wife Sarah were scolded, reassured, and advised by the scribe who took dictation for George's letters to his wife. Their marital conflict was less serious, but it demonstrates the tension that might result from being apart. She was berated by a controlling husband for overstepping her wifely duties while her husband's scribe, unasked, interjected himself as a referee in their dispute. Sarah took no offense at this interposition between herself and her illiterate husband. Such involvement was accepted and even encouraged by working-class couples. Forced to dictate letters to his wife Sarah, George used many scribes who performed invisibly, but one man intruded during Deal's dictation. Acting in many ways like a marriage counselor, Henry J. Souder encouraged, supported, scolded, and advised

168 LOVE AND THE WORKING CLASS

both George and Sarah when they expressed unhappiness with each other. Unlike a modern marriage counselor, however, who is invited to penetrate the invisible barriers of privacy around a couple, Souder saw no barriers between himself and the Deal's marriage. Granted, asking that he take dictation was an invitation to eavesdrop on their conversation, but his transcription service was not an automatic invitation to interject his advice.

Immediately after George once again reassured his wife that he would "cum home just as soon as i can," the scribe pounced on Sarah. "H. J. Souder will write a little ad vise to you and that is, I dont think it is ad visible for you to rite disscorageing letters to him for if a solger gites disscorage it is ten chance to one if he ever gites over it." Insouciantly confident in his mediating role, Souder issued a stern directive: "Now dont rite to him for to desert nor to run off or to cum home any sooner then i can." By nagging and criticizing her husband, Sarah had violated her wifely duty to cheer and support him. Souder let her know it. Then he suddenly shifted the narrative voice back to George. "I will cum home just as soon as i can that is shure," the husband spoke reassuringly, and then gently warned, "but i hope i can cum home on a ferlow in the fall but it is doubtful if we or i git to cum home then." Using a small x in place of a period to indicate his contributions, Souder again inserted a comment: "George he is a buly for cocks or ony other man or woman and so am i," he bragged and continued: "so I must quit scribbling to you . . . sutch foolishness." In this context, the slang phrase "bully for cocks" likely meant "ready for anything."[79] The scribe scolded as well as reassured George's wife, empowered by the cultural acceptance of third-party mediation, not only in working-class courtship but in marriage.[80]

Less than two weeks later, Souder again addressed Deal's wife Sarah: "you rote some thing about thanking me for riting for George Deal your husband, he wall always comes to me for a faver be for he goes any other plase, i will rite for George ever chance i can git and do all i can for him when i can."[81] Sarah took no offense at Souder's intervention in their marital communications, and Souder enthusiastically merged the job of scribe and mediator. Responding to Sarah's concern that George had forgotten her because the latest gap between his letters was four weeks, Souder admonished her in a postscript: "George has don the best he could about sending you letters that is shure i have rote good many of his letters and i love to yet as far as i can . . . i will try to answer all of his letters I can."[82]

Some of Souder's interruptions were innocent. After Deal conjured an image of eating "a big pot pie" baked by "old mam" for dinner, Souder

FIGHTING TO STAY TOGETHER 169

(a)

(b)

George Deal, a Union soldier, could not write and thus dictated all his letters to his wife Sarah. One of his scribes, Henry Souder, identified himself in this March 31, 1863, letter and explained that George sometimes helped him cook for their mess. Souder regularly took dictation for George and had no compunction about commenting on the couple's marital tensions.

George Deal Papers, Newberry Library.

170 LOVE AND THE WORKING CLASS

interjected, "iges I will cum witch george and help him to eat his pie fur pot py I am fon of and other thinges to."[83] The gabby scribe was having some fun, but he also exhibited no awareness of any special constraint that might separate a married couple from him or from their larger community.

"I dont know what you ment a seling the mar before you let me no any thing about it," George scolded Sarah in another letter, "but now you have sold her and you diden git what she was worth i wouldnener took Sixty five dolars for her." Sarah sold the mare for thirty-five dollars. Souder immediately intruded, "but i H.J. Souder thinks if you needed the money it was all rite and i don't blame you for it."[84] Sarah had assumed her husband's commercial role by selling the horse without asking him, but in spite of George's displeasure, Souder saw her role violation as an emergency measure that was wholly justified.

Being unable to write created extra vulnerability when the illiterate person was outside his face-to-face community. It is possible that George was not privy to the contents of Souder's written commentary, especially when the scribe supported Sarah. But because Souder respected no separation between himself and the Deals, he may have felt comfortable expressing his opinion directly to George.[85] The scribe had adopted membership in their tribe by virtue of his transcription service. That membership, Souder assumed without compunction, opened up the role of intermediary and marital counselor. No ethic of privacy seemed to hinder Souder or bother the Deals. Married couples encouraged and supported this characteristic boundary fluidity between themselves and their community.

Loyalty, constancy, and reliability—the qualities of an unchangeable relationship—were highly valued in working-class culture. Yet loss and change often contradicted these aspirations of permanency. There were manifold sources of disruption, including death, illness, war, personal conflict, and economic failure. It is understandable, then, that kindness, help in sickness, and economic constancy were seen as prime descriptors of a good marriage. Husbands as well as wives were oriented to household and community attachments. "Regardless of their work or political roles, or the number of hours spent away from the home," one historian of workingmen concluded, "household and neighborhood relationships defined their principal obligations."[86]

In troubled marriages, the community often got involved. This involvement was sometimes welcomed, sometimes resisted, and serious strains could result. Difficulties in nonromantic marriage commonly originated from one spouse's failure to satisfy traditional role obligations. The working-class husband or wife believed that love had been withdrawn by such a deficiency. Mates communicated love by meeting their compulsory duties within marriage. The failure of one spouse to perform his or her customary tasks was as much an emotional as a behavioral lapse. In responding to their marital discord, couples might turn to their tribe for material assistance but also for advice, peer counseling, and mediation. They might also call down group censure on their errant partners.

In nonromantic marriages, care and concern could be actively demonstrated by pragmatic, concrete behaviors. Working-class spouses often communicated their affection when they verbalized their desire to be of service to their partner, for example, cooking their favorite meal or getting the vegetable garden ready for planting. During the Civil War, wives would send "care packages" and the husband money home. Performing the duty-bound roles of husband and wife adequately conveyed nonromantic love to a majority of couples. In a mirror image of these positive behaviors, failure to fulfill their spousal obligations conveyed the absence of love. To address this gap, often the source of marital conflict, working-class couples looked to their partners for changes in behavior that met their relationships' practical needs. Thus they had a path, if they were willing and able, to reconcile and live together in peace.

7

Roses Are Red / Violets Are Blue

Emotional History in Rhyme

Poetry was ubiquitous in nineteenth-century America. Poems were scattered through newspapers and magazines. Students recited verses they had been asked to memorize. Children sang or spoke rhymes that structured their play. Americans of all ages could recall poems learned in nursery, in school, and on the playground. Poetry was popular in almost every social class, region, and ethnic and racial community.[1]

The poetic impulse of working-class people should come as no surprise. Poor, unschooled Americans regularly included poems in their letters. They favored short rhymes that followed the familiar meter of "Roses are red / violets are blue." These rhymes circulated by word of mouth and did not require any education to learn or to modify.[2] Participants in this oral tradition had no concern for an author and did not receive a stable text attributed to an individual poet. They repeated vernacular rhymes that were essentially "owned" by the group. This anonymity encouraged creative alterations and many variations of the same rhyme.[3]

The literary repertoire of working-class folks also included the lyrics of popular songs and ballads. These were commonly published on small sheets, one six-by-eight-inch page per song, which had words but no music. (Sheet music had both.) They were cheap, and their popularity soared in the early nineteenth century.[4] It is just as likely, however, that poor folk learned popular songs not from print sources, but from hearing the music performed.

Oral transmission demands the ability to remember words without recourse to a written text—and thus promotes repetition, rhyming, and rhythmic patterning. Research in cognitive psychology and neuroscience has substantiated that rhymes and rhythmic patterning promote recall.[5] Sound patterns cue memory and auditory rhythms focus attention and thus improve the ability to remember. Repetition lessens the "memory load" of both the reciter and the receiver.[6] The short rhymes favored by a number of working-class correspondents reflected the limits and rewards of a culture of memory.

Love and the Working Class. Karen Lystra, Oxford University Press. © Oxford University Press 2024.
DOI: 10.1093/oso/9780197514221.003.0008

ROSES ARE RED / VIOLETS ARE BLUE   173

The working class was partial to anonymous folk poems that were orally transmitted and absorbed by them, sometimes from an early age. Rhymes in an *abab* or *aabb* pattern were common, as was the singsong meter of short word groups accented on the second or third syllable. Exact consonance was not required, and any similarity of sound was permitted to stand for the rhyme. But long (meaning more than one stanza) poems with literary vocabulary ("wonted current" or "deeply wrought"—drawn from an original middle-class love poem) and a more complex meter line were rare in working-class communication.[7] It was short rhymes, usually in iambs (two syllables, with the accent on the second) cast in the "my love to you / no tongue can tell" mold, that appealed to poor, undereducated correspondents.

What is most striking about nineteenth-century Americans who operated outside the conventions of middle-class romantic love is their use of rhymed couplets to convey their feelings of attachment.[8] They most often trusted these anonymous folk poems to structure their communication of love. Easy to dismiss and difficult to plumb, short vernacular poems are sometimes called "doggerel" today. Often characterized as trivial, awkward, and even laughable, such a belittling attitude misses the genuine effort to convey feeling that such poetry embodies. Their value does not derive from some literary abstraction but rather from how effectively they communicated the intended meaning of the people who used them.[9]

However humble, vernacular poetry is part of the project that includes all literature, which one scholar has eloquently summarized as the affirmation that "we are not alone: though we may be 'poor, bare, forked animals,' we can try and hope to get in touch. And this," as that insightful critic observed, "though it may not at first glance seem to have much to tell the student of society, has a significance for him which he would neglect to his enormous cost."[10] Indeed this need to communicate is the impetus behind the sometimes awkward, sometimes tortuous, sometimes fiercely arduous work of a barely literate person who sits down to write a letter.

Poetry was given a special status and used in a variety of ways in working-class letters. Sarah Deal asked her illiterate soldier husband to carry some of her verses on his right side, no doubt as a talisman of her affection and a good luck charm in battle. He responded that it would work just as well "if I carry it between my leges, or on my left side or any other side."[11] He met her request with scorn, even as she evoked the magical power of verse. Though it was not commonly regarded as a good luck charm, poetry was regularly employed as a conduit for emotional expression during courtship and marriage.

George Deal, like many common soldiers, posed with his bayonet to enhance his military image. He was a private in the Twentieth Regiment, Ohio Infantry, enlisting in October 1862. He never made it home, dying near Atlanta in July 1864.
George Deal Papers, Newberry Library.

Widely circulated vernacular rhymes were exchanged in letters as genuine affirmations of affection and appeals for connection. These rhymes provided a common language of feeling. Correspondents drew upon this language, specially marked by rhythmic beats and rhymes, to communicate love, affection, longing, and connection in a predictable, yet distinctive manner. Having learned short rhymes from speech and song lyrics from musical

Sarah Deal may have sent this picture to her husband George while he was serving in the Union army. Sarah had a Native American grandparent according to her family's oral history.

George Deal Papers, Newberry Library.

176 LOVE AND THE WORKING CLASS

performance, undereducated Americans forced to communicate across spatial divides translated their oral culture into writing. Letters attest to the role that poetry played in their intimate lives.

The widow Peebles, a poor southern white woman, recounted two well-known rhymes when she wrote to Daniel Turner, a man whom she hoped to marry. The first was *not* the most popular poem in working-class letters, though most Americans (then and now) could easily recite it: "the rose is red the vilent is blue shugar is swete but not like you," she crooned. By slightly modifying the line following "shugar is swete"—from "and so are you" to "but not like you"—she was adopting a Black variant of the poem.[12] Making that small change, she joined African Americans in accentuating the exceptional appeal of their intended receiver. This couplet underlined her special feelings for Turner.

Her second rhyme was even more favored by working-class correspondents. "When this you sea remember / me tho fare a pre webe [far apart we be]" was how the widow closed her letter. Variants of this poem were also found in African American letters. Peebles hoped that she had some worth in Daniel's eyes and that her letter would remind him of her value. But she was actually a much more ardent admirer of the young soldier than either popular poem disclosed.[13]

Peebles was extremely poor and recently widowed. But her physical and emotional attraction to Daniel reached beyond the role requirements of a spouse. The language of poetry helped her express her erotic fantasy. After confessing obsessive thoughts of Turner, she launched into another rhyme: "the world is wide the sea is deape in your arms I long to sleape."[14] This couplet communicated her desire for sexual intimacy. Vernacular poems that conveyed sexual desire were a conduit of individual longing but also possessed the paradoxical quality of anonymity. There may have been some reassurance, perhaps even protection against group ridicule, if not self-consciously acknowledged, in using rhyming verse that was part of public memory.

Conveying their amorous feelings, African Americans also recited this rhyme, but they recalled another couplet that they sometimes added after "in your arms I long to sleep": "not fer one time, not fer three; / But long as we-uns can agree." Thomas Talley, a Fisk University professor and folklorist, collected this poem in the early twentieth century along with many others, including the "Roses are red" variant. A son of former slaves, he believed that a majority of what he called "Negro folk rhymes" were circulating in nineteenth-century Black communities as far back as "the dark days of American slavery." According to Talley, the two couplets amounted to an "antebellum marriage proposal." Though she did not use the additional rhyme, Peebles hoped for a long-term relationship.[15] Black informants, and their white counterparts in the South, knew and trusted similar folk rhymes about love.

Simeon Tierce, a young African American man, lived in the Hills community of Westchester County, New York, with his wife, Sarah Jane. A Civil War soldier who became a sergeant in the Fourteenth Regiment, Rhode Island Heavy Artillery (Colored), Tierce sent home a fuselage of vernacular rhymes, bunching six poems at the end of one letter to his wife.[16] He began his poetic medley with a verse that was well loved and oft used: "The rose is read, the violets blue / Sugar is sweet and so are you."[17] This message of affection was down-to-earth, direct, and reassuringly familiar to both Black and white Americans.

But then he added five more couplets, demonstrating that he was not satisfied—emotionally, aesthetically, or both—with this solo rhyme. Two other poems, more ephemeral rhymes that may have circulated only during the Civil War, affirmed the strength and durability of his love: "And if in war by battle slain / my love for you shall never frain." This verse suited the specific situation of the soldier who wanted to express endless love for his spouse, even in the afterlife. The prospect of dying in battle also animates the next poem. "As blood and water will not blend / my heart is true unto the end."[18] He again affirmed, without reservation, his faithfulness, loyalty, and commitment to his wife.

But Tierce did not have as much faith in his wife's fidelity as his own, declaring in the next well-known couplet, "if you loved me as I love you / no knife would cut our love into."[19] He chose to use only the short version of the "knife" couplet, the common form in white (and perhaps northern Black) working-class practice.[20] Unfortunately there is no way to know whether he was familiar with the longer call-and-response poem that Thomas Talley collected from Black informants in the South. The male suitor in the more elaborate African American version of the courtship poem was willing to surmount greater obstacles than his female counterpart. She feels the need for parental approval before marriage and he replies: "Rabbit hop an' long dog trot! / Let's git married if dey say 'not.'" Though Tierce is married and not an eager suitor, the point he makes is still strikingly similar. He insisted that his love could resist all tests while questioning the strength of his wife's devotion to him. Was Simeon's misgiving tied to the fact that he was Sarah Jane's second husband? Was he afraid she would hear rumors or discover some problematic conduct? Perhaps he had some bottled-up anxiety about his relationships within the African American community of Westchester County.

In another rhyme, he directly expressed suspicion of female motives and actions in general: "Since woman to man is so unjust / it is only you that I can trust."[21] Here he exempts his wife in the second line from the blanket condemnation of women in the first. Months after he sent this poem to his wife, a local midwife told her that a woman in labor had called out Simeon as the father.[22] Traditionally, such testimony was given great respect, though Tierce seems unconcerned. Affirming Sarah Jane's faithfulness and loyalty, however, might have been a preemptive strike. At the same time, he seems sincere in delivering an intimate message, something akin to "Trust me—no matter what you hear," to his wife through the poems he selected.

Tierce illustrates the overlap as well as distinctiveness of Black and white working-class culture, which included regional and event-specific variations. He displays a northern example of the intersection of Black and white culture. He also demonstrates that the poetry he sent his wife may have felt safer than a prose account of his emotions.

A single white Kentuckian, interested in a woman but unable or, what is more likely, unwilling to court her directly, also indicates that poetry was safer than a prose declaration of emotion. His cousin Jaspar, acting as an intermediary, had already warned him that a number of boys in his tribe were after her. "I am sorrow to hear of so many boy's after my darling M J though I cannot help my self," James wrote. "I wish I could rite something inticing you to tell her, I have not the time at the present, I will rite a verce for her."

> Believe me this I do protest, believe me what I say;
> You are the girl I do love best, untill my dying day.[23]

James sent a vernacular love poem meant for his "darling M J" in a letter to his cousin Jaspar. He expected Jaspar to communicate the rhyme verbally; his instruction was "to tell her." Obviously he was happy to be the ventriloquist putting words in the mouth of his cousin. As expected, he did not feel the need for privacy.

Though cousin Jaspar was his go-between, the poem itself also functioned as an intermediary in James's relationship with MJ. He was happy to have

Jaspar recite the poem to the girl because the rhymed couplet was given a singular status as a conduit of love. The poem's stylized structure marked it off from everyday expression at the same time that it had a public provenance. Thus the rhyme carried feeling from James to his girlfriend in a protected format that was safely personal and communal. James never married MJ, settling in his birthplace, Wayne County, Kentucky, with Elizabeth Hicks.[24]

One woman, who called herself "your affectionate friend," followed in the footsteps of many plain-spoken nineteenth-century correspondents, stating simply that she was thinking of love and marriage with Mr. Bleckley.[25] She elaborated her declaration of love with three vernacular rhymes, plainly indicating that using such poems was the conventional way to signal strong feelings of attachment. "As sure as the vine gows round the stump you are my darling sugar lump" combined a reliable natural occurrence representing steadfast commitment with an image of Mr. Bleckley's appeal.[26] The vine rhyme was part of the folklore of Black and white Americans. It was recited by African Americans along with another couplet: "W'en de sun don't shine de day is cold, / But my love fer you do not git old."[27]

Affectionate friend's second poem—"thar is plenty of boys that is true but thare is none that soots my eye like you"—was an affirmation of Mr. Bleckley's strong physical appeal. But after the letter writer's first two poetic confessions, she revealed another emotional layer that suggested a greater sense of risk and possibility of failure than appears at first glance. "[I]t is sweet to love but ohow biter it is to love aboy and then not get him." Burying several layers of expectations, feelings, and fears in this irregular rhyme, she most likely morphed hers from a version closer to "Love is sweet but oh how bitter / To love a boy and then can't get him."

"Your affectionate friend" demonstrated courage in communicating her feelings directly to Mr. Bleckley, closing with the plainspoken, "meeting gives me pleasure parting gives me pain." Was he responsive or not? The record is silent.[28] Working-class men and women often favored the safer choice of speaking through an intermediary, precisely because of the risk of being personally rejected. But if they did choose to communicate directly, they seem to prefer rhymed verse for a similar reason. It was safer to express feeling through conventionally structured channels than to articulate raw emotions in uniquely personal ways.

William Amos, a young Hoosier staying with North Carolina relatives in the late spring of 1869, boldly began a letter to Miss Nancy Doolittle: "Mad am I take my pen in hand to in form you that I have been in love with you for

180 LOVE AND THE WORKING CLASS

along time and never had the cour rage to tell you sow I have nothing left but my pen."[29] What he meant was demonstrated by the rest of his letter, which was composed of a series of poems with no breaks, no punctuation, and no transitions of any kind. Poetry made up the entirety, with one short interruption, until the closing line. For Amos, and indeed most of his working-class contemporaries, the best way to express love was in rhymes.[30] His unusual letter (whether a copy or a draft) takes the value of love verse to the furthest extreme.[31]

After candidly expressing his unspoken love for Nancy, Amos determinedly followed the cheerful first stanza of a printed poem he had memorized with a long chain of vernacular love poems.[32] Three of these rhymes drew their dominant theme from nature.[33]

> *The flowers were made to bloom dear / the stars were made to shine / the girls were made for boys dear / and maybe you were made for mine
> *The oak is tall the vine is green / the time is past that we have seen / I hope the time will shortly come / that I and you may Join as one
> *If I was an Apple and Miss N was another / what a pretty pair we would make upon a twig together.[34]

Only the first rhyme had a discernible provenance. It was a snippet from "Molly Bawn," a song written by the Irish painter, author, lyricist, and composer Samuel Lover. The lyric appeared in his 1839 *Songs and Ballads,* which had multiple editions stretching to 1902.[35] Amos's spelling errors indicate he wrote the extract from memory. Along with the second rhyme, the first suggested that mating was part of a determinate order in nature, a developmental sequence that had a natural progression. But doubt entered the poet's mind at two points: "*maybe* you were made for mine" in the first poem and "I *hope* the time will shortly come" in the second. The adverb "maybe" was especially effective at suggesting self-doubt because it so awkwardly broke the forward momentum of the poem's rhyme.

The natural satisfaction of coupling was invoked in the third poem, a pleasant rural image of two apples hanging side by side. This rhyme, with additional stanzas, was also appreciated in the African American community.[36] Amos favored the poem, sending it to both Nancy and another young woman, MB, who had spurned his earlier overtures. Selecting the same rhyme to express duplicate feelings to different women is instructive. William was apparently ready to love either MB or Nancy. So the apple poem with its image of bucolic coupling could honestly be sent to both women. Amos was not in romantic love with either woman when he chose this poem. He was willing to love the one who wanted to love him.

Vernacular love poems can often appear interchangeable, even if the content is distinctive. The common rhyme and meter patterns convey a universal relevance. Identical poetic meter and rhyme scheme can dominate the words, and even different content can end up sounding alike. In this sense, vernacular rhymes are perfect conveyors of nonromantic love, which by its nature did not demand a highly differentiated voice.

One young Virginia woman, writing in 1867, carried the fungibility of love across gender boundaries. She linked her boyfriend, Sem, and her twenty-one-year-old girlfriend in a popular vernacular poem about love. "[R]ound is the ring that has no end so is my love to you and Sem." She treated them interchangeably in this poem and made no distinction in the love she gave to each.[37] Amos, as expected, did not cross the gender divide, sending the same love poem to two women.

Showing a marked preference for the iambic couplet, working-class Americans used these short, rhymed lines to signal a special attachment. Amos included the favorite poem of plain folk in his poetic sampler: "when this you see / Remember mee / tho meny long miles apart we bee."[38] This poem's brief, repetitious, and singsong meter had deep appeal to the working-class correspondent. The structure of sound no less than the content appealed to their sensibility and communicated something meaningful.

A young white southern woman, Mollie D. Gaither, sent her soldier friend the common poetic tribute: "When this you se remember / me though many miles apart / we be." She followed this rhyme with another variation on the same theme: "I cant forJet one look of / thine though many miles / apart we be as long as life shal / last and memory reign I will / remember the."[39] Memory defined caring in the working-class world of intimacy. The common feeling of anxiety over being forgotten when living outside the face-to-face community predominated in this popular poem.

After becoming engaged to Burgess, Mollie D. used the poem in a slightly different way: "when this you se remember Mollie D. and think that she remember you."[40] By naming herself, she gave the poem a more individual focus. She even dropped the last rhyming couplet in favor of a personal affirmation in prose: "and think that she remember you." Her courtship blended romantic and nonromantic elements, and her treatment of the poem reflected that mix.

182 LOVE AND THE WORKING CLASS

Other working-class correspondents chose to abandon meter and rhyme in favor of plain-spoken prose with a similar theme. "Have you forgoten me," W. M. C. wrote to Maggie, "if not—remember."[41] With few words and a direct command, W. M. C. had apparently satisfied his need to get in touch. Edward Francis, a Black Kentuckian, was equally direct: "Dear Lizy, I hope you will remember me."[42] He reiterates the same message, with more emphasis, the next year. "I want you to remember me."[43] By contrast, a rhymed couplet could seem "fancy" or even ornamental. Vernacular poetry was a form of elevated speech in working-class letters, moving well beyond the basic requirements of comprehensible prose. One person's doggerel is another's literature.

Remembrance embodied many working-class emotional aspirations. Leonard Caplinger, a poor farmer fighting for the Union, wrote tenderly to his wife after many months of separation: "i hope that it Wonte be long tell i Can take holde of your softe hand." His physical expression is closely followed by verse: "When this you see / remember me tho / many a miles / aparte we beas." The context of physical longing indicates that Leonard meant to express intense feeling in this vernacular rhyme.[44]

Remembering was an act that defined their mutual desire to be together. Thus Mary Caplinger also included the well-loved rhyme in her letters. In late April 1863 she followed the "remember me" poem with the more puzzling "the rose is red the stem is green the day is pas that we hav seen."[45] Perhaps Mary meant that they were not together now, or perhaps the rhyme is a literal invocation of the end of the day. But it is a poem that dwelled on endings and was somewhat pessimistic in tone if not intent.

By the spring of 1863, Leonard's declarations of affection had become increasingly bold and creative. "When this you see my [drawing of a sideways heart] allwars Will be til death shal parte the."[46] Closing another letter with the familiar poetic admonition to remember, he unexpectedly became more open and forthright:

> When this you see remember
> me tho many amile aparte
> We be my love nite
> and day is of you and
> my sweete babs and i
> Hope wont be long
> Tell you all I can see[47]

Leonard Caplinger never used the word "love" outside this poem. Evidently the poetic line demarcated some distinctive emotional freedom that gave him permission to proclaim his love for his wife (and children), which "nite and day is of you." He was even inspired to add a rhyme of his own to close the poem: "Hope wont be long / tell you all I can see."

As their separation lengthened, the couple's feelings of attachment to each other intensified. Both Mary and Leonard exhibited a deeper awareness of their inner lives. Each of them found a need to modify the "remember me" poem by adding other rhymes. Several months after Leonard's poetic innovation, Mary broke through her emotional reticence. After she penned the familiar "remember me" rhyme, she added "where ever I / go What ever / I do nobody / else can love / you as I do."[48] Mary celebrated the lone individual who loved another without ambiguity. In penning this second rhyme, she singled him out as her romantic partner. For the very first time she named her feelings "love." But like Leonard, she expressed this romantic love only within the boundaries of a poem.

Tellingly, both Leonard and Mary had to modify the "remember me" poem to meet their growing and deepening emotional exclusivity. For this couple, the most oft-quoted coda of affection was a springboard to which they added another rhyme more expressive of their romantic attachment. Mary also embodied her special emotional connection to Leonard in a material form by sending some of her hair, which she wanted him to wear around his wrist: "think of me when ever you look at it," she instructed. "I braided it myself."[49] To be remembered at a distance was considered a convincing affirmation of individual value.

Peter Van Wagenen, a young African American man, shipped off on a whaler after getting in numerous scrapes with the law for his hijinks and carousing in New York City. Far away from home, he directed his mother: "Notice—when this you see, remember me, and place me in your mind."[50] Writing in the early 1840s, Peter made explicit one of the purposes of the most common vernacular rhyme by ending the poem with a nonrhyming command: "place me your mind." There was a pervasive anxiety in working-class culture of being forgotten. Geographical or physical separation triggered the fear of "out of sight, out of mind."

Like Wagenen, other correspondents sent this rhyme to their extended family and creatively modified the verse according to their own needs. If memory was the storehouse and speech spread the poems, then this rhyme had a remarkable staying power, though the constant drift from oral to written form and back again produced countless alterations. Confederate soldier Alfred N. Proffitt, working as a cook in a Lynchburg, Virginia, hospital, closed a letter to his sister with "When this you see think of me for in Lynchburg I bee A.N. P."[51] He cleverly incorporated his location and the initials of his name into the common rhyme, giving it a personal touch. "Remember me while part we be" closed a Black Pennsylvania soldier's letter to his sister during the Civil War.[52] He excised the first and third couplet without changing the import of the poem, making it his own through verbal parsimony. Ten years after the conclusion of the Civil War, thirteen-year-old Mary Dewalt was helping her illiterate mother take care of sixteen boarders as well as do laundry for a local Indiana hotel. She was still using a version of this rhyme.[53]

"When this you see / Remember me / Tho many a mile / a part we be" was repeated endlessly because it was aesthetically satisfying.[54] But it was also a substantive statement of fear, hope, and longing. These words held exceptional meaning for working-class Americans. Urging memory and connection in the face of physical separation, the poem signaled a fear of forgetfulness when tribal intimacy was broken. Most of all, it was a plea for love, highlighted or given emphasis because of its rhyme and meter. The words encoded a yearning for personal attachment that was oriented to courtship and marriage but could also involve specific family members as well as the larger community.

Members of the working class favored the short vernacular rhyme, but they also showed a strong preference for popular songs and ballads. At times, the line between poems and songs was almost indistinguishable, especially during the Civil War when poems were often set to music.[55] Song lyrics and vernacular rhymes would frequently appear in the same letter, but the lyrics seemed to answer a broader spectrum of expressive needs. Most of the longer poems in working-class letters were drawn from song and ballad lyrics that had likely been memorized. Often the correspondent creatively combined fragmentary lyrics of several stanzas from one or more songs.

William Amos remembered the lyrics to a song called "The Rose Will cease to Blow," which appeared in more than a dozen nineteenth-century English and American songbooks. One American collection claimed it had sold upwards of thirty thousand copies between 1835 and 1839, doubtless an exaggeration that was good for selling books.[56] The lyric was popular, however, and appealed to Amos and others by invoking the natural order to underline a lover's constancy and steadfast love: "the rose will cease to blow /

the eagle turn a dove / the stream will cease to flow / ere I will cease to love / the sun will cease to shine / the world will cease to move / the stars their light resign / ere I will cease to love."[57] The wide appeal of this lyric may be due to its versatility: it could be used to convey both romantic and nonromantic love. People yearned for stability and permanence within both approaches to love.

Like Amos, Mollie D. Gaither used vernacular rhymes and song lyrics to communicate her feelings. She sent Burgess, her fiancé, the lyrics to a popular ballad, "Absence," in her June 1864 letter. This was her one extended and frank articulation of love. "Days of absence sad and dreary,, / clothed in sorow dark array,, / Days of absence I am weary,, / when my love is far away," she crooned unexpectedly. The song continued by asking plaintively when the pain of absence would end. The answer was supposedly upbeat but echoed with the uncertainty of the soldier who might never return from battle.

> Not till that loved voice can greet me
> Which so oft has cheered my ear
> Not till those sweet eyes can meet me
> Telling that I still am dear
> Days of absence then shall vanish/
> Joy shall all my pains repay
> From my idol bosom banish
> Gloom but felt when he away.[58]

What was most striking about Molly's recitation of the lyrics from "Absence" was their sharp contrast with the unsentimental and restrained emotion of her own writing. The ballad verse that she posted was more sentimental and romantic than any feeling she ever conveyed in her own words. Seemingly suspicious of romantic feeling, she mocked the older suitor who was courting her fiancé's sister. "He would not eat any thing but milk and homley he was so taking on that he could not eat." She also mocked the sister's reaction: "The funny part of it he talked so mutch loving talk that it made Mollie [the sister] cry she went of to the woods and took a good cry it must have bin very loveing if it would make her cry."[59] Writing to her fiancé, she scoffed at the emotional drama of other courtships.

Mollie D. Gaither cautiously maintained many nonromantic elements in her own courtship. But the song lyrics she sent Burgess appear to be safe emotional territory. They channeled her sentiment and also protected her from

186   LOVE AND THE WORKING CLASS

too much emotional exposure. The poetry of songs and ballads functioned as an organized, shared, and transferable structure of feeling for anyone who found their own multifaceted emotions difficult or risky to express.

Young southerner John Fuller ran away from his Alabama home to join the Confederate army. (He was the wayward son of Solon and Elizabeth Fuller whose behavior caused considerable parental frustration and spousal conflict.) Writing to Miss Frances, a woman he had singled out from the tribe, he twice reassured her in straightforward prose that he remembered her. Like Mollie D. Gaither, he also included both vernacular rhymes and song lyrics in his letter. Asking that Miss Frances "remember me" in the popular poem, he also penned a variant of "the ring is round that has no end / so is my love to you my friend." This was the second most popular poem in letters exchanged between working-class couples. A gold ring became a simple but effective metaphor for the constancy and purity of love.[60]

Fuller turned to song lyrics, however, when he wanted to describe how his own feelings intersected with the emotions he supposed Miss Frances would experience if he died. He used modified snippets from two popular Civil War ballads: "The Rebel Soldier" and "The Southern Soldier Boy," plus a common phrase that appeared in several forms, including the New Testament.[61] His creation is an example of bricolage, a piece composed of bits and pieces from a variety of sources, all perhaps heard rather than read.

John's poem opens with an implied lament for the soldier who is far from home, stressing his geographical separation from the tribe. "i am A solgr so fier from mi hom." This line comes from "The Rebel Soldier." Being away from home was his first misfortune, followed immediately by recognition of an even greater calamity: his death on the battlefield. "A weep not for me if in som Batl field i shood fall." This is a stoic appeal that signals manly strength and courage. But the command to "weep not" is paradoxical because it is based on the expectation that Miss Frances would in fact be overcome with grief if he was killed. What "redeems" his death is both her tears and his belief that he is fighting for a glorious, in other words, a righteous cause. "i wod dy in this gloires caus o weep not for me if i shood fall in this gloires caus."[62] These are lines drawn from the third stanza of "The Southern Soldier Boy."

John skipped the first stanza, perhaps because the lyrics were written from the perspective of a woman. If her soldier sweetheart dies, the woman in the song affirmed her continuing attachment. "He still would be my joy, / For many a sweetheart mourns the loss / Of a Southern Soldier Boy."[63] If Fuller had any doubts, the first stanza instructed him to believe that Miss Frances would weep freely and mourn his loss.

Fuller ended his poetic bricolage with the forthright demand, "O remembr me." Though the phrase did not fit the poem's unpolished meter, it was the letter writer's last and perhaps most significant wish.[64] In this case, the imperative command to remember was also about memory beyond the soldier's death. Fuller betrayed an understandable nervousness about dying in an upcoming battle. But that nervousness seems to extend to the poetics of meter and rhyme. His abrupt prose command to remember at the end of his letter indicates an unwillingness to trust the versification he used earlier to convey his meaning. In most instances, however, the rhymed couplet served as an emotionally and aesthetically satisfying expression for its users.

John's father, Solon Fuller, who earlier enlisted as a substitute, also combined song lyrics and vernacular rhymes in letters to his wife. One poem expressed an open yearning for home: *"O that I was where I would be then I would be where I am not / here I am where I must be for where I would be I cannot."[65] This is a classic vernacular creation. But his next lines were inspired by an old Scottish ballad called "The Galley Slave." The opening lines of the first stanza were originally sung like this: "Oh, think on my fate! Once I freedom enjoy'd, / was as happy as happy could be, /But pleasure is fled! Even hope is destroy'd, / A captive alas! on the sea."[66] Though he modified the original to fit his military role on land, John's father used the poem to insist he was as much a captive in the military as the galley slave.

The next poem began as a published verse that became the lyrics of a popular ballad.[67] The central image was also a captive, an Indian youth who demanded (and then pleaded in subsequent stanzas) for freedom to be with his people in the natural environment that he claimed as his birthright. Peter Van Wagenen, a young African American man, was on a whaling vessel far from home when he included a version of this poem (as well as the variant on "remember me") in a letter to his mother, Sojourner Truth.[68] He was undoubtedly drawn to the poem's explicit racial lament and defiant racial censure. He made the lyrics his own, however, by synthesizing a creative variant of the original first stanza.

> Get me to my home, that's in the far-distant west,
> To the scenes of my childhood, that I like the best;
> There the tall cedars grow, and the bright waters flow,
> Where my parents will greet me, white man, let me go![69]

188 LOVE AND THE WORKING CLASS

The son of Sojourner Truth embraced this poem in the early 1840s when slavery was legal and the phrase "white man, let me go!" was an open challenge to the racial subjugation of African Americans. Perhaps his most interesting alteration occurred in the first line, where he substituted "Get me to my home" for "Let me go to my home." His assertive opening is much more congruent with the poem's insistent demand for freedom.

Van Wagenen and the Fullers—father and son—illustrate how working-class Americans adapted musical lyrics—both traditional ballads and popular songs. These lyrics were often encountered aurally through musical performance, thus giving wide access to people who may have had little time or inclination or even skill to read a text. Song lyrics also had a second advantage. They were frequently repeated, which facilitated memorization. Lyrics most often followed some common rhyming scheme that also made them easier to remember. Song lyrics were an important help in expressing complicated feelings about love, death, and in certain situations, oppression and confinement.

Occasionally working-class correspondents composed an original verse. George Deal, the illiterate Union soldier from Ohio, recognized that he was obligated to express special feelings for his wife Sarah through poetry. But he wrongly assumed he had to create an original poem. "[Y]ou wrote some verses," he acknowledged, immediately followed by a negative self-appraisal: "I haint good to makin verses." Then, as if he wanted to get it over with as quickly as possible, he gamely launched his attempt: "i think the dove will cum to the nest and to your armes for i no i want to be witch you as much as you do witch me."[70] Calling on his observations of nature or some remembered snippet of verse, he represented himself as the dove who returned to his symbolic nest because he wanted to be with his mate. His brief poem, however charming and tender-hearted, was missing the overriding requirement of nineteenth-century poetry: rhyme. This was why he judged that he "haint good to makin verses."

Though Deal's short poem was unrhymed, another Union soldier, a hired hand before the war, wrote a whole letter in rhymed verse to his brother Calvin, who was thinking of learning the cooper's trade. Delos Lake's original creation was unusual for its length and originality. One portion was a tribute to a "person of interest."

> there is another both young bright and fair
> while my thoughts they will rome she comes in for a share

the sweet hours we have spent seem now like a dream
in contrast with the present so hollowed they seem
I wonder if ever she thinks of the one
Who is now standing picket alone with his gun[71]

Six months after penning his poetic tribute, Delos was purposely checking out the girls in a cotton factory in Tennessee, where he was stationed.[72] "I don't know but that I will have to look arround for another girl," he told his brother, "for the one in Ill[inois] has gone south to learn the milenars trade and may be has gone over into the Confeneracy. any how I don't hear from her any more. I guess she is too soon a bird for me."[73]

"Bird" had several meanings in nineteenth-century slang, but in this case it carried the sense of a "person or thing of excellence."[74] To be "too soon" a bird for him likely meant that she and he paired off too quickly. The Illinois girlfriend moved south and, as Delos recognized, had likely reconstituted her tribal loyalties. He acknowledged that he should have maintained his relationship with the eligible girls (plural) of his tribe and waited to isolate a singular "girl."

B. W. Ellison was also fighting in the Civil War, but on the losing side. The bird was not too soon for him. After Appomatox, he married the girl he corresponded with during the war. A man of few words, he told her simply: "Nanie I would rather see you than any one else in the world. I could tell you more in an houre than I could write in a week." His letter was short and he wrote mostly about his lack of stamps, envelopes, paper, and the money to buy them. But he closed with two poetic expressions. The first was a vernacular rhyme in the standard iambic couplet form: "if you love me like I love you there is nothing can tare our love in too." The second was an evocative metaphor drawn from the Old Testament book of Solomon: "Many watters cannot quench love, Neither can the floods drawn it."[75] The line was likely written from memory and not copied from a text as both "waters" and "drown" were misspelled. Both poems affirmed the need to resist the forces that might try to end their relationship.

Poetry is not just for lovers. In working-class culture it was used to communicate affection for a variety of family members. Lois Richardson had two sons, Luther and Henry, to whom she had a particularly deep attachment because she raised them as a single parent after her husband abandoned her. When her boys joined the Union army, she penned a classic vernacular rhyme in support of the cause and their choice. "Twas hard my son to say

Adiew / And see you march away / But what true womman in the land / Has heart to bid you stay."[76] To fit the occasion, Lois put her patriotic feelings into poetic form.[77]

Her grandson sent her a rhyme in a postscript to his 1864 letter: "like aman without a wife / like aship without a sail / the oddest thing in life / is a shirt without a tail."[78] This imagery must have tickled the ten-year-old's funny

Clarence Stone, grandson of Lois Richardson Davis and son of Eunice Richardson Stone [Connelly], sports a bow tie in this formal studio photograph taken when he was around eleven years old. He included a poem in one of the lively letters he wrote at this age to his grandmother.
Lois Wright Richardson Davis Family Papers, Rubenstein Library, Duke University.

bone. By sending the rhyme to grandma, he put a value on its content as well as its aesthetic. Though the poem promoted marriage and disparaged bachelorhood, the youngster was likely attracted to the anomalous ships and odd-looking shirts. The form of the poem—a classic iambic couplet—appealed to both young and old.

As the poetry in their letters makes clear, the contrast between written and oral culture is often more theoretical than historical.[79] Classical scholars, folklorists, and cultural historians have all demonstrated that the two co-exist and overlap in the past and present.[80] This overlap of oral and written culture was certainly operating in the lives of working-class Americans who straddled both worlds. One woman who worked in a bonnet factory copied seven verses of poetry in her diary and wrote enthusiastically about reading Wordsworth's poems.[81]

Most unschooled Americans, however, favored short, rhymed vernacular verses of the "Roses are red" variety. The psychodynamics of oral culture—including a reliance on formulary expression, repetitive phrases, rhythmic patterning, and redundancy—plainly influenced their poetic preference for brief, simple rhymes.[82] Nursery rhymes spoken or sung (as in a lullaby) and games that were played in childhood shared sound patterns that established lasting commitment to certain poetic properties. The pioneering folklorist William Newell recorded firsthand observations of games in a variety of nineteenth-century American settings.[83] He collected hundreds of children's rhymes in his travels. Popular game rhymes were usually formed as two couplets or four lines in which the last word in the second and fourth line rhymed.[84] Newell believed most American game rhymes were of English origin, and that the many local variations throughout the country were selected from a common stock of rhymes that were often sung. The same pattern could be found in nursery rhymes.[85] While certain verses expressed their cultural values, working-class writers did not use the content of nursery or game rhymes in their letters.[86] It was the form of the rhymes that attracted them. They shaped working-class aesthetic preferences as adults.

The widespread practice of repetitious rhyming in songs, games, and playful childhood poems, without the mediating influence of middle-class literary education and print culture, deeply influenced working-class taste and poetic imagination. Adults showed a strong preference for the sound patterns of short iambic couplets as demonstrated in countless letters to and from spouses, friends, and family. They used these rhymes to express feelings that they often did not articulate in their own words.

192 LOVE AND THE WORKING CLASS

Though exposed to similar nursery rhymes and games, middle-class Americans with formal education beyond elementary school usually disdained the rhyming patterns that their undereducated peers appreciated into adulthood. One advice book writer, who called himself the Master of Hearts, hoped that it was "almost time for the 'roses red and violets blue to wither." He scorned the use of what he called "vile doggerel" and admonished his readers, "Do thou more than this, or else do nothing."[87]

A North Carolina woman recalled an important literary task that engaged her and other southern ladies during the Civil War. They wrote as well as read love letters for illiterate wives whose husbands were fighting for the Confederacy. She remembered "the little love messages and bits of poetry" such as "Roses red, and violets blue, Pinks are pretty and so are you, and such like" that "would cause a smile many times."[88] The smiles of these middle-class scribes were benign, but they also had a strong whiff of class condescension.

In writing middle-class love letters, privacy was a sacred trust, and original emotional expression, including poetry created by the letter writer, was an important sign of authenticity.[89] However, Victorians maintained an essential distinction: vernacular rhymes were acceptable expressions in the nursery, playground, and adolescent friendship or autograph albums. The latter were blank books often inscribed with short rhyming poems by teachers, friends, and adolescent schoolmates.[90] But brief rhyming couplets were *not* welcome as a demonstration of romantic love in middle-class courtship or marriage.[91]

Working-class people did not share this negative attitude. A sizable majority ended their education in elementary school.[92] As students, they would have used McGuffey's *First* and *Second Eclectic Reader* (or something similar), both first published in 1836.[93] The *First Reader* had no poetry. It relied on word recognition to teach reading and emphasized comprehension and spelling.[94] The *Second Reader* also focused on word recognition, spelling, and reading comprehension. Vocabulary instruction was more ambitious in the *Second Reader* and a few multistanza poems were included in later lessons.[95] Writing instruction was *not* offered in early editions of the *First* or *Second Reader*.[96] Content was conservative, giving special emphasis to honesty.[97] Many correspondents would have ended their formal schooling before they got past the first reader.

American education in most of the nineteenth century was focused on mandatory recitation of texts, both prose and poetry. In all likelihood,

ROSES ARE RED / VIOLETS ARE BLUE   193

vernacular rhymes would have been rejected in elementary school because they were too easy to memorize. Teachers in the lower grades may not have inculcated a hierarchy of literary texts so much as a hierarchy of memorization tasks.[98] Though they were aware of, and shamed by, their educational deficiencies, including their uncertain compositional and writing skills, working-class correspondents never showed any embarrassment about their use of short rhymes to express love and affection.

Vernacular couplets used in letters, especially the "roses" and "vine" rhymes, were frequently found on homespun American valentines in the 1840s and 1850s. The growing popularity of Valentine's Day stimulated the sale of commercial valentines, but it also inspired the use of homemade cards.[99] Dealers sent traveling salesmen out with samples of their product around 1840, at a time when most Americans they encountered had never seen a mass-produced valentine.[100] Increasing commercialization in the 1840s actually encouraged the simultaneous creation of more homemade objects.[101]

Later in the decade, the commercial valentine market was booming, not just in big cities like New York and Philadelphia but in smaller towns and rural areas. In 1853, the publisher T. W. Strong advertised an assortment of 180 valentines that cost between one and twelve cents and over five hundred varieties priced between twenty-five and fifty cents.[102] With his headquarters in New York City, Strong was not shy about sending agents to the hinterland. Cloth cutter and tailor Charles Dudley, a New Englander who did piecework for the local factory in Cheshire, Connecticut, near New Haven, likely purchased the valentine cards he sent to ten young women in 1856.[103] George Deal purchased a handcrafted valentine for his wife seven years later. With a paper doily and little flowers pasted on the cover, it opened to reveal a verse glued to a small sheet of paper:

> The rose its blooming tints discloses
> Let me put my tulips to your roses

The reader soon realizes that this poem, innocuous at first glance, is an invitation to physical intimacy. Flower metaphors had a variety of uses in the working-class imagination.[104]

The commercial production of inexpensive cards soon overwhelmed the folk artifact.[105] Nonetheless, mass-produced valentines did not replace the love rhymes sent in letters.[106] The few poems in the letters of laboring folk that can be traced to their source originated in traditional English valentine

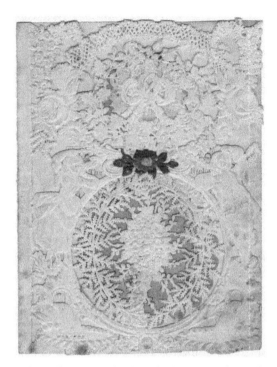

George Deal sent this valentine with a lace doily cover to his wife Sarah in 1863 while he was a Union soldier. Little flowers are pasted in the center cutout. He asked her to save this valentine until he returned home.
George Deal Papers, Newberry Library.

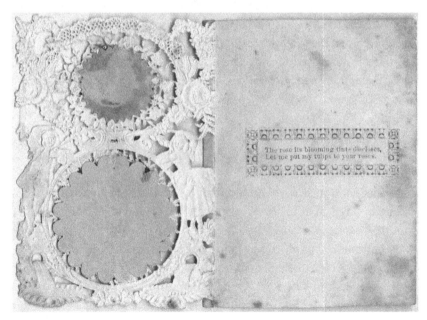

The valentine doily opens to reveal a suggestive verse pasted on a little slip of paper.
George Deal Papers, Newberry Library.

verse. The working class was conservative in its preference for old ballads and in their choice of vernacular rhymes. One vendor claimed that the old songs "sell steadily and pay us best in the end."[107]

Nineteenth-century correspondents drew from an older folk tradition when they used "Round is the ring that has no end / so is my love to you my friend" and "As sure as the vine grows round the stump / you are my darling sugar lump," as well as "Roses are red."[108] Many of their favored rhymes had been circulating for generations. "Roses are red" appeared in a late eighteenth-century nursery rhyme chapbook, but experts affirm it was a valentine rhyme before it was codified for the nursery.[109] More ephemeral rhymes may have had limited regional or ethnic circulation or were spread only within the confines of a certain historical event—the Civil War, for one. Nonetheless some rhymes were not only passed around for hundreds of years, but were shared across racial divides.

African Americans absorbed traditional valentine verse, often adding their own innovations. Thomas Talley noted this addition to "Roses are red": "De vi'lets fade, de roses fall; / But you gits sweeter, all in all." He collected an added verse to "darling sugar lump": "W'en de sun don't shine de day is cold / But my love fer you do not git old."[110] Seven love rhymes circulating in the Black community around 1920 were in active use by white and Black letter writers before 1880. This demonstrates again that working-class Americans with different racial and ethnic backgrounds had a separate as well as a common cultural heritage.

A group of soldiers in the Georgia Eighth Regiment from Floyd County held a Valentine's Day lottery in which each man drew an eligible young woman from their pool.[111] This lottery was a literal act of tribal courtship in that the men agreed to send a valentine, not to a woman of their choice but to anyone they drew from their box.[112] Drawing lots to choose a valentine was widely practiced in Britain during the seventeenth and eighteenth centuries. Part of the fun was that the couple paired by the drawing was supposed to be destined for a future marriage.[113] This folk practice had been preserved for more than 250 years when the Georgia Eighth decided to hold their valentine lottery. What had also survived was the meaning of "valentine," which was formerly a person or relationship, and not the object of exchange itself.[114]

After getting Miss Olivia's name, the fortunate swain began his letter: "Miss O. Espy this is the first of my undertaking efforts to Exspress my entire ignorance to you."[115] After the unintentional humor in his inauspicious opening, the Georgia soldier continued self-effacingly, "but as we are maney miles

196 LOVE AND THE WORKING CLASS

aparte I shall endver to Scrible a shorter message to you by candle ligh however I excspect you have fergotten me I have not fergotten you, Shall we ever meete again I hope so." The anxious suitor had met Miss Olivia in Floyd County, no doubt at her cousins, and she had left an indelible impression.

During the Battle of First Bull Run or Manassas, the first great battle in the Civil War, he was attending to the wounded "crying for help" and at the same time thinking "of one that I Left behind that I so dearley Love."[116] But the Georgia soldier acknowledged that, while he loved her above all others, he "was very delicate in leting you know aney Thing a bout me ever thinking a bout such a sweet subject." In the interactions that constituted tribal courtship, his behavior was not unusual.

As the apprehensive suitor closed his love letter, his spirits sank. "Mis Olevia I would give my Self to you if I could but I doant supose that my harte would be excepted This knight . . . but doant get maired before I can kill a few moor of the yanks for I want to be at the weding your most obediant Servant in the war tell death."[117] His standard letter closing was followed by a love poem:

> No chaing [change] my constant harte can own
> For the it beats and the aloan
> mid joy and grief this truth Ill prove
> Yet ever lasting is my love[118]

Although his prose was gloomy or perhaps more accurately expressed an overwhelming expectation of failure, the clumsy soldier still ended with an earnest poem that conveyed his undying love for Miss Olivia. Poetry was a privileged realm where a correspondent might express emotions without having to be constantly "on guard." Poems were a medium of expression that reduced the working-class fear of being laughed at or criticized for being unperceptive or unrealistic. Within its structure, poetry granted these nineteenth-century men and women some emotional freedom. The poem was a vehicle that externalized unformed or tentative feelings. Especially if the poems were widely known vernacular rhymes, the shared memory was reassuring and safe precisely because it was communal.

The short, rhymed couplets of vernacular poetry were repeated endlessly in working-class letters for a reason. Such poems satisfied or articulated certain deeply held values and beliefs. They were usually employed with utmost sincerity. The sender seemed confident in the rhyme's ability to communicate effectively to the receiver. He or she invested the repetitious phrases and rhythmic patterning of the poems with a significant power to convey feeling and, more surprisingly, to affect behavior. Repetition was also a form of emotional reassurance in the fraught arena of courtship and marriage.

Shorter rhymed couplets belonged to the folk.[119] Their familiarity and easy memorization were part of their authenticity and charm, not the opposite. Sent in letters by hopeful suitors and affectionate spouses, these rhymed couplets were "social actions" initiated by people who were often trying to create, strengthen, expand, and deepen their intimate relationships. In this, they satisfied a basic human need. The rhymes they could all recite by heart were storehouses of feeling that connected them to individuals and to their community.[120]

8

Imagining the Eternal Village

Death, Longing, and Loss

In the nineteenth century, the vernacular rhyme "when this you see / remember me" was an appeal for love from the living, but in the previous century the same rhyme (or a variation) was strongly linked with death. "When I [am] / dead and in my grav /-e and all my bones / are rotten *For / this you sea remem / ber me* That I are / not forgottin" was the verse stitched in the late 1780s onto a decorative sampler.[1] These were fabrics on which young girls practiced needlework by embroidering various designs, letters, and even rhymed verse.[2] Martha Earl, a school-age girl under ten, chose this rhyme to sew on her sampler as a reminder of the constant possibility of death.

By the time Mary Caplinger sent the "remember me" rhyme to her soldier husband in 1863, it had morphed into a plea, not for remembrance after death, but for feelings of attachment in this life.[3] Memory was a pivotal refrain in both sampler and letter, but separation caused by temporary mobility or permanent relocation replaced death in the call to remember. What remained constant over two centuries was the need for reassurance that absence would not result in being forgotten by loved ones. The second most popular rhyme found on American samplers from the seventeenth through the nineteenth centuries became the most popular love poem in working-class letters.[4]

Even so, an association of memory and mortality continued to resonate with many Americans. One young Hoosier, Mollie Dawalt, closed an 1880 letter to Ella Buck, her Pennsylvania cousin, with this rhyme: "Remember me when this you see / And think of one that thinks of thee / And when the grave becomes thy bed / O think of me when I am dead."[5] Neither Mollie Dawalt nor Ella Buck was yet twenty years old and the Civil War had ended when they were toddlers.[6] Mollie married at the exceptionally young age of fourteen and had been a widow for two years when she wrote this poem. Though the link between memory, attachment, and death had been reinforced in her

Love and the Working Class. Karen Lystra, Oxford University Press. © Oxford University Press 2024.
DOI: 10.1093/oso/9780197514221.003.0009

An early nineteenth-century American sampler includes the popular poem "When this you see / remember me," which is stitched in silk on plainly woven linen. It is one of many pieces of embroidery with this vernacular rhyme. Phebe Hart (American), Early nineteenth century, Sampler (8$^{11}/_{16}$ × 9$^{1}/_{16}$ in.), U.S., Museum of Fine Arts, Boston, Accession No. 50.4007.
https://collections.mfa.org/objects/65833/sampler.

at an early age, the connection of love and death was deeply embedded in a broad class-based sensibility.[7]

Working-class Americans routinely emphasized the impermanence of life and the transience of human connection when they said goodbye. "Yours until death" was their pervasive farewell in letters to family and friends. But paradoxically, the popular valediction also conveyed the permanence of the sender's feelings for the recipient. The emotional commitment to family and friends in "yours until death" was linked with the recognition of inevitable loss. While belief in the continuation of intimate relationships in heaven re-solved the tension between permanent commitment and mortality for many, no correspondent ended a letter with "yours until heaven." Utopia was pushed aside in favor of the here and now. On earth they knew that they would have to cope with temporal loss. In an earthly frame, death always threatened to sever the relationship of letter writer and recipient. This may explain their preference for a farewell that acknowledged life's impermanence and simul-taneously emphasized the durability of their worldly commitments.

Poor, undereducated correspondents used "yours until death" more than any other sign-off in their personal letters. The persistent refrain was pop-ular across a wide swath of the country and in a broad range of relationships. Wyatt Brantley, a free Black man, closed his 1830s letter to a former North Carolina neighbor who had moved to Indiana, "remaining your friend until death."[8] One white sharecropper wrote his southern neighbor in 1867: "Nothing more at present But Remaines your friend until death."[9] "We ever remain your loving Father and Mother untell death," a Georgia mother assured her Confederate son.[10] J. B. Roberts, a member of the Twenty-Eighth Indiana "colored" Infantry Regiment, signed off a letter to his father during the Civil War with "I Remain your Deare Sun until Death."[11] "I remain you affectionate untill deth, Mary R Brophy," a western widow resolved to her sister-in-law two years after the major conflict.[12]

Such language was commonplace in southern letters, but the goodbyes of northern correspondents were more diverse.[13] Nevertheless, a number of northerners also peppered their letters with the standard incantation, acknowledging the transience of all human relationships and the fragility of love. Closing a letter with this ritualistic valediction indicated that senders felt their level of affection for the recipient merited a remarkable promise: a lifelong commitment to their emotional bond.

Joshua Jones, a common soldier in the Nineteenth Indiana Volunteer Infantry, finished his earliest extant letter to his wife, written in August 1861, with this line: "So farewell friends and Relations yours till Death."[14] Significantly, he closed his next letter, written eight days later to his brother-in-law, with "Yours with Respect."[15] The contrast is telling. "Yours till death" carried a level of affection and intimacy that Jones did not feel for his brother-in-law. Working-class correspondents used the familiar phrase to commu-nicate an emotional connection that was affirmative. "Yours until death" was a declaration of love before death became an uncomfortable subject in American culture.

Jones, a poor Hoosier living near Muncie, Indiana, before the Civil War, expressed love more freely and directly to his wife than a majority of working-class husbands. He self-identified as "your Ever loving husband."[16] Occasionally he would voice a markedly middle-class version of romantic love: "Dear Celia I want you to write me if no body Else does for I love you more than all the world & I am content when I can hear from you."[17] But he nonetheless felt the pull of working-class culture. Straddling the nonromantic and romantic conventions of attachment, he used both in letters to his wife. "I will Ever Remain your affectionate & Loving husband until Death" combines the working-class "yours until death" with the middle-class "your affectionate and loving husband." This was followed by the classic working-class rhyme of remembrance, the vernacular "remember me" poem.[18] Love, death, and memory combined in this amalgam of feeling at the end of his letter.

The precariousness of life in nineteenth-century America was dramatically magnified by the Civil War, which gave the letter ending a special twist. During the war 182 out of every 10,000 Americans were killed by combat, infectious diseases, or untreatable injuries.[19] This was a death rate six times that of World War II.[20] When Hillory Shifflet, a white soldier in the First Regiment of Ohio Volunteers, wrote his wife, "So no more only I Remain your Husband un tell Death," they both recognized that their marriage might soon end on a battlefield.[21] David Demus, an African American soldier serving in the Massachusetts Fifty-Fourth closed a letter to his wife with a similar benediction: "yor Dear husben untill deth yor frend."[22] "Until death" took on an immediacy that contained both poignancy and power in the Civil War.

Mollie D. Gaither illustrated the merging of death, love, and memory in the closing lines of a letter to her boyfriend Burgess, a Confederate soldier from North Carolina. "I hope to hear from you soon I cant forSet [forget] one look of thine though miles apart we are as long as life shall last and memory reign I will remember the) . . . so fare you well my Dear Burg yours truly untill Death."[23] Mortality was especially visible when correspondents closed a letter to a soldier with the phrase "yours until death." This sign-off was a simultaneous acknowledgment of death as an always imminent possibility, even more ruthless in war, alongside an almost incongruous emphasis on the living. "Yours until death" was a paradoxical benediction. The first word conveyed personal commitment; the second and third were reminders of the limits of time and history. The high value placed on stability and

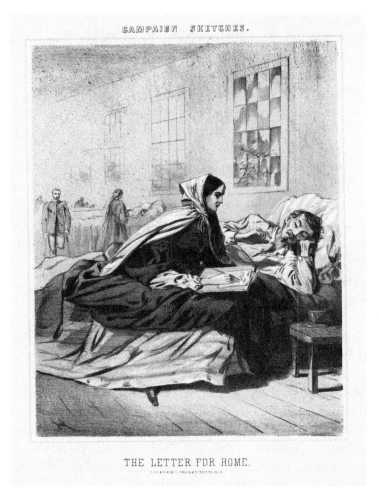

THE LETTER FOR HOME.

A woman takes dictation from a hospitalized soldier in this drawing by Winslow Homer. It is based on Homer's five-week sojourn with McClellan's Army of the Potomac in 1863. Titled *The Letter for Home*, this is one of six lithographs Winslow published in a book called *Campaign Sketches*.
Library of Congress 2013650300, LC-DIG-03009.

permanence in working-class relationships was confirmed by emphasizing their precariousness.

The specter of death often gripped the working-class American as he or she said goodbye to family and friends. Recognition of the possibility of death was tough-minded realism in the nineteenth century. Young and old were dying in the home, where avoidance was a virtual impossibility, and death was a quotidian experience. Not surprisingly, working-class men and women incessantly invoked their own mortality. This was true before, during, and after the Civil War.

Long before the outbreak of the war, death permeated everyday life. The reality of death was constant and pressing in the nineteenth century. "Thare is no news," Luther Trussell wrote Delia Page. "Nobody dead or married."[24] Birth, marriage, and death were the essence of hometown news, but death often trumped the lot. Reliable mortality rates are notoriously difficult to establish in antebellum America, but estimates in rural towns in the North run around 150 per 10,000 Americans annually. The estimates of mortality rates in larger northern cities are even higher: 200 to 400 deaths per 10,000.[25] These noncombat figures were comparable with, and may actually exceed, death rates associated with the Civil War. This was due, in large part, to high infant mortality rates. The Civil War death rate was exceptional and devastating because it struck an unimaginable number of adults in the prime of life.

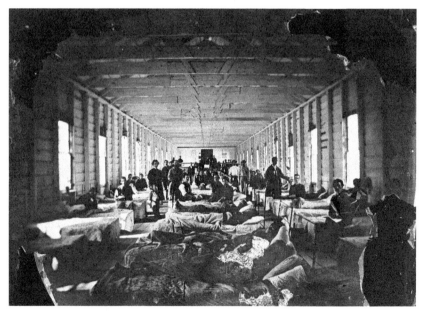

Mathew Brady photographed wounded Civil War soldiers in a hospital ward.
A few of the men staring at the camera likely never recovered from their injuries.
National Archives Identifier 524705.

204 LOVE AND THE WORKING CLASS

Epidemics, however, could fell both adults and children in spectacular fashion. Cholera outbreaks in 1832, 1849, and 1866 were classic American examples. Though vaccination had reduced the smallpox threat and yellow fever had died out in the North, cholera had not been tamed, and it struck every age, class, race, and gender. Victims could die within hours of the onset of first symptoms, which included diarrhea, intense vomiting, and severe cramps. Cholera was not an everyday affliction, but when the infection was spreading, it killed civilians with a speed that was exceeded only by battlefield deaths in war.[26] By contrast, malaria and tuberculosis were constant threats to the health of nineteenth-century Americans. One study, which focused on nineteenth-century New England, found that infectious diseases caused the vast majority of deaths. The top five killers included tuberculosis, scarlet fever, and pneumonia.[27]

Positive news of the health and prosperity of relatives, neighbors, and friends was highly prized, and yet reports on sickness and death sometimes received more attention, space, and weight in working-class letters. One correspondent, responding to his father's letter, actually explained the importance of writing about death. "I consider my self verry much respected by you for writing the affliction death and buriel of my poor unfortuneate mother," he solemnly intoned. "Respected" is the watchword here. The son felt valued by his father's letter because he took the time to write about his mother's death and suffering. "I am verry sorrow to hear of her death," James continued, "and verry much surprise ed to think she died from the affect of a snake bite."

James Gatewood had not lived with his parents for ten or eleven years but he still had positive memories of his mother, whom he credited for his moral upbringing. "I have not for gotten her kind hand that raised me from the cradle and her most be love ed voice which all ways commanded me from all corrupt maners and evil language." While his tribute to her was standard fare, he was unusually sensitive to his father's loss of companionship. His mother had "gone and left" his father, he observed, a strangely willful description of her accident but one that likely captured how his father felt. James granted that his father had "children enough" to keep him company, understanding that he was still alone because "the rite companion is gone." He fully sympathized with his father's loneliness, even identifying the difference between visible companionship and inner isolation. He added that even if all their friends and neighbors were around, "the[y] would not be of much compiney to you for the rite companion is not there."[28] The son twice acknowledged that his father was not missing people in general but his life-long companion. This is a rare articulation of the emotional satisfaction of nonromantic love.

If writing about death and suffering was an act of respect in working-class culture, it could take two very different forms. One was collective, focusing on the group instead of the individual. This collective approach incorporated the multiple deaths of family, friends, neighbors, and other associates, usu-ally within the boundaries of a specific place. Mortality was seen in terms of a network, and the treatment of death was cumulative and inclusive. This resulted in a group portrait of death that created its own emotional impact. Correspondents who related one death after another were focused on the community, not the individual.

These Americans did not express special feelings about one death but rather portrayed death as part of a life cycle that never ended. This style tended to be factual, distant, and repetitive: "i have but 3 Children living i have two in abetter world than this," one sister wrote another. She continued to detail the family roster of dead children: "luke had 3 children and one beried washington has 3 living and 3 dead Jane East has 8 living and one dead Robert has one child he labled it katy it is 2 years old."[29] The effect was cumu-lative. Not focused on any one event, repetition created its own emotional impact.[30]

"John Coin is ded," one widow informed her sister-in-law, and "hampton and lewis Rogers is ded Martha is maried last weak the horses ranaway Jane [her horse] fell down and broke her leg it is a 2 hundred dolars loss to me."[31] In the widow's litany of calamity, both death and marriage were on an equal footing with the loss of her horse. Death was conveyed with the same signif-icance as other news and events. This had a flattening effect that is discon-certing to a modern sensibility.

A Midwestern wife followed the same approach in conveying death to her friends. "Uncle Jessie Hannie is dead, died of paralissis, Mrs Seders died of consumption in Ohio Malachi Spence is dead. Old Mrs Loura is very sick with dropsy Mr Bewells family have left . . . for Iowa have been gone some time Emma Archer was married last tuesday."[32] The writer recounts death, mobility, and marriage without emotional distinction but with a cumulative affirmation of community connection. This aggregate approach expressed a larger acceptance of the life cycle—a stoic attitude and a sense of detachment from the individual death but attachment to the collective life of the commu-nity, which was the "organism" that counted most.

206   LOVE AND THE WORKING CLASS

Martha Burgess was literate but still recruited one daughter to take dictation for a letter to another. "[T]here a heep of sickness in this Co and a heep of deaths I never heard tell of so much Sickness in my life I was sorry to hear of little mary's death but that is a det that we all have to pay sooner or later," declared Martha. "I will be gain to tell you of deaths that has been William Shippy Wife is dead jo hippys Son Dalpers is dead old Mrs Canada is dead old Barba Duncan is dead old Mr Baly Nederson is dead jo Hopper is dead one of mot Lands daughters are dead old Cos Sanders is dead old Mac Manions is dead and two young men that died sudent [sudden] all the rest died with the fever." She interrupted her litany of death to discuss the state of the potato, cotton, and corn crop. Then she returned to her death count: "Coline is dead She has ben dead a bout five Months tell Berry that his Mother is dead I never heard what was the matter with her they are all dead now but Harret."[33] She treated death as something worth reporting or relaying on the level of other facts, such as crop prices and yields, weather, or accidents. Mortality was simply part of a cycle of planting and harvests that was seasonal and recurrent, a continuum of past to present that was reassuring because it modulated loss through continuity.

Elizabeth Sterling, self-conscious about the guilty pleasure in reporting the news of death and suffering, began her litany: "woren lord is ded he died with tha treamers [tremors] and tha butcher chimerhorn is all most gon tha don't think he will git up a gain," but then she stopped and joked with her father, "and if tha was a fiew more would go it would be a good thing."[34] With tongue in cheek, Sterling captured the paradoxical pleasure of toting up the local deaths. The foundation of her humor was the multilayered community history she shared with her father. Dense local knowledge was inherent in small-town relationships, which almost always included a tangled web of allies and adversaries. The intimacy of place transcended the demise of any one individual.

The community approach to death was reassuring because death was understood as part of the human life cycle that included the renewal of birth and marriage. Itemizing multiple deaths in succession was also a great equalizer in that it conveyed the feeling that all deaths mattered. In these collective tallies, no one was "more dead" than another, whatever their wealth or status while they were alive.

Working-class correspondents observed death in clusters or networks, but they also took an individual approach, often focusing on a specific person—child or adult—who died. Correspondents probed the meaning of individual death for themselves and their family members through eye-witness accounts of dying. Nineteenth-century Americans, whatever their station in life, gathered around the dying. This experience was commonly referred to as "the good death."[35] Curiosity mingled with sympathy and fear as family, friends, and neighbors watched and interpreted the meaning of life. Obviously the particulars were unique, but the comfort sent and received was a valued ritual.

The standards of a good death were broadly shared by middle- and working-class Americans. A good death usually meant that the dying (verbally or behaviorally) displayed a positive attitude that included joyful anticipation, willingness to take leave of earthly attachments, and resignation toward pain and suffering. Their common source was a generalized religious faith in a peaceful, pain-free afterlife.[36] To be completely valid, however, a positive attitude toward imminent death had to be ratified by some hint of mental clarity. It was important to know that, as one sister reported, "she had hir senses untill the last."[37]

"She was in a calm and happy frame of mind," twenty-four-year-old Anna Mason told her mother. This was the most reassuring news she could pass on about her aunt's death. Anna kept busy gathering news about her former hometown. "Few families," she told her mother "have not been visited by death or <u>matrimony</u>." A young single woman working in the Manchester, New Hampshire, cotton mills, she was naturally interested in matrimony, but she did not stint on descriptions of death in letters to her parents.[38] Filling two pages on the illness and death of Mr. Corliss, Anna closed her missive with the ritualized observance of the dying man's state of mind. "While he was breathing his last Mrs. C asked him if he could not speak to her once more he looked at her then raised his eyes and such a heavenly expression came over his face that (to use her words) it seemed as heaven opened and disclosed to his view the glories of another world He has patiently borne poverty and affliction and faithfully served his Master now he gone to his reward."[39] Stoic suffering was a paramount value in working-class eyewitness accounts of death. The working class also valued deathbed testimonies of piety and religious faith. But they were willing to take the measure of demeanor at the end of life if dying persons displayed some awareness of their passing.

Observations of the dying were linked to assurances of a rewarding afterlife, based primarily upon a happy frame of mind and some stoicism toward suffering. "I feel gratified to inform you," one brother wrote another concerning their mother's death, "that she left the wourld in the triumfs of faith." In her dying moments, she sang her favorite hymns, clapped her hands, and "shouted give glory to god and retained her senses while she had breath." She met or exceeded every requirement of the good death, and the happiness she exhibited "gave us all a great deel of Satisfaction."[40] Her positive attitude and mental clarity offered eyewitnesses considerable satisfaction, not least because they could report on the "good death" to friends or relatives.

In reality, the standards of a good death were often difficult to achieve. "I have one consoling thought," G. E. Hollis wrote a young female friend about his mother's death, "she expressed a willingness to go and said she would be happy which you know must fill my heart with joy." But he qualified his "consoling thought" with an admission. "[B]ut if I could saw her once more before she died I would hav been better reconciled to her death."[41] The problem was that he had not expected her to die, even though he knew she was sick, and he had not been able to witness her death, a comfort that he sorely missed.

One wife reported to her husband about his mother's death: "John, how we wished for her to come to enough to know and talk to us & tell what her wishes were, but it could not be. she had done her work in this world."[42] Witnessing the death of an unconscious person was a disappointment, perhaps even a substantial letdown, as all the anticipated drama of the ritualized farewell was gone, replaced by a blankness that was hard to interpret at that moment and perhaps even harder to impart to family and friends.

"My husband is no more," Ursula Terry informed her father-in-law in 1843. "And his death was peculiar." She describes how he had gone to the field and was at work when a neighbor approached. They both spotted a deer that they decided to track. Ursula's husband got the first shot and wounded the animal. When he prepared to shoot again, according to Ursula, he "fell on this face and expired without uttering but one word he died in the midst of health and I am left poor and disconsolate." The meaning Ursula took from her loss was very typical. "Oh how transient is human happiness and fading is all earthly honour and glory," she reflected, "how soon are our brightest prospects blasted by the hand of death Lord help us to consider our ways and ponder well our steps."[43] Ursula had practical economic concerns, but she was also struggling to find meaning in her husband's death. Her husband's sudden demise, lacking any verbal cues or familial witnesses, made it difficult to emotionally shape and to intellectually validate her personal loss.

IMAGINING THE ETERNAL VILLAGE 209

Civil War soldiers' wives had to cope with even more difficult circumstances than their civilian counterparts. One cultural historian has argued that the standard of the good death was strained during the Civil War but continued to be creatively applied for the comfort it might give to the grieving family.[44] This was no doubt true for middle-class soldiers and support staff—including military officers, doctors, and nurses—writing letters of condolence under various circumstances. They generally sought to improvise a good death for soldiers in the letters they wrote to loved ones.[45] One Confederate nurse reported that a dying soldier under his care "saw Jesus standing with his arms open and inviting him to come declaring that all was piece with him on erth,, and died as easy as a man could with a smile on his face and there is no doubt but he is at rest with his father in heven."[46] The soldier's smile, his dying declaration of peace, and his vison of Jesus welcoming him to heaven perfectly conform to the model of a good Christian death. Such symbols provided comfort to the grieving family regardless of their veracity.

In spite of the potential reassurance they could offer, working-class letter writers were much more literal and less inventive (perhaps less literary) than their middle-class compatriots. They did not demonstrate an urgent need to fit the facts of *sudden* death into a "good death" paradigm.[47] "[I]it become my painful duty to inform you that Mr. Catenhead is nomore," a Confederate soldier wrote his sister Faney about her husband's death: "he was killed on yesterday, in A charge on the enemy I do not know where he was struck, but from what I can learn he was shot through the chest with A miney ball." This brother did not attempt to gloss over the painful facts. "I saw him lying on the field, but we was retreating and there was no time for me to examin him further then to see that he was dead his boddy was left in the hans of the enemy." Sudden death associated with war did not fit the model of the good death, and many working-class soldiers did not pretend otherwise. Working-class combatants were often less tactful than their middle-class counterparts and more willing to report honestly to a widow about her husband's death. Some hope of heaven was often the only comfort they could provide. "[L]ook to A kind providence for protection in time," C. Dicken advised his sister, "and ever lasting, bliss in A world to come."[48]

Joseph Jones was a very devout man, but he did not try to invent a good death for his best friend Jo. While Jones was on a burial detail (most likely after the Second Battle of Murfreesboro) he discovered his friend's body: "jo was shot through the breast i dont know how long he lived or any thing a bout it i did not see him fall." Jones was very sympathetic to the dead soldier's wife, but he did not sugarcoat the facts: "i dont know how in the world phebe jane wil stand it," he confessed to his wife, "for it appeared as though it would narely kill me to loose such a good friend as him."[49] The body of the dead soldier had been completely stripped of all personal items; for that reason he cut a locket of hair for the grieving widow's comfort. Though Joseph was sensitive to Phebe Jane's suffering, he did not create a story to soften her grief.

Hair was a common way to represent the deceased. It was a mourning object in its own right, but it was also used in a variety of ways—brooches, bracelets, watch fobs, and other objects—that could be carried on the person of the bereaved and bring the living into physical as well as emotional contact with the dead. Embedding hair in decorative objects was a common middle-class ritual that may also have been familiar to working-class mourners.[50]

Nine months later, Joseph Jones was a battle-weary veteran who had survived Murfreesboro, the Tullahoma campaign in middle Tennessee, and the Battle of Chickamauga in Georgia.[51] He explained to his wife how his emotional reaction to death had changed: "it is nothing to a soldier to here of the death of a friend or comrad for he has enough of such before his eyes continualy to harden him so that he cannot mourn for the dead."[52] This was a principal reason why the good death no longer mattered to many foot soldiers in the war. Later in the war, certain women were also hardened to death. "I am vory sorrow to hear of Tomas Brit Death but it is no more that what I expected," one woman informed a soldier friend, "for I would Not be supprised to hear of you all being dead at no time."[53]

George Fluent, a working-class nurse assigned to the Jefferson Barracks General Hospital Ward in St. Louis, Missouri, described a soldier's death to his father as "very Eesy," but he included graphic details that might have been excluded by a middle-class writer: "he did not make eny remarks whatever he bled to death through his wound," George wrote. He emphasized that they did everything in their power to save him and then offered the father a piece of skull that was taken out of his son's head.[54] Sending the father a souvenir bone shard after remarking that his son said nothing while he bled to death through his head wound certainly compromised the consolation of a good death. Apparently this nurse did not feel the need to remake the actual circumstances for the father's peace of mind.

An African American man openly grieved for his dead comrade in the famed Massachusetts Fifty-Fourth: "i miss him as much as though he Was my own brother," William Davis wrote Violet Hall, his dead friend's wife. Davis's consolation letter to Violet mixed elements of the good death with

IMAGINING THE ETERNAL VILLAGE   211

a more troubling description of her husband's physical and mental state. On the one hand, Davis assured Violet, "he has Sufferd for nothing at any time" including his medical treatment. Furthermore, Davis was there to take "care of him night and day as i would of a brother."[55] Hall had been sick for several months and died in a hospital in Beaufort, South Carolina. Slow death sometimes allowed for a closer approximation of the standards of the good death.

Davis reassured Violet that her husband's "only wish and prayer" was to be with his family and friends when he died. But after a comforting and calming account of Hall's good death, Davis seems compelled to add negative information. "[H]e had one of the worst Diseases there is in the World that is the dropsy and i never saw any one Stand their Suffering as long as he has and not want to give up till the morning he died." (In this context, "dropsy" probably meant he had congestive heart failure or a kidney disease.)[56] Davis's judgment that Violet's husband had suffered at length away from home from "one of the worst diseases . . . in the world" could not have been a comforting thought.

Sudden death in battle resisted the ideal of the good death, and even the slower deaths of soldiers among peers might be hard to assimilate, but at least when the lifeless were identified and their families informed, grief could take its course. Untold numbers of Americans continued to search for kin and hold out hope long after their loved ones had disappeared. Eyewitnesses sent Faney, Violet, and Phebe accounts of their husbands' death. Such verification was precious. Many other wives, parents, siblings, and friends had no news or waited months, even years, to find out what had happened to their missing relatives.[57]

The currently accepted estimate of two hundred thousand Civil War widows means that large numbers of husbands died far away from home. Though thousands were never identified, many who were known still could not be buried in hometown graveyards. The shared rituals of grief were seriously disrupted by the Civil War.[58] "People do not mourn their dead as they used to," one elite southern woman observed. "Everyone seems to live only in the present—just from day to day—otherwise I fancy many would go crazy."[59] The most serious disruption came from the absence of a body to bury.[60] This hardship may have greatly inhibited Americans' ability to mourn their dead.[61]

In all likelihood, widows and their families did not hold funeral services at home without a corpse. Wealthier Americans expended their time and treasure to retrieve the remains of loved ones for another chance at a "normal farewell."[62] The common army practice of burying the body of a fallen soldier on or near the battlefield created havoc with later identification, however, as most graves were unmarked in spite of official policy.[63] Some poorer women turned this material and cultural affront into a cause, demanding that federal and state officials help them find and return the bodies of their husbands and sons.[64] The complications were many and the expense was great, so this was not an endeavor undertaken by the vast majority of widows, whatever their heartfelt wishes.

Matthew Brady photographed the graves of Civil War soldiers buried near City Point, Virginia General Hospital. The background graves have headstones, while the freshly dug burial mounds in the foreground are unmarked. Grave markers were precious to families as historians estimate that at least half of the Civil War dead were never identified.
Library of Congress, LC-DIG-01872.

It is not hard to conceive that wives whose husbands died in places and circumstances they had problems even imagining, without their help or care, were deeply distressed.[65] The scarcity of letters written by working-class widows about the deaths of their husbands may indicate that they avoided putting their emotional trauma into words.[66] The other possibility is that the letters wives wrote to relatives and friends mourning their spouse's death were not saved by families or collected by historical archives. The collection bias that favored soldiers over wives existed for decades, and widows' letters might have been discarded as a result. Collection bias no doubt reduced the survival rate of widows' correspondence, but it may not adequately account for their rarity.

Several historians have observed that numerous southern letter writers and diary keepers simply stopped writing after the war.[67] They attributed this phenomenon to an attempt by southerners to avoid a reminder of their loss. Perhaps a similar emotional logic could be applied to Civil War widows on all sides of the war. Writing about the loss of their husbands may have been an activity they wanted to avoid.

One modern grief theory helps in understanding how these Civil War widows coped with bereavement. It suggests that grieving should be viewed both as an orientation to loss (the past) and as an orientation to the life changes (the future) needed to adjust to the loss.[68] Oscillation between past misfortune and future restoration is a common response to grief. But many Civil War widows were under pressure, because of their economic vulnerability, to give restoration their full attention. They might have deliberately avoided the emotional stress of writing about the loss of their husbands.

Contrary to popular beliefs, some current psychological studies indicate that writing (or talking) about the death of a spouse has little or no effect on a person's adjustment to bereavement.[69] In fact working-class widows may not have had a high need for emotional disclosure. Living in nonromantic marriages, they likely had some residual sense that they could have wed a number of men from their local community (even if that was not necessarily accurate). Furthermore, they would not have believed, as in marriages based on romantic love, that their emotional well-being was dependent, in large part, on their husbands' love. Working-class wives also looked to their tribe for affective bonds, and as longtime local residents would have expected support from the community. Still, as James Gatewood observed after his mother died of a snakebite, absence could create loneliness, even in a nonromantic marriage with strong external familial and community bonds.[70]

Although alleviating loneliness (and perhaps depression) was surely a significant motivation, the central orientation of many working-class widows had to be their family's basic needs. The urgent problem they confronted was how to replace the economic contribution of their deceased spouse. To lose a husband in his prime was a financial disaster. Many wives experienced serious economic stress when a soldier husband died in the Civil War.[71] Union legislators recognized their economic struggle and passed the first Civil War pension program in 1862.[72] The median time between their husband's death and the filing of a pension application was four months, an indication of these widows' urgent need.[73] The average payout of eight dollars per month should have helped allay some of their anxiety. (The widows of Confederate soldiers were not eligible.) But in terms of 1870 income, this amounted to less than half the monthly paycheck of a typical farm laborer.[74] During the war, the Confederacy paid a death claim based on unpaid back pay to soldiers' widows or other family members. In a case study of Virginia's claimants, two-thirds received less than $100 in shaky Confederate currency.[75] The widespread belief that it was possible to meet one's spouse in heaven might have been an antidote to the downheartedness of poor widows. But heaven was not an antidote to providing basic needs in this world, which required an orientation to future restoration of a deceased husband's economic contributions to the family.

The most obvious path to replacing a late husband's economic support was to find another. But demographic data suggest that the majority of women over thirty who were widowed by the war were unable to marry again. Solving the restoration problem with another spouse was apparently quite difficult over a certain age. Low remarriage rates indicate that middle-aged widows had to find other solutions to their economic loss. Male relatives, especially fathers, brothers, and sons, played a critical role, as did government subsidies.[76]

In the case study of Virginia's claimants, only 1 of the 1,297 widows who filed death claims owned property in her own name and only 13 had jobs that paid a salary.[77] Most of the deceased husbands had no property and did not leave a will. In that case, common law dictated that wives had the right to one-third of their husband's estate. In many instances, that was one-third of "not enough." County governments in Virginia attempted to fill the gap by giving monthly food allotments to soldiers' wives and widows. In one county with the best surviving records, it appears that almost all widows asked for and received aid in the middle of the war.[78] Food riots broke out in Richmond, the Confederate capital, and smaller disturbances took place daily in other areas.[79] By the end of the war, only the Union army could provide poor southern widows the food they desperately needed. Eyewitnesses testified to the fact that widows were begging for work in almost every southern town or city a year after Appomattox.[80]

The remarriage records are incomplete for those Virginia wives who filed death claims, but of those women who can be traced, 156 married again and another 163 women remained widows. Restoration was an urgent priority successfully met by those who substituted one husband for another as quickly as possible. Seventy-three percent remarried between 1863 and 1868.[81] But what about the 163 who definitely did *not* remarry? Whether this was by choice or circumstance cannot be decided definitively, but clues reside in their age and in the economic outcome of second marriages. Predictably, Virginia women who remarried were better off financially in 1870 than widows who had no second husbands.[82] This economic advantage would not have escaped the notice of anyone in a tight-knit community. More than half of the women who were over thirty by the end of the war never remarried. Some older widows may have chosen to rely on their children (or older male relatives), but others likely failed in their attempts to find a second mate.[83]

The widow Peebles was poor and so desperate to remarry that she was courting a local soldier from her North Carolina Piedmont neighborhood in September 1864, eleven months after her soldier husband had died. Her attraction to Daniel Turner was multilayered, including his strong physical appeal. Neither owned property, but he was ten years her junior and had the advantage of youth. She was around thirty years old when she wrote him. He rejected her advances, eventually marrying another widow even older than Peebles. Supported by her son in 1870, clearly the widow Peebles did not choose to rely on her children over Turner. She did not find a man who was willing to marry her after her husband died. Perhaps as a consequence, she was the head of a household with no real estate and so little personal property that the census taker did not bother with a valuation.[84]

A northern study of nearly one thousand pension claims filed by enlisted soldiers (or their families) from the Iowa cities of Dubuque and Des Moines concluded that the payouts were not adequate to meet the pensioners' subsistence needs.[85] This suggests that many working-class widows did not have the luxury of choosing an independent lifestyle. Class bias against enlisted men and in favor of officers was endemic in the federal pension system.[86] Most enlisted men or their widows received payments that were woefully inadequate, sometimes as low as one dollar per month, and the neediest veterans and their families had the most trouble getting their claims approved.[87] While considered speedy by nineteenth-century standards, still only 39.4 percent of the widows of enlisted men received a decision on their pension case in one year or less.[88]

Restoration of a husband's economic contribution to the family was a pressing task for the working-class widow. This may have meant that adapting to life changes took precedence over emotional responses to loss. Indeed, grief work may have been a luxury for poorer wives. It makes sense that these widows would have handled their fundamental emotional disquiet through avoidance. But other working-class correspondents also practiced a strategy of avoidance. Sometimes the less educated soldier preferred to say as little as possible in a condolence letter to keep from disclosing details that might hurt the recipient.

After quickly describing the battlefield death of his friend, who died at Vicksburg from a bullet wound to the head, C. W. Spiker continued: "we all Join in unison [to] say there could not be a more peaceable and better soldier nor better liked than was friend lewis B but he is nomore he was buryed by the side of those of the Regt. that fell on the same day (the 16th of May)." Spiker was suddenly self-conscious about writing this much to his friend's sister and declared: "I will add nomore on this subject for I no how it will make you feal tho I could not have said less." He believed that fewer words would inflict less pain. But Spiker also claimed defensively, "I could not have said less."[89] Noting the manner of her brother's death and burial, he made no effort to go beyond his friend's popularity to create a good death for his comrade's sister. Brevity in discussing death may have been a deliberate strategy of many working-class correspondents, replacing the middle-class reliance on formulaic tropes of cheerful anticipation and stoic suffering.

One soldier explained why he was not saying more about his mother's death: "it is an unplesant thought for me to dwell upon," he explained; "therefore I will say as little as possible." Note the revelation that followed: "not withstanding I will often feel the loss of a kind Mother." The unpleasant thought drove him to avoid long exposition, yet he still maintained that he would "often feel the loss."[90] This strategy of avoidance may be one explanation for the brevity of some correspondents when they commented on death.

A taciturn style was widely shared among the folk before the Civil War. *"With sorrow we have to inform you," James Reed wrote his son in 1834, "that your brother Calvin departed this life after the illness of two nights and one day with an inflammation in the head. . . . All has gone smoothly with us since you left," he added, "with the exception of the loss of Calvin. So Calvin is no more."[91] Terse descriptions of death did not preclude an emotional reaction. Reed indicated that he was writing "with sorrow," a succinct summary of his feelings. Moreover the line "So Calvin is no more" is laden with a powerful, if unnamed, sense of loss.

In a postscript to his mother, sister, and brother-in-law, William Cates reported that his baby was taken sick the previous Sunday morning. He continued: "last Friday it turned black on one side of its face before it died so no more at this time write soon."[92] The half-blackened image of his baby's face is unambiguously disturbing by contemporary standards. Though Cates did not react overtly to his baby's death, he signaled his emotional discomfort by a headlong rush to put the topic behind him. He was remembering in order to forget. The highly unusual placement of the baby's death in a postscript probably bespoke a deep uneasiness about the infant's end of life.

Taciturn reports on children's deaths were deliberately brief, yet strangely revealing. "[M]y daughter Rebecah had a Child the 27 day of July 1833 in the morning and died in the Evening," a free Black farmer informed his former neighbors who had moved to the Midwest, "the child lived two weks and dide." A simple and unadorned report, yet the detail about his granddaughter's morning birth and evening death had a quiet sensitivity. This grandfather noticed the diurnal symbolism of her life.[93]

Conveying a child's death seemed to elicit the widest variation in attitude: from calm acceptance to deep disquietude, from hysterical grief to silent pain or even horror. Calm acceptance characterized this postpartum mother. "the 10th of January last I was confind to my bed with a boy baby which was dead born," a daughter informed her mother, "but that did not cause me any trouble at that time for I new it was better off than me or the rest."[94] This woman held a strong conviction that death had given her baby something better than life. Whether that improved condition was avoidance of life's pain and sorrow or a heavenly afterlife is unclear.

Brevity was one way to cope with grief but so too were elaborate descriptions of an unnerving death scene. Shaken by the accident that killed his infant son, John Barksdale, a poor Tennessee farmer, struggled to regain his equilibrium by writing a letter to his cousin. He revealed that their little son Augustus "burnt up" this spring. Seeming to blame his wife's "bad luck," he quickly acknowledged their mutual "misfortune," admitting that their baby's death was very hard on them both. "[T]o think how he was burnt and

218   LOVE AND THE WORKING CLASS

to die such a life as that is very distressing to think abought but we could not help it," he wrote defensively.

Barksdale was upset by the way his son died and took on the burden of recounting his death. On Thursday morning after breakfast he left to chop some hoop pine for barrels to store and transport tobacco. America finished breastfeeding her son and laid him down on a pallet in front of the fire. She left to milk the cow, but raced back to the house after hearing loud screams: "she found the child lying whare she had swep up the coldz of fire burnt so bad that he did not live longer than Friday evening," Barksdale reported. "[W]e done everthing we could for a burne but all failed but we have to give him up it is to distressing to think abought but the lord giveth and lord taketh and blessed be the lord." He took solace from the idea that his infant son was in the hands of a merciful God "whare we will have to appeare in that great & notaable day of the lord."[95] Torn between confession and suppression, this poor farmer mixed guilt, regret, Christian fatalism, and a hint of final reckoning in this description of his child's death. High infant mortality suggests that such a grisly and tragic accident was not unique.

Young children perished in numbers that were actually higher than that of Civil War soldiers, and their deaths were almost a constant in working-class families. Though imprecise, figures on the death of infants before the age of one range from 15 to 20 percent of those born on American soil in the second half of the nineteenth century.[96] It is useful, for comparison, to apply these percentages to a statistically reliable data set. In one year of the late twentieth century, 38,300 of the 3,855,000 infants born in the United States died. If the mortality rate had been 15 percent, as it was in the nineteenth century, well over half a million babies would have perished.[97]

Barely literate but nonetheless eloquent, Mary Cruse was exceptionally vulnerable after her three children died. The letter she wrote to her brother and sister reads like an open wound, so powerful is her expression of grief. Yet she was on the cusp of literacy, demonstrating once again that the barest writing skills can be applied to conveying the most heartfelt feelings. *"I would have written sooner but I have not been able," Mary explained. "O how can I write this morning? My hand trembles as I hold this pen, my eyes are dim with tears, and my heart is almost broken."[98] Thus began her agonized lament. "O to think of this journey, it has broken my peace forever. Scarcely had we reached the shores of this country than sickness seized hold of my poor children."[99] Mary had recently moved from Shannon to Weston

County, Missouri, and she felt so isolated and forlorn that she called it another "country."

"O Sally Ann, had my poor children sickened and died at home I would have tried to give them up and had them laid at Shannon with our mother and sisters where I could have went and knelt over their little graves and shed tears for them."[100] Mary believed that if death had taken them at home and not in some strange location, she would have been calmer and better able to make peace with her loss. She intuited that visiting their graves in the family burial ground would have given her some sense of continuity with the past.

Her grief was magnified by the disruption of a move that created severe emotional discontinuity in her time of need. She was surrounded by strangers and she lacked the intimacy of place to help support her and give her a sense of community. Wracked with guilt and sorrow, Mary Cruse poured out her feelings to her sister. "I cannot give them up. Oh, my dear children, how well I loved them. I brought them here to die." She was inconsolable. "This world has no chance for me now. I have no desire to live. My life is only a misery to me." Only her new baby, just a few weeks old, gave her any reason to go on. "You wished to know where the little ones were buried. O my heart will break," she cried.[101]

Mary was compelled to name each child who died, giving her son and two daughters individual identities. "Their names are sweet to me. I cannot stop with calling them over to you. My dear little Elisabeth and James and little Rachel Amanda, all lay suffering at the same time. We did not know which would die first."[102] This naming ritual seemed to give some meaning to her terrible heartbreak. She named them again and described the order of their death. "O Sally Ann shed one tear for me. On Monday morning about ten o'clock my little James died. O then I thought of you, and Amanda, Uncle, Pap, and the graveyard where he [James] had to be laid. O I thought I could not lay him there alone with strangers. In a few hours my dear Rachel was taken with him. O that sweet tongue child how well I loved her. They were both laid in their little black velvet covered coffins."[103] Each child received some tribute and was mourned by a mother who testified to her love for them as unique individuals. "My dear Lisa . . . O this affectionate child how she suffered. With her thought and joys, she was my good child. That same night she died. I never can get over the death of this child." She felt especially close to Lisa (Elizabeth), who prompted her most unqualified grief and despair. "This disease seized hold of my dear baby and tore it from my arms on the bluffs of the river. O was not this hard."[104]

220 LOVE AND THE WORKING CLASS

Mary's sense of broken community, and the isolation and estrangement that resulted from her move, made her children's demise even more devastating. She was deeply disturbed by their sudden death in the midst of strangers. "They are buried at a country graveyard. There is no church in that country. I never will close my eyes in peace until they are born back and laid in Shannon Church yard."[105] Confiding to her sister was some comfort, but she found no solace in thoughts of a heavenly reunion. She was intent on achieving a symbolic reunion, more physical than spiritual, in the family graveyard. Guilt and homesickness were intermingled with despair and heartache in her determined pledge. The dislocation of death was deepened by the isolation of living as a newcomer in a place that lacked even the rudimentary institutional support of a church. Mary had lost the familiarity of people as well as places like the church graveyard, and this loss magnified the desolation she felt over her children's deaths.

Unlike Mary Cruse, Susan Jones had the consolation of visiting the graves of her three children in an intimately familiar locality. With several years to mourn and grieve their passing, her pain was not as raw as Mary's. June brought sad thoughts of her dead children, and her emotions remained at odds with the summer season.[106] "June is my favorite month but I shall be glad when it is gone," Susan admitted to her husband.[107] The simple gesture of sending him a rose that was growing on their dead son's grave was a material commemoration of the child's death and the intimacy between his parents.[108] She drew considerable comfort from visiting her children's graves. Living in Harrison Township, Ohio, for at least eleven years before her three children died, the small local community (pop. 1,650) gave Susan the continuity, comfort, and familiarity that Mary Cruse missed so deeply.[109]

Both Susan and Mary lost three children in quick succession, and the contrast between them is instructive. Whereas Susan had all the emotional comforts her community could offer, Mary Cruse experienced a deep, overriding disquiet at her children dying away from the place she called home. Her gut-wrenching despair was, as she herself recognized, directly related to where they died. "[H]ad my poor children sickened and died at home I would have tried to give them up," she wrote plainly. They would have been buried with her mother and sisters in a kinship community that was comforting for its continuity with the past but also because she could "visit" her family and "shed tears for them" in the proper place. Mary's feelings may capture the early emotional turmoil of war widows when they heard that their husbands were dead: oscillating between animosity and fatalism, defeated but unable to find peace in their "good death" or burial at home.

Both Mary and Susan suffered acutely after the deaths of their children and did not practice the next mother's emotional withdrawal. After an arduous move from Massachusetts to Alabama, Ellen Richardson Merrill suspected that her young son might be dying. In this exceptionally revealing letter, she articulated a rarely acknowledged process of distancing that was probably quite common. Ellen's child fell ill with some stomach ailment on the family's journey from Massachusetts to Alabama, and he seemed to be getting worse with every passing day. She reported to her mother that he wanted her to hold him "all the time he growed poor all the time but it was a busey time with me and I tried to think he was ugly and turned him of[f]." She was obviously preparing for his death. "[B]ut all at once he took a turn he began to eat and grow fat and a better child you never saw than he is now."[110]

Ellen gave up hope for his recovery and tried to distance herself from him. Her description of this distancing process was deeply insightful: she "turned him of[f]" physically and psychologically, striving "to think he was ugly." She admitted her young son was very needy and she was very busy, which implied that she did not have the time or take the time to attend to him. Suddenly he began eating again and grew fat, and she exulted in his health and appearance. She reattached proudly to her little boy after she thought he was *not* going to die. Ellen's process of distancing and reattaching to her young child was likely a common defense against the pain of loss that someone like Mary Cruse suffered.[111]

Although distancing was also a defense against loss on the battlefields of the Civil War, soldiers were less prepared for death on the home front. Confederate John Cotton was thunderstruck to hear that Cricket (a nickname for his five-month-old daughter Nancy) was dead. "I no not how to address you on the subjectt," he told his wife. Cotton was heartbroken "to think I could not bee at home and see the last of her."[112] Witnessing death was a vital part of the life cycle in nineteenth-century families, and this was another comfort denied to Cotton because of war. It is easy to forget that Civil War soldiers had to deal not only with the slaughter of war, but with the death of loved ones living far from the fight.

"If you hant had little crickets funeral preached yet," he wrote eight months later, "don't have it preached till I come home." A popular custom in the southern hill country, the deferred funeral was also practiced in other rural areas by necessity.[113] Cotton, an Alabama yeoman, was still grieving the loss of his little Cricket and saw the funeral as a consolation he could yet obtain, if he ever returned home from the war. Vivid memories still played in his mind. "I can't hardly rite or talk about her without shedding tears I never shal forget how she use to fondle on my knees and her antic motions and her little prattling tongue," he reminded his wife, "but all this is past and she is at rest and is better off than her bereaved parents."[114] Cotton believed she was "at rest," but he made no mention of an afterlife. Fathers might react as emotionally as mothers to the death of a young child. Being unable to witness his baby daughter's death, or visit her grave, or attend a funeral surrounded by family and friends kept him in a state of fundamental disquiet.

Midwesterner Jonathan Labrant consoled his wife over the death of their baby son, Wallace. "I do not wish him back for I know he has gone home where his sufferings will end where wars turmoils & sorrow never come." The carpenter was sad and shed a tear but hoped to follow his son's little footprints to heaven.[115] Such an afterlife vision was often missing from poor folks' reactions to the death of young children. Working-class parents did not routinely talk about meeting their infants and young children in the afterlife. This was a middle-class trope.[116] What they frequently expressed was the hope and expectation of meeting their adult spouses, older children, siblings, and friends in heaven.

A definite sense of the reunification of adults after death permeated both northern and southern letters. "I had not ought to wish him back," Harriet Buck wrote from Minnesota about her dead son, for "he is better off than in this world of truble we know not how long it will be before we may all have to follow we ought to be prepaired to meet him in heaven."[117] "I hope you Will ont forget your pore Brother," Ambrose Garriot fretted. "[R]emember him in you payers for he exspects to meet you With his famley in a Better World than this whre thare will Bee no parting from friends No Ware to fight all will Bee peace."[118] Working-class longings clustered around an afterlife that was almost totally about personal relationships. Death was the vehicle for a utopian future where delayed gratification found its fullest expression.

For the working-class American, the complete expression of this delayed gratification was heaven.[119] "I sometimes think that it matters not, what becomes of our friends here," one brother wrote of another killed in the Civil War, "it matters not when, or where, they fall if we can only meet them in Heaven."[120] The most important geography outside their local village or town, heaven was a place of family intimacy. "[S]ofarewell forawhile," one Confederate soldier wrote his parents, "but ihope not all ways I remain your son until death ifinever se no more in life i hope i will see you in heaven where there is no war nor nuthing to morrow the peace of man kind there to Rain [reign] frrever in fool ness of Joy."[121] Even if they dropped the ritualized phrasing of "yours until death," northerners frequently emphasized mortality and an afterlife. "I preay that wemay bee granted the privleg of meatting feas to feas," Sydney Osmond closed her letter to her son and his family, "in a better world whear partting knowmoer is."[122]

No idea was more important to the working class in nineteenth-century America than the belief in "heavenly recognition."[123] Most correspondents thought they would know people at a celestial reunion. This was the hub of their response to death. "If not on earth we mey meet in heaven," John Shumway hoped after wondering whether his wife missed his kisses as much as he did hers. "Yes and that we shall know each other thair O what a pleasant thought."[124] This midwesterner's views of heaven were actually quite earthy. For in contemplation of heavenly delight, he expected to continue his spousal relationship.[125] So did James Masey, an African American husband who may have taken the Underground Railroad to Canada. "No more at present But yours in Body and mind," he declared to his wife, "and if we no meet on Earth I hope that we shall meet in heven."[126]

The hope of meeting in heaven was at the heart of the most dramatic exchange concerning death between husband and wife. "My dear wife, don't grieve after me. I am going to rest, I want you to meet me in Heaven," Asa V. Ladd wrote on the day he was scheduled to be executed. "I want you to teach the children piety, so that they may meet me at the right hand of God." Ladd was in Burbridge's Fourth Missouri Cavalry and ended up in the wrong place at the wrong time.[127] A Confederate prisoner of war, he had been chosen at random, along with five other enlisted men and one officer, to be shot in retaliation for the execution of seven Union prisoners of war taken at Pilot Knob. "I don't want you to let this bear on your mind no more than you can help, for you are now left to take care of my dear children," he continued practically. "Tell them to remember their father. I want you to go back to the old place and try to support yourself and the children. Leaving you in the hand of God," he became very tender at his last goodbye, "I send you my best love and respects in the hour of my death. Kiss all the children for me. You need not have no uneasiness as to my future state for my Faith is well founded and I fear no evil. God is my refuge and hiding place. Good by, Amy."[128] He wanted her to meet him in heaven, a place he imagined they could reunite as husband and wife.

Death was regularly seen as a religious gateway to a family reunion. Some correspondents emphasized the necessity of spiritual beliefs. "If we never meet again in this world," Louisa Downing advised her niece in 1872, "let us try to be prepared to meet in a better world than this whore parting is no more.... I want to no if your Mother is a profesor of religion and if you are if you are you posses more than this world goods it is good to live by and better to die by."[129] Louisa's husband also emphasized the hope of meeting his mother "beyond the grave ... & what a glorious meeting it will be."[130] The preparation for heaven so often referred to was Christian and part of a long tradition in American culture.

Some nineteenth-century correspondents, steeped in a worldview that concentrated on a theology of salvation, required a special born-again experience of Jesus to get to heaven.[131] In a later example of the importance of Christian doctrine, Georgia sharecropper J. M. Pearson admonished his sister and brother-in-law in the 1880s: "You have no Idea how much we all want to see you all but we are not able to go to see you so let us all live for Christ so that we may meet beyond jorden where there will be no more parting, neither sickness, suffering, nor sorrow, but where we can praise God forever through Christ our Redeemer."[132]

While the theological basis for admission to a celestial home was paramount to some, other working-class correspondents seemed to rely more on gut-level feelings than well-defined religious standards. After one Confederate soldier's death on the battlefield of the Atlanta campaign, a brother tried to reassure his sister that her husband was spiritually prepared to die. Though her husband was not a church member and had never taken the prescribed doctrinal path to salvation, friends and relatives paid minimal attention to his religious deficiencies.[133] His sergeant, based on the belief that God "knoweth them that trust in him," hoped that the soldier's wife would receive "that spirit to inable you to meet with them that have gone before."[134] Outward religious conformity was swept aside by God's way of knowing as well as man's feelings. This would seem to be another effort to make sudden deaths on the field of battle conformable to the model of the good death. But more divergence in class-based religious practices was at stake here.[135]

The rigors of godly judgment were considerably softened in working-class versions of an afterlife. Whereas past Calvinist teachings about death promoted an awareness of sinners confronting the terrible judgment of the Almighty, evangelical revivalism of the period was more sentimental and conciliatory.[136] The evangelists who urged their congregations to "come to

Jesus" assumed a personal agency that opened the gates of heaven to individual will. Grace was free and always available. This belief was "nurtured in the warm tides of revival fervor" and applied to Methodists, most Baptists, and all but Scotch Presbyterians.[137]

Though there were those who saw heaven as a restricted club for "members only," many working-class folk conceived of it as a place that was open to those who wanted to be there. They repeatedly admonished each other to meet there. "Dear Sister," one man wrote, "I some times feel just like I want to die and go meet those have gone before."[138] "When called from earth," another sister closed her letter with this wish, "may we meet in heaven where we Shall part no more."[139] After losing her "love," Elisabeth Cates confessed to her family that "some times I never can give him up; he is all my study day and nite But I keep it to my self I shead meny a tear aBout him." Her solution was celestial. "I wante all my friends to meet me in heaven for heven I beleave is my home."[140]

There was a voluntary aspect to many working-class conceptions of meeting friends in heaven, as if it were something they could agree upon in advance. This was based on three central beliefs: the existence of a specific location where loved ones could reunite after death; a continuation of personal identity that included recognition of family and friends in the afterlife; and the ability of most adults to go to that gathering place if they exercised their will and, perhaps as important, loved the people they wanted to meet. The ingredients that formed belief in a voluntary heaven were shared across the color line. Tillman Valentine, a sergeant in the Third US Colored Troops, composed a poem to honor his wife's father:

> Your aged father is gont to rest
> We his face weal no mor see
> but when we meete in hevens streetes
> O we shall hapy be
> his body is low beneath the sod
> his solde [soul] is floen [floating] on hye
> disturbe him not but let him rest
> let every tear be drye

The central theme of Valentine's poem is the belief that family and friends will meet "in heaven's streets" where they "shall hapy be." An afterlife where loved ones were reunited was an almost universal conviction in the American

Wearing his Grand Army of the Republic medal, Tillman Valentine, a sergeant in the Third US Colored Troops, is dressed for his meeting, likely located in Jacksonville, Florida, where he remained after the Civil War. This veterans' organization was open to all Union soldiers who had fought in the war.

Accessed on eBay by Jonathan White, published in *Pennsylvania Magazine of History and Biography* 139, no. 2 (April 2015).

working class.[141] Many, like Valentine, had no doubt about the ultimate outcome, expressing certainty by using "when" rather than the conditional "if," and ending the poem on a note of triumph.

The certainty of a heavenly home was often based on gut feelings. "[F]ather sayes he nows that they are to gether fore they loved each other so," a sister assured her sibling about the heavenly reunion of their mother and brother. Heaven was a place of love, and loving was the way to reunite in the afterlife. But if some put their emphasis on loving God, more people emphasized loving each other. "O let all of us make heaven our homes," she advised, as if this were a geographical choice under the control of everyone in her family.[142]

Specific Christian images of judgment were sometimes highlighted in descriptions of death and dying, but many of the folk spurned the threat of godly justice, seeming to believe they had already confronted a "terrible justice" on earth. The subtext of their writing about death and the afterlife was that they had paid their dues in the coin of pain and suffering in this life, and thus "deserved" a better future in a place where intimacy of all kinds— conjugal, familial, parental, and communal—would be experienced forever without fear of disruption.

What is unexpected and, at first glance, a contradiction is the hopefulness behind their constant fixation on death. One North Carolina Confederate, a devout and dutiful Christian father, admonished his sons: "be good boys and repent of your sins and do no sin afterwards." But even with such high standards, he was optimistic about their chances to reunite in the afterlife. "[Y]ou pa hopes to meet you in heaven where we will always be together and have no trouble."[143] Three months later, he had relaxed his theological scruples, telling his brother-in-law that he was often preoccupied with thoughts of his "Dear Wife & little wons at home. I dream of them often." He believed that the odds were against him surviving the war. But he added, "if I do not I *feal* that I shall meet them in heaven."[144] Fearful of death, he clutched the common consolation of a family reunion in heaven based on his feelings, not on religious doctrine. Most working-class Americans had been schooled in the theology of sin and salvation, but feelings often outweighed theology in their anticipation of a heavenly reunion with their loved ones. "I feel that I shall meet them in heaven" was a widely shared assumption, based on love that was familial and also communal.[145]

Significantly, heavenly admission was rarely limited by religious absolutes in working-class letters. Though their source was biblical, working-class versions of heaven had few of the trappings of traditional Christian iconography. Angels were scarce; the pearly gates and God's throne were missing; no harps were playing, and music was infrequent.[146] Moreover, knowing and loving God sometimes seemed secondary. In fact, heaven was rarely pictured as a place of worship.[147] What was important was meeting family and friends and being together—in a state forever unchanged—after death. Working-class heaven was not an otherworldly abstraction; it was an American village—only better—because relationships with family and friends were permanent.

The social aspects of the church were often more important to working people than religious ideology.[148] The church was, for many, more valuable as a gathering place than a doctrinal incubator. This is consistent with the unimportance of theology in working-class considerations of heaven. Injunctions such as "Let us meet" were more common than theological qualifiers or doctrinal limits based on restrictive admissions policies. One white female mill operative simply stated about her brother, "he is gone no more to return to us but we must meet him sooner or later."[149] In many cases, though not all, admission to heaven seemed wide open. This was true for working-class whites as well as people of color. Jesse McElroy, an African American who moved from South Carolina to Texas, was determined that the time he had left on earth "shall be spent in preparing myself for 'that house not mad with hands eternal in the heavens.' I want to meet you thare," he wrote his sister-in-law after the Civil War. He reminded her that they were old "and will probably never meet in this world but thare is nothing to hinder us from meeting in Heaven."[150] The preparation he had in mind was no doubt religious, but his sense of personal control over an afterlife reunion was quite worldly.

One of the more striking aspects of both Black and white conceptions of the afterlife is the silence surrounding race. This omission was not an enlightened projection of racial equality and harmony, at least on the white side, but a reflection of the tribalism that remained the bedrock of working-class feeling. People expected to meet extended family and friends who looked like them. This assumption was so taken for granted that no one had to mention it. A tombstone put up to honor the memory of white North Carolinian James Sydney Beavers, who died of a lingering illness months after fighting in the Second Battle of Manassas, was an exception that boldly illustrates the point.[151] Sid, as he was called, had been excommunicated in absentia from the Mt. Pisgah Missionary Baptist Church on October 26, 1861, "for opposing white and coloured equality in the church." His family proudly chiseled this fact on his tombstone, followed by the declaration: "then died his Father God to meet."[152] Relatives demonstrated their support for Sid's prejudice by displaying it on his grave. Moreover they flouted his official church expulsion, insisting on God's welcome in an afterlife where they never doubted the race of his heavenly companions. Their defiant announcement revealed an unwavering belief in a racially homogenous hereafter. There are

IMAGINING THE ETERNAL VILLAGE 229

hints that heaven was more integrated in the Black community. For example, several African American students in the postwar South imagined a reunion with their northern white teachers: "I hope that We Will be able to see each other again in this Life and if not I hope we may in heaven."[153]

While heaven was thought to be an attainable utopia, it was never deemed within reach on earth. Life in the here and now was always tending toward misery and want. Economic circumstances were often precarious. And survival could never be taken for granted. An ailing Mary Easterwood confessed to her sister that she had no money, but she could sell what she owned—her crops, horse, and hogs, even her "bed clothing"—to raise money for medicine. She was desperate to improve her physical condition but accepted her economic straits with a dose of future optimism if she recovered: "and i get my health i can go to woark and make them back again." Like many of her peers, she assumed full responsibility for the burden of her poverty and ill health. She hoped she could scrape together the money to buy enough medicine to cure her. But suspecting she might have consumption, and knowing it was an incurable disease, she closed her letter with a more fatalistic attitude toward the future: "i remain your Sister tell death So far you well if I never write again."[154]

The foundation of many working-class responses to life and death was a profound sense of powerlessness, perhaps best explained by Mary Caplinger in a letter to her soldier husband: "there is no use of complaingin about it for I will have to take whatever comes good or bad."[155] His absence created hardships and heartache, and she recognized her inability to change her condition. Feelings of powerlessness varied from situation to situation but what remained constant was an acceptance of the vagaries of existence. "I have nothing to write to you but greaf and trouble," one woman declared in 1844.[156] "[W]e must not expect all of the comforts in the world," another reflected in 1857, "if we do we shall be disapointed."[157] A Lowell mill girl warned her brother in the previous decade, "the world is cold pitiless and miserliy what I have suffered no one knows."[158] Widowed twice, another woman contemplated her mother's death in 1873 with these thoughts: "O well thare is not mutch real plasure in this beautful world sicknes sorow pain and death is our porsun here God grant that we will find rest by and by."[159] Working-class folk did not expect to escape misfortune or avoid trouble. Little wonder that they routinely closed their letters with "yours until death," a ubiquitous reminder of the impermanence of life and human connection.

230   LOVE AND THE WORKING CLASS

Heaven was the antidote for working-class pessimism. It was the utopian future where sickness, sorrow, and pain would be banished.[160] The promise of an untroubled afterlife, especially one that was restful and happy, was an important source of comfort in the present.[161] But perhaps it was also a source of self-esteem. The belief that you and your loved ones would eventually meet in heaven, whether based on doctrinal achievement or individual love, might offer a sense of pride and self-affirmation as well as a buffer against anxiety and self-doubt.[162]

Comparing otherworldly feelings to anticipations of joy at the end the war, one brother concluded, "How mutch more joy it will be when we meet in heaven where we will not part any more."[163] To say in 1864 that his eagerness to experience the end of the war could not compare to his joyful anticipation of meeting in heaven was a remarkable testament to his hunger for permanence in human relationships. This yearning for changelessness was the emotional lodestone of many common folk. Charles Watson's feelings were endlessly repeated: "May my life be spared through this campaign," he wrote his father. "[I]ff not may I so live so as to meet you all in that upper and better world where meeting and parting is no more. and where there is no war or any thing to disturb."[164] The central attraction of working-class heaven was the permanence of love. This was not mere rhetoric. Belief in the afterlife was a crucial coping mechanism on earth for Americans who were exposed to the constant loss of children as well as the deaths of young adults on an unprecedented scale during the Civil War.[165]

Middle-class Americans were also anxious for ways to cope with the death of men in their prime. Less than one book a year was published about heaven in the antebellum period; while in the ten years after the war, ninety-four books with detailed descriptions of heaven as a middle-class home were available to readers.[166] Americans of all classes were eager for reassurance that their Civil War dead were not really lost or abandoned.

But there were subtle differences in the class-based feelings about an afterlife. Two historians, studying the intellectual history of heaven, concluded that for middle-class Victorians "heaven was not earth transformed, it was earth stripped of the nonessentials."[167] Studying middle-class consolation literature, another cultural historian determined that heaven was depicted as "a continuation and a glorification of the domestic sphere."[168] Working-class heaven differed from its middle-class counterpart in that it was most often conceived as a dramatic transformation of earthly conditions. It was not the sense of continuity but of discontinuity or contrast with this life that was emphasized. There was a longed-for divide between earth and heaven, especially the absence of pain and suffering. For the working class, heaven was unequivocally earth transformed, rid of its essential misery and physical burdens.[169] Even in the domestic conceptions of heaven, where there was significant overlap in middle- and working-class ideas of the reconstituted family, the former emphasized the continuation of human love, while the latter focused on the elimination of loss and change.[170]

Terse or expansive in their descriptions, reassured or distressed in their judgments, many working-class correspondents focused on the individual death. Others, however, placed single deaths in a larger context of community life. Whichever approach they took, death was central to their experience of intimate family relationships. Newborn infant death was thought to be a release from the burdens of living. The death of the aged, often predicted in advance and witnessed by a circle of intimates, was frequently received with equanimity. It was thought that the elderly were relieved of life's burdens and could expect compensations in an afterlife of peace, rest, and the enjoyment of permanent relationships with kin. The sudden death of a child, as well as an adult in the prime of life, was more unsettling, especially as the model of a good death was difficult to impose. This included working-class soldiers whose responses to death ranged from sympathy to hardened detachment. Death was often stripped of the hazy filters of middle-class conventions by their honest and blunt reports.[171]

If the plain folk had an intimacy with death, then death may have been their most significant expression of intimacy with the living. That is, they often projected the clearest sense of their feelings about living relationships through the medium of death. Reflected in the mirror of death was the most intense emotional expression in working-class correspondence: a painful yearning for personal attachment without loss.

Their mordant drumbeat of death often masked an unexpected hopefulness. Death held a utopian promise for working-class Americans: an afterlife where they were rewarded by the capacity to give and receive love without fear of change. The most-repeated image of heavenly bliss was collective— the goal was to rejoin a group—to reconstitute an eternal village of family and friends outside of time. Working-class heaven contained a dramatic transformation of earthly relationships. And fundamental to the longed-for divide between earth and heaven was relational permanence. Unattainable on earth, their letters ritualistically closed with a paradoxical affirmation of emotional commitment within the boundaries of time. "Yours until death" was a recurrent reminder of the impermanence of life, and the always imminent loss that lurked behind any human attachment. The irony, however, was that many people expected to be together after death. But the contradiction was reconcilable in the here and now. Those who closed their letters with "yours until death" affirmed a willingness to take their connection with husbands, wives, friends, and relatives to the limits of earthly time. Maybe that is as meaningful a promise as we mortals can make to one another.

Epilogue

Nineteenth-century Americans with little education and modest means wrote many extraordinary letters. They almost never achieved prominence in the world at large. Nonetheless, families and friends preserved their expressions of hope, their feelings of sorrow, their avowals of affection, and their enjoyment of the funny side of life. Sometimes they corresponded during momentous events, like the Civil War, but often they wrote amid the mundane, quotidian grind of ordinary life. Whatever their outward circumstances, they struggled, with no other channels of communication, to stay connected to family and friends who were no longer part of their face-to-face community.

After reading thousands of their letters and tapping a large number for this book, perhaps it is fitting that the shortest letter in this bulky stack of mail should end the volume. Written by Isaiah Francis Wilson, it has a singular language, style, and content. His two-line letter was composed in the Mohawk language of Kanien'kéha, part of a Northern Iroquoian linguistic group. Unique in itself, his message in Mohawk was followed by a one-sentence English translation: "I guess there is a great many miles between here and your home, is not that so Friend."[1]

Luckily for us, the teacher who received his dispatch, Esther Hawks, had a deep appreciation for the humanity of her correspondents and the value of their letters. Although we know immeasurably more about her than we do about Isaiah F. Wilson, she bequeathed us an invaluable gift by saving his letter. The letter, together with his military service record and a variety of supplementary material, creates a surprisingly rich and historically significant account.

From his US Colored Troops military service record, we know that Wilson was a Canadian who identified his birthplace as Brantford, named for a famous Mohawk chief. This village was situated on land once owned by the Iroquois First Nations in the province of Ontario.[2] At the time he was mustered into the Union army, he was five feet, four and one-half inches tall, with brown eyes, black hair, and a light complexion.[3]

Love and the Working Class. Karen Lystra, Oxford University Press. © Oxford University Press 2024.
DOI: 10.1093/oso/9780197514221.003.0010

234   LOVE AND THE WORKING CLASS

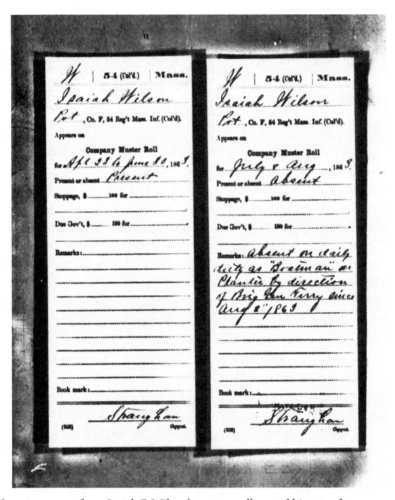

These two pages from Isaiah F. Wilson's muster roll record his attendance, special assignments, and other circumstances of his military service. He was logged "Present" in Company F of the Fifty-Fourth Massachusetts Infantry in late April through June and then "Absent" in July and August. The notation indicated he was serving as a boatman on the *Planter* beginning August 2, 1863.
US Colored Troops Military Service Records, 1863–1865, National Archives.

We know from his letter that Isaiah Francis Wilson could write in both English and his native tongue. The linguistic order of the letter, first Mohawk followed by English, signals Wilson's primary ethnic identity. The birthplace listed on his official US military service record vouches for Wilson's Mohawk heritage; so does the 1851 Canadian census, which indicates that Isaiah

EPILOGUE   235

Wilson was born in Grand River, as was his mother.[4] Grand River was the home of the Six Iroquois Nations, which included the Mohawk. The entirety of Wilson's Civil War soldier's file, however, represents him as a Black man. This is not surprising, given that Wilson volunteered for the first northern regiment of Black troops, the famous Massachusetts Fifty-Fourth.[5]

The Massachusetts Fifty-Fourth is recognized as an all-Black regiment, and Wilson's service may indicate that he had some African ancestry and recognized his multiracial heritage. This is plausible because Mohawks were known to have welcomed runaway slaves and may have encouraged or at least accepted intermarriage with them.[6] Isaiah was living in Oberlin, Ohio, and working as a laborer just before he volunteered for military service in 1863.[7] Oberlin was a hotbed of abolition sentiment, and the distinguished Black lawyer (and later state representative) John Mercer Langston was actively promoting the enlistment of Black soldiers.[8]

Wilson was likely recruited in a group. Throughout the country, men joined with friends and family in the expectation of staying together for support. He was one of eighteen soldiers from Oberlin who joined the Massachusetts Fifty-Fourth.[9] He was twenty-one and single at the time. If he had some African ancestry, joining a regiment with his Black comrades and coworkers would have seemed natural. Even without African lineage, Wilson would have been marginalized by his Indian ancestry in an all-white regiment. Clearly he found acceptance in the Black regiment.

Esther Hawks, the recipient and preserver of his missive, was teaching African American soldiers to read and write in Beaufort, South Carolina, in January 1863.[10] Three months later, she began practicing medicine at the hospital for "colored soldiers" she helped establish in Beaufort with her husband.[11] After the assault on Fort Wagner, wounded soldiers from the Fifty-Fourth were transported to the hospital in Beaufort. According to a compilation of the injured, Wilson was not wounded in the legendary assault on Fort Wagner by the Massachusetts Fifty-Fourth.[12] It is likely, therefore, that he helped transfer the wounded men and met Esther in a Beaufort classroom.

At the time he wrote his teacher, September 15, 1863, Wilson was a boatman on the steamship *Planter*.[13] Mohawk men had reputations as skilled boaters.[14] Though not conclusive, this assignment might signal that Wilson's Indian identity was well known among the officers in his regiment. The *Planter* was a special boat in several respects. It was a Confederate ship that was hijacked for the Union cause in an extraordinary tale of heroism,

236 LOVE AND THE WORKING CLASS

boldness, and smarts. It was also special because, in combining size and a shallow draft, it was capable of hauling fourteen hundred bales of cotton or its equivalent weight in troops and material along shallow coastal waters.

The story of how the *Plantar* went from Confederate hands to Union control is one of the more daring exploits of the Civil War, On May 13, 1862, Robert Smalls, a bondsman serving as a rigger and stevedore on the crew of this Confederate craft, impersonated the rebel captain, who was ashore with his officers, and sailed the steamship out of Charleston Harbor under the noses of twenty guards on the wharf.[15] He continued to execute his ruse and boldly sailed toward Fort Sumter, where a Confederate officer on duty gave the Plantar a signal to pass. Rather than heading toward Charleston's outer Confederate forts, Smalls eventually picked up speed and swung straight into the lines of the Union blockade, flying a white flag of surrender. Luckily the Union troops saw *Plantar*'s white bedsheet in time. The captain of the Union blockader boarded the steamship while the Black crewmen shouted triumphantly. After the US flag was hoisted at the crew's urging, a Black woman and three small children emerged from the hold.[16]

Robert Smalls carried off an amazing escape that included six of his enslaved crewmen as well as his wife and children. But he did more than deliver people and a boat into Union hands. He brought cargo that included a canon, a howitzer, additional guns, ammunition, and a book of secret signal flag codes being used by the Confederates. Most important, Smalls knew where all the Confederate fortifications in Charleston Harbor were located as well as where booby traps were hidden. The army bought the *Plantar* from the navy in the fall of 1862 and Smalls became the boat's captain in December after more heroics at the helm. This was the remarkable history of the boat where Isaiah Wilson was serving as a crewman when he wrote Esther Hawks.

"I guess there is a great many miles between here and your home, is not that so Friend" was his English translation of the Mohawk text that began his letter.[17] Deeply embedded in a sense of place, his message is one of sympathy for her separation from family and friends. But by asking her a question, he opened up the conversation to her feelings as well as his own. "[I]s not that so Friend" connected him to her perception of reality. "How are you doing so far from home?" could be the mundane American translation of Wilson's poetic line.

But another interpretation, based on a Dakota Sioux linguistic convention, might be closer to Wilson's intention. In the Dakota tradition, "It is so" is a sign of kinship and often ended a declarative sentence. Though Wilson's tribal lineage was Mohawk, the Dakota parallel is suggestive. When Wilson finished his one-line letter with the phrase "is not that so Friend," he might have been saying that his teacher felt like part of his family. And by turning the phrase into an interrogative, he may have been asking whether she shared similar feelings.[18]

Beginning his letter with the words "I guess . . ." encourages a reciprocal exchange of feelings. The number of miles between her home and where she is now is a fact. But the question embedded in the narrative implicitly recognizes that home is also an emotional state. The uncertainty has to do with Esther's feelings of home. The distance "between here" and Esther's home may shrink if Esther is happy and safe. Wilson communicates sensitivity to her state of mind, openness to her reality, and a powerful invitation to share her feelings in this one line.

Isaiah's artful message is striking for its quiet listening and loving acceptance of whoever Esther is and whatever she feels. There may be distant echoes of the popular vernacular poem: "When this you see remember me / tho many miles apart we be." But the difference is striking. The "remember me" poem centers on the sender, while Wilson's note is focused on the emotions of the receiver. But he is also expressing something of his own emotional affinity. Writing in the Mohawk language, Wilson asserts his Indian identity and the powerful pull of the people he has left for toil and adventure.[19] His empathy for Esther is grounded in his own yearning to return. The lines have power because he expressed a relatable longing for the comfort and belonging of home, not only as a location or place, but as an emotional state. Isaiah F. Wilson connected to Esther Hawks by imagining that she too wanted to go home. It is the act of shared imagination combined with the need and effort to know the feelings of another human being that makes his brief letter so affecting.[20]

Wilson definitely returned to his First Nation roots in Canada after the Civil War. The 1881 Canadian census closely matches what is known about him from his US military record. He is thirty-nine, living in Brantford, Ontario, his birthplace, and is employed as a sailor. He is identified as African, which no doubt refers to skin color, and his country or province of origin is registered as West Indian, which in the 1881 census "refers to individuals descended from Aboriginal peoples of Canada."[21] This is a category that includes the First Nations, or Indigenous people of North America, and corresponds with his Mohawk heritage. He is single and living with two

238 LOVE AND THE WORKING CLASS

First Nation women. The youngest, age eighteen, shares his surname and is likely a relative.[22]

Following Wilson's life course after the 1881 Canadian census is more challenging and requires a willingness to accept anomalies in records that otherwise fit the known facts. A register for Isaiah F. Wilson, created by the US National Home for Disabled Volunteer Soldiers in 1907, exactly renders the details of his military service, including his racial identification as a member of the Massachusetts Fifty-Fourth.[23] The Hampton, Virginia, branch of the old soldier's home, where he was sent, had been established to serve African Americans.[24]

Personal details in the Hampton profile include his prior residence in New Jersey, his work as a carpenter, and his marriage to a woman named Lizzie. She was a second-generation Irish American who was born in Pennsylvania, according to the 1900 US census. They married in 1893 but apparently had separated by 1905, when he told a New Jersey state census worker that he was a widower. He was more forthright with the Hampton registrar two years later, admitting that he was still married but had no idea where his wife was. Sometime in the last half dozen years of his life, and certainly by the last two, Wilson claimed Michigan as his birthplace.[25] The timing was closely linked to the start of his chronic kidney disease, which the Hampton ledger clerk, whether medically accurate or not, dated to October 1905. Reinventing himself as a US citizen was a prudent fabrication for a poor, single man seeking medical assistance and help with daily life from the US government. We know today that being an Indigenous person who may have had Black ancestors increased his risk of kidney disease. We also know that the early stages of this disease may produce few symptoms and that Isaiah may not have realized how sick he was until his illness was quite advanced.[26]

Wilson forthrightly claimed his Canadian birthplace and heritage as a young man in the Civil War. His late life reinvention was likely prompted by his desperate circumstances. The aging Isaiah was visibly struggling with the very concept of home that he so sensitively limned in his long ago letter. "I guess there is a great many miles between here and your home, is not that so Friend" speaks to Wilson's plight. His much younger wife had left him. He had no children, and no members of his family or tribe lived nearby to support him. Chronic nephritis would kill him, and as his kidneys failed, he turned to the veteran's home, the one American community that offered him

EPILOGUE 239

support. One hopes that he found some solace from the comrades-in-arms who took refuge beside him.[27]

Today it is easy to bridge spatial separation with talk. For the average American in much of the nineteenth century, only words on paper could cross expansive physical boundaries. These words were often sounded out phonetically by the barely literate. Because of this, the reader can listen to poor, working people before any recording device was available to capture their spoken language. Readers can also observe the rituals of courtship and marriage before the progression of urbanization and industrialization forever changed the physical and emotional landscape of America. Entering the lives of these humble correspondents through their writing fosters an understanding of their intimate feelings.

Paradoxes and contradictions abound in their lives. Nonromantic attachments were demarcated by group identity and heavily mediated by group support. Nonetheless, working-class mate selection demanded a narrowing focus on one individual while at the same time remaining loyal to one's tribe. Couples marrying for nonromantic love were sometimes caught in the push-pull of the individual versus the collective.

The common practice of defining one's tribe by geographical boundaries—towns, villages, or neighborhoods—gave working-class Americans an established identity. Most often, however, only racially similar people were considered group members. The field of choice in mate selection almost always excluded different races. However diverse the actual place they called home, color was their tacit inner boundary.

Other paradoxes in working-class mate selection were less durable and had fewer negative consequences. Men voluntarily disrupted their communal attachments for adventure, dreams of riches, or economic survival, as well as war, yet they continued to maintain their emotional connections to marriageable women at home. Young men often intended to return, even if this proved a false hope. Young women mostly stayed home, waited for the men to return, and accepted the available pool of eligible men. If they moved, women quickly reconstituted their tribal loyalties in their new location. Once married, however, they held tightly to their communal identity.

Though romantic love did not dominate the majority's choice of mates, it hovered in the background and could sometimes exert a pull away from community bonds. For the majority, love inhered in the act of choosing the best available person from the group to marry, not in deep devotion to a unique combination of specific qualities that the loved one possessed. While the majority married under the old rubric, a minority were adopting some romantic courtship beliefs and behaviors.

The minority who engaged in romantic practices during courtship and marriage was in the vanguard of a change that may have been unstoppable as small towns and villages across America gave up their young people to larger cities, immigration to urban centers skyrocketed, and mass culture advanced its tentacles at the turn of the twentieth century.[28] The old mate selection system was based on strong community ties that would weaken, not with migration per se, but with the permanent waves of out-migration of the young. Tribal courtship still existed, but the growing power of mass culture combined with a strengthening education system promoted the individualism of romantic love. Personal feelings began to trump social commitments and communal obligations.

Romantic love was making inroads in working-class culture, but the individualism it both reflects and inculcates was not yet ascendant in 1880 when waves of immigration, growing urban centers, a national market economy, and the expansion of mass culture were poised to noticeably change the American social landscape. Community attachments, whether in rural towns, villages, or urban enclaves, were still the emotional core of working-class intimacy. But the love that satisfied their hunger for connection was being redirected by social and cultural forces beyond their control. Basic conceptions of what it meant to be a person were shifting, growing from and being nurtured by a romantic ethos that promoted self-expression and personal fulfillment over collective bonds. The transition, however halting, to a different practice of intimacy had begun.

Acknowledgments

This book has been a labor of love (in content and in purpose) from the research to the final draft. In some ways it was a solitary journey. And yet, like most history books, the research and writing involved people at libraries, archives, conferences, internet sites, publishing houses, book groups, and more. Even an attempt to list all the names of the known contributors to *Love and the Working Class* would still be to miss the individuals, unknown to me, who made a contribution by coming to work and doing their job well. In recognition of their oft-overlooked assistance, I would like to thank

The extremely efficient interlibrary loan department at California State University, Fullerton, who provided an invaluable service by finding and sending (with lightning-fast speed) the articles and book chapters I requested.

The canvassers at Ancestry who copied and digitized a Grand Canyon's worth of primary sources and the programmers who organized the data in algorithms that allowed me to undertake wide-ranging and diverse record searches with only a computer and Wi-Fi.

The visionary librarians, the computer techs, and the staff who helped digitize thousands and thousands of nineteenth-century letters with more coming online every year. They provided ready access to valuable evidence located throughout the country.

The many librarians and archivists who organized, maintained, and protected manuscript collections in the institutions I visited.

The unidentified academics who judge the scholarly merits of book manuscripts for publishers. They carry out essential and undervalued work. Mine offered very helpful suggestions for improving my manuscript.

The unsung workers who turned nineteenth-century photographs and letters into high-resolution TIFF files that the designers in the art department adapted for my book.

242 ACKNOWLEDGMENTS

I cannot name all the organizers of major conferences where I gave papers, but I am grateful for their efforts, and especially those of their staff and helpers, whose hard work behind the scenes is usually underappreciated. I was especially thankful for the opportunity to present a paper based on my research for this book at the first History of Emotion Conference in the United States, held at George Mason University in 2018 and organized by Peter Stearns and Susan J. Matt. Over the years I gave other papers on my research at the European Association for Early American Studies, the California as well as the National American Studies Association, the American Historical Association, and the Western Association of Women Historians. These were opportunities to think about my letters, dig for cultural patterns, and present my ideas to audiences of professional scholars.

Many types of professionals helped bring this book to press. My Oxford University Press acquisition editor, Nancy Toff, had many hats to wear as a senior vice president but found the time for what I would call a "tough love" content edit that resulted in a stronger manuscript. She has a steely-eyed approach to prose that was very valuable in the late revision process. My project manager, Zara Canon-Mohammed, never wavered in her support and encouragement. I cannot thank her enough for her gracious efficiency and her timely follow-up to my questions, worries, and difficulties. Her gentle kindness and tactful interventions were a constant source of reassurance. Ponneelan Moorthy and Kalpana Sagayanathan were in charge of production, and their continued attention to detail was critical to the quality of the finished volume. In addition, they kept the book-making "trains" running on time.

My intellectual life has been sustained by several scholarly interest groups. I presented a paper to the Huntington Library Senior Scholars Seminar and benefited from the lively discussion that followed in the seminar room and at lunch. Mac Rohrbough started the group and has always been a source of encouragement and a model of scholarly commitment, as has Sarah Hanley, who was especially generous to lesser-known scholars. Sarah has a searching intellect and is a fierce defender of intellectual excellence wherever she finds it.

Carol Rigolot took over the Senior Seminar from Mac and continued the tradition of scholarly excellence and dialogue. The graciousness of her nuanced leadership skills was striking. Carol is another generous listener whose affirmation of my work, given her own achievements, has meant a great deal.

ACKNOWLEDGMENTS 243

The mantle of leadership has passed to Dan Horowitz, who has kept up the tradition of lively presentations accompanied by robust question-and-answer sessions. My colleague and friend Leila Zenderland gave a brilliant presentation last year based on her remarkable book project that focuses on the participants from twelve countries who attended an important seminar at Yale. Leila never settles for glib answers and tackles the hard questions in all her work, with intellectual honesty and a probing intellect. She has finely honed editorial skills, an ear for language, and a special willingness to help younger scholars.

Other Huntington Library friends and scholars whom I have known for many years and whose interest in and support of my scholarship has been important to me include Helen Horowitz, Colleen Jaurretche, Judy Raftery, and Barbara Donagan. What a joy it was to travel with Geoff Shrager and Colleen to Ireland and Sicily and with Judy to the old Hapsburg Empire as well as to conferences around the United States. And what a joy it was to share Huntington lunches and Pasadena dinners with Helen, Colleen, Judy, and Barbara Donagan, an independent scholar whose conversation was informed by first-rate scholarship, a keen intellect, and a wry sense of humor.

There were many other personal connections and long-standing relationships that were important to making this book. Carole Srole was instrumental in organizing the sessions at the Berkshire Conference on the History of Women and the Western Association of Women Historians, where I presented papers. We have always shared a keen appreciation of the history of emotions. Carole is a key contributor, along with Nancy Fernandez, to the Southern California American Women's History Reading Group, which has been vital to my scholarly life by providing a place for intense dialogue on the latest books in the field. Other members of this professional reading group include Peggy Renner, whose goodwill and positive outlook toward any challenge has been an inspiration. I could say the same about Lois Nettleship, another longtime member, whose astute intelligence and dedication to scholarly excellence were regularly displayed in our book group and in private conversations, which always included our shared passion for opera and classical music. Nancy Fernandez has always been a generous listener in group and individual settings. She responded thoughtfully to descriptions of my book in various stages of development. I hope she and other good listeners know that they are irreplaceable.

I am also a member of a small but mighty general book club that spun off from a larger group sponsored by the Indianapolis Public Library. It has been

244 ACKNOWLEDGMENTS

a privilege and a joy to discuss twelve books a year on Zoom with Mary and Jim Kenny, Mike Przbylski, John Sturman, Rachel Kenny Turner, and Cindy Eversman. Mary preceded Rachel in a leadership role, and each member has brought special insights to our discussions. Mary (with Jim) raised twelve children and that, along with the rich panoply of other life experience, informs her discerning analysis of literature. She is a wise woman. Rachel, our current leader, is pursuing her PhD in epidemiology and works with data on traumatic brain injuries and seizure disorders. She brings her observational skills to discussions in which members grapple with the complexities of human experience.

Though I am retired, the Department of American Studies at California State University, Fullerton, is another group that has a special place in my heart. I regularly attend the Faculty-Graduate Student Colloquium and find that the presentations continue to swirl in my brain long after the occasion has passed. Faculty whom I see regularly at these talks (in person or on Zoom) include Susie Woo, Kristin Rowe, Carrie Lane, Alison Kanosky, Terri Snyder, Jesse Battan, Elaine Lewinnek, Sarah Fingal, Dustin Abnet, Eric Gonzaba, Leila Zenderland, Adam Golub, Randy Baxter, Arlene Ring, and Craig Loftin. American Studies continues to be a link that joins some of my lifelong friends. Mike Steiner, a beloved colleague, and Lucy Steiner, a beloved friend, nurtured community in the department for decades with unselfish generosity. They have a talent for friendship that includes bringing people together in their home over good food and wine. They give of themselves with a joyful energy and commitment to relationships that is extraordinary. I cherish their presence in my life.

I also cherish other friends who were my colleagues. Allan Axelrad relishes discussing his deeply thoughtful scholarship and is an enthusiastic supporter of his colleague's academic work, mine included. Inside and outside the classroom, Pam Steinle is committed to asking key cultural questions. Pam gave unstintingly to the master's degree program and tirelessly nurtured the PhD aspirations of many American Studies graduate students before she retired. She read my introduction and gave me positive feedback when it counted. Carolyn Thomas joined the Fullerton faculty this year, and her very quick mind and penetrating intellect, allied with David Spight's good-natured observations and wry wit, enliven any discussion. John Ibson and Steve Harrison also bring their talents to rewarding dialogue. John is a natural storyteller who sees the humor around him and can relate narratives of human foibles inside and outside the academy. He also delights in probing the

ACKNOWLEDGMENTS 245

cultural patterns of diversity. Steve often asks incisive questions and follows up with observations and queries that reflect a curious mind and a willingness to listen and understand other people's experience. I have unbounded respect for Doug Temple, who worked in a support staff role for many years at Fullerton. His sweet honesty, integrity, kindness, and unwavering courage in confronting obstacles have truly been an inspiration.

I have friends scattered across the country who have encouraged my work by accepting the tempo of my research and writing and by giving me warmhearted support. In Indianapolis these friends include D. Paul and Debby Thomas, Katherine and Fred Scott, and Susan Lawson. Paula Sturman, another Hoosier, loaned me her ancestral Civil War letters, which found their way into my book. Other Indiana family members include her husband, Steve Sturman, Jim and Emily Sturman, and Susan Beeman, who spends most of her year in Virginia. Since moving to St. Louis from graduate school in Cleveland, Mary Ruckdeschel, Linda Lindsey, and I have continued to share our work and family life.

I had many a lunch with Tiffany Benedict Browne in downtown Indianapolis (and phone calls since) as we hashed over our mutual writing experiences and other adventures in living. She brings a passion to the history of Indianapolis and an ear for lively prose. Benton Marks, my office landlord in Indianapolis, loaned me a huge antique desk where I did research and wrote on my aged laptop; his executive manager, Mandy George, was always a steady presence in the building and a congenial lunch pal.

I see Carolyn and Jim Payton and Will and Arlene Brewster every summer at the Stratford Theatre Festival in Ontario, Canada, where we share long conversations over breakfasts at our B & B. Our discussion sometimes continues at pre-theater dinners. This is a renewal experience that has enhanced my work and enriched my life.

In California, friends who tracked my book's progress include Jane Bryson in San Francisco; Denise and Bob Zondervan in Claremont; Will Nettleship in Placentia, Kitty Brennan in Laguna Beach, Gerlinda Carr in Garden Grove, Linda Schultz in Fullerton; and another Fullerton denizen, Pat Haley. Pat is a voracious reader who always has a book to recommend. We share a passion for detective fiction, a genre I sometimes call "brain candy," though I have considerable respect for many authors of the craft.

Family is precious and even though mine are geographically scattered, like many of my friends, we maintain connections through phone calls and visits. My brother, Torrey Lystra, is a remarkable visual artist and an author who has listened with curiosity, insight, and sympathy to all the minutiae of doing my book from contract to page proofs. He has lived a life of exceptional courage and love, using his artistic and spiritual gifts to empower others. My nephews—Matthew, Joshua, and Seth Lystra, their spouses Lindsey, Jaida, Holly, and their children—add smarts and fun to the family circle in Washington State.

My brother is very special and so is my sister, Gaylen Mollet. She sent a previous book I wrote on Mark Twain and his family to Oprah, urging her to adopt my book for her national book club. I was deeply touched. As this illustrates, she is a caring defender and advocate for her family. Her husband, Ralph, is her rock. My nephew Lucas Mollet, his spouse Jaime, and their children, and my niece Amanda Foster and her husband Nathan, add smarts and fun to the Texas circle. Adding to the Texas family album are my partner's daughter Kristina Nelson, her husband Mark, and their children. New York is where we visit my partner's son Gregory, his wife Elizabeth, and their children.

My life-partner John has never wavered in his support and encouragement for this project. Authors who do long-term projects will understand how much his steadfast belief in my work has meant to me. John patiently listened to my small and large gripes and to an assortment of writing quandaries. He has tracked my hopes, disappointment, elation, and deflation through the publishing process. It is often the little things that make or break a couple who live together over many years. John does little things that make me smile; he also good-naturedly undertakes the little things that I badly want to avoid, like pest control. His optimistic spirit is heartening and his belief in people's goodness is infectious. I am grateful for his companionship and most of all, his love.

And gratitude for love is the truest way to close this book.

APPENDIX A

Writing, Education, and Literacy

"Literacy" and "illiteracy" are slippery terms. In the United States today literacy is judged by a variety of standards. Those who read a little but cannot fill out an application or decipher a food label, or are unable to follow a simple children's story, are considered functionally illiterate. Other more complicated measures of literacy include the ability to understand the instructions on a traffic ticket or to interpret an insurance policy accurately. (This might qualify some PhDs as illiterate.) Such modern criteria, whatever their contemporary efficacy, are unworkable when applied to more distant eras. In the nineteenth century, for example, the army enlisted men who could not sign their names. During World War II, the US Army rejected persons who were unable to read the written instructions necessary to accomplish a military mission.[1]

Historians who have examined reading and writing before the nineteenth century most often use the distinction between a signature and a mark—the classic X—to measure literacy in large groups. The scholarly consensus (with a few passionate dissenters) is that a signature indicates reading literacy. The logic is that teaching reading, because of its importance, would receive priority over learning to write a signature, which would generally occur after learning to read. Therefore those who could sign their names were judged to be "reading literate," and those who made a mark instead were considered illiterate.[2]

Writing is a more complicated skill set and requires more training than a simple signature. For that reason historians generally maintain it is unsafe to count signatures as a measure of writing literacy but practical to use them as indicators of an ability to read. Experts argue that a significant proportion of people who could sign their names would have already learned some basic reading skills. This is a convention of literacy research that may not hold up in individual cases but is the bedrock assumption behind the consideration of large numbers of official documents such as wills and military enlistment forms. Using the signatures on wills, for example, scholars have shown that a gender gap existed in the reading skills of ordinary Americans, with women lagging far behind men throughout the seventeenth and eighteenth centuries.[3]

Measuring the extent of basic writing skills is more problematic than gauging reading literacy. The study of writing literacy has faltered because of the problem of evidence.[4] Some historians have insisted that understanding writing literacy requires a "practice-based approach" in which the process of writing is studied as an experience, not just an abstract skill.[5] When approached through writing practices, such as the actual creation of letters by specific correspondents, clear-cut dichotomies between the literate and illiterate disappear.

An indispensable tool to evaluate literacy in large populations became available in nineteenth-century America. In 1840, fifty years after the census was initiated, the census takers began to ask ordinary Americans: "Can you read and can you write?"[6] The census enumerators concluded by 1870 that respondents consistently overestimated their ability to read even as they truthfully evaluated their writing skills. "Taking the whole country together, hundreds of thousands of persons appear in the class 'Cannot write' over and above those who confess that they cannot read," the 1870 census concluded. "This [cannot

248   APPENDIX A

write] is the true number of the illiterate of the country."[7] The problem is that reading was in all likelihood a much more common skill than writing. It was taught very early in American schools and had the cultural backing of a Bible-oriented religious culture. (Simply consider George Deal, a poor Ohio farmer who could probably read but definitely could not write.)

The census, whatever its limitations, has nonetheless proved to be an essential source for assessing overall rates of literacy in America.[8] Using census data, demographers Leo Soltow and Edward Stevens have estimated that the United States entered the nineteenth century with a white illiteracy rate hovering around 25 percent in the North but almost double that figure (40 to 50 percent) in the South. (This refers to reading illiteracy. Writing illiteracy would be higher still.) By 1840, however, these rates had dropped dramatically. They estimated that white southern illiteracy plummeted to 19 percent at the same time as northern illiteracy fluctuated between 3 and 9 percent. While the North-South divide was significant, wide variations in literacy also existed within those regions before the Civil War.[9]

Distinctions within regions tended to reflect differences in population density. Areas of high population density usually had higher literacy rates. This was due to the influence of churches, libraries, newspapers, businesses, and especially schools. Reading literacy lagged in areas that lacked these institutional resources and social networks. In 1840 white North Carolinians led the nation with a whopping 28 percent illiteracy rate. Predictably, the state of North Carolina was next to last in the number of schools per white children aged five to eleven.[10]

Other indispensable tools to evaluate nineteenth-century literacy in large scale male populations were the military records and soldiers' aid reports of the Civil War. A survey of northern soldiers by the US Sanitary Commission found that the educational mean for white soldiers was 4.4 years of schooling. Almost half the soldiers clearly had a limited common school education. The literacy rates of southern soldiers were much lower than their northern counterparts. Consequently, the unschooled warrior might sometimes find that letter-writing was harder than fighting.[11]

White soldiers born in New England had the highest literacy rates, averaging 5.2 years in school.[12] Connecticut had the lowest self-reported level of illiteracy at 0.3 percent and one of the best systems of public education. By contrast, up to 20 percent of the soldiers born in Kentucky and Tennessee had never attended school. Soldiers from those states averaged only 3.3 years of schooling.[13]

The opportunity for education was routinely denied to those in bondage. But free Black literacy was rising before the Civil War. In 1850, 63.8 percent of free Blacks aged twenty to twenty-nine were literate; the corresponding rate in 1860 was 70.9 percent.[14] After emancipation, education became a top priority in the lives of freedmen and women, especially for their children. Nineteen percent of Black Americans reported themselves to be literate in the first census (1870) after they were free. This compares to the 89 percent of self-reported literacy among whites. In the next twenty years Black Americans increased their literacy by an impressive 24 percent.[15]

In antebellum America, a great majority of northern children attended school from age five to nine, regardless of the wealth of their parents. Those who attended regularly probably received close to eleven hundred hours of reading instruction by age eleven, more than enough to achieve reading literacy. This is reflected in the 1840 census, which found northern states leading in literacy counts.[16]

In the South, reading literacy among the poor was much more precarious than in the North or West. Between ages five and fourteen school enrollments in the South were half what they were in the North. Both before and after the Civil War, according to Soltow and Stevens, "the average southern child was more likely *not* to attend a school in any given year than to attend one."[17] "I am glad Clarence is going to School," New Englander Henry Richardson wrote about his young nephew in 1862. "[T]ell Mother to pay his tuition as long as the school lasts and charge it to me do not let him grow up in ignorance there are hundreds of Children in this City [New Orleans] that are from ten to 16 years old and cannot read a word." Richardson's observations about southern children led him to conclude sarcastically, "so much for the glorious institutions of the south."[18] Only southerners whose families owned twenty or more slaves had a literacy rate that compared favorably to northern states.

Regular school attendance (associated but not always determined by the number of schools) was the greatest predictor of literacy rates in mid-nineteenth-century America. Faithful attendance produced basic reading literacy regardless of the wealth or ethnicity of parents.[19] And a large majority of northern children in all economic circumstances attended school from age five to nine.[20] Parental wealth played an increasingly important role, however, from ages ten through nineteen, years crucial for learning grammar and composition. The educational opportunity of nineteenth-century adolescents was strongly linked to the wealth and occupation of their parents.[21]

In 1853 the state of Ohio asked teachers to classify the number of schoolchildren who were literate. They were supposed to evaluate whether a child was able to read and write and to enumerate the student's individual coursework. Mid-nineteenth-century Ohio teachers did not give writing instruction to a majority of their pupils until age nine. Since school attendance began to drop off around age ten, as work-related activities competed for school time within working-class families, writing literacy had a precarious foothold, especially among poorer children.[22]

These mid-nineteenth-century teachers most often judged children to have achieved literacy when they were enrolled in a course on grammar. Less than 10 percent of their students studied grammar before age twelve, and the proportion of male students enrolled in a grammar course grew to only 27 percent by age sixteen. The Ohio teachers set a standard of writing proficiency at mid-century that excluded a majority of working-class children. Yet American adults wrote letters, no matter what their level of proficiency. For their willingness to brave their teachers' (and better educated contemporaries') scorn, I am grateful.

APPENDIX B

Literacy and Oral Culture

D. Brads, an African American man living in Indiana, offers an especially dramatic example of someone who melded oral and written communication. In 1852 he composed an entire letter, possibly to his brother-in-law, by means of words that he sounded out syllable by syllable.[1] Standard spelling is bracketed below each line.

ita ke this oper tu in ity to sem dy ou af ew lines to let you
[*I take this opportunity to send you a few lines to let you*]

kno whow iam geit ing aloing iam w elel at this time except
[*know how I am getting along. I am well at this time except*]

avery Bad ha ond iha ve m ot u sed it for to w eeks
[*a very bad hand. I have meant to send it for two weeks*]

ho ping that these few lin es May gow safe to hamd andfind you
[*hoping that these few lines may go safe to hand and find you*]

w elel tim es is ve ry hard here i x pect to go to del fy im to
[*well. Times is very hard here. I expect to go to Delfy in two*]

orthree w eeks iam sory to say that Mary is very low m owch of
[*or three weeks. I am sorry to say that Mary is very low much of*]

iw amt you two rit as soonas you gethis amd let mee kmo whow
[*I want you to write as soon as you get this and let me know how*]

th a re gettimg aloing
[*they're getting along.*]

I m cam Marind ud k I ncle p as fu rds en er writ as soo as you
[*(Name) married (name) as far as I know. Write as soon as you*]

get thi
[*get this.*]

Writ am let M kmo w Wher Marindu is hrot to Mee tha t he unds im
[*Write and let me know where Marinda is. He wrote to me that they were in*]

Mo B eles rile Whem he rote
[*Mobile's Isle [?] when he wrote*]

Nomore at this time

D Brads [to]

BurWick RoBerts

Jordain is ahard roab
[*Jordan is a hard road*]

252   APPENDIX B

Very few words are indecipherable—a testament to the power of phonetic spelling to communicate meaning. D. Brads had the usual working-class priorities in writing a letter—health, economic conditions, and news of family and friends. His last line, a postscript of sorts, was likely his metaphor for living an exemplary Christian life in order to reach heaven. He may also be alluding to the difficulties of living in the here and now. In Black culture, the metaphor of the road had many applications to the idea of both earthly and spiritual deliverance.[2] Clearly Brads was familiar with the phrase "Jordan is a hard road" and expected his family and friends to understand his meaning.[3]

With a strong will to communicate, John Fuller, a young white soldier, was also on the cusp of literacy. He too wrote a letter with the most basic alphabetic and phonetic skills. (Standard spelling is again bracketed below each line.) "OU ar," opened Fuller's love letter to Miss Frances in 1864.

i this mornin grasp mi pn in hand to pn you A few lins thos few lins leafs me
[*I this morning grasp my pen in hand to pen you a few lines. Those few lines leave me*]

well I hop thos few Lins may Reash your fur Distut hand And fin you in Joyen the
[*well. I hope those few lines may reach your far distant hand and find you enjoying the*]

sam Life Blesin . . . i Am destitut of nus thu Army is Anoop in we expect A fight
[*same life blessing. I am destitute of news; the army is a napping. We expect a fight*]

in A few Das Al tho tha solgrs ses tha Dnt think we will have mush fitn hier.
[*in a few days although the soldiers say they don't think we will have much fighting here.*]

"tll ma i Ritn to hier A few Das A go Also to Pa tll ma i Am in fin Sparets tlll ma if
[*Tell Ma I [have] written to her a few days ago, also to Pa. Tell Ma I am in fine spirits. Tell Ma if*]

she hiers from bruthers to writ to me wher tha Or . . . tll hier to B shoer to writ to me."
[*she hears from brothers to write to me where they are. . . . Tell her to be sure to write to me.*][4]

This is dialect writing at its purest, because it is created by the speaker as he attempts to recreate the sounds of his speech. It is a challenge to decipher because writing literacy requires visual memory—spelling words in a definite alphabetical pattern—as well as aural perception. Both Brads and Fuller were still in a world of sound when they sat down to write and were mostly guided by their ear.

What courage and audacity to write a letter after learning the alphabet and a little phonetic spelling. We witness the result of these barely literate men working more than 150 years ago to convert speech into text. Reading Fuller's first line "OU are," I was reminded of modern text messaging. Nineteenth-century correspondents, however, used pencil or pen and a sheet of paper. Surprisingly, no one down the generations tossed these sheets. So we inherit two vivid examples of letters that are remarkable testaments to the human need to be in touch.

Notes

Abbreviations

In view of the time it took to prepare this manuscript, some collections may have been reorganized or recataloged, augmented with additional material, as well as digitized. Citations reflect my individual research experience both in brick-and-mortar repositories and online. Collections I read in a digital format are clearly indicated by the URL in endnotes or in the identifier below.

Unless otherwise indicated, **all citations** of census data, military and pension documents, and the numerous records of births, deaths, marriages were accessed online through Ancestry.com.

ADL	Auburn Digital Library, Civil War Letters Collection, at http://content.lib.auburn.edu/cdm/compoundobject/collection/civil2/id/22267/rec/10
Amos	Amos Family Letters
Bronson	Anna Dorothy Mason Bronson Papers
Buck	Ella E. Buck Papers
Caplinger	Leonard T. Caplinger Papers
Coolidge	Oliver S. Coolidge Papers
CivWar	Civil War Collections
Confederate	Confederate Papers
CWLJ	Eugene H. Berwanger, ed., "Absent So Long from Those I Love": The Civil War Letters of Joshua Jones," *Indiana Magazine of History* 88 (September 1992): 205–39.
D. Lake	Delos W. Lake Papers
Duke	David M. Rubenstein Rare Book & Manuscript Library, Duke University
Downing-Whinrey	Downing and Whinrey Family Papers
EHHP	Esther Hill Hawks Papers
Flint	Francis S. Flint and Family Papers
Gaither	Gaither Family Papers
Garriott	John W. Garriott Letters
GDP	George Deal Papers
HEH	Henry E. Huntington Library, San Marino, California

254 NOTES

Hillman	Levi C. Hillman and Family Letters
IDL	Iowa Digital Library, Civil War Diaries and Letters, University of Iowa, at https://digital.lib.uiowa.edu/islandora/search/Civil%20War%20letters?type=edismax&cp=ui%3Aroot
IHS	Indiana Historical Society, Indianapolis, Indiana
ISL	Indiana State Library, Indianapolis, Indiana
JWL	John Wilson Letters
Johnson	William Lee Johnson Letters, Photocopies
Labrant	Jonathan B. Labrant Papers
Lipscomb	Lipscomb Family Papers
LC	Library of Congress, Washington, D.C.
LMGL	Lowell Mill Girl Letters, Center for Lowell History, University of Massachusetts Lowell Libraries, at http://library.uml.edu/clh/all/alet.htm
LWRD	Lois Wright Richardson Davis Papers
Mellish	George H. Mellish Papers
MHS	Minnesota Historical Society, Saint Paul, Minnesota
MOHS	Missouri Historical Society Library & Research Center, St Louis, MO
Newberry	Newberry Library, Chicago
Osmond	William R. Osmond and Family Papers
Photocopies	Ph
Reeves	Elizabeth Reeves and Andrew J. Reeves Papers
RLC	Riley Luther Correspondence
Saxton	Saxton Family Papers
SFL	Strayer Family Letters privately held by Paula Sturman, Culver, Indiana
Shattuck	Eliza Shattuck Correspondence
SLFP	Solon L. Fuller Papers
SHSM	The State Historical Society of Missouri. It has research centers in Cape Girardeau, Columbia, Kansas City, Rolla, St. Louis, and Springfield. The Western Historical Manuscripts Collection has been incorporated into the holdings of the State Historical Society. This collection includes correspondents located throughout the trans-Mississippi West.
Shumway	John P. Shumway Papers
TP	Typescript
UNC	Southern Historical Collection, Wilson Library, University of North Carolina at Chapel Hill
Upchurch	Isham Simms Upchurch Letters
Vanhorn	Arthur Vanhorn Family Papers

VS/UV	"Valley of the Shadow: Two Communities in the American Civil War." A digital archive of primary sources sponsored by the Virginia Center for Digital History, University of Virginia, http://valley.lib.virginia.edu/ (this is the portal web address and the best way to enter the website). The project is exceptionally well organized and the letter collections are easy to find. The key sorting device of letters, other than date, is location. The Guide to the Valley Project is found at http://valley.lib.virginia.edu/VoS/usingvalley/valleyguide.html.
VTLL	Virginia Tech Special Collections "Civil War Love Letters," found at http://spec.lib.vt.edu/cwlove/
Watson	Charles H. Watson Letters
Woods-Holman	Woods-Holman Family Papers

Introduction

1. Motoko Rich, "Colum McCann Wins National Book Award," *New York Times*, November 18, 2009, http://www.nytimes.com/2009/11/19/books/19awards.html. The phrase McCann used in his acceptance speech was "anonymous corners of human experience."
2. Eileen Boris, "Class Returns," *Journal of Women's History* 25 (Winter 2013): 74–87, esp. 81. Boris would, I believe, classify my work as the study of "intimate labor."
3. She continued: "for every thing is giting so deer that tha cant By hardly a naughf to gan." Watson was living in Jackson County, North Carolina, and her husband had joined the Confederate army. Elizabeth Watson to James Watson, October 29, 1861, Southern Appalachian Digital Collections, Western Carolina University, https://southernappalachiandigitalcollections.org/browse/search/elizabeth-watson-to-james-watson-october-29-1861.
4. Seth Rockman, "Class and the History of Working People in the Early Republic," *Journal of the Early Republic* 25 (Winter 2005): 527–35, quotation on p. 535.
5. Christopher Clark, "Comment on the Symposium on Class in the Early Republic," *Journal of the Early Republic* 25 (Winter 2005): 558.
6. Jennifer L. Goloboy argues for a cultural definition of the middle class in "The Early American Middle Class," *Journal of the Early Republic* 25 (Winter 2005): 537–45.
7. Elizabeth Alice Clement, *Love for Sale: Courting, Treating and Prostitution in New York City, 1900–1945* (Chapel Hill: University of North Carolina Press), 10.
8. See, for example, Christine Stansell, *City of Women: Sex and Class in New York, 1789–1860* (Urbana: University of Illinois Press, 1982). She used legal records, moral and labor reform reports, social welfare surveys, and case histories; Kathy Peiss relied on a wide range of reports by vice reformers, government agencies, and special investigative committees in *Cheap Amusements: Working Women and Leisure in*

256 NOTES TO PAGE 3

Turn-of-the-Century New York (Philadelphia: Temple University Press, 1986); Melissa A. Hayes found some remarkable evidence of sexual attitudes in "Sex in the Witness Stand: Erotic Sensationalism, Voyeurism, Sexual Boasting, and Bawdy Humor in Nineteenth-Century Illinois Courts," *Law and History Review* 32 (February 2014): 149–202; Robert Griswold deftly employs divorce records in *Family and Divorce in California, 1850–1890* (Albany: State University of New York Press, 1982); Beverly Schwartzberg examines evidence that resulted from the government investigation of Civil War pension applications in "'Lots of Them Did That': Desertion, Bigamy, and Marital Fluidity in Late-Nineteenth-century America," *Journal of Social History* 37 (Spring 2004), 573–600.

9. For example, see the classic studies by Bell Irvin Wiley, *The Life of Billy Yank: The Common Soldier of the Union* (Indianapolis: Charter Books, 1962); Wiley, *The Life of Johnny Reb: The Common Soldier of the Confederacy*, updated ed. (Baton Rouge: Louisiana State University Press, 2008); Lewis O. Saum, *Popular Mood of Pre–Civil War America* (Westport, Ct: Greenwood Press, 1980); and Saum, *Popular Mood of America, 1860–1890* (Lincoln: University of Nebraska Press, 1990); James M. McPherson, *For Cause and Comrades: Why Men Fought in the Civil War* (New York: Oxford University Press, 1997); Reid Mitchell, *Civil War Soldiers: Their Expectations and Their Experiences* (New York: Viking, 1988); Edwin S. Redkey, *A Grand Army of Black Men: Letters from African-American Soldiers in the Union Army, 1861–1865* (Cambridge: Cambridge University Press, 1992); Christopher Hager, *I Remain Yours: Common Lives in Civil War Letters* (Cambridge, MA: Harvard University Press, 2018); David Williams, *Rich Man's War: Caste, Class and Confederate Defeat in the Lower Chattahoochee* Valley (Athens: University of Georgia Press, 1998), esp. chapter 4; also Thomas E. Rodgers, "Civil War Letters as Historical Sources," *Indiana Magazine of History* 93 (June 1997): 105–10.

10. George C. Rable, *Civil Wars: Women and the Crisis of Southern Nationalism* (Urbana: University of Illinois Press, 1989); Elizabeth D. Leonard, *Yankee Women: Gender Battles in the Civil* War (New York: Norton, 1994); Drew Faust, *Mothers of Invention: Women of the Slaveholding South in the American Civil War* (Chapel Hill: University of North Carolina, 1996); Judith Ann Giesberg, *Civil War Sisterhood: The U.S. Sanitary Commission and Women's Politics in Transition* (Boston: Northeastern University Press, 2000); Carol K. Bleser and Lesley J. Gordon, eds., *Intimate Strategies of the Civil War: Military Commanders and Their Wives* (New York: Oxford University Press, 2001); Jane Schultz, *Women at the Front: Hospital Workers in Civil War America* (Chapel Hill: University of North Carolina Press, 2004); Catherine Clinton and Nina Silber, eds., *Battle Scars: Gender and Sexuality in the American Civil War* (Oxford: Oxford University Press, 2006); also their earlier *Divided Houses: Gender and the Civil War* (New York: Oxford University Press, 1992); LeeAnn Whites, *The Civil War as a Crisis in Gender: Augusta, Georgia, 1860–1890* (Athens: University of Georgia Press, 1995); Leslie Schwalm, *A Hard Fight for We: Women's Transition from Slavery to Freedom in South Carolina* (Urbana: University of Illinois Press, 1997); Jane Turner Censer, "Finding the Southern Family in the Civil War," *Journal of Social History* 46 (Fall 2012): 219–30; Stephanie McCurry, "Women Numerous and Armed:

NOTES TO PAGES 3–4   257

Gender and the Politics of Subsistence in the Civil War South" in *Wars within a War: Controversy and Conflict over the American Civil War*, ed. Joan Waugh and Gary W. Gallagher (Chapel Hill: University of North Carolina Press, 2009), 1–26; McCurry examines poor southern women's letters to governors in Virginia, North Carolina, and Georgia as an expression of class and gender that coalesced into a new political identity: the soldier's wife. Rita Roberts transcribes a diverse selection of African American letters in *"I Can't Wait to Call You My Wife": African American Letters of Love and Family in the Civil War Era* (San Francisco: Chronicle Books, 2022).

11. Albert L. Hurtado, *Intimate Frontiers: Sex, Gender, and Culture in Old California* (Albuquerque: University of New Mexico Press, 1999), esp. chapter 4; Malcolm J. Rohrbough, *Days of Gold: The California Gold Rush and the American Nation* (Berkeley: University of California Press, 1997); Susan Lee Johnson, *Roaring Camp: The Social World of the California Gold Rush* (New York: Norton, 2000). The three review essays cited below focus on gender, race, and ethnicity, suggesting that these are frequent concerns in western history (even as some essayists critique their absence). Class has not been given the same prominence. See Margaret Jacobs, "Western History: What's Gender Got to Do With It?," *Western Historical Quarterly* 42 (October 2011): 297–304; Karen J. Leong, "Still Walking, Still Brave: Mapping Gender, Race, and Power in U.S. Western History," *Pacific Historical Review* 79 (November 2010): 618–28; Elizabeth Jameson, "Looking Back to the Road Ahead," *Pacific Historical Review* 79 (November 2010): 574–84; Raúl A. Ramos argues for a new narrative in "Chicano/a Challenges to Nineteenth-Century History," *Pacific Historical Review* 82 (November 2013): 566–80. The narrative of western history has long included the US-Mexico borderlands. See Margie Brown-Coronel's argument for the importance of letters as an historical source in "Intimacy and Family in the California Borderlands: The Letters of Josefa del Valle Forster, 1876–1896," *Pacific Historical Review* 89 (Winter 2020): 74–96; and Erika Pérez, "The Dalton-Zamoranos: Intimacy, Intermarriage, and Conquest in the U.S.-Mexico Borderlands," *Pacific Historical Review* 89 (Winter 2020): 44–73.

12. Thomas Dublin, ed., *Farm to Factory: Women's Letters, 1830–1860*, 2nd ed. (New York: Columbia University Press, 1993); Dublin, *Women at Work: The Transformation of Work and Community in Lowell, Massachusetts, 1826–1860* (New York: Columbia University Press, 1979), esp. 47–48; Dublin, *Transforming Women's Work: New England Lives in the Industrial Revolution* (Ithaca: Cornell University Press, 1994). Dublin is an incisive analyst and far-sighted pioneer in the use of letters to study working-class Americans. Historical sociologist Karen V. Hansen also used working-class letters with insight and sensitivity in *A Very Social Time: Crafting Community in Antebellum New England* (Berkeley: University of California Press, 1994).

13. I have been encouraged and informed by the burgeoning field of emotional history. Its theoretical underpinnings are articulated by Susan Matt and Peter N. Stearns, *Doing Emotions History* (Urbana: University of Illinois Press, 2014); Jan Plamper, *The History of Emotions: An Introduction*, trans. Keith Tribe (New York: Oxford University Press, 2015); William M. Reddy, *The Navigation of Feeling: A Framework for the History of Emotions* (Cambridge: Cambridge University Press, 2001); Barbara

258   NOTES TO PAGE 4

H. Rosenwein, *Emotional Communities in the Early Middle Age* (Ithaca: Cornell University Press, 2006); Rosenwein, *Generations of Feeling: A History of Emotions, 600–1700* (Cambridge: Cambridge University Press, 2016).

Epistolary studies, a field with a more literary bent, has also been instructive. See, for example, the forty-four essays in Celeste-Marie Bernier, Judie Newman, and Matthew Pethers, eds., *The Edinburgh Companion to Nineteenth-Century American Letters and Letter-Writing* (Edinburgh: Edinburgh University Press, 2016).

14. Suzanne M. Stamatov, *Colonial New Mexican Families: Community, Church, and State, 1692–1800* (Albuquerque: University of New Mexico Press, 2018); Antonia I. Castañeda, "Engendering the History of Alta California, 1769–1848: Gender, Sexuality, and the Family," *California History* 76 (Summer–Fall 1997): 230–59; Deena J. Gonzalez, *Refusing the Favor: The Spanish-Mexican Women of Santa Fe, 1820–1880* (New York: Oxford University Press, 1999); Lee M. Penyak and Verónica Vallejo, "Expectations of Love in Troubled Mexican Marriages during the Late Colonial and Early National Periods," *The Historian* 65 (Winter 2003): 563–86; Miroslava Chavez-Garcia, *Negotiating Conquest: Gender and Conquest in California, 1770s to 1880s* (Tucson: University of Arizona Press, 2004); Maria Raquel Casas, *Married to a Daughter of the Land: Spanish-Mexican Women and Interethnic Marriage in California, 1820–1880* (Reno: University of Nevada Press, 2007); Andres Resendez, *Changing National Identities at the Frontier: Texas and New Mexico, 1800–1850* (New York: Cambridge University Press, 2005); Ramon A. Gutierrez, *When Jesus Came, the Corn Mothers Went Away: Marriage, Sexuality, and Power in New Mexico, 1600–1846* (Stanford: Stanford University Press, 1991); Rebecca Earle, "Letters and Love in Colonial Latin America," *The Americas* 62 (July 2005): 17–46. Earle's fascinating article compares terms of endearment in sixteenth- and eighteenth-century letters sent to wives in Spain from husbands in the Spanish Indies. These were privileged correspondents. Erika Perez sensitively analyzes the effects of social class on intimate relationships in *Colonial Intimacies: Interethnic Kinship, Sexuality, and Marriage in Southern California, 1769–1885* (Norman: University of Oklahoma Press, 2018). Jumping to the late twentieth century, Larry Siems in *Between the Lines: Letters between Undocumented Mexican and Central American Immigrants and Their Families and Friends* (Tucson: University of Arizona Press, 1992) has collected, translated, and edited letters of working-class people (most undocumented). These letters were written in Spanish in the late 1980s to early 1990s when long-distance phone calls to other countries were very expensive and the digital revolution was just beginning. The United Kingdom Science and Technology Council reported that the internet was used by 0.05 percent of people in 1990. While far removed from the nineteenth century, these Mexican and Central American correspondents illustrate that letter-writing is common where the need exists. I was intrigued by several parallels between their letters and the working-class correspondence in this book. They used almost no punctuation and included long lists of people whom they greeted or who sent greetings back. Siems cut these lists but he comments that they are an illustration of "the deep interconnectedness of the communities." See pp. ix–x. Another example of correspondence, including love

NOTES TO PAGES 4–5   259

letters, translated from Spanish but written in the early 1960s, is Miroslava Chavez-Garcia, *Migrant Longings: Letter Writing across the U.S.-Mexico Borderlands* (Chapel Hill: University of North Carolina Press, 2018).

15. See for example, Kathryn A. Sloan, *Runaway Daughters: Seduction, Elopement, and Honor in Nineteenth-Century Mexico* (Albuquerque: University of New Mexico Press, 2008); Martyn Lyons, *The Writing Culture of Ordinary People in Europe, c. 1860–1920* (Cambridge: Cambridge University Press, 2013); David A. Gerber, "Acts of Deceiving and Withholding In Immigrant Letters: Personal Identity and Self-Presentation in Personal Correspondence," *Journal of Social History* 39 (Winter 2005): 315–30; and Gerber's *Authors of Their Lives: The Personal Correspondence of British Immigrants to North America in the Nineteenth Century* (New York: New York University Press, 2006); Emma Griffin, "The Emotions of Motherhood: Love, Culture, and Poverty in Victorian Britain," *American Historical Review* 123 (February 2018): 60–85; Mary Blewett, "Yorkshire Lasses and Their Lads: Sexuality, Sexual Customs, and Gender Antagonisms in Anglo-American Working-Class Culture," *Journal of Social History* 40 (Winter 2006): 317–36; Barry Reay, *Microhistories: Demography, Society and Culture in Rural England, 1800–1930* (New York: Cambridge, 1996); Ginger S. Frost relies on lawsuits in *Promises Broken: Courtship, Class, and Gender in Victorian England* (Charlottesville: University Press of Virginia, 1995); Steve King, "Love, Religion and Power in the Making of Marriages in Early Nineteenth-Century Rural Industrial Lancashire," *Rural History* 21 (April 2010): 1–26; Peter Ward, "Courtship and Social Space in Nineteenth-Century English Canada," *Canadian Historical Review* 68 (March 1987): 35–62; Stephen Lassonde, *Learning to Forget: Schooling and Family Life in New Haven's Working Class, 1870–1940* (New Haven: Yale University Press, 2005); Francoise Barret-Ducrocq uses foundling hospital files in *Love in the Time of Victoria: Sexuality, Class and Gender in Nineteenth-Century London* (London: Verso, 1991); Steven E. Rowe offers a conceptually rich and sophisticated analysis of literacy in "Writing Modern Selves: Literacy and the French Working Class in the Early Nineteenth Century," *Journal of Social History* 40 (Fall 2006): 55–83; Richard B. Stott, *Workers in the Metropolis: Class, Ethnicity, and Youth in Antebellum New York City* (Ithaca: Cornell University Press, 1990), constructs the urban culture of young male (mostly) Irish and German immigrants, including language, clothing, food, and sports. Keith Breckenridge, in "Love Letters and Amanuenses: Beginning the Cultural History of the Working Class Private Sphere in Southern Africa, 1900–1933," *Journal of Southern African Studies* 26 (June 2000): 337–48, finds that intimate correspondence was collaborative and that personal letters were often read aloud, which leads him to reconsider the meaning of the private sphere in early twentieth-century South Africa.

16. David Henkin estimates that 161 million letters were mailed in 1860, with a per capita average of 5.15. By contrast he cites an estimate (made by Mary Livermore) that "a hundred and eighty thousand letters a day were sent or received by soldiers in the Civil War." Her claim would have resulted in a number that seems larger than life. See *The Postal Age: The Emergence of Modern Communication in Nineteenth-Century America* (Chicago: University of Chicago Press, 2006), 3, 137.

260   NOTES TO PAGES 5–8

17. Christopher Hager, *I Remain Yours: Common Lives in Civil War Letters* (Cambridge, MA: Harvard University Press, 2018), 4. This figure would mean that 2.75 million soldiers, one estimate of those who fought in the Civil War, had written and received an average of 181 letters. Of course the total number of soldiers who served is not the same as the figure in any one year of the four-year war. Enlistment and discharge dates, as well as death and desertion, would all affect a soldier's length of service. The number actually serving in any one year would vary. I doubt that this average applies to the working-class foot soldier.

18. James McPherson, *The War That Forged a Nation: Why the Civil War Still Matters* (New York: Oxford University Press, 2015).

19. Marcellus Mitchell to Rebecca, September 15, 1865, Marcellus Mitchell Correspondence, LC. Refer to chapter 1 for more details.

20. George to Sarah Deal, March 31, 1863, comments by Henry J. Souder, scribe, DL, Newberry. Sarah's ancestry (based on family lore) found in an undated, handwritten note on the back of her photograph, authored by an unidentified (maternal) great granddaughter. I give credence to the family's oral history. Refer to chapter 1.

21. Peter Van Wagenen to Mother, September 19, 1841, printed in *Narrative of Sojourner Truth, a Bondswoman of Olden Time, with a History of Her Labors and Correspondence Drawn from Her "Book of Life"* (New York: Oxford University Press, 1991; originally published 1850), 78–79. It is spelled Van Wagener in the 1850 edition. Also Carter G. Woodson, ed., *The Mind of the Negro: As Reflected in Letters during the Crisis, 1800–1860* (Washington, DC: Association For the Study of Negro Life and History, 1926; reprint, New York: Dover, 2013), 553. Consult chapter 7 for more details.

22. William J. Walker to John [his son], February 2, 1850, in Woodson, *Mind of the Negro*, 522. Refer to chapter 2 for more details.

23. Elizabeth Rawlings to Robert Rawlings, February 1, 1858, Brophy-Beeson Papers, HEH. Refer to chapter 2.

24. Seth Eastman to Horace Dresser, November 15[?], 1862, transcribed in *Private and Amorous Letters of the Civil War*, ed. Thomas P. Lowry (self-published, 2009), 28–30. See chapter 4.

25. H. H. to Miss O. Espy, February 14, 1863, Joseph Espey Papers, UNC. Consult chapter 7 for more details.

26. William Wood and J. R. Littlejohn to Cousins & friends, September 6, 1856, Lipscomb, UNC. Refer to chapter 4.

27. Eliza Bixby to brother, March 3, 1852, LMGL. Consult chapter 4 for a more detailed narrative.

28. Edward H. Spencer to Friend Barney, January 31, 1862, Saxton, HEH. Though their marriage appeared unstable, they were still together seventeen years after he was discharged from the army. Consult chapter 6 for more evidence.

29. Asa V. Ladd to Wife and Children, October 29, 1864, TP, Asa V. Ladd Papers, SHSM. The punctuation was likely added at a later date. Refer to chapter 8.

30. Tillman Valentine to Elizabeth Valentine, April 24, 1864, in Jonathan W. White, Katie Fisher, and Elizabeth Wall, eds., "The Civil War Letters of Tillman Valentine, Third US Colored Troops," *Pennsylvania Magazine of History and Biography* 139 (April 2015): 183–86. See chapter 8 for a more developed context.

NOTES TO PAGES 8–13   261

31. He was living in District 47, Lawrence County, Missouri, when the 1850 census was taken June 1.

32. Jasper Bell to William and Caroline Warm, July 5, 1851 [Jasper and Franklin Bell wrote separate messages in the same letter], Downing-Whinrey, SHSM. Refer to chapter 2.

33. Widow Peebles to Daniel Turner, September [1864], filed with Will H. Cobb's letter to Bettie V. Herring, October 11, 1864, Wright and Herring Family Papers, UNC. This letter required extensive research in census, demographic, and military records in order to provide the missing facts and indispensable details of contextualization. The research process and results are explained in chapter 1.

34. J. F. Gros to J. H. Creighton, February 12, 1888, J.H. Creighton Letters, SHSM.

35. Thomas Gaither to Mother, March 27, 1863, Gaither, UNC.

36. Sarah Barksdale to Son [William Holman], May 13, 1854, Woods-Holman, SHSM.

37. Riley to Mary Ann Luther August 4, 1862, RLC, Duke.

38. Unidentified Friend to Josh [Lipscomb], October 10, 1858, Lipscomb, UNC.

39. John Fuller to Miss Frances, April 19, 1864, SLFP, Duke.

40. Charles Henry Richardson to Mother [Lois Davis], January 1, 1864, LWRD, Duke.

41. See the superb series Labor Studies and The Working Class in American History published by the University of Illinois Press. Their backlist includes more than a hundred examples. Classic books on work in America include Alice Kessler-Harris, *Out to Work: A History of Wage-Earning Women in the United States* (New York: Oxford University Press, 1982); Susan E. Hirsch, *Roots of the American Working Class: The Industrialization of Crafts in Newark, 1800–1860* (Philadelphia: University of Pennsylvania Press, 1978); Jacqueline Jones, *American Work: Four Centuries of Black and White Labor* (New York: Norton, 1998); Susan Estabrook Kennedy, *If All We Did Was to Weep at Home: A History of White Working-Class Women in America* (Bloomington: Indiana University Press, 1979); Bruce Laurie, *Working People in Philadelphia, 1800–1850* (Philadelphia; Temple University Press, 1980); Sean Wilenz, *Chants Democratic: New York City and the Rise of the American Working-Class, 1788–1850* (New York: Oxford University Press, 1984); David Montgomery, *The Fall of the House of Labor: The Workplace, the State, and American Labor Activism, 1865–1925* (New York: Cambridge University Press, 1987). For a more recent classic in the field, see Seth Rockman, *Scraping By: Wage Labor, Slavery, and Survival in Early Baltimore* (Baltimore: Johns Hopkins University Press, 2009).

42. Violating the unspoken racial boundary in working-class courtship confirmed its presence. See chapter 3 for evidence in the familial and community response to the marriage of Eunice Richardson Stone to the Black sea captain William Connolly.

43. Folk songs (e.g., ballads) and folk literature (e.g., jokes or oral narratives) must stand rather abstractly for the whole group unless specific performers, along with their performance text and audience response, can be documented.

44. Susan J. Matt, *Homesickness: An American History* (New York: Oxford University Press, 2011), introduction, esp. 3–6. The difficulty of leaving home is explored in James Davis, "Music, Homesickness, and American Civil War Soldiers, *Lied und Populäre Kultur* 63 (2018): 35–52; also Frances Clark, "So Lonesome I Could Die: Nostalgia and Debates over Emotional Control in the Civil War North," *Journal of Social History*

262 NOTES TO PAGES 13-22

41 (Winter 2007): 253–82; Chad Montrie, "'I Think Less of the Factory Than of My Native Dell': Labor, Nature, and the Lowell Mill Girls," *Environmental History* 9 (April 2004): 275–95.

45. The 1880 statistic is striking. See Eric H. Monkkonen, *America Becomes Urban: The Development of U.S. Cities and Towns, 1780–1980* (Berkeley: University of California Press, 1988), 70–72.

46. See chapter 8 for evidence and analysis. The two most important books on death in the Civil War are Drew Faust, *This Republic of Suffering: Death and the American Civil War* (New York: Knopf, 2008), and Mark S. Schantz, *Awaiting the Heavenly Country: The Civil War and America's Culture of Death* (Ithaca: Cornell University Press, 2008).

47. Russell J. Johnson, *Warriors into Workers: The Civil War and the Formation of Urban-Industrial Society in a Northern City* (New York: Fordham University Press, 2003), 12.

48. Troy Rondinone, *The Great Industrial War: Framing Class Conflict in the Media, 1865–1950* (New Brunswick, NJ: Rutgers University Press, 2009), esp. chapter 2. His argument is that the Civil War provided the language and metaphors for constructing the relationship of labor and capital in postwar America.

49. See Justina Woods in chapter 2.

50. E. P. Thompson, *The Making of the English Working Class* (New York: Random House, 1963), 9, 11.

Chapter 1

1. Research on the social and cultural history of literacy is ample. Among the many works are Richard Brodhead, *Cultures of Letters: Scenes of Reading and Writing in 19th Century America* (Chicago: University of Chicago Press, 1993); Kathy Davidson, ed., *Reading in America: Literature and Social History* (Baltimore: Johns Hopkins University Press, 1989); William Merrill Decker, *Epistolary Practices: Letter Writing in America before Telecommunications* (Chapel Hill: University of North Carolina Press, 1998); Konstantin Dierks, *In My Power: Letter Writing and Communication in Early America* (Philadelphia: University of Pennsylvania Press, 2009); I. J. Gelb, *A Study of Writing: The Foundations of Grammatology* (Chicago: University of Chicago Press, 1952); Jack Goody, *The Interface between the Written and the Oral* (Cambridge: Cambridge University Press, 1987); Harvey J. Graff, *The Literacy Myth: Literacy and Social Structure in the Nineteenth-Century City* (New York: Academic Press, 1979); Harvey J. Graff, *The Labyrinths of Literacy: Reflections on Literacy Past and Present*, rev. ed. (Pittsburgh: University of Pittsburgh Press, 1995); Edward E. Gordon and Elaine H. Gordon, *Literacy in America: Historic Journey and Contemporary Solutions* (London: Praeger, 2003); Erik A. Havelock, *The Muse Learned to Write: Reflections on Orality and Literacy from Antiquity to the Present* (New Haven: Yale University Press, 1986); Catherine Hobbs, ed., *Nineteenth-Century Women Learn to Write* (Charlottesville: University Press of Virginia, 1995); Jennifer Monaghan, *Reading for*

NOTES TO PAGES 22–24   263

the Enslaved, Writing for the Free: Reflections on Liberty and Literacy (Worcester, MA: American Antiquarian Society, 2000); Brian Street, *Literacy in Theory and Practice* (Cambridge: Cambridge University Press, 1984). Other works are cited where relevant to specific evidence and analysis.

2. Virgil P. [Pomrhon?] to P. C. Cameron, May 27, 1848, Cameron Family Papers, UNC.

3. For a significant study of the sense of place developed by enslaved people, see Anthony Kaye, *Joining Places: Slave Neighborhoods in the Old South*, (Chapel Hill: University of North Carolina Press, 2007); also Claude A. Clegg III, *The Price of Liberty: African Americans and the Making of Liberia* (Chapel Hill: University of North Carolina, 2004).

4. Joseph to Abby Cross, March 6, 1865, published in "The Civil War Letters of J.O. Cross, 29th Connecticut Volunteer Infantry (Colored)," ed. Kelly Nolin, *Connecticut Historical Society Bulletin* 60 (Summer–Fall 1995): 230–31.

5. The mileage is based on modern street and freeway routes. Pomrhon's letter was addressed to Paul Cameron, who ran the family plantation near Durham, North Carolina, from 1837 until the late 1850s, according to UNC biographical information.

6. Nolin, "Letters of J.O. Cross," 215–18.

7. William Johnson to Maggie, October 16, 1869, Johnson, MHS.

8. Lieut. S. Y. Seyburn, "The Tenth Regiment of Infantry," in *The Army of the US Historical Sketches of Staff and Line with Portraits of Generals-in-Chief*, ed. Brigadier General Theo[Philus] F[Rancis] Rodenbough and Major William L. Haskin (New York: Maynard, Merrill, & Co. 1896), 541–42. https://history.army.mil/books/R&H/R&H-10IN.htm.

9. Ann Osmond's mother to children, January 4, 1846, Osmond, MHS.

10. Amy Galusha to Parents, May 9, 1851, LMGL.

11. John Garriott to Samuel and Gulda Meginety, March 7, 1862, Garriott, SHSM. John lived with his sister and brother-in-law before he joined Company G, Eighteenth Missouri Volunteer Cavalry. His middle name was Washington.

12. Elizabeth Sterling to Ann Osmond, May 10, 18[??], Osmond, MHS.

13. Isaac Osmond to William and Ann Osmond, February 9, 1846, Osmond, MHS.

14. Polly Lanphear to Eliza Shattuck, October 29, 1854, Shattuck, MHS.

15. George Lanphear to Eliza Shattuck, April 1, 1858, Shattuck, MHS.

16. John Christy to David Demus, November 19, 1863, VS/UV.

17. B. A. Campbell [cousin] to Sara Kesterson, February 21, 1870, CivWar, MOHS.

18. John C. McCracken to Samuel Culberson, August 27, [circa 1845], John and Samuel J. Culberson Papers, Duke.

19. Sara Reed & Ann Reed to Anna Bronson, September 1857, Bronson, HEH.

20. Henry Jones to [Andrew and Elizabeth Reeves], May 18, 1860, Reeves, UNC.

21. Mary Jane to David Demus, December 6 [probably 1863], VS/UV. She was around twenty years old when she wrote this letter.

22. E. H. and A. L. Barkley to J. B. O. Barkley, September 27, 1861, Barkley Family Papers, UNC.

23. Caroline Emerson to Sister and Brother, August 1, 1886, Lipscomb, UNC.

24. Hillory to Jemima Shifflet, November 6, 1861, CivWar, MOHS.

264 NOTES TO PAGES 24–26

25. David Gerber makes an important distinction between writers who were apologizing for technical errors and those better-educated writers who lamented an inability to "think effectively enough to express the larger range of concerns that they were experiencing as they wrote." While American working-class correspondents were usually focused on their technical deficiencies, they also regularly lamented that they could think of nothing to write. See David Gerber, *Authors of Their Lives: The Personal Correspondence of British Immigrants to North America in the Nineteenth Century* (New York: New York University Press, 2006), 170.

26. Don Hall to Mary Vanhorn, January 17, 1863, Vanhorn, LC.

27. Cousin to Edward Francis Bailey, December 10, 1853, Sarah Bailey Papers, IHS. "Excues my bad wirting for this is the second letter that I ever wrote," one sister declared. Pestena Webb to William Holman, August 3, 1857, Woods-Holman, SHSM.

28. Frank Flint to Jennie Russell, August 24, 1864, Flint, MHS. His age was recorded as fourteen in the 1860 US Federal Census.

29. Frank Flint to Jennie Russell, October 9, 1864, Flint, MHS.

30. Frank Flint to Jennie Russell, October 22, 1864, Flint, MHS.

31. John to Louisa Shumway, March 19, 1865, Shumway, MHS.

32. Silas to Clara Browning, February 6, 1863; Silas Browning to Wife, March 2, 1863; Silas Browning to Wife, February 27, 1863, Silas W. Browning Papers, LC. His wife was letting their daughters read his letters without a second thought. Working-class boundaries of privacy after marriage were much more loosely drawn than in middle-class culture. See chapter 5.

33. See William J. Gilmore, *Reading Becomes a Necessity of Life: Material and Cultural Life in Rural New England, 1780–1835* (Knoxville: University of Tennessee Press, 1989), 292–301. Gilmore's amazingly detailed research and precise analysis ends where this study begins, but his findings on print culture, family libraries, and the most popular authors and books in the early Republic are suggestive. The poor and geographically isolated in his sample of rural New England families averaged three to four books in "collections surviving at inventory" (147). By contrast, professional households averaged sixty-five volumes and wealthy farmers forty-seven (391). Gilmore's analysis of one occupational category, artisans, is most surprising. He claims they "took great advantage of print culture and sustained the most active intellectual interests of any occupational group except professional and manufacturing families" (349–50). Nevertheless, artisans averaged nine books in their family libraries, placing their average holdings fourth from the bottom on his occupational scale (391). The production and consumption of print culture increased spectacularly over the course of the nineteenth century, but the reading habits of working-class Americans between 1830 and 1880 remain somewhat opaque. I am certain they read and cherished their Bibles and their correspondence. At least during the Civil War, ordinary soldiers read and shared newspapers, some books, and magazines. They did not mention fiction in their letters. The classic work on the importance of dime novels in shaping nineteenth-century working-class culture is Michael Denning's *Mechanic Accents: Dime Novels and Working-Class Culture in America* (New York: Verso, 1987).

NOTES TO PAGES 26–27   265

34. Isaac Osmond to William Osmond, January 21, 1844, Osmond, MHS. Isaac moved from Pennsylvania, his birthplace, to New Jersey, New York, and finally to the promised land of Wisconsin.

35. William Littlejohn to Uncle, August 12, 1876, Lipscomb, UNC.

36. Hansel Roberts [dictated to Ransom Roberts], March 17, 1833, Roberts Family Papers, LC.

37. Mollie D. Gaither to J. B. Gaither [her cousin], December 6, 1862, Gaither, UNC; W. F. Cates to Mother, December 21, 1850, H. N. Epps Family Letters, SHSM; Isaac Osmond to William Osmond, November 30, [18??] and February 25, 1855, Osmond, MHS; Marcellus Mitchell to Rebecca, September 15, 1865, Marcellus Mitchell Correspondence, LC.

38. See Appendix B for two vivid examples.

39. See Walter Ong, *Orality and Literacy: The Technologizing of the Word* (London: Methuen, 1982); Ruth Finnegan, *Oral Poetry: Its Nature, Significance and Social Context*, rev. ed. (Bloomington: Indiana University Press, 1992), 111; Carl F. Kaestle, "Studying the History of Literacy," in *Literacy in the United States: Readers and Reading since 1880*, ed. Carl F. Kaestle et al. (New Haven: Yale University Press, 1991), 3; Brian Stock, *The Implications of Literacy: Written Language and Models of Interpretation in the Eleventh and Twelfth Centuries* (Princeton: Princeton University Press, 1983), 12. Literary critics and cultural historians see a significant overlap between written and oral culture, but the opposition persists in more general cultural criticism.

40. D. A. Carey to Joshua Lipscomb, January 12, 1860, Lipscomb, UNC.

41. Joan E. Cashin suggests that in antebellum America "literacy is neither expected nor rewarded" in some communities. She believes that St. Peter's Parish in Beaufort District, South Carolina, was one such place. See her "Widow in a Swamp: Gender, Unionism, and Literacy in the Occupied South during the Civil War," in *Occupied Women: Gender, Military Occupation and the American Civil War*, ed. LeeAnn Whites and Alecia P. Long (Baton Rouge: Louisiana State University Press, 2009), 171–84.

42. Sarah Barksdale to William Holman February 27, 1854, Woods-Holman, SHSM.

43. Another important synthesis of oral and written culture is the widespread practice, at least in New England, of reading out loud. This practice is thoroughly documented in Ronald J. Zboray and Mary Saracino Zboray, *Everyday Ideas: Socioliterary Experience among Antebellum New Englanders* (Knoxville: University of Tennessee Press, 2006), 127–44, 153–73. The Zborays include a number of working-class examples, but they do not make explicit class distinctions in their analysis.

44. Elizabeth Fuller to Solon Fuller, November 1862 [cataloger's date but likely written in late October 1862; internal evidence of October 27, 1862]. After admitting she had no idea what month or numerical day it was when she began her letter, Elizabeth evidently asked for help and then added a date: "Novemb 7 1862"; her add-on date may have referred to the month and day of a second sitting when she ended her letter. SLFP, Duke.

45. Note, however, that Elizabeth Fuller clearly dated a letter she wrote Phillip, her son, on July 20, 1862. Her use of a calendar date in this letter (and others) obviously indicates a recurrent orientation to numerical time.

266 NOTES TO PAGES 28–30

46. Joseph Cross to Abby Cross, December 31, 1864, published in Nolin, "Letters of J.O. Cross," 223–24.

47. The personal dates of birth and marriage might also become an issue for those immersed in an oral culture. Thus Leonard Caplinger directed his wife: "set down our ages and when we as married Bill was born Set them all down rite so thare will be no truble about it for if I warnt to get hoam they mite of agreat use and you mite forgit." Leonard to Polly [Mary] Caplinger, [no date but probably around March or April 1863], Caplinger, HEH.

48. Thomas T. Bigbie to wife [Mary Jane Bigbie], September 21, 1863, ADL.

49. Thomas T. Bigbie to wife, March 12, 1864, ADL.

50. George Deal, US Civil War Soldier Records and Profiles, 1861–1865. He enlisted in October 1862 in the Ohio Twentieth Infantry and died during the Atlanta Campaign twenty-one months later, on July 22, 1864.

51. George to Sarah Deal, April 8, 1863, DL, Newberry.

52. George to Sarah Deal, July 30, 1863, DL, Newberry. Italics are mine. I am assuming that George was referring to himself when he used the first-person singular pronoun and not a surrogate reader.

53. See January 20, 1863, letter "ritten by Thom Corban a strange to you." The scribes were invisible in all Deal's letters before this date. The most active scribe by far was Henry J. Souder, who announced himself on March 31, 1863. Souder's numerical competence was sometimes shaky when forming the numbers 1 and 7.

54. George to Sarah Deal, March 31, 1863. This letter included Henry J. Souder's commentary as scribe. DL, Newberry.

55. George to Sarah Deal, April 20, 1863, comments by Henry J. Souder, scribe, DL, Newberry.

56. George to Sarah Deal, March 31, 1863, comments by Henry J. Souder, scribe, DL, Newberry.

57. Handwritten note on her photograph by an unidentified great granddaughter [maternal] of Sarah Deal. "Hearsay has it that she was ¼ Indian." DL, Newberry.

58. The 1870 US Federal Census indicates that Sarah Deal could not read or write. George Deal's July 30, 1863, letter indicates otherwise. There are several other discrepancies in this couple's records, including age variations. But after exploring a number of alternatives, I concluded that I had correctly identified the Sarah and George Deal of the Newbery letter collection in census, military, and demographic records.

59. The literacy category in both the 1850 and 1860 census is "Persons over 20 yr's of age who cannot read & write." George was approximately twenty years old as recorded in the 1850 census, so his age may have kept him from being classified as illiterate. In 1860 it is possible that he lied about his ability to write or perhaps the census taker thought his reading literacy was enough, even though both reading and writing were enumerated separately.

60. A practice-based approach to literacy based on actual letters has many advantages, and one disadvantage. What this micro-approach to literacy based on actual letters cannot offer is large-scale population statistics. The biggest gain is the ability to track nuances of expressive skill and to observe the specific experiences of writing. Only

NOTES TO PAGES 30–32   267

through George's offhand comment about reading his wife's letter can his partial literacy be ascertained. (I am interpreting his "I" as self-referential and not an allusion to his scribe.)

61. Widow Peebles to Daniel Turner, September [1864], filed with Will H. Cobb's letter to Bettie V. Herring, October 11, 1864, Wright and Herring Family Papers, UNC.

62. I searched the relevant online databases with only the information provided by her letter and found that the plethora of possibilities was head-spinning.

63. One Sallie A. Peebles was visited on August 8, 1860. But another separate federal census record existed for a second Sallie A. Peebles who also lived in North Division, Guilford County, North Carolina, when the census taker called in July. She was also married to an Albert Peebles, who was a laborer with a personal estate worth only fifty dollars more than the first Albert. This Sallie was twenty-seven (the census taker visited her household on July 14) and she appeared to have five children. Small age differences should not be given much weight since birth dates were notoriously inaccurate at the time. Nonetheless, there was a two-year discrepancy in the ages of the Sallies and a three-year discrepancy between the two Alberts.

Children seemed to be the best means to distinguish the two women, since the August Sallie had four children at home and the July Sallie five. What a surprise, then, to discover that three of their children had the same first names in the identical birth order: David, John, and Malinda. There was some difference (not much) in the boys' ages (one to two years) but the two Malindas were the same age. The youngest children in both families were two-year-old girls with different names. July's youngest child was identified as Catherine and August's was called Menerva. Andrew, age thirteen, was the only July child who had no counterpart in the August family.

Were these two Sallie's the same woman? One household was visited on July 14 and the other on August 8. The August 8 census taker found another adult woman, Menerva Halbrook and her child, Samuel, living with the Peeples. The oldest boy, Andrew, was missing in the August record. The same man questioned both families and each had a different set of neighbors. (Households were surveyed by geographical proximity.) I spent several days trying to track down the Sallie (and her family) who was visited on July 14 with no success.

My colleague and friend Leila Zenderland suggested at the end of my frustrating search that perhaps Sallie and Albert moved to a new location in the three weeks or more between visits by the census taker. If he interviewed a different adult in the two locations, he may not have realized the overlap. This now seems to me to be the most plausible explanation: the two Sallies and Alberts were one couple with four children (possibly a fifth) and relatives who came and went. I concluded that the youngest girl was known as both Catherine and Menerva.

64. This discovery came after a long search for Sallie's maiden name, which was Meredith. Pursuing information on Minerva Peeples, the most distinctive given name among Sallie's children, turned up her death certificate. She was identified as Minerva Cook, her married surname, and her birth was charted around 1859, which meant that she had been included in the 1860 census. Her father was identified as Albert Peeples, and her mother's maiden name was given as Sally Ann Meredith. Following this lead,

268 NOTES TO PAGES 32–33

the 1850 census indicated that Sallie A. Meredith and Minerva Meredith were sisters who were living with their parents in Guilford, North Carolina. Sallie's youngest child was also named Minerva, which suggested that Sallie's sister was her child's namesake and that her married sister was living in their household in August. But there was a hitch. The North Carolina Marriage Records indicated that Minerva Peeples married William Halbrook in 1852. If this Minerva had been Sallie's sister, her maiden name would have been Meredith. (Note the variable spelling of Peebles.) This raised the possibility that Minerva was a relative of Albert Peebles, Sallie's husband. However, none of Albert's sisters (listed in the 1850 census) were named Minerva. After many fruitless searches in a wide variety of documents, a note in a family genealogy provided the key. Albert and James Peeples had a sister named Mary whose middle name was Minerva. Sallie's sister-in-law, Minerva Peeples, had married William Halbrook in 1852 and was residing with them in August 1860. James was his sister's official witness, and Halbrook, Sallie and Albert's brother-in-law, performed the same function for them when they married in 1852. The Merediths and Peebles had been neighbors. See the 1850 US Federal Census and a "Public Members Genealogy Tree" under Albert Peeples.

65. According to my analysis above, August would have been the second visit by the census taker, only in a location different from the first.

66. The most obvious place to look for evidence of Albert Peebles's death was the military records of the Civil War. Again, many Peebles served—Benjamin, Robert, J. A., Albert W., James, Walter, Thomas, William, Selburn, Ashley, Henry—but no one matched the husband of the 1860 census. Adding the Second Regiment, North Carolina Infantry, to the search (as indicated on the envelope) still did not produce results. Combing through the Second North Carolina Infantry regimental lists was also fruitless. Sometimes patience and determination pays off. Combining and recombining key words in numerous web searches, the notation "Albert G. *Peoples*" appeared at the bottom of an entry tag line "By Battle Unit Name, Search for Soldiers, The Civil War (US)." Using *Peoples*, a close soundalike to Peebles, to search a National Park Service database proved to be a dead end. But an entry in the US Civil War Soldier Records and Profiles database finally yielded the widow Peeble's husband. He was listed as Albert Peoples of Guilford County, North Carolina, enrolled July 23, 1861, in Company E, North Carolina Second Infantry Regiment. He did not survive the war. His location, regiment, and company checked out. However, no death date was given. But an online index of cemetery and burial details gave Peoples's death as November 16, 1863. See Albert G. Peoples in US Find a Grave Index, 1600s–current.

67. "The Civil War in North Carolina—2nd Infantry Regiment," http://www.researchonl ine.net/nccw/unit21.htm.

68. Widow Peebles to Daniel Turner, September [1864], Wright and Herring Family Papers, UNC. The poetry that ended this letter is discussed in chapter 7.

69. The US Federal Census Mortality Schedules Index, 1850–1880.

70. Will H. Cobb to Cousin Bettie [Herring], October 11, 1864, Wright and Herring Family Papers, UNC.

NOTES TO PAGES 33–34   269

71. North Carolina Troops, 1861–1865: A Roster, compiled by Louis H. Manarin et al., https://familysearch.org/search/catalog/147534?availability=Family%20History%20Library.

72. Enslaved men might also enlist together or join the same company or regiment as other refugees from their neighborhoods. See Kaye, *Joining Places*, p. 199.

73. Jean V. Berlin, ed., *A Confederate Nurse: The Diary of Ada W. Bacot, 1860–1863*, as cited in J. David Hacker, Libra Hilde, and James Holland Jones, "The Effect of the Civil War on Southern Marriage Patterns," *Journal of Southern History* 76 (February 2010): 39–70, esp. 46.

74. According to the North Carolina Wills and Probate Records, 1665–1998, Robert Humphries died in 1863. Mary's son, James A. Humphries, was living in another state when he enlisted in November 1862. See US Confederate Soldiers' Compiled Service Records, 1861–1865.

75. In the 1850 federal census Turner was listed as five years old in August; in the 1870 census taken in July he gave his age as twenty-six. This slight discrepancy in Turner's age may indicate nothing more than the common confusion about birthdates in the nineteenth-century working class. It is also possible that he added a year to his age because his wife was so much older.

76. See Robert Humphries, 1860 US Federal Census. His real estate was valued at $160. The 1860 census taker left Albert Peebles's real estate column blank. Both widows would have had a dower's right to one-third of their husband's land until they died, but only Robert Humphries owned real estate. Unfortunately for Mary Humphries, her husband's property was sold to pay his debts. All sales and cash disbursements appear to be in Confederate money. See Robert A. Humphreys, North Carolina Wills and Probate Records, 1665–1998. She received $700, presumably in Confederate script, and had to pay her husband's estate $10 for a cart and $150 for an ox. There was a balance of $26.71 due the administrator after all their debts were paid.

77. Sally Peeples, 1870 US Federal Census.

78. US Civil War Soldier Records and Profiles, 1861–1865.

79. Another example of the class superiority exhibited by educated Americans toward the working class is found in Elvira J. Powers, *Hospital Pencillings: Being a Diary While in Jefferson General Hospital . . .* (Boston: Edward L. Mitchell, 1866), 147–52. Three Confederate love letters were sent from a captured post office in Virginia by a Union officer to his sister in Rockford, Illinois, who shared them with the author of this memoir. She transcribed them and then mocked their spelling, punctuation, and feeling. I first came across this source in Christopher Hager, *I Remain Yours: Common Lives in Civil War Letters* (Cambridge, MA: Harvard University Press, 2018), 97.

80. Leo Soltow and Edward Stevens, *The Rise of Literacy and the Common School in the U.S.: A Socio-economic Analysis to 1870* (Chicago: University of Chicago Press, 1981), 24–26, 128–29, and 178, Table 5.11. Also see Appendix A, n. 21.

81. Patrick M. Horan and Peggy G. Hargis, "Children's Work and Schooling in the Late Nineteenth-Century Family Economy," *American Sociological Review* 56 (October 1991): 583–96.

270 NOTES TO PAGES 34–39

82. See David Henkin's excellent discussion of the social and cultural significance of correspondence during the Civil War in *The Postal Age: The Emergence of Modern Communication in Nineteenth-Century America* (Chicago: University of Chicago Press, 2006), 137–47.

83. Samuel to Sophie Potter, October 19, 1862, Samuel Potter Papers, LC.

84. Oliver Coolidge to [Father and Sister], May 28, 1862, Coolidge, Duke.

85. Marcellus Mitchell to Rebecca, September 18, 1864, and September 15, 1865, Marcellus Mitchell Correspondence, LC.

86. Sydney Fuller to Solon Fuller, February 6, 1863, SLFP, Duke.

87. See William J. Collins and Robert A. Margo, "Historical Perspectives on Racial Differences in Schooling in the United States," National Bureau of Economic Research Working Paper 9770, June 2003, 8, 41, Table 4, computed from the Integrated Public Use Microdata Series IPUMS samples, http://piketty.pse.ens.fr/files/CollinsMargo2003.pdf.

88. Edward Francis to Liza Francis, August 8, 1865, in "'I Don't Fear Nothing in the Shape of Man'": The Civil War and Texas Border Letters of Edward Francis, United States Colored Troops," ed. Marshall Myers and Chris Propes, *Register of the Kentucky Historical Society* 101 (Autumn 2003): 465–66. In addition, see Private Edward Francis in the US Descriptive Lists of Colored Volunteer Army Soldiers, 1864. Information about Francis supplied in two categories support the likelihood that he was not free until he enlisted: "Name of Owner of A Slave" (Edy Francis) and "Residence of Owner of a Slave" (Madison Co., K). See also Victor Howard, "The Civil War in Kentucky: The Slave Claims His Freedom," *Journal of Negro History* 67 (Autumn 1982): 245–56.

89. Chump Pugh to Esther Hawkes, June 15, 1864, EHHP, LC.

90. Elizabeth Hyde Botume, *First Days Amongst the Contrabands* (Boston: Lee and Shepard, 1893), 151, https://archive.org/details/firstdaysamongst00botu.

91. T. D. Eliot, *Report of the Committee on Freedmen's Affairs, to the House of Representatives, March 10 1868* (Washington, DC: Government Printing Office, 1868), 22–25, as quoted in John Blassingame, "The Union Army as an Educational Institution for Negroes, 1862–1865," *Journal of Negro Education* 34 (Spring 1965): 152–59.

92. Zboray and Zboray, *Everyday Ideas*, 19–20.

93. James to Mary Lockwood, March 8, 1865, James Lockwood and Family Papers, MHS.

94. Lewis to Nancy McDaniel, December 24, 1863, Confederate, UNC.

95. David to Mary Jane Demus, June 4, 1864, Franklin County, Pennsylvania, VS/UV.

96. Frank Flint to Jennie Russell, January 19, 1865, Flint, MHS.

97. O. S. Coolidge to Father & Sister, January 30, 1862, Coolidge, Duke.

98. Oliver Coolidge to [Sister], May 15, 1862, Coolidge, Duke. See chapter 4 for more details and analysis.

99. George T. Beavers to Brother-[in-law], September 22, 1861, Upchurch, Duke. I discuss the issue of privacy in more detail in chapter 4.

100. Frank Flint to Jennie Russell, October 22, 1864, Flint, MHS.

101. George Delavar to Mrs. Hawkes, March 17, 1864, EHHP, LC. He lived in New Bedford, Massachusetts.

NOTES TO PAGES 39–44   271

102. Mary to Leonard Caplinger, May 17, 1863, Caplinger, HEH. The common practice of reading printed material out loud likely influenced the practice of reading handwritten letters to nonrecipients. See Zboray and Zboray, *Everyday Ideas*, 127–44, 153–73, for documentation of the public reading of printed material. The Zborays include a number of working-class examples, but they do not make class distinctions in their analysis.
103. Frank Flint to Jennie Russell, October 30, 1864, Flint, MHS.
104. Louisa Sawyer to Cousin Sabrina [Edwards Bennett], December 1849, LMGL.
105. Edward to Liza Francis, January 31, 1866, in Myers and Propes, "Letters of Edward Francis," 476.
106. Ellen A. Everingham to Cousin, July 24, 1853, Woods-Holman, SHSM.
107. David Hall to Arthur Vanhorn, January 1, 1862, Vanhorn, LC.
108. William Littlejohn to Uncle Smith Lipscomb, February 17, 1871, Lipscomb, UNC.
109. J. C. Owens to parents, April 26, 1863, Confederate, UNC.
110. Riley to Mary Ann Luther, August 4, 1862, RLC, Duke.
111. Henry Martin to Elisabeth Martin [cousin], October 9, 1863, CivWar, MOHS.
112. Joseph Aid to Wife, May 28, 1864, TP, Joseph Aid Papers, SHSM.
113. Eunice Stone to Anne [McCoy?], December 23, 1860, LWRD, Duke.
114. Louisa Russ to John Shumway, October 21, 1855, Shumway, MHS.
115. Louisa Amorret Russ to John Shumway, June 2, 1856, Shumway, MHS.
116. John Shumway to Louisa Amorret Russ, April 18, 1858, Shumway, MHS.
117. Joseph Fardell to Parents, November 9, 1863, CivWar, MOHS.
118. Sarah E. Trask, March 31, 1849, journal entry, as quoted in Zboray and Zboray, *Everyday Ideas*, 11. I have returned the quotation to its original spelling. See chapter 4, n. 4, for relevant citations.
119. John Garriott to Samuel and Gulda Meginety, March 7, 1862, Garriott, SHSM.
120. Barsina to Jane, August 25, 1870, hand-copied letter in the Barsina Rogers French Journal, HEH. See Lucille M. Schultz, *The Young Composer: Composition's Beginnings in Nineteenth-Century Schools* (Carbondale: Southern Illinois University Press, 1999), esp. chapter 5.
121. A. D. Buck to Brother Marco, August 25, 1865, Saxton, HEH.
122. Orra Bailey to Wife, June 17, 1863, Orra B. Bailey Papers, LC.
123. Carter Page to Mrs. Isabella Page [mother], July 10, 1876, TP, [Thomas D.] Page Family Papers, SHSM.
124. C. H. Richardson to Mother and Sister, June 29, 1865, LWRD, Duke.
125. Mother to C. H. Richardson, July 3, 1865, LWRD, Duke.
126. See Karen Lystra, *Searching the Heart: Women, Men, and Romantic Love in Nineteenth-Century America* (New York: Oxford University Press, 1989), 13–18.
127. Ann Osmond's mother to children, January 4, 1846, Osmond, MHS.
128. David Gerber found that his British immigrant correspondents were deeply committed to a reciprocal exchange of letters. He identified the threat when one side stopped writing as a "reciprocity crisis." My concept of the "reciprocity rule" was formulated independently of his study of immigrant letters, but the overlap is striking. See Gerber, *Authors of Their Lives*, 102–5.
129. John and Sally Kesterson to Joseph Kesterson, July 28, 1864, CivWar, MOHS.

272 NOTES TO PAGES 44–47

130. Isaac Osmond to William Osmond, February 25, 1855, Osmond, MHS.

131. Ann Osmond Russell Estabrooks to Ann Osmond, July 25, 1875, Osmond, MHS.

132. Elizabeth Sterling to Ann Osmond, April 1, 1872, Osmond, MHS.

133. Mary Walker to Friend, 18[??], Woods-Holman, SHSM.

134. Matthew Marvin to Brother, December 27, 1861, Matthew Marvin Papers, MHS.

135. Father to Children, June 20, 1858, Levi Colburn Hillman Papers, MHS.

136. M. Garland to William Garland, May 16, 1844; also October 2, 1844, William Harris Garland Papers, UNC.

137. W. H. Kesterson to Joseph Kesterson, August 10, 1864, CivWar, MOHS.

138. George Delavar to Mrs. Haweks [*sic*], January 13, 1864, EHHP, LC.

139. Jesse Skinner Wilkerson to Brother and Sister, November 26, 1863, Civil War Diaries and Letters, IDL.

140. Karen V. Hansen, *A Very Social Time: Crafting Community in Antebellum New England* (Berkeley: University of California Press, 1994), 62. She found that working-class correspondents and diary keepers "experienced acute insecurity regarding the reciprocity of feelings and attachment."

141. Jacob Christy to Mary Jane Demus, May 29, 1865, Franklin County, VS/UV. See Pennsylvania and New Jersey, Church and Town Records 1669–1999, for his baptism record; also see 1850 US Federal Census under Jacob E. Christer. His entire family is identified as biracial or, in the nineteenth-century census term, mulatto.

142. Simeon Tierce to Sarah Jane Tierce, November 24, 1863 in Edythe Ann Quinn, *Freedom Journey: Black Civil War Soldiers and The Hills Community, Westchester County, New York* (Albany: State University of New York Press, 2015), 136. Quinn published his five letters in an Appendix B (pp. 133–49) along with helpful annotations. She added periods and some commas but did not change his spelling.

143. Rufus Wright to Elisabeth Turner Wright, April 22, 1864, in *Families and Freedom: A Documentary History of African-American Kinship in the Civil War Era*, ed. Ira Berlin and Leslie S. Rowland (New York: New Press, 1997), 166.

144. J. C. to Susannah Owens, April 26, 1863, Confederate, UNC.

145. John to Mary Wilson, January 1, 1859 [actually 1860], JWL, Newberry.

146. James Randall to sister, April 26, 1863, TP, "The Civil War Letters of James Randall, Oakland, New York," Nunda Historical Society, http://www.nundahistory.org/randall63.html.

147. Henry Tolle to Jaspar Bertram, April 16, 1865. The 1890 Veterans Schedules (under Newton J. Bertram) indicated that Bertram was discharged from Union service on July 4, 1864. He was home in Kentucky when this letter was written. Jaspar N. Bertram Papers, University of Washington Libraries Digital Collections, https://content.lib.washington.edu/civilwarweb/collections.html.

148. Adeline Colburn to Sister [Mrs. Rebecca Knowlton], July 22, 1849, LMGL.

149. Sister [working in Lowell mills] to Brother living in Bethel Vermont, October 1, [1854], filed under Anonymous (Bethel, VT), letters; another variation from mill girl Hannah I. Williamson to Mary S. Fraser, April 3, 1836, LMGL, "give my respects to all who may enquire for me." Also see Thomas Dublin, *Women at Work: The Transformation of Work and Community in Lowell, Massachusetts, 1826–1860* (New York: Columbia University Press, 1979), esp. 47–48.

NOTES TO PAGES 47–50   273

150. G. W. Jones to Wife, May 7, 1863, in *The Sound of Distant Drums: Veteran's Voices from the Heartland, 1861–2003*, ed. Chuck Knox (Bloomington, IN: Author House, 2005), 14. He was a farmer in Rockcastle County, Kentucky. Also Henry H. to Mary E. A. Dedrick, April 7, 1862, VS/UV.

151. Lizzie to "All At-Home," April 16, 1866, LMGL.

152. Lydia Bixby to Mother [Mary Gilson Bixby], May 22, 1852[?], LMGL.

153. James Miles to Neighbour [presumably Reeves] July 21, 1867, Reeves, UNC.

154. Henkin, *The Postal Age*, 147, emphasized the personal letter as both "a vehicle and a model for . . . family intimacy in a mobile society." He is primarily referring to "[m]id-century American families, especially those of the emergent middle class" and highlights the "performance of family duty and the expression of family affection" in middle-class letters. Working-class letters often include family within a broader circle of communal intimacy defined by location.

155. See Lystra, *Searching the Heart*, chapters 1 and 2; also Henkin, *The Postal Age*, 11, 146–47. Nicole Eustace argues that eighteenth-century male elites commonly wrote public love letters, in *Passion Is the Gale: Emotion, Power, and the Coming of the American Revolution* (Chapel Hill: University of North Carolina Press, 2008), 107–8. She connects the public love letter to communal and role-bound conceptions of the self.

156. This failure to protect the private individual was baffling to middle-class readers in their time and in our own.

157. William Dunlap to Elizabeth Rife, May 12, 1861. Also see Augusta County, Virginia, 1870 Population Census, VS/UV.

158. Ruth Elson states that elementary spelling books (in editions spanning 1823 through 1872) referred to "rank of persons" and "station in life." See *Guardians of Tradition: American Schoolbooks of the Nineteenth Century* (Lincoln: University of Nebraska Press, 1964), 269. I did a cursory sample of the University of Pittsburgh digital collection of one hundred nineteenth-century schoolbooks but was unable to locate similar examples. http://digital.library.pitt.edu/collection/19th-century-schoolbooks.

159. Robert Karen, "Shame," *Atlantic Monthly*, February 1992, 40–70; online version, p. 9, http://www.empoweringpeople.net/shame/shame.pdf. He noted: "The crippling self-hatred that class subjugation often instills can be alleviated by class unity and closeness."

160. Peter N. Stearns, *Shame: A Brief History* (Urbana: University of Illinois Press, 2017).

161. See Lystra, *Searching the Heart*, chapters 2 and 8.

162. Many versions of this vernacular poem appear in nineteenth-century letters. See chapter 7 for multiple citations and a fuller discussion. For one example among hundreds, see Nancy Jane Rawlings to Rebecca Rawlings Brophy, April 11, 1858, Brophy-Beeson Papers, HEH.

Chapter 2

1. The 1880 statistic is striking. David Ward, *Cities and Immigrants: A Geography of Change in Nineteenth-Century* America (New York: Oxford University Press, 1971),

274 NOTES TO PAGE 50

6, Table 0-1; Eric H. Monkkonen, *America Becomes Urban: The Development of U.S. Cities and Towns, 1780–1980* (Berkeley: University of California Press, 1988), 70–72.

2. Patricia Kelly Hall and Steven Ruggles, "'Restless in the Midst of Their Prosperity': New Evidence on the Internal Migration of Americans, 1850–2000," *Journal of American History* 91 (Dec. 2004): 829–46, esp. 829, 839–40, 844. They aim to measure "permanent interstate migration" rather than temporary mobility for work, war, or school. Thus they use the fifty to fifty-nine age cohort in order to examine a presumptively stable age group, and thus eliminate (as much as possible) the inclusion of temporary migration and "retirement" or return migration after age sixty. Their study does *not* allow for a quantitative measure of short- or long-term mobility among marriage-age men and women in their twenties. However, several nineteenth-century community studies, as well as census data, suggest that Americans in their twenties and thirties were the most mobile. See Hall and Ruggles, p. 835 n. 14. Large-scale African American interstate mobility can only be measured by census information beginning in 1870.

3. Hall and Ruggles, "Restless in the Midst," 839–40, 844.

4. In New England, an area of significant out-migration, Hal Barron found that in a representative town almost 50 percent of male household heads ages twenty to twenty-nine who were residents in 1840 were still there twenty years later. A similar persistence level was found in a comparison of the 1860 to 1880 census. Hal S. Barron, *Those Who Stayed Behind: Rural Society in Nineteenth-Century New England* (New York: Cambridge University Press, 1984), chapter 5, esp. 80, 84, Table 5.4. Significantly these figures were adjusted for mortality, which yields a more accurate result. Persistence is only one element in the story of working-class courtship.

5. Jason Jindrich, "Suburbs in the City: Reassessing the Location of Nineteenth-Century American Working-Class Suburbs," *Social Science History* 36 (Summer 2012): 147–67. Kathy Peiss discusses the "importance of social clubs as mediators of urban courtship" in *Cheap Amusements: Working Women and Leisure in Turn-of-the-Century New York* (Philadelphia: Temple University Press, 1986), 48–49, 60–61.These clubs were organized around neighborhoods as well as the workplace. In low-density rural areas, community could encompass a county. Some highly mobile young men might even expand their geographical focus to a region or state.

6. The assumptions of race were broader than courtship and almost always tacitly assumed unless racial boundaries were violated. See Joshua D. Rothman, *Notorious in the Neighborhood: Sex and Families across the Color Line in Virginia, 1787–1861* (Chapel Hill: University of North Carolina Press, 2003), for violations of these racial boundaries and the role of the local community in accepting or rejecting those intimate relationships.

7. While statistical measures of this group bond are elusive, nineteenth-century working-class Americans (both skilled and unskilled) made permanent moves across state lines less than their white-collar, middle-class peers. The disparity in this measure of mobility between unskilled (nonfarmers) and white-collar workers in 1850 was almost twenty percentage points. See Hall and Ruggles, "Restless in the Midst," p. 842.

NOTES TO PAGES 51–53   275

8. Susan J. Matt, *Homesickness: An American History* (New York: Oxford University Press, 2011), 5–6. They called acute homesickness "nostalgia."

9. James S. Beavers to Brother [Isham Upchurch], July 2, 1861, Upchurch, Duke.

10. Nancy Glen to Emaline Boley, January 16, 1858, Uncatalogued Miscellaneous Collection, Archives of American Art, Smithsonian. Nancy was living in Creighton, Guernsey County, Ohio, when she wrote her letter. She was about twenty-eight miles from Noble County, Ohio, where her friend Emaline was located. (Distance is based on both county seats.) Creighton no longer exists. Emaline's location was determined from her brother's (Lewis Boley) military records and burial site, which is Ava, an unincorporated community in northwestern Noble Township. See U.S. Find A Grave Index, 1600s to Current.

11. Charles Smith to Martha and William Smith, April 4, 1851, Woods-Holman, SHSM. Another letter from Charles Smith to his Uncle dated May 15 [missing year] has a heading that indicates his home is Overton, Tennessee.

12. For confirmation of her local residence, see Samar Patterson, 1850 US Federal Census; also Tamer Smith, 1860 US Federal Census. A courthouse fire in 1865 destroyed all the Overton County marriage records from 1806 to 1866. I could not confirm the exact date of their marriage. See "Lost Records: Courthouse Fires and Disasters in Tennessee" https://sos.tn.gov/tsla/pages/lost-records-courthouse-fires-and-disasters-in-tennessee.

13. Henry Clay Russell to Sister, November 15, 1861, Civil War Diaries and Letters, IDL.

14. Total Population for Iowa's Incorporated Places, 1850–2010. The earliest record for Crawfordsville was 1870. http://www.iowadatacenter.org/archive/2011/02/citypop.pdf.

15. J. M. Watson to J. B. O. Barkley, November 8, 1863, Barkley Family Papers, UNC.

16. Ansel Safford to Parents, Brother, and Sisters, January 29, 1863, CivWar, MOHS. See the 1860 US Federal Census for identification of his hometown.

17. J. W. Estes to Mother and Father, March 28, 1837, H.N. Epps Family Letters, SHSM.

18. He was living in District 47, Lawrence County, Missouri, when the 1850 census was taken June 1.

19. F. L. Bell to Mother, Brothers, and Sisters, July 6, 1852, Downing and Whinrey, SHSM.

20. F. L. Bell to Mother, Brothers, and Sisters, July 6, 1852, Downing and Whinrey, SHSM. His hometown was probably the little village of Halltown, Missouri. Malcolm Rohrbaugh, an eminent gold rush scholar, pointed out that the scarcity of marriageable women in the early gold rush settlements would have played a role. See his *The California Gold Rush and the American Nation* (Berkeley: University of California Press, 1997) esp. chapter 6.

21. Charles Watson to Father [and sisters], June 27, 1864, Watson, MHS. He lived in Featherstone Township, Goodhue County, Minnesota, before the war. The county seat, Red Wing, had a population of 1,250 in 1860, by far the largest town in Goodhue County. Featherstone Township was not listed in *Population of the United States in 1860; comp. from the original returns of the Eighth Census . . .* at https://www.census.gov/prod/www/decennial.html.

22. Henry Clay Russell to Sister, February 2, 1865, Civil War Diaries and Letters, IDL.

276 NOTES TO PAGES 54–57

23. Polly Lanphear to Eliza Shattuck, September 21, 1854, Shattuck, MHS.

24. J. Trent Alexander, and Annemarie Steidl, "Gender and the 'Laws of Migration': A Reconsideration of Nineteenth-Century Patterns," *Social Science History* 36 (Summer 2012): 223–41, esp. 237.

25. Mary Lanphear to Eliza Shattuck, April 13, 1855, Shattuck, MHS.

26. George Lanphear to Eliphalet and Eliza Shattuck, December 17, 1857, Shattuck, MHS. Also see notes 70–72 below.

27. Unidentified young woman to Margaret Dunlap, June 7, 1860, Augusta County, Virginia, VS/UV.

28. Sarah H. Rice to Mother and Father, [n.d.], [internal evidence indicates that it was late in 1839], LMGL. Quotations in the next two paragraphs are drawn from this letter. Thomas Dublin comments on the Rice letters in *Women at Work: The Transformation of Work and Community in Lowell, Massachusetts, 1826–1860* (New York: Columbia University Press, 1979), 36–37.

29. Sarah Rice to Father, September 14, 1845, LMGL.

30. Sarah Rice to Father, February 23, 1845, LMGL.

31. 1850 US Federal Census, Boston; 1855 Mass. State Census, Brookline, Mass.; 1865 Mass. State Census, Worcester; Mass.; 1870 US Federal Census, Worcester, Mass.; Massachusetts Death Records, 1841–1915, Leicester, Mass.

32. Elizabeth Rawlings to Robert Rawlings, February 1, 1858, Box 2, Brophy-Beeson Papers, HEH.

33. Middle-class men, by contrast, could court long distance through letters. This was also true of a much smaller portion of working-class men.

34. Thomas Dublin, *Transforming Women's Work: New England Lives in the Industrial Revolution* (Ithaca: Cornell University Press, 1994), 146–50.

35. Hannah Williamson Wilson to Mary S. Fraser, April 3, 1836, LMGL. Birth, death, and marriage information is included in website footnotes. Hannah and her husband-to-be assumed the standard role of courtship intermediaries.

36. Hannah's husband was farming in Dracut soon after their marriage but sometime in the next decade they returned to his birthplace, living in Pelham, New Hampshire, for many years. See the New Hampshire Births and Christenings Index, 1714–1904 plus the 1840 and 1860 US Federal Census under Clifton Wilson; the 1850 census under Clefton Wilson. See also Silas Coburn, *History of Dracut, Massachusetts* (Lowell, MA: Courier Citizen Co., 1922), https://archive.org/stream/historyofdracutm00c obu#page/n7/mode/2up.

37. She married Issacher Adams. See 1840 US Federal Census under Issaker Adams. Only the head of household is listed by name, but the age spread of individual family members indicates that this was the household of the bridegroom's father who shared his given name. See also Vermont Historical Society Census by towns for 1840 at https://vermonthistory.org/explorer/discover-vermont/facts-figures/census-reco rds/census-by-towns.

38. All the statistics in this paragraph come from Dublin's *Transforming Women's Work*, 117–18, esp. Table 3.5.

39. Listed as Anonymous (Marcia) letter, LMGL. With a careful reading of this anonymous letter, I was able to reconstruct a fairly detailed narrative. I identified the letter

NOTES TO PAGES 57–61   277

recipient as Charles P. Wardwell of Lowell, Massachusetts. Through him I was able to find the sender in census and marriage records. Her name was Marcia B. Cole. Marcia wrote this letter before she and Charles were married on June 24, 1849. Only the year, 1849, was indicated in the typescript, but with the marriage date and the internal reference to wanting $20 "this spring," it was clear that the letter was composed in the winter of 1849, sometime between January and March. New England springs usually begin in April. Soon after their wedding in June, Charles and Marcia moved to Oxford, the Maine county where he was born. By 1860 they had moved to Belknap County, New Hampshire, where she was born. The letter identifies her location as Lake Village, New Hampshire, which is now a neighborhood called Lakeport in Laconia, New Hampshire. In 1860 they were very poor, reporting only $100 of personal wealth and no real estate. Ten years later their fortunes had sharply improved. See 1850, 1860, and 1870 US Federal Census under Charles P. S. Wardwell; also Maine, Birth Records, 1715–1922.

40. This figure is based on Thomas Dublin's sample of New Hampshire millhands.

41. Dublin, *Transforming Women's Work*, 113–18. See p. 114 n. 60 for a discussion of possible bias in determining the marriage age of female mill workers who returned home.

42. Dublin, *Transforming Women's Work*, 117, esp. Table 3.5.

43. Unidentified Friend to Josh [Lipscomb], October 10, 1858, Lipscomb, UNC.

44. Unidentified Friend to Josh [Lipscomb], October 10, 1858, Lipscomb, UNC.

45. I am basing this conclusion on the knowledge that he had a wood and iron shop connected to the blacksmith shop and employed one "hand" as well as the blacksmith.

46. Unidentified Friend to Josh [Lipscomb] October 10, 1858, Lipscomb, UNC.

47. William J. Walker to John [his son], February 2, 1850, in Carter G. Woodson, ed., *The Mind of the Negro: As Reflected in Letters during the Crisis, 1800–1860* (Washington, DC: Association For the Study of Negro Life and History, 1926; reprint, New York: Dover, 2013), 522.

48. The earliest version of the song is credited to Charles T. White, but the Juba project, an exploration of blackface minstrelsy sponsored by the University of Toronto, could not verify his authorship. https://minstrels.library.utoronto.ca/node/519146.

49. See "Minstrel Songs Old and New." This website attributes both the words and music of this song to an anonymous creator. www.pdmusic.org/minstrel.html.

50. For an insightful study of the importance of local affinity, see Anthony Kaye, *Joining Places: Slave Neighborhoods in the Old South* (Chapel Hill: University of North Carolina Press, 2007).

51. Parents, as well as other family members, often took a resigned attitude toward their children's marriage, in some cases even letting their children decide on a suitable marriage age. "She has not had a felo yet," one mother observed, "yet she mite of had but she sais that she will be eighteen first." [Ann Osmond Russell Estabrooks] to William and Ann Osmond, August 23, 1870, Osmond, MHS.

52. For a contrasting style of parental control in the Italian ethnic community, see Stephen Lassonde, *Learning to Forget: Schooling and Family Life in New Haven's Working Class, 1870–1940* (New Haven: Yale University Press, 2005), chapter 5.

53. Nancy Cott, *Public Vows: A History of Marriage and the Nation* (Cambridge: Harvard University Press, 2000), 37.

278 NOTES TO PAGES 61–64

54. R.A. Pearson to Miss M.A. Reeves, December 20, 1868, Reeves, UNC.

55. Mary Blewett, "Yorkshire Lasses and Their Lads: Sexuality, Sexual Customs, and Gender Antagonisms in Anglo-American Working-Class Culture," *Journal of Social History* 40 (Winter 2006): 322. Blewett reports that female weavers made detailed public evaluations of the looks and physical attributes of a strange man on the factory floor. Though this may have been a defense "against the condemnatory scrutiny of strangers," as she claims, it also reflects the intense value working-class women placed on the physical appearance of men who were potential objects of desire inside as well as outside marriage.

56. Mrs. Mary Baldwin to Ella Buck, December 29, 1879, Ella E. Buck Papers, Indiana State Library.

57. Mary Kesterson to Sarah Kesterson, September 19, 1880, Missouri Digital Heritage, St. Louis Civil War Project, http://cdm.sos.mo.gov/cdm/compoundobject/collect ion/ CivilWar/id/13268/rec/1.

58. A. W. Grubb to Maggie E. Grubb, May 31, 1877, John and Jacob Bingham Papers, SHSM. "i have bin to tow poties sice i have binn hear and i havent seen but one purty girl yet and she was from Mo.," a brother living in Texas told his sister. "Jack Barnes clames her and i clame her and i don't know how meny does gow to see her she is the best looking girl in Texas."

59. The 1860 and 1870 federal census points to an Adam W. Grubb as one of the most credible possibilities, but I was unable to make a definitive identification.

60. Matthew Marvin to Brother, February 10, 1862, Matthew Marvin Papers, MHS.

61. Matthew Marvin, US, Civil War Draft Registration Records, 1863–65.

62. Illinois, US County Marriage Records, 1800–1940.

63. Charles Watson to Brother, January 7, 1864, Watson, MHS.

64. Thomas Gaither to Burgess Gaither, November 30, 1862, Gaither, UNC. "There is some nice looking Girls here in old Virginia, but the most of them can not get a meals victuals cant spin a roal never seen a bur of cotton and they do nt suit a North Carolina boy I would not give a good North Carolina Girl for a half dozen of them I do not think of Va know now."

65. Thomas Gaither to Mother [and Molley], December 10, 1862, Gaither, UNC.

66. William Wood & J. R. Littlejohn to Cousins & friends, September 6, 1856, Lipscomb, UNC. "I am agoing to marry between now [September 1856] and spring if I can get the Right kind of a girl I want a girl that Knows something about domectic affairs that is just the sort of agirl that I wont for a wife & Dick says that is the only sot of a girl that he will marry."

67. William Wood & J. R. Littlejohn to Cousins & friends, September 6, 1856. Lipscomb, UNC.

68. James Brewer to Margaret Alley, July 27, 1863, Alley-Brewer Family Letters, SHSM.

69. James S. Brewer returned home to Fulton County, Illinois, and married Sarah M. Philips in October 1867. It is unclear whether Sarah was the woman he called a "snorter for fun" and full of "social glee." In 1860 James was a farm laborer living with his employer in Fulton County. See the 1850 and 1860 federal census for James S. Brewer; also Illinois, Marriage Index, 1860–1920. The summary report for the

NOTES TO PAGES 64–68   279

manuscript papers indicates that James L. Brewer served in the Twenty-Eighth Illinois Volunteer Infantry. But no James L. was listed for the Twenty-Eighth in the Illinois Civil War Muster and Descriptive Rolls. Based on the correct identification of Brewer's Illinois infantry, James Brewer's middle initial should be S. James L. served in the 102nd Illinois Infantry. Only James S. Brewer served in the Twenty-Eighth. Middle initials can be a crucial aid to distinguishing people with a common name. See Database of Illinois Veterans Index, 1775–1995 and the Illinois Civil War Muster and Descriptive Rolls, Illinois State Archives, Office of the Secretary of State at http://www.ilsos.gov/isaveterans/civilmustersrch.jsp.

70. George Lanphear to Eliza and Eliphalet Shattuck, December 17, 1854, Shattuck, MHS. Ellen Shattuck is Eliphalet's sister. His death certificate in the Vermont Vital Records, 1720–1908 database establishes that his parents were John and Lepha (variously spelled). Looking up John in the 1850 and 1860 census, I found Ellen was part of their household. Ellen's first name was Sarah. She was listed under her middle name in the 1860 census.

71. George Lanphear to Eliza Shattuck, January 1, 1856, Shattuck, MHS.

72. George Lanphear to Eliza and Eliphalet Shattuck, December 23, 1855, Shattuck, MHS.

73. *Dictionary of American History*, rev. ed., vol. 6 (New York: Charles Scribner's, 1961), 293.

74. Molly D. Gaither to John Burgess Gaither, March 7, 1864, Gaither, UNC.

75. William Wells Newell, *Games and Songs of American Children* (New York: Harper & Brothers, 1883), 61.

76. Newell, *Games and Songs*, 62. In Boston the variant went: "As many wives as the stars in the skies, / And each as old as Addam." And in Georgia, the game-rhyme began, "Many many stars are in the skies, / And each as old as Adam."

77. Women and men shared many group experiences in rural America. See Karen V. Hansen, *A Very Social Time: Crafting Community in Antebellum New England* (Berkeley: University of California Press, 1994), 18 n. 29. She cites Nancy Grey Osterud's conclusion that men and women were integrated in their "patterns of sociability" in rural upstate New York.

78. George Lanphear to Eliza and Elilphalet Shattuck, December 23, 1855, Shattuck, MHS.

79. George Lanphear to Eliza and Elilphalet Shattuck, December 23, 1855, Shattuck, MHS.

80. George Lanphear to Eliza Shattuck, June 20, 1856, Shattuck, MHS.

81. Still unmarried, George died at the Battle of Missionary Ridge on November 25, 1863.

82. Joseph Hall to Mary Vanhorn, March 30, 1865, Vanhorn, LC.

83. Joseph Hall to Mary Vanhorn [sister], March 30, 1865, Vanhorn, LC.

84. Jasper Bell to William and Caroline Warm, July 5, 1851 [Jasper and Franklin Bell wrote separate messages in the same letter], Downing-Whinrey, SHSM.

85. H. C. Hunt to Joe Whinrey, August 29, 1882, Downing-Whinrey, SHSM.

86. Holly Buck to Brother and Sister, September 3, 1854, Shattuck, Minn.

87. George Deen to Sister, May 22, 1857, Alley-Brewer Family Letters, SHSM. Lineville straddles the border between Missouri and Iowa.

88. Old Uncle Ned to Friend David, April 27, 1864, Unidentified Manuscripts Collection, LC.

280　NOTES TO PAGES 68–70

89. James and Elizabeth Ferguson to Russell Ferguson, February 5, 1855, TP, Russell Ferguson Letters, SHSM.

90. James and Elizabeth Ferguson to Russell Ferguson, October 29, 1856, TP, Russell Ferguson Letters, SHSM.

91. H. B. Ferrell to William D. Ferrell [postmarked May 17, 1884], Wanda Haney Harwood Coll., SHSM.

92. [A son, probably Phillip Fuller] to Mother [Elizabeth Fuller], July 10, 1862, SLFC, Duke.

93. Elizabeth Smith Fuller to Son [likely Phillip Fuller], July 20, 1862, SLFC, Duke. Margaret did not need to use Fuller's mother as a go-between. Even if she was illiterate, she could have dictated a letter to a relative or friend.

94. Rufus Wright to Elisabeth Turner Wright, May 25, 1864, in *Families and Freedom: A Documentary History of African-American Kinship in the Civil War Era*, ed. Ira Berlin and Leslie S. Rowland (New York: New Press, 1997), 166–67.

95. David Demus to Mary Jane Demus, July 27, 1864, VS/UV.

96. Samuel Christy to Mary Jane Demus, September 3, 1864, VS/UV.

97. Simeon Tierce to Sarah Jane Tierce, November 24, 1863, in Edythe Ann Quinn, *Freedom Journey: Black Civil War Soldiers and The Hills Community, Westchester County, New York* (Albany: State University of New York Press, 2015). Quinn published his five letters in an Appendix B (133–49) along with helpful annotations. She added periods and some commas but did not change his spelling.

98. Simeon Anderson Tierce to Sarah Jane Tierce, Undated Letter [written between March 27 and July 8, 1864], in Quinn, *Freedom Journey*, 146–47.

99. Jane Williamson, "African Americans in Addison County, Charlotte, and Hinesburgh, Vermont, 1790–1860," *Vermont History* 78 (Winter–Spring 2010): 15–72, esp. 28–29, 36.

100. Vermont, Race: 1850 Surveys; US Federal Census 1850; and Chittenden County, Vermont, Federal Census 1850 accessed through Social Explorer, an online demographic tool at https://www.socialexplorer.com/a9676d974c/explore. While the sample from 1790 to 1860 is very small, African American men occasionally married white women. Importantly, Vermont did not prohibit interracial marriage. See Williamson, "African Americans in Vermont," pp. 29–30.

101. Bell Wiley in *The Life of Johnny Reb: The Common Soldier of the Confederacy*, updated ed. (Baton Rouge: Louisiana State University Press, 2008), 276, briefly mentions the practice of using intermediaries. His sensitivity to this norm, though only one line, stands out, considering that the first edition of his work was published in 1943. I have come across no other historian who clearly recognized this pattern.

102. Caroline M. Richardson to Orrilla Varney, April 12, 1846, LMGL.

103. "Repeated visits implied commitment" among elites in early American culture, according to Martha Tomhave Blauvelt, "Making a Match in Nineteenth-Century New York: The Courtship Diary of Mary Guion," *New York History* 76 (April 1995): 164. Nancy Grey Osterud, in her study of rural New York farm women living in an agricultural community in the second half of the nineteenth century, also found this pattern. See *Bonds of Community: The Lives of Farm Women in*

NOTES TO PAGES 70–72   281

Nineteenth-Century New York (Ithaca: Cornell University Press, 1991), 95–96. Class was not a category of analysis in Osterud's study.

104. Mollie D. Gaither to J. B. Gaither, May 6, 1864, Gaither, UNC.

105. Public failure might translate into a personal sense of shame.

106. Ginger S. Frost, *Promises Broken: Courtship, Class, and Gender in Victorian England* (Charlottesville: University Press of Virginia, 1995), 61–62, 69–70, 92–93. She finds that the median English working-class engagement was one year, three months. But her contention that in England "[a] lower middle- or working-class woman might wait 5–10 years for marriage" after being engaged is astounding by American standards. Nothing even remotely similar occurred in the United States, where a long engagement period was rare. Perhaps the lawsuits for breach of promise are not normative evidence of working-class mate selection in England. If long engagements were deviant there as well, then it was exactly this deviance that would have provoked the lawsuits. Francoise Barret-Ducrocq found that more than three-quarters of the working-class Londoners in her sample of foundling hospital files had courtships that lasted longer than six months, and almost 54 percent lasted one to two years or more. Once again, it is likely that abandoning a child was not the end result of a normal courtship in England, and it was certainly not ordinary behavior in America. See *Love in the Time of Victoria: Sexuality, Class and Gender in Nineteenth-Century London* (London: Verso, 1991), 98. Unlike Frost's subjects, the women in Barret-Ducrocq's study did not have the resources to file a breach-of-promise lawsuit, but were most often promised marriage and then jilted after they became pregnant. If one to two years was a normative engagement period in England, then the American working-class courtship pattern differed from its Atlantic analogue in length. Moreover, the demarcation of courtship from engagement was blurred in America, where the presumption of future marriage was encapsulated within the third stage of working-class courtship. Engagement was almost never explicitly separated from courtship in American working-class correspondence. Regarding her English subjects, Frost acknowledges that she may have "put too definite a line between the two periods," that is, courtship and engagement.

107. Frost, *Promises Broken*, 62. The long engagement pattern in England is instructive in contrast to American patterns. "First," the English historian contends, "these couples had to save carefully before setting up a household." Working-class Americans showed little or no inclination to delay marriage in order to save money. Some men may have delayed the whole mate selection process because of economic deficiencies, but once they made a decision to marry and paired off with their intended, marriage followed within months rather than years.

108. John B. Gilman to Nelly, February 3, 1856, John Gilman and Family Letters, MHS. My emphasis.

109. George Lanphear to Eliza Shattuck, March 17, 1857 and October 27, 1857, Shattuck, MHS.

110. George Lanphear to Eliza Shattuck, September 6, 1857, Shattuck, MHS.

111. As far as I know, there is no way to quantify the time between courtship and marriage in working-class practice. My figures are based on rough estimates from the

282 NOTES TO PAGES 72–76

letters. See Beverly Schwartzberg, "'Lots of Them Did That': Desertion, Bigamy, and Marital Fluidity in Late-Nineteenth-Century America," *Journal of Social History* 37 (Spring 2004): 580, 585, 590. She documents several short courtships reported by wives to Civil War pension examiners.

112. Frank Flint to Jennie Russell, November 18, 1864, Flint, MHS.

113. Sarah E. Denham to Jaspar N. Bertram, July 20, 1862, University of Washington Digital Collections, Jaspar Bertram Papers, http://digitalcollections.lib.washington.edu/cdm/compoundobject/collection/civilwar/id/659/rec/25.

114. Charles Smith to Martha and William Smith, April 4, 1851, Woods-Holman, SHSM.

115. Juliaett Chaffer to Louisa Russ, February 12, 1857, Shumway, MHS.

116. Justina Woods to Zelia Woods, February 18, 1849, Woods-Holman, SHSM.

117. Justina Woods to Zelia Woods, September 17, 184[?] and February 18, 1849, Woods-Holman, SHSM.

118. Thomas Baldwin and J. Thomas, *A New and Complete Gazeteer of the U.S.* (Philadelphia: Lippincott, Grambo & Co., 1854).

119. Justina Woods to Sister, January 25, 1853, Woods-Holman, SHSM.

120. See Missouri Marriage Records, 1805–2002, and the 1850 and 1860 US Federal Census. Also Baldwin and Thomas, *Gazeteer of U.S.* Her father valued his real estate holdings at $5,000 in the 1850 federal census. It is difficult to assess the real value of his holdings, as the land was in an unincorporated area.

121. Missouri Marriage Records, 1805–2007, and the 1860 and 1870 US Federal Census. The spelling of her married name changed from McSwaine in the 1850 Marriage record to McSwainin in the 1860 census to McSween in 1870.

122. J. F. Sutton to Russell Ferguson, January 21, 1855, TP, Russell Ferguson Letters, SHSM. She is referring to Spring River, Lawrence County, Missouri.

123. F. L. Bell to Mother and all, May 1, 1859, Downing-Whinrey, SHSM. He was married by the 1870 US census and living in Empire, California, a small Central Valley town.

124. William Meeter to John Mcclure, December 20, 1827, William Meeter Letter, SHSM. Calloway County, where he was living, was organized in 1820.

125. Harriet Buck to Eliza Shattuck, January 14, 1857, Shattuck, MHS.

126. M[ary] M. Houser to James Houser [cousin], May 23, 1864, Augusta County, VS/UV.

127. Anna Mason to Mother, June 15, 1856, Bronson, HEH.

128. Carol Lasser, "'The World's Dread Laugh': Singlehood and Service in Nineteenth-Century Boston," in *The New England Working Class and the New Labor History*, ed. Herbert G. Gutman and Donald H. Bell (Urbana: University of Illinois Press, 1987), 72–88, esp. 73, 76–77; Susan L. Porter, "Victorian Values in the Marketplace: Single Women and Work in Boston, 1800–1850," in *Women of the Commonwealth: Work, Family, and Social Change in Nineteenth-Century Massachusetts*, ed. Susan Porter (Amherst: University of Massachusetts Press, 1996), 17–41; David J. Hacker, Libra Hilde, and James Holland Jones, "The Effect of the Civil War on Southern Marriage Patterns," *Journal of Southern History* 76 (February 2010): 52–54, Table 1.

129. Howard Chudacoff, *The Age of the Bachelor: Creating an American Subculture* (Princeton: Princeton University Press, 1999).

130. Mollie D. Gaither [girlfriend] to J. B. Gaither, April 30, 1864, Gaither, UNC.

NOTES TO PAGES 77–82   283

131. John Garriott to Brother & Family, January 17, 1862, Garriott, SHSM.
132. John Garriott to Sister, September 11, 1862, Garriott, SHSM.
133. John Garriott to Sister, September 11, 1862, Garriott, SHSM.
134. John Garriott to Sister, April 5, 1863, Garriott, SHSM.
135. John Garriott to Sister, April 5, 1863, Garriott, SHSM.
136. John Garriott to Sister Zarilda, April 30, 1864, Garriott, SHSM.
137. Missouri Marriage Records, 1805–2002; American Civil War Regiments, 1861–66, Eighteenth Infantry Regiment, Missouri, Muster date: July 18, 1865.
138. John W. Garriott, 1850, 1860, 1880 US Federal Census. In the 1860 census, his name is spelled "Garrett." See also 1885 Kansas State Census Collection, 1855–1925.
139. 1860 US Federal Census under Jas Bevers, National Park Service Soldiers and Sailors Database under James S. Beavers.
140. 1860 US Federal Census under Thos Bevers. George was also his father's name, and the son likely went by his middle name in the family.
141. All quotations in this paragraph are found in George T. Beavers to Brother[-in-Law], September 22, 1861, Upchurch, Duke.
142. George T. Beavers to Brother[-in-Law], September 22, 1861, Upchurch, Duke.
143. George Beavers to Brother [John Beavers], February 3, 1862, Upchurch, Duke.
144. George Beavers to Brother [John Beavers], February 3, 1862, Upchurch, Duke.
145. Mildred Yates, North Carolina, US Index to Marriage Bonds, 1741–1868. Mildred Yates lived with her parents in the Southern Division of Wake County, North Carolina, according to the 1860 federal census. The Beavers lived in the Eastern Division of Chatham County that census year. Chatham County shared an eastern border with Wake County. One possibility is that they were neighbors who lived on either side of an artificial county line with few natural barriers. See State Archives of North Carolina, North Carolina Maps (Digital Project), 1871 map of Wake County, https://dc.lib.unc.edu/cdm/singleitem/collection/ncmaps/id/241/rec/10. Another possibility is that Mildred spent considerable time in Chatham County with her mother's family. See birthplace of mother on Sarah Mildred Johnson's Death Certificate, North Carolina, US Deaths, 1906–30. On a hand-drawn map done at the beginning of the twentieth century, which included the names of landowners, people with the surnames Beavers and Yates were located near each other. Historic map of Williams Township, Chatham Co., North Carolina, 1903, https://dc.lib.unc.edu/cdm/ref/collection/ncmaps/id/270.
146. North Carolina Index to Marriage Bonds, 1741–1868 and US Civil War Soldier Records and Profiles, 1861–65. He was mustered out on February 10 and married on November 24, 1865.

Chapter 3

1. Frank Flint to Jennie Russell, November 18, 1864, Flint, MHS.
2. Quantification is difficult, but perhaps not more than a quarter of poor, undereducated Americans practiced romantic courtship or blended some aspect of romantic

284   NOTES TO PAGES 82–85

love and romantic courtship rituals into their nonromantic mate selection practices. This is an estimate based on a wide sample of letters, at least five thousand, that I have read for this study. Of course, no exact calibration is possible but some proportionality is helpful.

3. These groups often conformed to the boundaries of a small village or township but could, in the case of larger cities, be defined by neighborhoods, districts, or work environments.

4. Delos Lake to Mother, January 19, 1865, D. Lake, HEH.

5. Delos Lake to Calvin Lake, January 22, 1865, D. Lake, HEH.

6. Jacob Christy to Mary Jane Demus, May 29, 1865, Franklin County, Pennsylvania, VS/UV. See Pennsylvania and New Jersey, Church and Town Records 1669–1999 for his baptism record; also see 1850 US Federal Census under Jacob E. Christer. His entire family is identified as biracial or, in the census term, mulatto.

7. Samuel Christy to My Dear Friends, July 10, 1864, Franklin County, Pennsylvania, VS/UV.

8. Marriage Certificate of Rufus Wright and Elisabeth Turner in *Families and Freedom: A Documentary History of African-American Kinship in the Civil War Era*, ed. Ira Berlin and Leslie S. Rowland (New York: New Press, 1997), 165.

9. Rufus Wright to Elisabeth Turner Wright, May 25, 1864, in Berlin and Rowland, *Families and Freedom*, 166–67.

10. D. Ellis to Brother [Lemuel Ellis], December 11, 1852, Lemuel Ellis Papers, Duke. "I want to Come home wos then I ever did in life." "I am not satiffide at all and cant be with out I can git A wife I think I shall com hom an d look out for one bu for long."

11. Unidentified young woman to Margaret Dunlap, June 7, 1860, Augusta County, Virginia, VS/UV. See chapter 2 for her comments on the boys she left behind after she relocated.

12. See Betsy Ann Amos, North Carolina Marriage License (1867–1961), accessed at North Carolina Marriage Records, 1741–2011. Her father, Richard Amos, is identified on the license as deceased, but her mother is living in Stokes County, where the marriage took place on September 15, 1873. William Amos was visiting these relatives.

13. The two letters were written seriatim on the same sheets of paper. Amos addressed his first letter to Nancy Doolittle and his second to MB. My guess is that Amos was either practicing or copying real letters. They might also have been drafts of letters that he fantasized about but never mailed. Even if they were not posted, his texts illuminate a common thought pattern that undergirds nineteenth-century tribal courtship.

14. William H. Amos to MB, May 30, 1869, Amos, Duke. The first letter, addressed to Nancy Doolittle, was headed by two different dates. The second letter that followed, addressed to MB, had no date. Of the two dates, the one on the left, May 30, seems to belong to his second letter to MB. The April 29, 1869, date is situated further to the right in a position that might be expected for the first letter. Regardless of spatial position, the later date should logically belong to the later letter.

15. William H. Amos to MB, May 30, 1869, Amos, Duke.

NOTES TO PAGES 85–88   285

16. He was living in Howard County, Indiana, about eighty miles north of Shelby County, and working as a farm laborer when the census taker called. See William Amos, Ervin, Howard County, Indiana, in the 1860 and 1870 Federal Census. Close relatives lived in Shelby County, Indiana. Amos may have lived with them intermittently during his adolescence.

17. See Indiana Marriage Index, 1840–1941. There were many Eliza Millers around the right age living in Indiana in 1870. One likely candidate was working in Shelby County as a domestic. See the 1870 US Federal Census.

18. W. W. Hagood to Miss Ollevia, January 6, 1864; G. E. Hollis to Miss O. A., February 21, 1864, and several others, Joseph Espey Papers, UNC.

19. Richard P. Hays to Miss Olivia, January 5, 1862, Joseph Espey Papers, UNC. See US Census Bureau, Census of Population and Housing Publications, "Measuring America: The Decennial Censuses from 1790–2000," https://www.census.gov/libr ary/publications/2002/dec/pol_02-ma.html. I chose 1860 as the closest date to the letters sent to Miss Olivia. Using the fifteen to nineteen age range of the 1860 census as a rough estimate of eligible mates in Cherokee County, the local pool had a peak figure of 845 males and 885 females. Of course an individual resident would constitute a tribe within a subset of town, village, neighborhood, school, church, and family connections.

20. See Richard P. Hayes [spelled with an *e*], 1850 US Federal Census. In 1850 he was living in Cherokee County and was sixteen years old. He was listed as a farmer. His correspondence indicates he was better educated than many of his peers. Olivia married her cousin, Joseph Samuel Espey in October 1865. See Olivia Espy in the Alabama, Compiled Marriages from Selected Counties, 1809–1920. She moved to Texas Valley, Georgia, where her husband's family lived, according to the 1870 US Federal Census.

21. Jerome Farnsworth to Sister Mate, February 19, 1862, Jerome Farnsworth and Family Papers, MHS.

22. The county had a population of slightly over five thousand in 1860. His residence in the township of Elysian meant he would have been familiar with a smaller pool of eligible women. Le Sueur County Minnesota Genealogy and History, http://genealog ytrails.com/minn/lesueur/census.html.

23. US Census Bureau, Census of Population and Housing, "1860 Census: Population of the United States," 250, https://www.census.gov/programs-surveys/decennial-census/decade/decennial-publications.1860.html. The 1860 census did not provide counts of single or married populations within age categories. Therefore the fifteen-to nineteen-year division is the most reliable tally of eligible single residents. The age group that follows, twenty- to twenty-nine-year-olds, would include too many married people.

24. B. A. Campbell to Sarah Kesterson, February 21, 1870, CivWar, SHSM. In the early 1880s, Sarah lived in Boonville, Missouri. It is unclear where she was living in 1870, but she was likely situated in a small Missouri town.

25. Balus King Draper to Caroline Lipscomb, April 12, 1851, Lipscomb, UNC. All Draper's quotations below come from this letter. "[T]he wedding is over at last I wer at

286 NOTES TO PAGES 88–90

it wee had agrate deal of fun thare plaid tel 3 o clock in the nite," "thare wer about eight hundred Dollars worth of gulery thare that is bee sids what the gentlmen had One lady by the of Miss Elizabeth trus had One hundred and fifty seven Dollars worth of guelary she wos one of the waters."

26. "Miss Frances hague wood another water she had one hundred Dolers worth of guelary she is one of May bous [my beaus]," Draper bragged. "She is as pirty as apink and I lover her sohard hit all most mak my hart sink O whot pirty black Eyes she has got wot rosey cheaks to pirty pirty to ride apore horse I had the pleasure of Com versen with Her at the weding." "[P]irty as a pink" was a colloquialism that meant pretty as a pink carnation, which he rhymed with "makes my heart sink" another standard nineteenth-century colloquialism.

27. "give Altimirah My best love and reskek and tel her that I havent forgoten yer yet and don't in ten to[.] tel her to rite to mee and rite as wirck [quick] as you Can."

28. Baylis Draper, Alabama Marriages, 1809–1920 (Selected Counties).

29. 1870 Federal Census and Average Value of Land per Farm, Table 34, USDA General Report, 30, http://usda.mannlib.cornell.edu/usda/AgCensusImages/1959/02/01/888 /Table-34.pdf.

30. Henry Clay Russell to Sister, November 30, 1865, Civil War Diaries and Letters, IDL.

31. Henry Clay Russell to Sister, August 10, 1865. He revealed his engagement in Henry Clay Russell to Sister, October, 12, 1865. Her full name was Mary Jane Robinson McKinnie. Civil War Diaries and Letters, IDL.

32. Henry C. Russell married Amanda McCall, Iowa Selection Marriage Index, 1758–1996. They married November 25, 1868. Also see 1870 US Federal Census under Henry Russell.

33. Her hometown was Williamsburg, Massachusetts.

34. According to the 1860 Federal Census, Luther and Lucy were working in different locations. He was employed in Dracut, Massachusetts, and she was working in Shelburne, Massachusetts. They were close to ninety miles apart when the census was taken in July. See Lucy A. Smith and Luther L. Richardson in 1860 US Federal Census. It is possible that they worked together at some other time of the year, but unlikely, since summer was the prime season for Luther's labor as a temporary farmhand. Also the 1860 census indicated that Lucy was working for a man who had a wife. At the time that she wrote her letter to Luther (with no notation of the year), she was working for a widower and was looking backward at their employment together. It seems reasonable, therefore, to eliminate 1860 as the year that they became acquainted. My best guess is that her letter was written in 1861 and that they had been employed together in 1859. They could have worked together earlier, but the letter was clearly written before she married in June 1862.

35. Lucy A. Smith to Luther Richardson, June 16, [1861?], LWRD, Duke. For a general overview, see Carol Lasser, "The Domestic Balance of Power: Relations between Mistress and Maid in Nineteenth-century New England," *Labor History* 28 (January 1987): 5–22.

36. Lucy A. Smith to Luther Richardson, June 16, [1861?], LWRD, Duke.

37. See 1860 US Federal Census and Massachusetts Marriage Records, 1840–1915.

NOTES TO PAGES 90–95   287

38. Anson "Dyre" in the 1850 US Federal Census and Anson "Dyer" in the 1860 US Federal Census. He was living in the Vermont Asylum for the Insane at Brattleboro, founded in 1836. For more information on this institution see Constance M. McGovern, "The Insane, the Asylum, and the State in Nineteenth-Century Vermont," *Vermont History* 52 (Fall 1984): 205–24, https://vermonthistory.org/journal/misc/InsaneAsylum&State.pdf. Also Lucy A. Dyer, 1870 US Federal Census for a record of her husband's wealth.

39. Luther Richardson to Friend Oria [sometime around November 1863], LWRD, Duke.

40. Orie McCoy to Charles H. Richardson, February 21, 1864, LWRD, Duke.

41. Luther was killed in action on September 19, 1864, well after her February invitation to Henry. US, Registers of Deaths of Volunteers, 1861–1865.

42. Oreanna McCoy in the Massachusetts, Town and Vital Records, 1620–1988. She married Lowell Young on July 17, 1869.

43. Charles Henry Richardson to Mother, April 8, 1865, LWRD, Duke.

44. M[ary] M. Houser to James Houser, March 21, 1864, Augusta County, Virginia, VS/UV.

45. M[ary] M. Houser to James Houser, May 23, 1864, VS/UV.

46. Both Burgess Gaither's cousin (his fiancée) and sister are called Molly and spelled erratically. I have aimed for a consistent distinction by referring to his cousin and fiancée as Mollie or Mollie D. and his sister as Molly, regardless of how their names were spelled in the letters. Mollie D. to John Burgess Gaither, February 20, 1864, Gaither, UNC. Most of the marriage proposals captured in working-class letters were devoid of romantic imagery. Another example is Alexander Moody to Lois Richardson, April 15, 1855, LWRD, Duke. See Moody's proposal in chapter 6.

47. Mollie D. to John Burgess Gaither, March 7, 1864, Gaither, UNC. Another letter in the collection by Mollie D. to Burgess also appears to be dated March 7, 1864. The number 7 in this case might also be a 1.

48. Mollie D. Gaither to John Burgess Gaither, March 7, 1864, Gaither, UNC. Mollie D. was only willing to express her love directly through a love song, which she quoted. See chapter 7 for a full discussion of this poem.

49. John Burgess Gaither to Sister Molly, March 20, 1864, Gaither, UNC.

50. Mollie D. Gaither to J. B. Gaither, May 6, 1864, Gaither, UNC.

51. Mollie D. Gaither to J. B. Gaither, June 4, 1864, Gaither, UNC. Clarksbury is not a town but a Methodist church in Iredell County, North Carolina.

52. "Population of the United States in 1860: North Carolina," https://www2.census.gov/library/publications/decennial/1860/population/1860a-27.pdf. At its peak, the total pool of eligible boys in Iredell County numbered 605 and girls 611, which was the 1860 census figure for white males and females in the fifteen to nineteen age group. (The age group that follows, twenty- to twenty-nine-year olds, would include a large and indeterminate number of married people.) Only four free African Americans in this age bracket were living in Iredell in 1860. The county seat had a population of 320. Mollie D. and Burgess would have interacted with a subset of the county population of single young people: neighbors, classmates, friends, and family connections. In

288 NOTES TO PAGES 95–100

fact, the 1860 US Federal Census officially designated "East of Rockford Road, Iredell, North Carolina" as the home of Mary [Mollie] D. Gaither.

53. Mollie D. Gaither to J. B. Gaither, May 6, 1864, Gaither, UNC.

54. John Burgess Gaither to Sister Molly, March 20, 1864, Gaither, UNC.

55. Mollie D. Gaither to J. B. Gaither, June 4, 1864, Gaither, UNC.

56. J. B. Gaither to Molly, July 20, 1864, Gaither, UNC.

57. Mollie D. Gaither to John Burgess Gaither, February 20, 1864, Gaither, UNC.

58. J. B. Gaither to Molly, July 20, 1864, Gaither, UNC.

59. P. M. Sammery to Molly E. Gaither, July 28, 1864, Gaither, UNC.

60. Evidence for this analysis of middle-class courtship can be found in Karen Lystra, *Searching the Heart: Women, Men, and Romantic Love in Nineteenth-Century America* (New York: Oxford University Press), chapter 6.

61. US Census Bureau, *Statistics of the Population of the United States at the Tenth Census*, "Population by Race, Sex, and Nativity," Volume 1, 409, Table 5. https://www2.census. gov/library/publications/decennial/1880/vol-01-population/1880_v1-13.pdf

62. James le Renisan to Miss Lucious [Lucia] Knotts, October 17, 1887, Rhone Family Papers, Briscoe Center for American History, University of Texas, Austin. I first came across a quotation from his letter in Vicki Howard, "The Courtship Letters of an African American Couple: Race, Gender, Class, and the Cult of True Womanhood," *Southwestern Historical Quarterly* 100 (July 1996): 74. Howard spotlights the romantic love letters of Calvin Rhone and Lucia Knotts.

63. Though verification proved elusive, he might be the man recorded as James Renson who married Octava Floyd in Texas in 1903. See Octava Floyd, Texas, Select County Marriage Index, 1837–1965. Also Octavia Floyd, 1900 US Federal Census.

64. Shelton Martin to Elisabeth Martin, August 18, 1864, CivWar, SHSM. This correspondence has been digitized and can be found at the Missouri Digital Heritage site, Missouri History Museum, St. Louis Area Civil War Digitization Project. https://mdh. contentdm.oclc.org/digital/collection/CivilWar/search/searchterm/Shelton%20Mar tin/page/2.

65. F. I. Buber to I. S. and Diliza Upchurch, October 20, 1857, Upchurch, Duke. The letter writer is definitely Frances I. Beavers. He dramatically misspelled his name but his self-identification as the brother of Adelia Upchurch, nee Beavers, led through the database called Web: Netherlands, Genealogie Online Trees Index, 1000–2015 Birth, Marriage, & Death to a chain of US Federal Censuses, which allowed for the unambiguous verification of his identity. Frank Beavers was dubbed Baber in Civil War Records. Beavers was also a troublesome name for the 1850 census taker who called his family the Browers.

66. See the 1860 US Federal Census under the name J. F. Baber. His location, age, birthplace, and occupation check out, but the youngest child in his household, age two, could not have been born before he became a widower. He was living with a mysterious eighteen-year-old woman who was impossible to trace.

67. William Johnson to Maggie, March 4, 1869, Johnson, MHS. .

68. William Johnson to Maggie, May 20, 1869, Johnson, MHS.

69. William Johnson to Maggie, August 9, 1969, Johnson, MHS.

70. Romantic love resulted in a predictable emotional response pattern: jealousy and possessiveness, feelings of dependency, obsessive thoughts of the loved one, fluctuations of happiness and unhappiness, and fear for the well-being of a beloved. See Lystra, *Searching the Heart*, chapter 2.
71. William Johnson to Maggie, May 9, 1869, Johnson, MHS.
72. William Johnson to Maggie, May 20, 1869, Johnson, MHS.
73. William Johnson to Maggie, April 21, 1868, Johnson, MHS.
74. William Johnson to Maggie, April 21, 1868, Johnson, MHS.
75. William Johnson to Maggie, August [number unclear], 1868, Johnson, MHS.
76. These courtship tests usually involved identifying an obstacle that the partner in love was challenged to overcome. Evidence for testing in middle-class courtship can be found in Lystra, *Searching the Heart*, chapter 6.
77. William Johnson to Maggie, October 16, 1869, Johnson, MHS.
78. William Johnson to Maggie, August [number unclear], 1868, Johnson, MHS.
79. J. H. Benson to William Johnson, November 17[?], 1869, Johnson, MHS.
80. William Johnson to Maggie, January 19, 1870, Johnson, MHS.
81. The quotation is often cited without attribution. When any source is given, the citation is to Maya Angelou interview, Oprah Winfrey SuperSoul Sunday, February 3, 2013. Watching the entire Winfrey interview of Angelou on YouTube, I never heard her say it. It is possible that some other version was aired on the radio.
82. Eunice Stone Connolly to Mother, March 7, 1870, Richardson, Duke.
83. Eunice L. Richardson Stone, 1869, Massachusetts, US Marriage Records, 1840–1915. See Martha Hodes, *The Sea Captain's Wife: A True Story of Love, Race, and War in the Nineteenth Century* (New York: Norton, 2006) for the larger narrative.
84. Eunice Stone Connolly to Mother, December 15, 1871, Richardson, Duke.
85. Eunice Stone Connolly to Mother, March 7, 1870, Richardson, Duke.
86. Eunice Stone Connolly to Mother, March 7, 1870, Richardson, Duke; Martha Hodes, ed., *Sex, Love, Race: Crossing Boundaries in North American History* (New York: New York University Press, 1999).
87. Eunice Stone Connolly to Mother, March 7, 1870, Richardson, Duke.
88. Hattie to Mother and Sister [Lois Davis and Ann Putnam McCoy], January 26, 1872, Richardson, Duke.
89. Mr. Connolly to Mother [Lois Davis], February 2, 1874.
90. Eunice Connolly to Mother, March 27, 1875.
91. Ellen Merrill to Brother [Charles Henry Richardson], February 19, 1881. The information on the circumstances of their sister's death was provided by an enclosed letter from John Wood, a lawyer for Connolly's estate.
92. Eunice Stone Connolly to Mother, March 7, 1870, Richardson, Duke.
93. Eunice Connolly to Mother, January 3, 1873, Richardson, Duke.
94. Heather Andrea Williams, *Help Me to Find My People: The African American Search for Family Lost in Slavery* (Chapel Hill: University of North Carolina Press, 2012); Dylan Penningroth, "My People, My People: The Dynamics of Community in Southern Slavery," in *New Studies in the History of American Slavery*, ed., Edward Baptist and Stephanie Camp (Athens: University of Georgia Press, 2006), 166–76.

290 NOTES TO PAGES 110–113

95. See Joshua D. Rothman's valuable study, *Notorious in the Neighborhood: Sex and Families across the Color Line in Virginia, 1787–1861* (Chapel Hill: University of North Carolina Press, 2003), for violations of these racial boundaries and the role of the local community in accepting or rejecting intimate relationships.

Chapter 4

1. William Wood and J. R. Littlejohn to Cousins & friends, September 6, 1856, Lipscomb, UNC.
2. Mary Blewett, "Yorkshire Lasses and Their Lads: Sexuality, Sexual Customs, and Gender Antagonisms in Anglo-American Working-Class Culture," *Journal of Social History* 40 (December 2006): 325. She reports on a female factory ritual called "sunning" where the women seize a new lad on the job and pull down his pants, exposing his genitals to ridicule. Apparently the ritual could sometimes include pouring machine oil and vigorously rubbing his privates before letting him go. See J. B. Priestley, *Margin Released: A Writer's Reminiscences and Reflections* (London: Heinemann, 1963), 61.
3. Karen Lystra, *Searching the Heart: Women, Men, and Romantic Love in Nineteenth-Century America* (New York: Oxford University Press, 1989), 84–91.
4. "I don't care if I do get laugh at, for looking so soon," Sarah Trask wrote defiantly, referring to her oft-thwarted predictions of the imminent return of her sailor boyfriend. See Sarah Trask Diary, May 7, 1849, as quoted in Karen V. Hansen, *A Very Social Time: Crafting Community in Antebellum New England* (Berkeley: University of California Press, 1994), 122. This diary entry is a clear example of public ridicule related to sexual attraction. For a fuller exploration of the Trask diary, see Mary H. Blewitt, "'I Am Doom to Disappointment': The Diaries of a Beverly, Massachusetts Shoebinder, Sarah E. Trask, 1849–1851," *Essex Institute Historical Collections* 117 (July 1981): 192–212; also Mary H. Blewett, *Men, Women, and Work: Class, Gender, and Protest in the New England Shoe Industry, 1780–1910* (Urbana: University of Illinois Press, 1988), 88–94.
5. Frank Flint to Jennie Russell, October 9, 1864, Flint, MHS.
6. Frank Flint to Jennie Russell, August 2, 1864, Flint, MHS. See Francis S. Flint in 1860 US Federal Census.
7. Cambridge became a city in 1846, uniting three rival villages—Old Cambridge, Cambridgeport, and East Cambridge—according to the Cambridge Historical Commission at https://www.cambridgema.gov/historic/cambridgehistory. See also The Reverend Nicholas Hoppin, *An Anniversary Sermon Preached in Christ Church, Cambridge, Mass.* (Boston: E.P. Dutton & Co., 1861), 10 n. 1, for a breakdown of population in each distinct settlement within the city.
8. Alfred Roe, *The Twenty-Fourth Regiment* (Worcester, MA: Twenty-Fourth Veteran Association, 1907), 497–506. See Company E roster of noncommissioned officers and privates.

NOTES TO PAGES 113–114   291

9. Campbell Gibson, "U.S. Census Bureau Population of the 100 Largest Cities and Other Urban Places in the United States, 1790–1990," Population Division Working Paper no. 27, June 1998, https://www.census.gov/library/working-papers/1998/demo/POP-twps0027.html.

10. This was also true of Lowell, which in 1860 was the twenty-sixth largest city in the United States with a population of 36,827. Charles Henry Richardson asked his mother to find out if there was any truth to the rumor that some young woman in Lowell, who fit the description of his old girlfriend, was claiming they were married. This gossip had all the characteristics of a small-town setting. Evidently tribalism existed among young single men and women in Lowell, so much so that Henry instructed his mother: "do not say any thing about this." Charles H. Richardson to Mother, May 29, 1863, LWRD, Duke.

See Jason Jindrich, "Suburbs in the City: Reassessing the Location of Nineteenth-Century American Working-Class Suburbs," *Social Science History* 36 (Summer 2012): 147–67. For a discussion of the urban village in a contemporary context, see Clement Homs, "Localism and the City: The Example of 'Urban Villages,'" *International Journal of Inclusive Democracy* 3 (January 2007), unpaginated, https://www.inclusivedemocracy.org/journal/vol3/vol3.htm.

11. "Formation and Ranks in Civil War Units" maintains that a company may have started out as one hundred men but was soon reduced to sixty in camp and forty or so after the first battle. See www.angelfire.com/wv/wasec5/formations.html and "Life in a Civil War Army Camp," www.civilwarhome.com/camplife.html. Twenty men might be assigned to a Sibley tent that was designed for twelve. The men in Coolidge's tent may also have been passing around explicit sexual material. See Judith Giesberg, *Sex and the Civil War: Soldiers, Pornography, and the Making of American Morality* (Chapel Hill: University of North Carolina Press, 2017), chapter 2.

12. Oliver Coolidge to [Sister], May 15, 1862, Coolidge, Duke. Though I found several prospects in the US Federal Census and other online databases, I could not conclusively identify the letter writer. This is not surprising given the available information. The recipient, Bill Jennings, was indeed a member of the Twenty-Fourth Massachusetts Volunteer Infantry, as was Shubael Snow, another man referred to in the letter. I believe it is authentic.

13. Coolidge indicated her age before he copied the letter.

14. David J. Hacker, Libra Hilde, and James Holland Jones, "The Effect of the Civil War on Southern Marriage Patterns," *Journal of Southern History* 76 (February 2010): 52–54, Table 1.

15. Oliver Coolidge to [Sister], May 15, 1862, Coolidge, Duke. Jennings may have preferred his middle name, William, to his first name, Otis. See Otis W. Jennings, 1870 Federal Census and Massachusetts Town and Vital Records, 1620–1988. Also Otis N. Jennings, US Civil War Draft Registration Records, 1863–1865. His residence, age, and occupation match these records. If my identification is correct, he died a bachelor.

16. Leslie M. Janes and James M. Olson, "Jeer Pressure: The Behavioral Effects of Observing Ridicule of Others," *Personality and Social Psychology Bulletin* 26 (April 2000): 474–85, esp. 484.

292 NOTES TO PAGES 115–120

17. [Sister] to Oliver Coolidge, [December 1862?], Coolidge, Duke.

18. The girls seem to be writing letters to soldiers whom they regarded as part of their community. Tellingly, Oliver's sister did not condemn the boys as individuals but as a group. Her heated reaction is a sign that she considered at least some of the soldier boys to be members of her tribe. Friends usually enlisted together, and companies were formed from recruits who lived in specific places. See James I. Robertson, Jr., *Soldiers Blue and Gray* (Columbia: University of South Carolina Press, 1998), 12.

19. Dorte Marie Søndergaard, "The Thrill of Bullying: Bullying, Humour and the Making of Community," *Journal for the Theory of Social Behaviour* 48 (March 2018): 48–65, esp. 63.

20. Coolidge to [Sister], May 15, 1862, Coolidge, Duke.

21. The girls' feelings of insecurity, usually tamped down by help and support from intermediaries, were increased through the act of sending personal letters directly to the boys.

22. Janes and Olson, "Jeer Pressure," 474–485.

23. Jaspar Barritt to William Barritt, September 14, 1864, Jasper N. Barritt Correspondence, LC.

24. Joseph Fardell to Parents, May 28, 1864, CivWar, SHSM.

25. Jonathan Blyth to Father and Mother, June 5, 1865, George O. Jewett Papers, LC.

26. Mary Mellish [mother] to George Mellish, February 8, 1865, Mellish, HEH.

27. Luther Richardson to Mother, September 20, 1863, LWRD, Duke.

28. William Meeter to John Mcclure, December 20, 1827, William Meeter Letter, WHMC. This is a typescript of the original letter, which was not in the collection. The transcriber censored what was obviously a crude expression for a woman's "tail." I am guessing the word was "ass." "Salt on its tail" was a slang expression that meant to catch or capture.

29. Joseph Sewell to Thomas Gaither, April 20, 1862, Gaither, UNC.

30. Joseph Sewell to Thomas Gaither, April 20, 1867, Gaither, UNC.

31. Joseph Sewell to Thomas Gaither April 20, 1862, Gaither, UNC.

32. William Crawford to Father and Mother, undated but probably July 1863, Henry Clay and William H. Crawford Letters, WHMC.

33. William Crawford to Brother Edward, July 21, 1863, Henry Clay and William H. Crawford Letters, WHMC.

34. J.[ames] H. Mansfield to Horace Dresser October 17, 1861. Transcriptions of letters to Horace Dresser can be found in Thomas P. Lowry's *Private and Amorous Letters of the Civil War* (self-published, 2009), 23. (Lowry was an associate clinical professor of psychiatry at the University of California, San Francisco, when he retired.) The originals can be read in the Lovell Historical Society. See John and Liz McCann, "Dear Hod: The Civil War Letters of Horace Dresser" *Yesterday's News*, published by the Lovell Historical Society, Spring 2011, 5–6. https://www.lovellhistoricalsociety.org/wp-content/uploads/2015/12/Spring-2011.pdf.

35. Seth Eastman to Horace Dresser, December 11, 1861, Lowry, *Private and Amorous Letters*, 21–22.

36. Seth Eastman to Horace Dresser, June 1, 1862, Lowry, *Private and Amorous Letters*, 25–26.

NOTES TO PAGES 120–122 293

37. Seth Eastman to Horace Dresser, July 6, 1862, Lowry, *Private and Amorous Letters*, 27.
38. Seth Eastman to Horace Dresser, November 15?, 1862, Lowry, *Private and Amorous Letters*, 28–30.
39. J. B. K. to Horace Dresser, July 26, 1863, Lowry, *Private and Amorous Letters*, 31–32.
40. Melissa A. Hayes, "Sex in the Witness Stand: Erotic Sensationalism, Voyeurism, Sexual Boasting, and Bawdy Humor in Nineteenth-Century Illinois Courts," *Law and History Review* 32 (February 2014): 149–202, esp. 149–50, 187, 161, 169, 176, 196–97. This richly sourced and astutely argued article does not attempt to distinguish working from middle-class participants. I have only included evidence of explicit sexual expression from witnesses—all community bystanders—who reflected working-class speech patterns.
41. Nahum Trask Wood Diary, January 24, 1871, Daily Journal of Nahum Trask Wood for the Year 1871, HEH, hereafter cited as Nahum Wood Diary. The neglect of sheep in western iconography and historiography is discussed in Susan Lee Johnson, "Brokeback Mountain," *Journal of American History* 93 (December 2006): 988–90.
42. Anaheim's first census (1870) counted a population of 880, only 3 of whom were nonwhite, though an untold number of Hispanics and Native Americans were likely ignored or avoided the government agent. Campbell Gibson and Kay Jung, Historical Census Statistics on Population Totals by Race, 1790 to 1990, and by Hispanic Origin, 1970 to 1990, for Large Cities and Other Urban Places in the United States," Population Division Working Paper no. 76, Washington, DC, US Census Bureau, February 2005), Table 5, unpaginated.
43. Peter Boag, *Same-Sex Affairs: Constructing and Controlling Homosexuality in the Pacific Northwest* (Berkeley: University of California Press, 2003), 23–24; Peter Boag, *Re-dressing America's Frontier Past* (Berkeley: University of California Press, 2011), 4–5.
44. Mary W. Blanchard, "The Soldier and the Aesthete: Homosexuality and Popular Culture in Gilded Age America," *Journal of American Studies* 30 (April 1996): 25–46. This article has more relevance for a middle-class study, but her point about tolerance of the "invert" in the 1870s and 1880s is applicable to working-class culture.
45. Nahum Wood Diary, January 22, 1871. Dean Walter F. McCullock, "Woods Words: A Comprehensive Dictionary of Loggers Terms," Oregon Historical Society, 1958, 80, https://archive.org/stream/woodswordscompre00mccu/woodswordscompre00mc cu_djvu.txt.
46. See Boag, *Same-Sex Affairs*, p. 23, Figure 2.
47. Boag, *Same-Sex Affairs*, p. 24. Boag has done extensive research on same-sex relationships in the American West between 1880 and 1930.
48. Nahum Wood Diary, January 22, 1871. A bum is late nineteenth-century slang for buttocks or intercourse with a woman.
49. Nahum T. Wood, California, Death Index, 1905–1939.
50. William Turner to J. B. O. Barkley, February 18, 1863, Barkley Family Papers, UNC.
51. I could not establish their genealogical relationship, but his familiarity strongly suggests a family connection.
52. George to Sarah Deal, January 3, 1864, DL, Newberry.
53. See Hayes, "Sex in the Witness Stand," p. 189, for more examples. She argues for a strong double standard within the legal system.

294　NOTES TO PAGES 122–128

54. Justina Woods to Sister, May 7, 1852, Woods-Holman, WHMC.
55. The straight line distance from Nashua, New Hampshire to Lowell, Massachusetts, is around twelve miles.
56. Blewett, "Yorkshire Lasses," 317–36, esp. 321, for evidence of female victimization in Yorkshire and Lancashire textile factories.
57. Eliza Bixby to brother, March 3, 1852, LMGL.
58. Blewett, "Yorkshire Lasses," 321. Her evidence comes from the Lancashire cotton textile industry. Also Daniel E. Bender, "'Too Much of Distasteful Masculinity': Historicizing Sexual Harassment in the Garment Sweatshop and Factory," *Journal of Women's History* 15 (Winter 2004): 91–116, esp. 100–101.
59. Sister to Brother, October 1, 1854, Anonymous (Bethel, VT) Letters, LMGL.
60. William H. Simon to Sister [Abby Cross], undated but probably written in June 1864, published in "The Civil War Letters of J.O. Cross, 29th Connecticut Volunteer Infantry (Colored)," ed. Kelly Nolin, *Connecticut Historical Society Bulletin* 60 (Summer–Fall 1995): 234–235 and 223 n. 56. "[B]ut orange has got ripe yet to bout Hazeard garels you orter see the wemen out hear that have large tit as a cow."
61. Jestena Webb to William Holman, October 5, 1857, Woods-Holman, WHMC.
62. Pennsylvania Counties: History and Information—eReferenceDesk.com, www.ereferencedesk.com/resources/counties/pennsylvania/.
63. Sallie Seeper Scott to Robert James Barnett, April 15, 1865, VTLL. Sally's letter did not contain an open declaration of love, but she called her correspondent, Robert James, her "only lover" and "loving Bob" and pledged her steadfast commitment. However, Sally gave no indication that she and Robert were engaged. The letter's recipient is cataloged on the website as Robert Bennett, but Sallie referred to him as Robert Barnett in the body of the letter.
64. Lystra, *Searching the Heart*, chapters 3 and 4.
65. Lystra, *Searching the Heart*, 249.
66. George to Sarah Deal, July 30, 1863, DL, Newberry. See John Morrish, ed., *The Folk Handbook: Working with Songs from the English Tradition* (New York: Outline Press, 2007), 233.
67. George to Sarah Deal, July 30, 1863, DL, Newberry.
68. George to Sarah Deal, February 10, 1863, DL, Newbery. The sexual behavior of male pigs is discussed in P. H. Hemsworth and A. J. Tilbrook, "Sexual Behavior of Male Pigs," *Hormones and Behavior* 52 (2007): 39–44, quotation p. 40, https://www.researchgate.net/publication/6333350.
69. Joseph O. Cross to Abby Cross, December 31, 1864, full letters presented in Nolin, "Letters of J.O. Cross," 216, 223–24. For information on Lester and his wife, see p. 224 n. 64.
70. Simeon Tierce to Sarah Jane Tierce, undated letter [written between March 27 and July 8, 1864] in Edythe Ann Quinn, *Freedom Journey: Black Civil War Soldiers and The Hills Community, Westchester County, New York* (Albany: State University of New York Press, 2015), 146–47. Quinn published his five letters in an Appendix B (133–149) along with helpful annotations. She added periods and some commas, but did not change his spelling.

NOTES TO PAGES 128–130   295

71. Quinn, *Freedom Journey*, 53.
72. Ann Stevens to Walter Knight, May 4, 1882, and May 23, 1882, quoted in Robert L. Griswold, *Family and Divorce in California, 1850–1890* (Albany: State University of New York Press, 1982), 88–89. My friend and colleague Michael Steiner first alerted me to this evidence.
73. Ann Stevens to Walter Knight, May 4, 1882, and May 23, 1882, quoted in Griswold, *Family and Divorce*, 88–89.
74. See Walter Knight in California Voter Registers, 1866–1898, Residence Year, 1890; also California Voter Registers, 1900–1968, Residence Years, 1900–1912; and the 1920 US Federal Census. The most reliable estimate of his birth year seems to be around 1860. Also Ann Eliza Stevens, 1880 US Federal Census.
75. US, Quaker Meeting Records, 1681–1935 for Mary Samms.
76. Mother [Mary Samms] to Ann S. Osmond, January 4, 1846, Osmond, MHS. See also US, Quaker Meeting Records, 1861–1935, under John Samms, Ann S. Osmond's brother, for confirmation that Mary Samms is the correspondent.
77. Vern Bullough, ed., *The Encyclopedia of Birth Control* (Santa Barbara, CA: ABC-CLIO, 2001), 79–86; Andrea Tone, *Devices and Desires: A History of Contraceptives in America* (New York: Hill and Wang, 2001), 52, 84–85.
78. Byberry, still a separate township at the time, was relatively close to the city center of Philadelphia (twenty miles or so by today's road maps).
79. Mother [Mary Samms] to Ann S. Osmond, January 4, 1846, Osmond, MHS.
80. Steven Mintz, *Huck's Raft: A History of American Childhood* (Cambridge, MA: Harvard University Press, 2004), 77.
81. Karl Ittmann, *Work, Gender and Family in Victorian England* (New York: New York University Press, 1995), 230–31. The consensus is that female-controlled networks of sex information predominated in late nineteenth-century England. Blewett, "Yorkshire Lasses," 318; Patricia Knight, "Women and Abortion in Victorian and Edwardian England," *History Workshop*, Autumn 1977, 57–68, esp. 60, 62. She concluded that the use of abortifacients—including drugs, herbs, and other homegrown remedies—was the major form of family limitation in these English communities. Ittmann, in *Work, Gender and Family*, 230–35, believes the most likely methods of working-class birth control were coitus interruptus and abstinence, with abortion being "a final recourse in case other methods fail."
82. Of course strong female networks were formed in support of American women during and after childbirth. See Laurel Thatcher Ulrich, *A Midwife's Tale: The Life of Martha Ballard, Based on Her Diary, 1785–1812* (New York: Knopf, 1990); and Judith Walzer Leavitt, "Under the Shadow of Maternity: American Women's Responses to Death and Debility Fears in Nineteenth-Century Childbirth," *Feminist Studies* 12 (Spring 1986): 129–54, esp. 144–48. The birth control of choice for Americans below the middle class remains unknown. See James C. Mohr, *Abortion in America: The Origins and Evolution of National Policy* (New York: Oxford University Press, 1979), 46–118. He argues that a dramatic upsurge of abortion occurred between 1840 and 1880 in America, which he largely attributes to middle- and upper-class white, married Protestants.

296   NOTES TO PAGES 130–131

83. Eliza Adams to The Family, September 19, 1857 as quoted in Hansen, *A Very Social Time*, 114. She thinks the comment on dropsy is serious. I have a different interpretation.

84. Sharon Block, "Lines of Color, Sex, and Service: Comparative Sexual Coercion in Early America," in *Sex, Love, Race: Crossing Boundaries in North American History*, ed. Martha Hodes (New York: New York University Press, 1999), 141–63.

85. See Description, "Plan of the City of Lowell, Massachusetts, 1850," Norman B. Leventhal Map Center Collection, Boston Public Library Digital Collections, https://collections.leventhalmap.org/search/commonwealth:wd3761962.

86. Hansen, *A Very Social Time*, 115–16, 137. Hansen argues for the inadequacy of the public vs. private "model," but the "model" she refers to is different from the actual boundaries constructed and negotiated by people in the nineteenth century. She seems to see private as "not social," but this formulation has inherent difficulties. For example, romantic love is a social construct acquired through social means but communicated privately between two individuals in courtship and marriage according to social rules and beliefs.

87. He is supposed to have told Al Smith to give his friend Bob "a God Dam." Claiming he never said it, he warned Bob to keep his mouth shut at home. Unidentified Male to Friend Bob, 1861, John McEwen Papers, LC.

88. Monroe population drawn from 1860 Federal Census. This young man's concern for his reputation in the local village he called home indicates a level of organic social control that Richard Stott argues was absent in certain all-male milieus, especially the California Gold Rush and urban countercultures. See *Jolly Fellows: Male Milieus in Nineteenth-Century America* (Baltimore: Johns Hopkins University Press, 2009), 36. Stott's evidence and analysis is perceptive, wide-ranging, and imaginative, but even if, as he claims, the regular jolly fellows in villages were "diverse in social rank," the majority did not appear to be poor, uneducated, or lacking in financial resources. The problem for single working-class men was that letters as well as returning kinfolk and friends could bear witness in their local communities to their drinking, carousing, gambling, and whoring and therefore make it more difficult to marry within the tribe. Stott recognized that sexual aggression was less tolerated in villages than in cities. See p. 26.

89. For almost one hundred pages of documented cases of prostitution in Civil War court-martial records, see Thomas P. Lowry, *Sexual Misbehavior in the Civil War: A Compendium* (Lexington, KY: Xlibris, 2006), 15–113. The practice was widespread and involved large numbers of privates, enlisted men, and noncommissioned officers as well as the higher ranks. Lowry makes no distinction among military grades in his reporting. Also see articles on prostitution in New York City published by the flash press twenty years earlier. Patricia Cline Cohen, Timothy J. Gilfoyle, and Helen Lefkowitz Horowitz, *The Flash Press: Sporting Male Weeklies in 1840s* (Chicago: University of Chicago Press, 2008), 129–58. I doubt that many readers were working-class men. The excerpts on prostitution, for example, were *not* pitched to working-class taste culture, and the writers used a vocabulary and assumed a pose that was pseudo-sophisticated. The piece on chambermaids is especially revealing

of class bias (161–65). Also see the excellent review essay by Katherine Hijar, "Flash Men, Jolly Fellows, and Fancy Books: Nineteenth-Century New York, the Nation, and Sexuality in Print," *Journal of Urban History* 37 (May 2011): 451–59.

90. Clare A. Lyons, *Sex among the Rabble: An Intimate History of Gender and Power in the Age of Revolution, Philadelphia, 1730–1830* (Chapel Hill: University of North Carolina Press, 2006), 312, 316–18. Lyons finds that "inexpensive popular print" was full of tales of seduction leading to prostitution. The question of readership outside Philadelphia remains uncertain.

91. Lyons, *Sex among the Rabble*, 348, 353–54, 391–92. She argues this association was constructed by the middle class and became an uncontested cultural assumption. I have found no evidence that the working class, Black or white, thought they were more lustful or sexually profligate than the middle class or elites.

92. Hayes, "Sex in the Witness Stand," 176.

93. Kathy Peiss, *Cheap Amusements: Working Women and Leisure in Turn-of-the-Century New York* (Philadelphia: Temple University Press, 1986), 50, 136. Vice reformers found that the frank discussion of sexuality among laboring women in urban centers such as New York was common at the turn of the century. These activists observed that sexual knowledge was routinely communicated in restaurants, laundries, factories, and department stores through networks of female employees. This included "[r]isque jokes, swearing, and sexual advice."

94. Søndergaard, "Bullying, Humour," 48–65, esp. 56, 58.

Chapter 5

1. The clearest discussion of these obligations from a legal perspective is Hendrik Hartog's "Marital Exits and Marital Expectations in Nineteenth-Century America," Philip A. Hart Memorial Lecture, April 10, 1991, http://scholarship.law.georgetown.edu/hartlecture/8. For an influential historical survey of American marriage and public policy, including civil rights, citizenship, state laws, and federal legislation, see Nancy F. Cott's *Public Vows: A History of Marriage and the Nation* (Cambridge, MA: Harvard University Press, 2000); for an indispensable study of African American marriage, see Tera Hunter, *Bound in Wedlock: Slave and Free Black Marriage in the Nineteenth Century* (Cambridge, MA: Harvard University Press), 2017.

2. Samuel Potter to Sophie Potter, November 23, 1862, Samuel Potter Papers, LC.

3. Their letters were full of complaints about their health, relatives, economic scarcity, domestic burdens, or the dearth of letters received at home. Confederate wives had even more difficult economic challenges to surmount, as Stephanie McCurry demonstrates in her insightful essay "Women Numerous and Armed: Gender and the Politics of Subsistence in the Civil War South," in *Wars within a War: Controversy and Conflict over the American Civil War*, ed. Joan Waugh and Gary W. Gallagher (Chapel Hill: University of North Carolina Press, 2009), 1–26. McCurry examines poor southern women's letters to governors in Virginia, North Carolina, and Georgia

298   NOTES TO PAGES 133–139

as an expression of class and gender that coalesced into a new political identity: the soldier's wife. As she notes, there is no similar study of poor women in the Union states.

4. Susan to Wallace Jones, June 2, [1864], Susan Alice Jones Coll., HEH.

5. Mary to Leonard Caplinger, June 7, 1863, Caplinger, HEH.

6. See the website "Identifying Phototypes–Phototree.com" for a brief guide to these distinctions. http://www.phototree.com/identify.htm.

7. L. Wisstover to wife, October 5, 1862, CivWar, SHSM.

8. Hillory to Jemima Shifflet, November 19, 1862, CivWar, SHSM.

9. Leonard to Polly [his wife Mary's nickname] Caplinger, April 16, 1863, Caplinger, HEH. He sent fifty dollars home.

10. Hillory to Jemima Shifflet, April 12, 1863, CivWar, SHSM.

11. Hillory to Jemima Shifflet, May 2, 1863, CivWar, SHSM.

12. Hillory to Jemima Shifflet, May 9, 1863, CivWar, SHSM.

13. Jane Lull to Lois Davis, April 15, 1855, LWRD, Duke.

14. Ellen Merrill to Mother [Lois Davis], March 14, [1858], LWRD, Duke.

15. Nellie [Ellen Merrill] to Mother, October 9, [1859], LWRD, Duke.

16. Olive Brown to Sabrina Bennett, May 15, 1839, in *Farm to Factory: Women's Letters, 1830-1860*, 2nd ed., ed. Thomas Dublin (New York: Columbia University Press, 1993), 65.

17. William H. Scott to Brother [James H. Parker] and Sister, May 1, 1849 [accessed as St. Louis History Coll., Box 2], SHSM.

18. Hillory to Jemima Shifflet, March 18, 1862, CivWar, SHSM.

19. For example, David Hafer to Wife, July 5, 1865, Franklin County, "Aftermath," VS/UV.

20. The origin of this taboo may be religious. The idea that it is blasphemous to love a spouse more than God was an early rationale for *not* expressing love directly to one's mate. See Karen Lystra, *Searching the Heart: Women, Men, and Romantic Love in Nineteenth-Century America* (New York: Oxford University Press), 240–46 for a fuller explanation. Unlike the middle class, which left abundant evidence in antebellum letters of their religious motives, the working class never gave any hint of a religious source for this practice.

21. "Yours until death" was the most widely accepted convention of nonromantic love. It was commonly used in other important relationships as well, including parents, children, siblings, relatives, and friends.

22. Riley to Mary Ann Luther, May 20, 26, 29, 1862; July 23, 1862; August 3, 1862, RLC, Duke.

23. Riley to Mary Ann Luther, August 3, 1862, RLC, Duke.

24. Riley to Mary Ann Luther, February 22, 1865, RLC, Duke.

25. Mary Ann to Riley Luther, October 13, 1862, RLC, Duke.

26. Riley to Mary Ann Luther, October 25, 1863, RLC, Duke.

27. John to Lucinda Boley, March 7, 1860, Uncatalogued Miscellaneous Collection, Archives of American Art, Smithsonian.

28. Rhoda to Rowland Casey, October 13, 1863, Confederate, UNC. Their landlord thought he had a buyer for the land they occupied and he wanted Rhoda to move to another property.

NOTES TO PAGES 139–143   299

29. Rowland to Rhoda Casey, December 22, 1861, Confederate, UNC.
30. Rowland to Rhoda Casey, January 1, 1863, Confederate, UNC.
31. Rowland to Rhoda Casey, May 30, 1863, Confederate, UNC.
32. Rhoda to Rowland Casey, October 13, 1863, Confederate, UNC.
33. Rhoda to Rowland Casey, October 13, 1863, Confederate, UNC.
34. The box never arrived because Rowland's lieutenant, on leave in their local village, refused to transport it back to camp. This infuriated Rowland. See Rowland to Rhoda Casey, January 24, 1864, Confederate, UNC.
35. Rowland to Rhoda Casey, January 24, 1864, Confederate, UNC.
36. Rowland to Rhoda Casey, January 24, 1864, Confederate, UNC.
37. Orra Bailey to Wife, November 25, 1862, Orra B. Bailey Papers, LC.
38. Orra Bailey to Wife, October 22 and October 4, [1862], Orra B. Bailey Papers, LC. See Wendy Gamber, *The Boardinghouse in Nineteenth-Century America* (Baltimore: Johns Hopkins University Press, 2007), esp. chapter 3.
39. Orra Bailey to Wife, September 25, 1864, Orra B. Bailey Papers, LC.
40. Orra Bailey to Wife, November 25, 1862, Orra B. Bailey Papers, LC.
41. US Civil War Soldiers Records and Profiles, 1861–1865, and US City Directories, 1882–1995, Residence Year 1865.
42. Rufus to Elisabeth Turner Wright, [April] 2[2], 1864, in *Families and Freedom: A Documentary History of African-American Kinship in the Civil War Era,* ed. Ira Berlin and Leslie S. Rowland (New York: New Press, 1997), 165–66.
43. Rufus to Elisabeth Turner Wright, May 25, 1864, in Berlin and Rowland, *Families and Freedom,* 166–67.
44. Wife to Willie, May 1, 1883, Augusta County, Aftermath, VS/UV.
45. See Lewis Strayer to Wife, December 25, 1861; May 5, 1862, SFL.
46. Lewis Strayer to Wife, July 10, 1862, SFL.
47. Lewis Strayer to Wife, June 15, 1862, SFL.
48. Lewis Strayer to Wife, May 1, 1862, SFL.
49. Lewis Strayer to Wife, May 16, 1862, SFL.
50. He was willing to assert his love for individual children, telling his daughter Elizabeth, "dear daughter be A good girl for i love you" or his son, "Joseph be a good boy i love you and i no that you love me." Lewis Strayer to Wife, May 16, and May 5, 1862, SFL.
51. The number and length of their correspondence is an archival rarity. I believe, however, that large quantities of letters were written by African Americans during the Civil War. Due to the past bias and prejudice of American research institutions, and the understandable reluctance of African American families to entrust their letters to these public archives, their nineteenth-century correspondence is still hard to find. I am hopeful that family letters are being privately held.
52. David to Mary Jane Demus, October 17, 1863, Franklin County, VS/UV. Original spelling: "ant marrey and unkel sol harson" "ginney and ant marry harson."
53. David to Mary Jane Demus, March 4, 1864, VS/UV. "give mi love to fathr and lizabeth and to ant marry and to unkel solaman harson and Cusen gorge and Cusen rachel and to all the frends nothing more at present but reman yor Dear husben untill deth yor frend."
54. David to Mary Jane Demus, August 18, October 7, 1863, VS/UV.

300 NOTES TO PAGES 143–147

55. He tells his brother-in-law that his wound may never heal in David Demus to Jacob Christy, December 24, 1863; the discussion with his wife occurs January 9, 1864, VS/UV.

56. David Demus to Mary Jane Demus, November 10, 1863, VS/UV. "i Will fetch you Wan home if send me Ward Wat Cind you Want a Dubbel slol Wiy i Can get it as i Cum home i thig that i Can get it Cheaper on the Way."

57. Mary Jane Demus, December 6, [1863], VS/UV. Date ascertained from letter sequencing. No year in the catalog e-text.

58. Mary Jane to David Demus, December 6, [1863], VS/UV. Date ascertained from letter sequencing. No year in the catalog e-text. See also David to Mary Jane Demus, January 16 and March 4, 1864, VS/UV.

59. Mary Jane to David Demus, February 23, 1864, VS/UV. As the time of their separation lengthened, David and Mary became much more romantic. For a wider historical and cultural context, see Wilma King, *Essence of Liberty: Free Black Women during the Slave Era* (Columbia: University of Missouri Press, 2006).

60. Mary Jane to David Demus, March 15, [1864], VS/UV. Date ascertained from letter sequencing. No year in the catalog e-text.

61. Mary Jane to David Demus, March 15, [1864], VS/UV. Date ascertained from letter sequencing. No year in the catalog e-text. "when you rote the over tim you was coming i set up ever nigh looking for you till ten oclock then i woud give you up and go to bed and lay and lisen i cud not sleep haff for i was so shar you woud come father woud say he wont come to nigth o but i dou with [do wish] you cud come."

62. See comment on peddling in John to Mary Wilson, April 3, 1861, JWL, Newberry.

63. John to Mary Wilson, October 17, 1859, December 4, 1860, April 3, 1861 and May 19, 1861. See also John Wilson to Friend Haven, June 29, 1860, JWL, Newberry.

64. John to Mary Wilson, January 1, 1859 [actually 1860], JWL, Newberry.

65. John to Mary Wilson, January 1, 1859 [actually 1860], JWL, Newberry.

66. John to Mary Wilson, December 4, 1860, JWL, Newberry.

67. John to Mary Wilson, December 29, 1862, JWL, Newberry.

68. John to Mary Wilson, September 4, 1860 and February 23, 1861, JWL, Newberry.

69. John to Mary Wilson, April 3, 1861, JWL, Newberry.

70. John to Mary Wilson, May 4, 1861 JWL, Newbery.

71. John to Mary Wilson, December 4, 1860; Horace Mickel, "Conversation between Moore & Wilson, January 14, 1862; C. L. Ruhling & Co. to Mrs. Mary D. Wilson, March 1, 1862, JWL, Newberry.

72. Horace Mickel to Mrs. [Mary] Wilson, December 16, 1863, March 2, 1864, and November 11, 1864. JWL, Newberry.

73. J. C. to Susannah Owens, April 26, 1863, Confederate, UNC.

74. Isham Upchurch to "My Dear Wife," November 16, 1861, Upchurch, Duke. Emphasis is mine.

75. Simeon Tierce to Sarah Jane Tierce, November 24, 1863, in Edythe Ann Quinn, *Freedom Journey: Black Civil War Soldiers and The Hills Community, Westchester County* (Albany: State University of New York Press, 2015). Quinn published his five letters in an Appendix B (133–49) along with helpful annotations. She added periods and some commas, but did not change his spelling. Priscilla and William

NOTES TO PAGES 147–150 301

Brooks were married. Priscilla was home in the Hills and William, who was serving with Simeon, had been "all the time grumbling." I believe his grumbling was about receiving insufficient mail from home. My reading is that Tierce wanted his wife's letter forwarded to Brooks as a joke. The salient fact is that her letter was handed over to another husband. Simeon to Sarah Jane Tierce, November 24, 1863, in Quinn, *Freedom Journey*, 135–38. For the legal context of free Black marriage in the North, see Tera W. Hunter, *Bound in Wedlock: Slave and Free Black Marriage in the Nineteenth Century* (Cambridge, MA: Harvard University Press, 2017), 105–14.

76. Hillory to Jemima Shifflet, July 4, 1862, CivWar. SHSM.
77. Hillory to Jemima Shifflet, July 4, 1862, CivWar, SHSM.
78. Laura F. Edwards commented on the public lives led by many poor white and African American women in *Gendered Strife and Confusion: The Political Culture of Reconstruction* (Urbana: University of Illinois Press, 1997), 155–58.
79. Vicky Holmes, *In Bed with the Victorians: The Life-Cycle of Working-Class Marriage* (Cham, Switzerland: Palgrave Macmillan, 2017), 15–33. She uses inquest reports to determine the sleeping arrangements of working-class couples in England. Holmes discusses the "practical implications" of sharing a bedroom when newlyweds were compelled by finances or housing shortages to delay moving into their own home.

Chapter 6

1. After starting their dialogue with untouched quotations from their letters, I will switch to a standard English translation. My intention is to expose the reader to the original first, because their speech has power that a translated version sometimes lacks. I feel it is important to process some of their feelings of distress in their own voice.
2. Elizabeth to Solon Fuller, November 1862 [cataloger's date but likely written in late October 1862; internal evidence of October 27, 1862], SLFP, Duke. The quotations in the paragraphs that follow are all drawn from this letter, which is cited again at the end of the sequence.
3. Standard English translation of Elizabeth's writing commences here. I will forgo the asterisks in the quotations that follow. "I do not never expect to lay eys on you agane," she admitted in a postscript, "you promis me that you would get a furlow and come home I surpose you did not wont to come." "johson sed that ef you did not get in you might get home the lest way you could cludy ware hird him say so and you no that he was amean man."
4. "[Y]ou no that if I had ceard no more for you and john then you both ceares for me," she reminded her husband. "I could went to my children whare I coul uv liveed well no I stayed here and trye to do all I coul to my home agreeable." "I did not turne you and john loose in the world to purrish."
5. Elizabeth to Solon Fuller, November 1862 [cataloger's date but likely written in late October 1862; internal evidence of October 27, 1862], SLFP, Duke. After the last dig, her tone softened. She was glad to hear that his health was good and that he was not

302 NOTES TO PAGES 150–154

sleeping on the ground. She closed: "I must bid you fare well along alass fare well one moure time adue I remain your unhappy wife while life remaines." She added a postscript that his friend had promised to grind her corn and then reneged for no apparent reason. "[T]hank god that thare is a worme place for all such people," she quipped.

6. Solon to Elizabeth Fuller, November 15, 1862, SLFP, Duke.

7. Elizabeth to Solon Fuller November 24, 1862, SLFP, Duke. "I a hope that this leter will find you in good health and well sattisfide," she responded, "for it has been about 9 monts sence you have appeard to be sattisfide whare I was." "I have not got 1 grane of salt sence you left I am aliving apun parch meale coffee and bred with out salt I hav got no shoes yet and my feat is on the cold frosty ground," she complained. "I have not spent 1 dime of your money onely to pay the expence of your mair for I did not no wheather you wished me to live of ov it or not as john had left or not."

8. Elizabeth to Solon Fuller November 24, 1862, SLFP, Duke. "Mr fuller you sed that you thught I had cast you off which was vary far from me for I did not go off but I tried to stay with you but you wos deturme to leave for ef you did not go in the armey you intended to leve here for in my pressence you had reather go in the army and be shot then stay here and perish."

9. Elizabeth to Solon Fuller, November 24, 1862, SLFP, Duke. "[W]hile I live Mr fuller sleepe is a strange to my eyes for when I ly down at night I ly thare thinking whot was the cause of leaveing for I never did don thing nor say nothing to you that I ought naught no to sed."

10. Elizabeth to Solon Fuller, November 24, 1862, SLFP, Duke. "[I]t is all right," she noted mockingly, "I will bar it like I ought and hope I shall not be long in your way for if peace was made to morrow I never expect to see you agan for that was what you left here for to get shut of me so I dare not hope ever to see you agane."

11. Solon to Betsey [Elizabeth Fuller], November 30, 1862, SLFP, Duke.

12. Standard English translation of Solon's writing commences here. I will forgo the asterisks in the quotations that follow. Solon to Betsey [Elizabeth Fuller], November 30, 1862, SLFP, Duke. "[B]etsey if I hav don ronge I am sorrey forit for I cold note hav maid two hundred Dolers thar in two yeares and I have maid fifteen hundred and if I Die or gite cild you and Johnney will have it." "[I]f he will com back and Doo well." "I want you to do with the money as it suits you and when I come home I will bring some more. I don't want you to want for anything while the money lasts." "I want you to Doo with the monney as itsutes you and when I come home I will bring some more I Donte want you to want for eeney thing while the monney laste."

13. Solon to Betsey [Elizabeth Fuller], November 30, 1862, SLFP, Duke. "[W]hen I took the notion to cum in the armey," he added in a postscript, "cod see no other way to liv for thar was noe way to mak monney and i Did note blev thate war wood last longe and neither Doo I now." He predicted that the Civil War would end in March 1863, and "if ite Dose I hav maid a good winters worke if mey mind coold be contented bute ites is note."

14. Solon to Elizabeth Fuller, December 14, 1862, SLFP, Duke. "[Y]ou right that i left you to starv," he responded honestly, and "i cold see nothinge bute starvation whin i lefte

NOTES TO PAGES 154–156   303

home and how i cood hav gote monney to beuy corn or solte," "is all the time nighte and Day a bought you and the rest of them," "and that is all the way i now how to Doo."

15. Solon to Elizabeth Fuller, December 14, 1862, SLFP, Duke. She should get "control of him untill i com hom," "to bringe back an whip him savreley for i am determed that he shall note be a steroting a bout the cuntrey."

16. Elizabeth to Solon Fuller, December 25, 1862, SLFP, Duke. "[Y]ou speake of coming hom I cant flatter my selfe that I ever see you agan for that happy day is to fare ahead for me ever to so if you can get home make hast and let me se if I shall live to se that happy day."

17. The transcribed quotations in this paragraph come from Solon to Elizabeth Fuller, December 16, 1862, SLFP, Duke. "[W]e ar absent in destenest [distance] menney a mile but mi mind is with you continley," he wrote tenderly, "i want to com hom verrey mutch but i cant com home now for the small pox is ragin heare and thee wonnt late a solger lev the campe now." The quotations in the rest of the paragraph are drawn from this letter.

18. "Johnney omey sun whie wonte you Doo as i wanted you to Doo then i shold B happey but as ite is i cant but be misareble Johnney my sun doo bee a goD boy and Doas ma wantes you to Doo."

19. "[I]f you are a good boy all that i have shal be yours."

20. Elizabeth to Solon Fuller, December 15, 1862, SLFP, Duke.

21. Solon to Elizabeth Fuller, January 1, 1863, SLFP, Duke. "[I] recived youer letter and you was kind a nought to tel me that you wod not right noe letters til you gote one from mee," he scoffed. "[I]f it is a ganst youer wil to right to me Don't righte nomore for thare has not ben a weak but i hav rought a letter and sum weakes i have rought two," "fir i don't feit as tho i had one frend in the world"; he believed "that i shal git achane to com hom bee for long so fare well mey der wif and may god bless you."

22. Elizabeth to Solon Fuller, January 20, 1863, SLFP, Duke. "[J]ohn did not take them out it was some miss mangedment in the post master I hird from John he is well and aliving with aman in oxfordly the mame of Talor and gets 25 aday and that is all I no about him"; "you sed if I did not wish to wright I nede not do it it was aplane case to me that if you could wright to ware that you could write to me I thought that youceared not for me for you sed that john was to have all you had when you dyed I have children that will sur pote me if I will go to them."

23. Solon to Elizabeth Fuller, January 2, 1863, SLFP, Duke. "[I] think that i will be able to liv in a bet stit than when i was hom bee fouer for i coole se nothing but Desperration for i had maid nothing to eight nor nothing to war but now i shal hav sumthing to liv on so doo right as sun as you get this letter and let mee no how times is thar ... if you new how bad I want to hear from you you wod right a meditley but out of sit out of mind."

24. The transcribed quotations in this paragraph come from Elizabeth to Solon Fuller, February 2, 1863, SLFP, Duke. "Mr fuller you nead not think hard of me for not writing for I anser all of your letter soone as I can when the weather is cold I cant wright atall for my hand is so numb." "I must come to aclose for you see I cant hardley

304   NOTES TO PAGES 156–161

write atall I could fill the shete but my hand is in such afix you must right soon for if I cant see you I am glad to her from you."

25. Solon to Elizabeth Fuller, February 16, 1863, SLFP, Duke. "[Y]ou noe better what to doo withit than I Doo for I hav goe no mind ten minetes."

26. Solon to Elizabeth Fuller, February 16, 1863, SLFP, Duke. "[F]or girle she sese hard times But I hope that she will se meeney happey Dayes to wak up for these bad ones"; "it is a hard world to liv in," he opined, "but if it was not for hopes ef all beinges we wood bee the most miserable but god noes what is best for us all."

27. Solon to Elizabeth Fuller, February 22, 1863, SLFP, Duke. "[W]ewill in Joy selves better than we ever hav done."

28. Elizabeth to Solon Fuller, February 24, 1863, SLFP, Duke. "I wos mos destract ed for feare you wos killed Mr fuller you don't know how uneasy I am about you for I never go to bed but I think and pitty you liing on the cold ground and no a pillar to put under your pur old head and I d not no weather you have enny to cuver with or not"; "for my deare I feele that if it pleas God to spare your life and you get home agan it don't matter how pore weare I could bee happy."

29. The transcribed quotations in this paragraph come from Elizabeth to Solon Fuller, March 15, 1863, SLFP, Duke. "I am vary sory to here that you have got the each for iam as feared of it as I am the smallpox . . . Mr Fuller you don't know how bad I wont you to come home wors then tung can tell or pen can describe."

30. Solon may not have made it home. Duke's summary report gave no indication. One important Civil War website, "Private Voices," claimed he died during the war. I could not independently verify the date of his death.

31. Elizabeth to Solon Fuller, November 1862 [cataloger's date but likely written in late October 1862; internal evidence of October 27, 1862], SLFP, Duke.

32. Solon Fuller to "Respect Sur" [Mr. Ware], March 23, 1863, SLFP, Duke.

33. Edward H. Spencer to Friend Barney, January 31, 1862, Saxton, HEH.

34. Edward H. Spencer to Friend Barney, January 31, 1862, Saxton, HEH.

35. Edward to Jennie Spencer on same sheets as Edward Spencer to Barney, December 13, 1861, Saxton, HEH. I am uncertain whether Eddie's pet name for Jennie began with an M or an N. In a preponderance of cases, the letter looked like an *N*.

36. Edward to Jennie Spencer, February 14, 1862, Saxton, HEH.

37. Edward to Jennie Spencer, February 14, 1862, Saxton, HEH.

38. Edward to Jennie Spencer, June 26, 1862, Saxton, HEH.

39. Edward to Jennie Spencer, July 9, 1862, Saxton, HEH. Underlining indicates a correspondent's emphasis.

40. See Eddie to Jennie Spencer and Eddie to Cousin Rose, August 24, 1862; Eddie also wrote another intimate letter to his wife that was addressed to Cousin Rose, September 16, 1862, Saxton, HEH.

41. Edward to Jennie Spencer, August 4, 1862, Saxton, HEH.

42. Edward to Jennie Spencer, August 4, 1862, Saxton, HEH.

43. Edward to Jennie Spencer, August 4, 1862, Saxton, HEH.

44. Edward to Jennie Spencer, July 9, 1862, Saxton, HEH.

45. Eddie to Jennie Spencer, August 24, 1862, Saxton, HEH.

NOTES TO PAGES 161–164   305

46. E. H. Spencer to "Mrs. St. J Spencer" August 4, 1862, Saxton, HEH.

47. Eddie to Jennie Spencer, December 20, 1862, Saxton, HEH.

48. Ed to Jennie Spencer, June 21, 1863, Saxton, HEH.

49. Edward to Jennie Spencer, July 30, 1863, Saxton, HEH.

50. Edward to Jennie Spencer, July 30, 1863, Saxton, HEH.

51. 1880 US Federal Census. The town was Moravia, New York. His occupation was listed as machinist. See Wendy Gamber, *The Boardinghouse in Nineteenth-Century America* (Baltimore: Johns Hopkins University Press, 2007), esp. chapter 6.

52. See Hendrik Hartog, *Man and Wife in America*: A History (Cambridge, MA: Harvard University Press, 2002), 20–23, 29–39; Lystra, *Searching the Heart*, 206–26; Robert Griswold, *Family and Divorce in California, 1850–1890* (Albany: State University of New York Press, 1982), 79, Table 19. Desertion was the top complaint by men against women but nonsupport was women's top grievance in Griswold's sample of divorce filings.

53. Norma Basch, *In the Eyes of the Law: Women, Marriage, and Property in Nineteenth-Century New York* (Ithaca: Cornell University Press, 1982), 37, 87, 122. Married women's property reform was middle class but had broader implications in some states that included women's wages in their statutes. Working-class couples did not have the assets to use the courts to their advantage. Also Hartog, "Marital Exits and Marital Expectations in Nineteenth-Century America," Philip A. Hart Memorial Lecture, April 10, 1991, http://scholarship.law.georgetown.edu/hartlecture/8, 122–23, 128–29.

54. Beverly Schwartzberg, "'Lots of Them Did That': Desertion, Bigamy, and Marital Fluidity in Late-Nineteenth-Century America," *Journal of Social History* 37 (Spring 2004): 573–600, esp. 573–77, 582, 592–94, and n. 15; Norma Basch, "Relief in the Premises: Divorce as a Woman's Remedy in New York and Indiana, 1815–1870," *Law and History Review* 8 (Fall 1990): 1–24, esp. 8, 16; also Norma Basch, *Framing American Divorce: From the Revolutionary Generation to the Victorians* (Berkeley: University of California Press, 1999).

55. Lois Richardson, July [1851?], LWRD, Duke. This text began as a five-line letter dated in July with no day or year. [1851?] was added later in pencil. The rest of the document was an undated journal entry likely written in 1851, after her husband Luther walked out on her. She called him "my young hearts first Love" and described their relationship as "comfiding" and devoted. Obviously her perspective was not shared by him.

56. Basch, "Relief in the Premises," 8, 16. Desertion in the mid-nineteenth century was more prevalent among husbands, who had an easier time finding a new companion than wives.

57. See Daniel A. Severance to John Kittredge Esq., December 14, 1851, LWRD, Duke.

58. Lot Richardson [father-in-law] to Lois Richardson, December 15, 1851, LWRD, Duke.

59. Lois Richardson, July [1851?], LWRD, Duke.

60. Lot Richardson to Lois Richardson [note appended by Polly Richardson] January 29, 1853, LWRD, Duke.

61. Eunice Stone to Brother [Luther Richardson], December 14/15, [1858?], LWRD, Duke.

306 NOTES TO PAGES 164–170

62. See Alexander Moody to Mss Richson [Lois Richardson], February 5, 1855, and Jane Lull [daughter] to Lois Richardson Davis, April 15, 1855, LWRD, Duke. Jane admitted she heard rumors but had no direct knowledge that her mother was already married to Davis.

63. Alexander Moody to Mss Richson, February 5, 1855, LWRD, Duke.

64. Alexander Moody to Lois Richardson, April 15, 1855, LWRD, Duke. See chapter 3 for several other nonromantic proposals of marriage.

65. [Luther Richardson] to Mrs. L Richardson & Co, February 1, 1855, LWRD, Duke. Though the sender does not identify himself, it is none other than the wayward husband.

66. See Daniel A. Severance to John Kittredge Esq., December 14, 1851, LWRD, Duke. Martha Johnson was married in Northfield, Massachusetts, and died there. She was living in Northfield when the census taker called in 1850 and 1860.

67. Martha Johnson to Sister, April 3, 1855, LWRD, Duke.

68. John F. McClymer, "Late Nineteenth-Century American Working-Class Living Standards," *Journal of Interdisciplinary History* 17 (Autumn 1986): 379–98, esp. 387–88. This well-written article was based on the *Sixth Annual Report* of the Massachusetts Bureau of the Statistic of Labor, done in 1875. I am willing to assume that the consumption values, if not the actual behaviors, were similar.

69. Martha Johnson to Sister, April 3, 1855, LWRD, Duke.

70. See Lois Davis [mother] to Charles Henry Richardson, May 12, 1861, LWRD, Duke.

71. Lois Davis to C. H. Richardson, June 7, 1862, LWRD, Duke. See Gamber, *The Boardinghouse*, chapter 2.

72. C. H. Richardson to Lois Davis, August 4, 1862, LWRD, Duke.

73. C. H. Richardson to Lois Davis, August 19, [1862], LWRD, Duke. See also US, Civil War Soldier Records and Profiles, 1861–1865.

74. Lois Davis to C. H. Richardson, January 28 [1863], LWRD, Duke.

75. C. H. Richardson to Mother, June 10, 1863, LWRD, Duke.

76. Charles Henry Richardson to Mother, April 8, 1865 LWRD, Duke.

77. Mother to Charles Henry Richardson, May 15, 1865, LWRD, Duke.

78. Schwartzberg, "Desertion, Bigamy," 573–600.

79. "Bully for cocks" may be a variant of "bully for you," which meant "good for you." During this period, "bully" was slang for "Bravo!" or "terrific. See American Civil War Slang. www.citrus.k12.fl.us/staffdev/.../Slang%20of%20the%20American%20Civil%20War.

80. George to Sarah Deal, April 20, 1863, with comments by H. J. Souder, scribe, DL, Newberry.

81. George to Sarah Deal, June 2, 1863, with comments by H. J. Souder, scribe, DL, Newberry.

82. George to Sarah Deal, June 7, 1863, with comments by H. J. Souder, scribe, DL, Newberry. Souder's numbers are sometimes hard to decipher.

83. George to Sarah Deal, April 8, 1863, with comments by Henry J. Souder, scribe, DL, Newberry.

84. George to Sarah Deal August 6, 1863, with comments by H. J. Souder, scribe, DL, Newberry.

NOTES TO PAGES 170–172   307

85. Souder could have also given George the letter to read, as George indicated he could "purti well" read Sarah's letters in George to Sarah Deal, July 30, 1863, DL, Newberry. If he was referring to himself and not his scribe, George's reading skills were surely basic and his limited proficiency may have been at odds with the pressure to get his letters in the mail.

86. Joshua R. Greenburg, *Advocating The Man: Masculinity, Organized Labor, and the Household in New York, 1800–1840* (New York: Columbia University Press, 2007), 14. Though he was referring to New York workingmen in the early republic, his generalization applies to working-class husbands through most of the nineteenth century.

Chapter 7

1. Angela Sorby, *Schoolroom Poets: Childhood, Performance, and the Place of American Poetry, 1865–1917* (Durham: University of New Hampshire Press, 2005); William Wells Newell, *Games and Songs of American Children* (New York: Dover, 1963, unabridged republication of 1903 edition based on 1883 publication by Harper & Brothers); Ryan Cordell and Abby Mullen, "'Fugitive Verses': The Circulation of Poems in Nineteenth-Century American Newspapers," *American Periodicals* 27 (2017): 29–52. Cordell and Mullen write that "poems appear in nearly every issue of nineteenth-century US papers (30)." This is based on computational analysis drawn "from large-scale, digitized corpora of nineteenth-century newspapers and magazines." Andrew Hobbs in "Five Millions Poems, or the Local Press as Poetry Publisher, 1800–1900," *Victorian Periodicals Review* 45 (Winter 2012): 488–92, estimates that four to six million poems were published in the English provincial press (local newspapers) in the nineteenth century. His figure gives some dimensionality to the term "popular" and "widespread" across the Atlantic. It is likely, however, that poor workers were "not part of the newspaper-reading public" until late in the nineteenth century. See Richard L. Kaplan, *Politics and the American Press: The Rise of Objectivity, 1865–1920* (Cambridge: Cambridge University Press, 2002), 105–18; refer to Table 4.2, p. 112, for a fascinating chart on the cost of Detroit newspapers as a percentage of workers' daily wages from 1865 to 1905. By the late nineteenth century, the morning paper in Detroit and many other cities was oriented to the middle class and the evening to the working class (117). Alice Fahs has documented the popularity of poetry in both the North and South during the Civil War in *The Imagined Civil War: Popular Literature of the North and South, 1861–1865* (Chapel Hill: University of North Carolina Press, 2001), 61–62, 91; Faith Barrett and Cristanne Miller, eds., provide easily accessible examples in *"Words for the Hour": A New Anthology of American Civil War Poetry* (Amherst: University of Massachusetts Press, 2005); Matthew Frye Jacobsen examines Old and New World poetry and fiction in his *Special Sorrows: The Diasporic Imagination of Irish, Polish, and Jewish Immigrants in the United States* (Berkeley: University of California Press, 2002; orig. pub. 1995). For an excellent case study of poems in African American newspapers, see Hannah Wakefield. "'Let the Light Enter!': Illuminating the Newspaper Poetry of Frances Ellen Watkins Harper,"

308 NOTES TO PAGES 172–176

Legacy: A Journal of American Women Writers 36 (2019): 18–42. See also Ronald J. Zboray and Mary Saracino Zboray, *Everyday Ideas: Socio-literary Experience among Antebellum New Englanders* (Knoxville: University of Tennessee Press, 2006), 49–69; David Haven Blake, "When Readers Become Fans: Nineteenth-Century American Poetry as a Fan Activity," *American Studies* 52 (2012): 99–122, esp. 101–2.

2. Memory experts agree that a limited number of items can be stored at one time in short-term or working memory. Alan D. Baddeley, *Essentials of Human Memory* (Hove: Psychology Press, 1998), 77–78. Baddeley claims seven separate items can be retained in short-term memory at one time. See also Nelson Cowan, "The Magical Number 4 in Short-Term Memory: A Reconsideration of Mental Storage Capacity," *Behavioral and Brain Sciences* 24 (2001): 87–114; discussion 114–85. He concluded that three to four items are normal but strategies can be used to expand that capacity.

3. Folklorists are often concerned with the stability of oral transmissions. Christopher M. B. Nugent argues that while printed texts are closed, oral texts are always open to alteration. And "the constant flow of texts from oral to written form and back again" is bound to produce variance. See his impressive *Manifest in Words, Written on Paper: Producing and Circulating Poetry in Tang Dynasty China* (Cambridge, MA: Harvard University Press, 2011), 8, 117.

4. "America Singing: Nineteenth-Century Song Sheets," Library of Congress, at https://www.loc.gov/collections/nineteenth-century-song-sheets/about-this-collection/. For sheet music, which included both lyrics and musical notations, see "Historic American Sheet Music: Rare Book, Manuscript, and Special Collections Library," Duke University. This project site includes a wealth of information, including a fine bibliography. https://library.duke.edu/rubenstein/scriptorium/sheetmusic/about.html.

5. David C. Rubin, *Memory in Oral Traditions: The Cognitive Psychology of Epic, Ballads, and Counting-Out Rhymes* (New York: Oxford University Press, 1995).

6. Rubin, *Memory in Oral Traditions*, 231.

7. Zboray and Zboray, *Everyday Ideas*, 64–65.

8. See Ginger Frost, *Promises Broken: Courtship, Class, and Gender in Victorian England* (Charlottesville: University Press of Virginia, 1995), 67–69. Frost has found that in England "[e]ven poorly educated men wrote romantic verses as an expression of their affection."

9. Ruth Finnegan, *Oral Poetry: Its Nature, Significance and Social Context*, rev. ed. (Bloomington: Indiana University Press, 1992), 270; also Michael C. Cohen, *The Social Lives of Poems in Nineteenth-Century America* (Philadelphia: University of Pennsylvania Press, 2015); Joan Shelley Rubin, *Songs of Ourselves: The Uses of Poetry in America* (Cambridge, MA: Harvard University Press, 2007).

10. Richard Hoggart, "Literature and Society," in *A Guide to the Social Sciences*, ed. N. Mackenzie (London: Weidenfeld and Nicolson, 1966), 247–48 as cited in Finnegan, *Oral Poetry*, 271.

11. George to Sarah Deal, July 30, 1863, DL, Newberry.

12. Thomas W. Talley, *Negro Folk Rhymes: Wise and Otherwise* (New York: Macmillan, 1922), 128. See n. 15 below for more details.

NOTES TO PAGES 176–178   309

13. Widow Peebles to Daniel Turner, September [1864], Wright-Herring Family Papers, UNC. Her slight modification of the standard second line—"though many miles apart we be"—did not alter the poem's meaning.

14. Widow Peebles to Daniel Turner, September [1864], Wright-Herring Family Papers, UNC. The 1870 US Federal Census indicates that Turner was unable to read or write, which is why this letter was preserved by Will H. Cobb, a doctor in his regiment. Turner enlisted in Company E, North Carolina Second Infantry Regiment on June 24, 1861. See Civil War Soldier Records and Profiles, 1861–1865. He was married in September 1869 to a widow at least nineteen years his senior. Her name was Mary S. Humphries. He did not marry the widow Peebles. His nuptial to such an older woman was highly unusual. See more discussion of the widow Peebles and Daniel Turner in chapter 1.

15. Talley collected an additional stanza in *Negro Folk Rhymes*, 137, 229. A Fisk University chemistry professor, he was a member of the Fisk Jubilee Singers for a short time and also sang in a less famous Jubilee quartet. Talley was the compiler and editor of this collection as well as author of a long, concluding essay that analyzed the content of the volume. He noted that "[m]ost of the Rhymes were given by different individuals in fragmentary form" (274).

16. Simeon to Sarah Jane Tierce, November 24, 1863, in Edythe Ann Quinn, *Freedom Journey: Black Civil War Soldiers and The Hills Community, Westchester County, New York* (Albany: State University of New York Press, 2015), 135–36. Quinn published his five letters in Appendix B (133–50) along with helpful annotations. She added periods and some commas, but did not change his spelling. Tierce included no poetry in the other four letters that have survived.

17. He did not use the Black variant of this common rhyme.

18. Simeon to Sarah Jane Tierce, November 24, 1863, in Quinn, *Freedom Journey*, 135–36.

19. Among the many sources where this rhyme can be found is Edward Eggleston, "The Graysons: A Story of Illinois," *Century Illustrated Monthly Magazine* 35 (1887): 370. Eggleston serialized his novel in the *Century*. His narrator called the rhyme "a favorite with the swains of the country school-house." By this, I think he meant to disparage the rhyme by attributing it to country bumpkins. See also Talley, *Negro Folk Rhymes*, pp. 138, 245. He indicated that rural Black folk had more familiarity with vernacular rhymes than their city cousins.

20. E. C. Perrow, "Songs and Rhymes from the South," *Journal of American Folklore* 28 (April–June 1915): 185. This rhyme was collected in Mississippi from rural whites, documented in a manuscript dated 1909; a Black version using an ax was reported in Virginia in 1914.

21. The first line of the lyric to Bob Marley's "Who the Cap Fit," though it does not single out women, has a striking parallel to Tierce's rhyme: "Man to man is so unjust, children: Ya don't know who to trust." This could be a coincidence, or both men could be playing with a folk rhyme that spanned more than a century.

22. Simeon Tierce expressed distress that his wife had cursed at the news but otherwise seems unconcerned and even jokes about the incident. Simeon to Sarah Jane Tierce, undated [written between March 27 and July 8, 1864] in Quinn, *Freedom Journey*,

310　NOTES TO PAGES 178–180

146–48. Quinn suggests the letter might have been written closer to his death in July. Tierce received the midwife's news approximately three to seven months after he wrote his November 24, 1863, letter. See chapter 4 for more details.

23. James Bertram to Jaspar N. Bertram, June 10, 1861, University of Washington, Civil War Letters, Digital Collection, https://content.lib.washington.edu/civilwarweb/collections.html.

24. James Varner Bertram, in the US, Find a Grave Index, 1600s–Current; he married Elizabeth Hicks, February 4, 1864. See James V. Burtram in the Kentucky, County Marriage Records, 1783–1965. See also US Civil War Draft Registrations Records, 1863–1865 for James Butram.

25. Affectionate friend to Mr Elaxsandriie Blakley, April 30, [1880?], F. A. Bleckley Papers, Duke. The date appears to be 1880, which puts it outside the date range of almost all the letters and notes in this collection. I wondered if the affectionate friend had complete mastery of her numbers. She was not alone in finding "Bleckley" a challenging name to spell. It had many variations in official documents (e.g., marriage and census records), which I reviewed using North Carolina, where the correspondents enlisted in the Confederacy, as my geographical focus. The plethora of spellings, along with some caution about the date, made it impossible to determine the recipient of her note.

26. Helen Wheeler collected this poem in her search for "Illinois Folk-lore," published in *The Folk-lorist: Journal of the Chicago Folk-lore Society* 1 (July 1892): 67. A homeopathic doctor smirked at the thought of "love-lorn Little Billee" reciting this poem to the "cooing Trilby" in an after-dinner speech by H. B. Bryson titled "Mr. Toastmaster, Ladies and Gent—," printed in *Medical Indicator* 3 (May 1895): 24; C. D. Strode believed it was the verse on a fifteen-cent valentine he sent sometime in the last half of the nineteenth century. He described the result in "Strode's Moral Musings: His First and Only Valentine and the Sad Dwindling of Early Ideals," *The Packages* 6 (February, 1903): 29, 169.

27. It appeared under the "Love" section as part of "Roses Red" in Talley's collection, *Negro Folk Rhymes*, 128; he also found it in modified form as the last two lines of a nursery rhyme about a grasshopper (169).

28. Reviewing census and marriage records deepened the mystery of the recipient's identity. Several Bleckleys had been married for ten years or more in 1880 according to North Carolina, US Marriage Records, 1741–2011. One promising candidate in that year's Federal Census, Alex Blackley, was listed as a thirty-five-year-old widower living alone in North Carolina. Curiously, the census taker considered him insane.

29. William H. Amos to Miss Nancy Doolittle, April 21, 1869, Amos, Duke. His use of the word love is discussed at length in chapter 3.

30. William H. Amos to Miss Nancy Doolittle, April 21, 1869, Amos, Duke. I have inserted poetic breaks for easier reading.

31. Whether the poetry was a sampler of feelings he intended to draw upon in future correspondence, or a copy of a letter he had actually mailed, the texts are an opportunity to document a range of vernacular poetry in active use by a young working-class man attempting to court a young woman "of interest."

NOTES TO PAGES 180–183   311

32. Though it had some rhythmic and rhyming affinity with vernacular verse, the first poem in his letter contained literary language (for example: "bosom," "repose," and "bliss") and can be traced to an identifiable author. It was written by C. L. Spencer under the pseudonym of Frank Myrtle and was self-published as "The Proposition" in an 1858 collection of his poetry. Since a printed copy was available, Amos's multiple mistakes in spelling and syllabic spacing indicate that he penned the poem from memory. It is unclear, however, whether he memorized the poem from a written or spoken source. See "The Proposition" followed by "Her Answer" and "What He Said" in *The Poems of Frank Myrtle* [pseudonym for C. L. Spencer] (Nashville, TN: J.B. M'Ferrin, Agent, 1858), 116–17. The first stanza of Myrtle's poem was an expression of hope that the woman shared as much love and passion as the poet. But the poem had two more stanzas in which the lovers rejected and mocked each other. Amos included only the suitor's love-smitten proposal in the opening stanza. He ignored the humorous and sour exchange of the last two stanzas. Leaving them out resulted in a significant recontextualization of the original. Whatever caused the excisions, poetry was being actively shaped to the purposes of the user.
33. William H. Amos to Miss Nancy Doolittle, April 21, 1869, Amos, Duke. I have superimposed breaks in these poems for the reader's convenience and provided standard English spelling.
34. William H. Amos to Miss Nancy Doolittle, April 21, 1869, Amos, Duke.
35. Samuel Lover, *Songs and Ballads*, 4th ed. (London: Houlston and Wright, 1858), 153; Richard Nagle, ed., *The Popular Poets and Poetry of Ireland* (Boston: Richard Nagle, 1887), including a short bio of Samuel Lover, 123.
36. Talley, *Negro Folk Rhymes*, 133.
37. Mary Lamon to Cynthia Long, April 14, 1867, "Aftermath," Augusta County, VS/UV.
38. William H. Amos to Miss Nancy Doolittle, April 21, 1869, Amos, Duke.
39. Mollie D. Gaither to J. B. Gaither, December 6, 1862, Gaither, UNC.
40. Mollie D. Gaither to John Burgess Gaither, March 7, 1864, Gaither, UNC.
41. W. M. C. to Maggie, undated, John McEwen Papers, LC. This note was saved by a middle-class man who probably acquired it during the Civil War.
42. Edward Francis to Liza Francis, August 8, 1865, in "'I Don't Fear Nothing in the Shape of Man': The Civil War and Texas Border Letters of Edward Francis, United States Colored Troops," ed. Marshall Myers and Chris Propes, *Register of the Kentucky Historical Society* 101 (Autumn 2003): 465–66.
43. He added: "I have not forgot you and never shall forget it as long as long as I live." Edward Francis to Liza Francis, January 1866, in Myers and Propes, "Letters of Edward Francis," 474–75.
44. Leonard to Polly Caplinger, [undated but probably written in March or April 1863], Caplinger, HEH.
45. Mary to Leonard Caplinger, April 26, 1863, Caplinger, HEH.
46. Leonard to Polly Caplinger, April 22, 1863, Caplinger, HEH.
47. Leonard to Polly Caplinger [March?] 8, 1863, Caplinger, HEH.
48. Mary to Leonard Caplinger, June 15, 1863, Caplinger, HEH.
49. Mary to Leonard Caplinger, June 15, 1863, Caplinger, HEH.

312 NOTES TO PAGES 183–186

50. Peter Van Wagenen to Mother, September 19, 1841, in *The Mind of the Negro: As Reflected in Letters during the Crisis, 1800–1860*, ed. Carter G. Woodson (Washington, DC: Association For the Study of Negro Life and History, 1926; reprint, New York: Dover, 2013), 553; he was the son of Sojourner Truth. Also see Sojourner Truth, *Narrative of Sojourner Truth, a Bondswoman of Olden Time, with a History of Her Labors and Correspondence Drawn from Her "Book of Life"* (New York: Oxford University Press, 1991; originally published 1850), 78–79. It is spelled "Van Wagener" in the 1850 edition.

51. A.[lfred]N. Proffit to R. L. Proffit [sister], July 1864, Proffit Family Letters, UNC. Andrew and Alfred were in Company D, Eighteenth North Carolina regiment, and survived the war.

52. Jacob Christy to Mary Jane Demus, July 2, 1864, Franklin County, VS/UV.

53. Mary Dewalt to Ellen Buck, August 18, 1875, Buck, Indiana State Library.

54. One of the most fascinating variants on the "remember me" rhyme is found in a friendship album created in 1824 by a Chinese exchange student, Wu Lan, for his teacher. "Dear friend, I write in this Book for you to remember me by. Take my pen to write these few lines for you to open the eyes see that kingdom of the high place. *I hope you will remember the me say these few words.* I acquainted you few weeks, I can say to so much for you, you much give the new spirit to self. I hope you never forget me." As quoted in Karen Sánchez-Eppler, "Copying and Conversion: An 1824 Friendship Album from a Chinese Youth," *American Quarterly* 59 (2007): 328.

55. Fahs, *The Imagined Civil War*, 51.

56. See *The Singer's Own Book: A Well-Selected Collection of The Most Popular Sentimental, Patriotic, Naval, and Comic Songs* (Philadelphia: Thomas Cowperthwait & Co., 1839), preface to the Thirtieth ed., v.

57. William H. Amos to Miss Nancy Doolittle, April 21, 1869, Amos, Duke. I've corrected his myriad spelling mistakes. This lyric's appeal to Amos can be understood by comparing the parallel themes of his vernacular rhymes. See *The Singer's Own Book*, p. 230.

58. Mollie D. Gaither "Song Ballet," June 1, 1864, Gaither, UNC. The lyrics she inscribed in her letter were minor variations of the print versions of "Days of Absence" in popular songbooks. For example, she substituted "voice" for "vow," and "idol" for "idle." See John Grigg, *Southern and Western Songster* (Philadelphia: Grigg & Elliot, 1834), 93. Also *The Eolian Songster: A Choice Collection of the most Popular Songs, with Music* (Cincinnati: U.P. James, 1852). This poem was also included in a November 18, 1861, letter from John W. Truss to Rebecca Truss found in "Civil War Letters from Parsons' Texas Cavalry Brigade," ed. Johnette Highsmith Ray, *Southwestern History Quarterly* 69 (October 1965): 211–12. According to his daughter, John Truss was "an educated man who could talk in poetry if he chose." He is *not* included in this study.

59. Mollie D. Gaither to J. B. Gaither, April 30, 1864, Gaither, UNC.

60. The version that I used in the text was written by William H. Amos to Miss Nancy Doolittle, April 21, 1869, Amos, Duke. John Fuller's reworking is "mi lov to you no tonng can tll mi lov is As Pur as A Ring of gold hit is Round hit is Pur hit has no end so is my lov to you mi Darlin Frend." John Fuller to Miss Frances, April 19, 1864, SLFP,

NOTES TO PAGES 186–187   313

Duke. Another variation penned by Mollie D. Gaither is "round as a ring that has no end so is my love to you my friend." Mollie D Gaither to J. B. Gaither, October 25, 1863, Gaither, UNC.

61. He began with a modified version of two repeating lines from the popular song "The Rebel Soldier." The lines "I am a Rebel soldier / And far from my home" end each stanza and would have rung in the ears of many Confederate fighters, including John. See lyrics for "The Rebel Soldier" at https://www.battlefields.org/learn/primary-sour ces/civil-war-music-rebel-soldier. Also see Bruce C. Kelley and Mark A. Snell, eds., *Bugle Resounding: Music and Musicians of the Civil War Era* (Columbia: University of Missouri Press, 2004), 64, for the full lyrics of "A Southern Soldier Boy." Another song with the same title was published in 1882. It was written from the omniscient perspective as a paean to the sacrifice of a young Confederate soldier during the war. The song affirms that his memory lives on in his mother. Father Ryan and W. Ludden, "The Southern Soldier Boy" (Savannah, GA: Ludden & Bates, 1882), Civil War Sheet Music Collection, Library of Congress, https://www.loc.gov/resource/ihas.200002433.0?st= gallery. "Oh weep not for me" can be found in hymns, a ballad, and the King James Bible, Luke 23:28.

62. John Fuller to Miss Frances, April 19, 1864, SLFP, Duke.

63. C. W. Alexander, "The Southern Soldier Boy" (Richmond: Geo. Dunn & Company, 1863), Civil War Sheet Music Collection, Library of Congress, https://www.loc.gov/ item/ihas.200000728/. The entire first stanza follows:

> Oh! If in battle he was slain,
> I am sure that I should die,
> But I am sure he'll come again
> And cheer my weeping eye;
> But should he fall in this our glorious cause,
> He still would be my joy,
> For many a sweetheart mourns the loss
> Of a Southern Soldier Boy.
> Yo! Ho! Yo! Ho! Yo! Ho! Ho! . . .
> I'd grieve to lose my joy,
> But many a sweetheart mourns the loss
> Of a Southern Soldier Boy.

64. In England during this period, working-class poetry was also focused on the theme of "forget me not." See Frost, *Promises Broken*, pp. 67–69.

65. "O that I was whar I wood bee then I wood bee war I am not / her iam whare I mut bee for whare I wood be I can not."

66. Solon Fuller to Elizabeth Fuller, March 6, 1863, SLFP, Duke. "The Galley Slave" is found in *The Musical Banquet or Choice Songs* (Glasgow: A. Macgoun, 1790), 90. John's father changed the words to "how hard is mey fat hoo once fredom injoid / I was happey as happey coold be but pleser is fled / a captiv alas you may see."

67. *The Frank C. Brown Collection of North Carolina Folklore: Folksongs from North Carolina*, volume 3, eds. Henry M. Belden and Arthur Palmer Hudson (Durham, North Carolina: Duke University Press, 1952), 319. Brown cites George Lyman

314 NOTES TO PAGES 187–191

Kittredge, who claimed this was first printed in an 1835 songbook. In fact, the first printed version was a poem that appeared in an article in December 1833. See John Perry, "The Indian's Entreaty," *New-York Christian Messenger, and Philadelphia Universalist* 3 (December 28, 1833): 68. Apparently the subject of the poem was an unhappy American Indian youth who was persuaded to leave his natal home to matriculate in the East at a religious seminary. He begged to leave, according to this article, but no one listened, so he finally ran away. The incident supposedly resulted in this poem, which was put to music and, according to Brown, appeared in a great many songbooks from 1835 to 1890. See "White Man Let Me Go" in "The Traditional Ballad Index" eds. Robert B. Waltz and David G. Engle. http://balladindex.org/Ballads/FJ032.html. Notes on this song suggest that there was likely an earlier folk version.

68. Letter from Peter Van Wagenen to Mother, September 19, 1841, printed in *Narrative of Sojourner Truth*, 78–79. See pp. 75–76 for the circumstances that led to his employment on a whaling ship.

69. *Narrative of Sojourner Truth*, 79.

70. George to Sarah Deal, April 20, 1863, DL, Newberry. Several months before he composed his original poem, George sent Sarah a commercial valentine verse that is discussed later in the chapter.

71. Delos Lake to Calvin Lake, September 3, 1863, D. Lake, HEH.

72. Delos Lake to Calvin Lake, February 28, 1864, D. Lake, HEH.

73. Delos Lake to Calvin Lake, April 9, 1864, D. Lake, HEH. The Illinois lady surprised him by writing in late March 1865. Delos Lake to Mother and Brother, March 26, 1865, D. Lake, HEH. His commitment was weak, however, and his expectations were low. "Calvin says his girl has deserted him," Delos wrote his mother less than one month after receiving the Illinois lady's letter. "I expect mine has also." Delos Lake to Mother, April 22, 1865.

74. This was the meaning of "bird" for the last half of the nineteenth century, according to Robert Hendrickson, *The Facts on File Encyclopedia of Word and Phrase Origins*, 4th ed. (New York: Infobase, 2008). Using other reference works, "bird" can be interpreted differently.

75. B. W. Ellison to Nannie Hope, January 26, 1865, Bradley County, Tennessee, TNGenInc, found at "This That and T'other: Letters from forgotten Ancestors, Pre-1920 letters," https://www.tngenweb.org/tnletters/bradtn3.htm.

76. Lois Davis to Charles Henry Richardson, April 4 [actually early May], 1861, LWRD, Duke. This poem was likely part of the folk culture of the Civil War. See a longer poem from Lois R. Davis to her "boys," April 1, 1860, LWRD, Duke.

77. Her turn to patriotic poetry was apparently widespread in the North. See Fahs, *The Imagined Civil War*, pp. 4, 64, 122.

78. Clarance Richardson to Grandmother, March 2, 1864. This poem appeared in an almanac. See William Martin Anderson, *They Died to Make Men Free: A History of the 19th Century Michigan Infantry in the Civil War* (Berrien Springs, MI: Hardscrabble Books, 1980), 180.

79. Albert Lord, *The Singer Resumes the Tale* (Ithaca: Cornell University Press, 1995), 202. Though Lord acknowledges a transitional category, he believes the distinction between oral and written traditions in literature is essential "in order to correctly

NOTES TO PAGE 191   315

appreciate its aesthetics and to describe and edit its texts." I have much more intellectual congruence with the work of Ruth Finnegan. See Finnegan's *Oral Poetry* and "What Is Oral Literature Anyway? Comments in the Light of Some African and Other Comparative Material," in *Oral Literature and the Formula*, ed. Benjamin A. Stolz and Richard S. Shannon III (Ann Arbor: Center for the Coordination of Ancient and Modern Studies, University of Michigan, 1976), 127–66. See also the discussion that follows the article on pp. 167–76. Finnegan insists on the relativity of the concepts of oral and written literature and that "oral literature is not a single, clear-cut category, nor is it opposed in any absolute way to written literature" (161). I appreciate her emphasis on empirical evidence. The wide-ranging cross-cultural data she presents are consonant with the evidence I have gathered for this study.

80. See Zboray and Zboray, *Everyday Ideas*, pp. 39–41, 43–45. The contrasts between an oral and a fully literate culture have significant ramifications in emotional history. Working-class Americans, who were on the cusp of literacy, as well as those with better writing skills, were influenced by oral or nonliterate speech patterns in their writing. See Walter Ong's classic *Orality and Literacy: The Technologizing of the Word* (London: Methuen, 1982).

81. Zboray and Zboray, *Everyday Ideas*, pp. 32–33.

82. Rubin, *Memory in Oral Traditions*, chapter 4.

83. Newell, *Games and Songs*, 1–3; Gary Alan Fine, in "Children and Their Culture: Exploring Newell's Paradox," *Western Folklore* 39 (July 1980): 170–83, analyzes and supports Newell's claim that children's folklore is both conservative and innovative; Fine points out that "some genres seem to be particularly conservative (rhymes)" (183); Sylvia Ann Grider comments on the methodological changes in the field since Newell in "The Study of Children's Folklore," *Western Folklore* 39 (July 1980): 159–69.

84. Newell, *Games and Songs*, 10–11. The verse was often accompanied by a refrain, which could be one line or two, repeated at the end of each stanza.

85. Rosalie V. Halsey's *Forgotten Books of the American Nursery: A History of the Development of the American Story-Book* (Boston: Charles E. Goodspeed & Co., 1911), is oriented toward print culture and the narrative story. Percy B. Green's classic *A History of Nursery Rhymes* (London: Greening & Co., 1899) is exclusively British. Another modern classic, Iona and Peter Opie, *The Oxford Dictionary of Nursery Rhymes* (London: Oxford University Press, 1951; 2nd edition, 1997), included some American examples, plus a long discussion of Mother Goose. I have found no evidence that nursery rhyme books were read by working-class parents or children, though any of these rhymes could have been transmitted orally. *Mother Goose's Melodies: A Facsimile Reproduction of the Earliest Known Edition*, ed. Col. W. F. Prideaux (London: A.H. Bullen, 1904), https://archive.org/details / mothergoosesmelo00pridiala; also Mahlon Day, *New York Street Cries in Rhyme* (New York: Dover, 1977; facsimile reprint of 1825 edition).

86. All the content of the adolescent kissing or love games that Newell documented are found in his section on "Love-Games" in *Games and Songs*, 39–62. Though not a kissing game, "Paper of Pins" was another popular children's rhyme with many variations that, Newell reported, he had heard "from persons of all classes and ages."

316   NOTES TO PAGES 191–192

Calling this poem a love-game, Newell's transcription revealed a lighthearted cynicism about women's motives for marriage. The rhyme features a male suitor who offers to give his girlfriend a "paper of pins," "an easy chair," "a silver spoon," and "a dress of green," all of which are rejected by his future mate. He finally offers the key to his heart, which is still refused in this cynical children's rhyme. But money brings her assent to marriage, followed by the mocking admission of the last stanza: "Ha, ha, ha, money is all / And I won't marry you at all." The final stanza almost shouted that the game was a joke. The penultimate verse, however, was quite serious in defining economic gain as the "preferable" motive for marriage. There was at least one variant with a happy ending based on romantic love. Newell, *Games and Songs*, 51–55.

87. Master of Hearts, *A Collection of New and Original Valentines, Serious & Satirical, Sublime & Ridiculous* (London: Ward and Lock, 1858), 9, 15.

88. Alice Campbell, "Return of the Bethel Heroes," in *War Days in Fayetteville, North Carolina: Reminiscences of 1861 to 1865*, complied by J.E.B. Chapter, United Daughters of the Confederacy (Fayetteville: Judge Printing Co., May 1910), https://docsouth.unc.edu/fpn/chapter/chapter.html.

89. Victorians also saw poetry drawn from the work of well-regarded authors as legitimate expressions of romantic love.

90. "Roses Are Red / violets Are Blue: A 'Sampler' from Friendship Albums," Tredyffrin Easttown [Pennsylvania] Historical Society, *History Quarterly*, Digital Archives 26 (April 1988): 55–68, https://tehistory.org/hqda/html/v26/v26n2p055.html.

91. Karen Lystra, *Searching the Heart: Women, Men, and Romantic Love in Nineteenth-Century America* (New York: Oxford University Press, 1989), chapter 1.

92. See Appendix A.

93. Carl F. Kaestle, "McGuffey Readers," in *The Oxford Companion to United States History* (New York: Oxford University Press, 2001); Carol Kammen, "The McGuffey Readers," *Children's Literature* 5 (1976): 58–63. The McGuffey series, eventually six in all, were not numbered according to grade level but according to difficulty. This meant that children of different ages might be working in the same reader. McGuffey quickly became one of the best-selling textbook brands and is still widely known today.

94. The earliest edition I had access to was William Holmes McGuffey, *The Newly Revised Eclectic First Reader* (Cincinnati: Winthrop & Smith, 1844); I also looked at *The New First Eclectic Reader* (Cincinnati: Sargent, Wilson, & Hinkle, 1857); and *McGuffey's First Eclectic Reader*, rev. ed. (New York: John Wiley & Sons, 1879). The 1879 edition is the most widely reproduced and widely available online. Moreover, it is the edition that is often used in scholarly analysis. However, the 1879 revision introduced significant changes to the original text. These alterations included the addition of phonics and lessons in writing the basic alphabet in script. The 1879 edition of the *First Reader* was not available to children during my study. Therefore I have based my description on the 1844 edition.

95. William Holmes McGuffey, *The Second Eclectic Reader* (Cincinnati: Truman & Smith, 1836). For example, Lesson 22, p. 43, is ambitious by working-class standards. Words included: loathes, skulks, yawns, creeps, ignorance, slovenliness, uncombed, garments, and eagerly. The first poem I found in the 1836 *Second Reader* was Lesson 58, p. 108. The poetry was composed of four-line iambic couplets.

NOTES TO PAGES 192–193   317

96. William Holmes McGuffey, *The Second Eclectic Reader*, rev. ed. (New York: John Wiley & Sons, 1879) The 1879 edition of the *Second Reader* included significant changes from the original including an emphasis on correct pronunciation, basic sentence construction, writing (called slate work), and punctuation. Poetry was introduced in Lesson 4, p. 16.

97. Virtuous behavior was emphasized in McGuffey readers. This included the values of industry, charity, and kindness. The sanctity of property was preached and the sins of alcohol and laziness were excoriated. Patriotism was also heavily promoted. Some New England children, the best educated in the country, were probably instructed in higher-level readers.

98. Catherine Robson, "On Difficulty," *Modern Language Quarterly* 75 (June 2014): 321–24; see also Catherine Robson, *Heart Beats: Everyday Life and the Memorized Poem* (Princeton: Princeton University Press, 2012), 35–40.

99. Ornate verses found in pamphlets and chapbooks (small, inexpensive booklets) called Valentine Writers were also available for copying. Valentine Writers were supposed to provide poetry for men and women to send in handwritten valentines and also poetic responses to those they received. These chapbooks offered an array of holiday poems for replicating in cards and letters. There is scant evidence, however, that poor folk used the Valentine Writers in creating their handwritten cards, and *no* evidence that they were the source of poetry in their letters. I am increasingly puzzled by the question of who actually used them. I believe finding poetry from Valentine Writers in working-class letters would be a rare discovery. Valentine Writer poems were too highfalutin'—ornate, pretentious, and grandiose—for working-class taste and too artificial and contrived for adult Victorians in courting relationships. Perhaps they were consulted by middle-class adolescents who copied some lines on their handwritten valentine's cards. Some of the valentine writers I have sampled include (online) By a Lady, *An Original Collections of Genteel and Fashionable Valentines* (London, 1820); *The Lover's Poetic Companion and Valentine Writer* (London: Ward, Lock and Tyler, 1875); *A Collection of Original Valentines* [London?, 1800?]; *The new English valentine writer, or the high road to love; for both sexes. Containing a complete set of valentines, . . . To which is added, several new songs in Honour of the day* (London, [1784]), Eighteenth Century Collections Online, Gale Facsimile. Also *The Ladies' polite valentine writer; or, A new collection of elegant valentines of the fair sex. Principally original* (London: Dean and Monday, 185[?]). It should be noted that they endlessly cribbed from each other. See Leigh Schmidt, "The Fashioning of a Modern Holiday: St. Valentine's Day, 1840–1870," *Winterthur Portfolio* 28 (1993): 209–45, 218–19, 223. Also Bruce David Forbes, *America's Favorite Holidays: Candid Histories* (Oakland: University of California Press, 2015), 66–70.

100. It is possible that some laboring folk learned their love poems from almanacs, which sometimes included valentine rhymes to mark the occasion.

101. Schmidt, "Fashioning," 209–45, esp. 213–14, 216–218, 222.

102. These numbers are based on an advertisement reprinted in Schmidt, "Fashioning," 226–27.

318   NOTES TO PAGES 193–195

103. Charles W. Dudley Diary, February 10 and 15, 1856, HEH. Cheshire had a population of 1,626 in 1850. See "Population of Connecticut Towns, 1830 to 1890," *Connecticut Secretary of the State*, 2013, http://www.sots.ct.gov/sots/cwp/view.asp?a=3188&q=392396.
104. George to Sarah Deal, January 30, 1863, DL, Newberry.
105. Schmidt sets that turning point at around 1860 ("Fashioning," 223). The *New York Times* argued that Valentine's Day was big business, and the popular belief that this holiday had been "resigned to chambermaids and their swains" after the Civil War was incorrect. "Valentines: Interesting Statistics of the Trade—the Practice of Sending Valentines Extending," *New York Times*, February 4, 1867; Barry Shank, *A Token of My Affection: Greeting Cards and American Business Culture* (New York: Columbia University Press, 2004).
106. A broadside cheaply printed by Strong in 1852 for hawking valentine rhymes to the humblest Americans contained more than 350 two-line couplets that were meant to be cut and pasted into homemade valentines. As far as I am aware, correspondents did not copy the couplets in the letters I read. See *Cupid's Chit Chat* (New York: T.W. Strong, 1852), Archive of Americana, American broadsides and ephemera, Series 1 no. 14433, Aubry R. Watzek Library, Lewis & Clark College. This crudely printed one-page sheet was also published in Boston. A note in pencil at the bottom right corner reads, "Valentine messages to cut out." Nothing was clipped in this sheet, however. I was alerted to the existence of this rare document in Schmidt's outstanding article, "Fashioning," 220 n. 21. I would not rule out the possibility that poor people cribbed a few of their rhymes from inexpensive commercial valentines.
107. Paul Charosh, "Studying Nineteenth-Century Popular Song," *American Music* 15 (Winter 1997): 478–82.
108. For the origin of "Roses" as a valentine, see Opie and Opie, *Dictionary of Nursery Rhymes*, p. 446. Working-class correspondents offered no nursery rhymes (at least none that were cataloged in the classic collections) as symbols of attachment in their letters; for "Ring" see James Hardy and G. Laurence Gomme, eds., "The Denham Tracts, 1846–1859," *The Folk-lore Society*, 35 (London: David Nutt, 1895), 348–49; for "Vine" see n. 26 above.
109. Opie and Opie, *Dictionary of Nursery Rhymes*, 446; G. F. Northall, *English Folk Rhymes: A Collection of Traditional Verses Relating to Places* . . . (London: Keegan Paul, Trench, Trübner, 1892), 210.
110. Talley, *Negro folk Rhymes*, 128.
111. Floyd County, Georgia, recruits joined Companies A, E, and H.
112. H. H. to Miss O. Espy, February 14, 1863, Joseph Espey Papers, UNC. He wrote: "we met at a caban to had a valentine drawing and it as a happe lot to Draw your Name from the Box."
113. Schmidt, "Fashioning," 211. Apparently drawing lots has a long history going back to a Roman festival celebrated on February 14 when young men would draw the name of a young woman who would be their partner for the day. See J. Hillis Miller, *Topographies* (Stanford, CA: Stanford University Press, 1995), 109.
114. Schmidt, "Fashioning," 215.

NOTES TO PAGES 195–198   319

115. H. H. to Miss O. Espy, February 14, 1863, Joseph Espey Papers, UNC. Spelling varied by family. Olivia Espy lived in Cherokee County, Alabama, and was a cousin of a large Floyd County clan of Espeys. Floyd, Georgia, and Cherokee County, Alabama shared a border and were carved out of Indian territory. See H.S. Tanner and assistants, "Georgia and Alabama," *American Atlas* (Philadelphia: H.S. Tanner, 1823) and "County Map of Georgia and Alabama" in Unidentified Atlas (Philadelphia: August S. Mitchell, Jr., 1860) digitized in the Virtual Vault, Historic Maps, Surveyor General, RG 3-8-65, Georgia Archives. https://vault.georgiaarchives.org/digital/collection/hmf/id/12/rec/13.

116. H. H. to Miss O. Espy, February 14, 1863, Joseph Espey Papers, UNC.

117. H. H. to Miss O. Espy, February 14, 1863, Joseph Espey Papers, UNC. See chapter 3 for her attitude.

118. The closest source I could find was a poem in George Pope Morris et al., eds., *The New Mirror*, vol. 1 (New York: Morris, Willis & Co., April 29, 1843), 51. "For ever thine this heart— / All else may change, and be: / But this, thy heart, no change can own, / For thee it beats, for thee alone, / And breaks, cast off by thee; / Thine, Thine alone."

119. See Barre Toelken's fine study *Morning Dew and Roses; Nuance, Metaphor and Meaning in Folksongs* (Urbana: University of Illinois Press, 1995), 28.

120. Willis Buckingham argues that poetry was "the preeminent literary medium for [heartfelt] social exchange" among middle-class Americans in "Emily Dickinson and the Reading Life," in *Dickinson and Audience*, eds. Martin Orzek and Robert Weisbuck (Ann Arbor: University of Michigan Press, 1996), 242. For a sophisticated literary defense of the uses of popular poetry by ordinary Americans in the first half of the twentieth century, see Mike Chasar, *Everyday Reading: Poetry and Popular Culture in Modern America* (New York: Columbia University Press, 2012). Chasar also argues for the importance of an oral culture of poetry in modern America in "Orality, Literacy, and the Memorized Poem" *Poetry* 205 (January 2015): 371–82.

Chapter 8

1. Jennifer Davis Heaps, "'Remember Me': Six Samplers in the National Archives," *Prologue Magazine* 34 (Fall 2002): 184–95. The online version (Part 1) has no pagination. Emphasis mine. www.archives.gov/publications/prologue/2002/fall/samplers-2.html.

2. A school-age girl practices her embroidery on samplers by stitching various designs and letters. These designs may be pictorial as well as abstract, while the letters can occur singly, as in a sample alphabet, and also in a rhymed verse.

3. Mary to Leonard Caplinger, June 15, 1863, Caplinger, HEH. See Ethel Stanwood Bolton and Eva Johnston Coe, *American Samplers* (Boston: Massachusetts Society of the Colonial Dames of America, 1921). Significantly, this classic sampler reference guide classifies "when this you see" under both categories: "In Praise of Love" (256) and "Reflections on Death and Sorrow" (279, 281). The ubiquity and longevity

320 NOTES TO PAGES 198–201

of this particular rhyme is illustrated by its use on samplers from the seventeenth through the late nineteenth century (though less often after 1825).

4. Barrett Wendell to Mrs. Bolton, June 20, 1920, in Bolton and Coe, *American Samplers*, 248. Toni Fratto, "Samplers: The Historical Ethnography of an American Popular Art" (PhD. diss., University of Pennsylvania, 1971), 37. According to Fratto's survey, "When this you see" reached its peak use in the 1830–1840 period, characterized by an emphasis on self-expression in samplers. See Heaps, "Remember Me," n. 11, for multiple examples from South Carolina (1743), Pennsylvania (1828, 1840), Massachusetts (1748, 1793), Virginia (1761), and Ohio (1837). "Different versions of this verse appear on samplers created in various geographic areas and time periods," Heaps observed. "It had incredible staying power."

5. Mollie Dawalt [Mrs. Mary Baldwin] to Ella Buck, April 17, 1880, Buck, ISL. The correspondent had returned to her maiden name.

6. See 1870 US Federal Census under Mary E. Dawald, who was eight years old. Dawalt's father was a laborer who owned no land or house, and her mother could neither read nor write. Indicated in 1870 federal census under John and Ann R. Dawald.

7. See Steve Conway, "Death, Working-Class Culture and Social Distinction," *Heath Sociology Review*, 21 (December 2012): 441–49, esp. 442. He believes cultural practices reflect and reproduce class distinctions in the face of death.

8. Wyatt Brantley to Willis Roberts, no date [likely sometime in the summer 1830], Roberts Family Papers, LC.

9. James Miles to Neighbour [presumably Reeves], July 21, 1867, Reeves, UNC.

10. Jane Espey to Maes Espey, January 28, 1862, Joseph Espey Papers, UNC.

11. J. B. Roberts to Father [Stephen Roberts], February 17, 1865, Roberts Family Papers, LC.

12. Mary R. Brophy to Mary Brophy Beeson, April 1, 1867, Brophy-Beeson Papers, HEH.

13. "I remain thy affectionate Brother," Pennsylvanian John Sammes signed off a letter to his sister, playfully spelling his name backward (John Sammes, to Sister, September 20, 1859, Osmond, MHS). "From your sister" was sufficient for one transplanted Vermonter (Hattie Buck to Sister, October 27, 1857, Buck, ISL). Another ended on an optimistic note: "I will draw to a close by wishing you good health good by" (Reuben Lanphear to Daughter Eliza, November 13, 1857, Shattuck, MHS).

14. Joshua Jones to Wife & little Boy & friends, August 11, 1861, CWLJ.

15. Joshua Jones to J. W. Abrell, CWLJ.

16. Joshua to Celia Jones, February 6 and April 2, 1862, CWLJ.

17. Joshua to Celia Jones, August 18, 1862, CWLJ.

18. Joshua to Celia Jones, April 2 and July 15, 1862, CWLJ. Southerner J. J. Asbill, a Confederate soldier, also merged the nonromantic and romantic conventions of attachment in his closing: "your loving husbin untell death." J. J. Asbill to Wife, May 11, 1862, J. J. Asbill Correspondence, LC.

19. J. David Hacker, "A Census-Based Count of the Civil War Dead," *Civil War History* 57 (December, 2011): 307–48. He offers a significant revision to the agreed-upon statistics of Civil War mortality.

NOTES TO PAGES 201–207 321

20. Drew Gilpin Faust, "'A Riddle of Death': Mortality and Meaning in the American Civil War," 34th Annual Robert Fortenbaugh Memorial Lecture, Gettysburg College, 1995. She was using the older figure of 620,000 deaths. Also Drew Gilpin Faust, "The Civil War Soldier and the Art of Dying," *Journal of Southern History* 67 (February 2001): 3–38, esp. 3–4.

21. Hillory Shifflet to Jemima Shifflet, May 2, 1863, CivWar, MOHS.

22. David Demus to Mary Jane Demus, March 4, 1864, VS/UV. See chapter 5 for a brief review of the closing lines in their correspondence.

23. Mollie D. Gaither to Burgess Gaither, October 25, 1863, Gaither, UNC.

24. Luther Trussell to Delia Page, June 20, 1860, in *Farm to Factory: Women's Letters, 1830–1860*, ed. Thomas Dublin (New York: Columbia University Press, 1981), 159–60.

25. Gary Laderman, *The Sacred Remains: American Attitudes toward Death, 1799–1883* (New Haven: Yale University Press, 1996), 24–25.

26. Charles Rosenberg, *The Cholera Years: The United States in 1832, 1849, and 1866* (Chicago: University of Chicago Press, 1962, 1987), 1–4; Mark S. Schantz, *Awaiting the Heavenly Country: The Civil War and America's Culture of Death* (Ithaca: Cornell University Press, 2008), 11.

27. Andrew Noymer and Beth Jarosz, "Causes of Death in Nineteenth-Century New England: The Dominance of Infectious Disease," *Social History of Medicine* 21 (December 2008): 573–78.

28. James Gatewood to Father, June 18, 1855, Amos, Duke.

29. What was left unsaid, but implied, was Katy's vulnerability to an early demise. Emiline Rawlings Goudie to Rebecca Rawlings Brophy, August 7, 1864, Brophy-Beeson Papers, HEH.

30. Additive syntax—and . . . and . . . and—is called parataxis. It is relied upon in oral cultures to aid memorization and promote social traditions. See Eric A. Havelock, *The Muse Learned to Write: Reflections on Orality and Literacy from Antiquity to the Present* (New Haven: Yale University Press, 1986), 76.

31. Mary Rebecca Rawlings Brophy to Mary Catherine Brophy Beeson, April 1, 1867, Brophy-Beeson Papers, HEH.

32. H. N. Coomer to Otis Mason and Francema Mason, September 11 and 17, 1868, Francema Mason–Otis Mason Correspondence, Newberry. Death usually trumped marriage in family communications with the exception of young singles writing to each other.

33. Martha Burgess [dictating] to Nancy E Burgess, October 8, 1865, Lipscomb, UNC.

34. Elizabeth Sterling to Father, undated, Osmond, MHS.

35. Laderman, *The Sacred Remains*, 28.

36. Pat Jalland, *Death in the Victorian Family* (Oxford: Oxford University Press, 1996), 25–38; for an added comparative perspective, see Pat Jalland, *The Australian Ways of Death: A Social and Cultural History, 1840–1918* (New York: Oxford University Press, 2002).

37. Ann Russell to William R. Osmond and family, [undated], Osmond, MHS. The dying woman was probably a sister.

38. Anna Mason to Parents, November 27, 1854, Bronson, HEH.

322 NOTES TO PAGES 207–210

39. Anna Mason to Mother, November 2, 1853, Bronson, HEH.
40. A quiet, easy death was best by working-class standards because it denoted future happiness. John and Rachel Ricketts to brother, December 23, 1838, as quoted in Lewis O. Saum, "Death in the Popular Mind of Pre-Civil War America," *American Quarterly* 26 (December 1974): 489–92, esp. 492.
41. G. E. Hollis to Miss O. A., February 21, 1864, Joseph Espey Papers, UNC.
42. Ann to John Larimer, March 7, 1865, Civil War Diaries and Letters, IDL.
43. Ursula Terry to Reuben Terry, April 5, 1843, George F. and Ursula Terry Letters, SHSM.
44. Drew Faust, *This Republic of Suffering: Death and the American Civil War* (New York: Knopf, 2008), chapter 1; Faust, "Civil War Soldier," 11–13, 16, 19. What was dominant in working-class letters before and during the Civil War was a belief in heaven as a real place where people could meet after life ended. See Schantz, *Awaiting the Heavenly Country*, chapter 2. Also James McPherson, *The War That Forged a Nation: Why the Civil War Still Matters* (New York: Oxford University Press, 2015), chapter 4; Gregory A. Coco, *Killed in Action: Eyewitness Accounts of the Last Moments of 100 Union Soldiers Who Died at Gettysburg* (Gettysburg: Thomas Pub., 1992).
45. See Faust, *This Republic of Suffering*, for one example of the many comforting condolence letters sent by Walt Whitman (123–24).
46. My hunch is that this was an imaginary account that he used repeatedly to comfort the grieving families of dead soldiers. Joseph Davis to Cousin and Aunt Jane, April 12, 1862, Joseph Espey Papers, UNC. See also Joseph William Davis, US Civil War Soldiers Records and Profiles, 1861–1865 and the 1850 and 1860 US Federal Census for Joseph W. Davis. His father owned $12,000 worth of land in 1850 and his brother $9,000 in 1860 if the census valuations can be believed.
47. Ashley Michelle Mays, "A Past Still Living: The Grieving Process of Confederate Widows" (PhD diss., University of North Carolina at Chapel Hill, 2014). Chapter 3, on condolence letters, is the most extensive collection I have found in the historical literature. Though she makes no distinction between middle- and working-class writers, Mays plainly observes that some of the eyewitness correspondents detailing the death of a husband in the Civil War "did not spare widows, supposedly of the more delicate gender, from gruesome details" (118).
48. C. Dicken to Mrs. Faney Catenhead, July 23, 1863, in I. B. Cadenhead, "Some Confederate Letters of I. B. Cadenhead," *Alabama Historical Quarterly* 18 (Winter 1956): 567–68. He was in Company H, Thirty-Fourth Alabama Infantry Regiment.
49. Joseph Jones to Nancy E. Jones, February 11, 1863, #: GLC02739.034. The Gilder Lehrman Institute of American History, hereafter cited as Gilder Lehrman. https://www.gilderlehrman.org/collection/glc02739034.
50. Adam Bradford, "Inspiring Death: Poe's Poetic Aesthetics, 'Annabel Lee,' and the Communities of Mourning in Nineteenth-Century America," *Edgar Allan Poe Review* 12 (Spring 2011): 72–100; Robert Kenzer, "The Uncertainty of Life: A Profile of Virginia's Civil War Widows," in *The War Was You and Me: Civilians in the American Civil War*, ed. Joan Cashin (Princeton: Princeton University Press, 2002), 119.
51. He was a private in the Seventy-Ninth Illinois Infantry, Company F. See Illinois Civil War Rosters, where the battles of each infantry regiment are listed. http://civilwar.ill inoisgenweb.org /reg_html/079_reg.html.

NOTES TO PAGES 210–213   323

52. Joseph Jones to Nancy E. Jones, November 10, 1863, #: GLC02739.084, Gilder Lehrman. https://www.gilderlehrman.org/collection/glc02739084.

53. Mary Chenoweth to Jasper N. Bertram, January 29, [probably 1864], University of Washington Libraries, Civil War Letters, Digital Collections, https://digitalcollecti ons.lib.washington.edu/digital/collection/civilwar/id/656/rec/24. See Drew Gilpin Faust, *Mothers of Invention: Women of the Slaveholding South in the American Civil War* (Chapel Hill: University of North Carolina Press, 1996), 189–91, for similar attitudes expressed by middle-class southern women.

54. George Fluent to Mr. McClane, August 26, 1864, Civil War Diaries and Letters, IDL. See also 1870 US Federal Census.

55. William A. Davis to Violet Hall, September 17, 1864, complete letter transcribed in Katie O'Halloran Brown, "Letters of Black Soldiers from Ohio Who Served in the 54th and 55th Massachusetts Volunteer Infantries during the Civil War," *Ohio Valley History* 16 (Fall 2016): 75–76.

56. John D. Comrie, "Remarks on Historical Aspects of Ideas Regarding Dropsy," *British Medical Journal* 2 (August 11, 1928): 229–32, http://www.jstor.org.lib-proxy.fuller ton.edu/stable/25329668.

57. Drew Gilpin Faust, "'The Dread Void of Uncertainty': Naming the Dead in the American Civil War," *Southern Cultures* 11 (Summer 2005): 7–32.

58. Middle-class female mourners had a defined clothing ritual that involved elaborate rules on the appearance and timing of mourning attire. See Karen Haltunnen, *Confidence Men and Painted* Women (New Haven: Yale University Press, 1982), 136–44; also Faust, *This Republic of Suffering*, 146–53. It is unclear what, if any, part of this clothing ritual was observed by working-class women. Whatever their customs, wartime shortages in the South would have made this symbolic gesture difficult for nonelite women. See Mays, "Grieving Process," pp. 77–80, 83, 85.

59. John Q. Anderson, ed., *Brokenburn: The Journal of Kate Stone, 1861–1868* (Baton Rouge: Louisiana State University Press, 1955, 1972), 277.

60. The importance of working-class funeral ritual is illustrated in two subcultures: Vincent DiGirolamo, "Newsboy Funerals: Tales of Sorrow and Solidarity in Urban America," *Journal of Social History* 36 (Autumn 2002): 5–30; and Michael K. Rosenow, *Death and Dying in the Working Class, 1865–1920* (Urbana: University of Illinois Press, 2015).

61. Faust, *This Republic of Suffering*, 144.

62. Laderman, *The Sacred Remains*, 152–53; Faust, *This Republic of Suffering*, 85–99.

63. Faust, *This Republic of Suffering*, 64–80, 161.

64. Judith Giesberg, *Army at Home: Women and the Civil War on the Northern Home Front* (Chapel Hill: University of North Carolina Press, 2009), 146–60.

65. Faust in *This Republic of Suffering* sensitively discussed a widow's despair (130–32).

66. I found no letters of working-class widows describing the facts of or reactions to the death of their husbands who were fighting in the Civil War. In her thoughtful narrative on both Union and Confederate Civil War widows for Virginia Tech's Essential Civil War Curriculum website, Angela Esco Elder quotes from the correspondence of only two Civil War widows. Most widow reactions were reported by observers. https://www.essentialcivilwarcurriculum.com/civil-war-widows.html.   See   also

324 NOTES TO PAGES 213–214

Jennifer Lynn Gross, "'Good Angels': Confederate Widowhood in Virginia," in *Southern Families at War: Loyalty and Conflict in the Civil War South*, ed. Catherine Clinton (New York: Oxford University Press, 2000), 133–53. This article contained no correspondence by a widow regarding her husband's death. The only evidence of a widow's reaction came from a diarist who witnessed one wife's emotional response to her husband's death in a hospital (136). Another article by Jennifer Gross, while rich in postbellum evidence, contains no letters by widows describing their husband's death. "The United Daughters of the Confederacy, Confederate Widows, and the Lost Cause," in *Women on Their Own: Interdisciplinary Perspectives on Being Single*, ed. Rudolph M. Bell and Virginia Yans-McLaughlin (Piscataway: Rutgers University Press, 2007), 180–200. Ashley Mays observes in "The Grieving Process of Confederate Widows," a dissertation that relies heavily on letters, "Widows' response to the news of their husbands' deaths were so intimate and emotional that only vague records remain" (76). Also see Mays, p. 131. As far as I can ascertain from the quoted material in Mays's chapter 4, "Emotion," she found six southern widows who wrote at least one letter expressing their grief, plus two diarists. None of these correspondents appear to be working-class women.

67. This parallels the "gap in evidence about postwar marriage patterns" that was pointed out in J. David Hacker, Libra Hilde, and James Holland Jones, "The Effect of the Civil War on Southern Marriage Patterns," *Journal of Southern History* 76 (February 2010): 39–70, esp. 50.

68. Norman L. Farberow, "Theories," a subset of the entry on "Grief" in *Macmillan Encyclopedia of Death and Dying*, ed. Robert Kastenbaum, vol. 1 (New York: Macmillan Reference, 2002), 373–80; Margaret Stroebe and Henk Schut, "Meaning Making in the Dual Process Model of Coping with Bereavement," in *Meaning Reconstruction and the Experience of Loss*, ed. Robert Neimeyer (Washington, DC: American Psychological Association Press, 2001), 55–73; Margaret Stroebe and Henk Schut, "The Dual Process Model of Coping with Bereavement: Rationale and Description," *Death Studies* 23 (1990): 197–224.

69. Margaret Stroebe et al., "Does Disclosure of Emotions Facilitate Recovery from Bereavement? Evidence from Two Prospective Studies," *Journal of Consulting and Clinical Psychology* 70 (2002): 169–79.

70. A twenty-first-century study of widows in Nepal, whose husbands died as a consequence of a long civil war, found that financial stress was significantly associated with depression and anxiety. S. Basnet, P. Kandel and P. Lamichhane, "Depression and Anxiety among War-Widows of Nepal: A Post-Civil War Cross-Sectional Study," *Psychology, Health and Medicine* 23 (February 2018): 141–53. There is no American Civil War equivalent, for the reason that evidence of widows' feelings in their own words is scarce.

71. Robert Kenzer's "The Uncertainty of Life," 122–25, provides a detailed description of the aid requested in Henry County, Virginia, by widows who desperately needed help to feed their families in the face of rising prices and the decreasing supply of foodstuffs.

72. Amy E. Holmes, "'Such Is the Price We Pay': American Widows and the Civil War Pension System," in *Toward a Social History of the American Civil War: Exploratory*

Essays, ed. Maris A. Vinovskis (New York: Cambridge University Press, 1990), 171–95. She provides a succinct overview of the evolution of the pension system and estimates that over 108,000 women became Union widows, of whom about 52,000 were listed on pension rolls in 1883. Megan J. McClintock's "Civil War Pensions and the Reconstruction of Union Families," *Journal of American History* 83 (September 1996): 456–80, is a cogent, well-written account of the evolution of pension laws during and after the Civil War. These pension studies do not typically utilize widows' correspondence. For the legal and cultural foundations of military widows' entitlement to government relief, see Kristin A. Collins, "'Petitions Without Number': Widows' Petitions and the Early Nineteenth-Century Origins of Public Marriage-Based Entitlements," *Law and History Review* 31 (February 2013): 1–60.

73. Laura Salisbury, "Women's Income and Marriage Markets in the United States: Evidence from the Civil War Pension," *Journal of Economic History* 77 (March 2017): 3–4, 17. According to Salisbury's economic analysis of federal pension records, Union widows had few good alternatives to remarriage. Thus, especially women with young children were pressured out of financial necessity to enter marriages that she termed "of very low value." The problem of course is that this judgment, while it may be valid in terms of economic behavioral analysis, might not be shared by the widows themselves. For example, Daniel Turner was illiterate, property-less, and far outside her age demographic, yet the widow Peebles badly wanted to marry him. See chapters 1, 7, and 8.

74. Salisbury, "Women's Income," 3.

75. Kenzer, "The Uncertainty of Life," 113–14.

76. Hacker, Hilde, and Jones, "Effect of the Civil War," 39–70, esp. 63–64, 68, and n. 59. These authors found that census evidence suggested low remarriage rates among southern women widowed by the Civil War; also Salisbury, "Women's Income," 30. In her detailed economic analysis of the federal Civil War pension program, she concluded that at age thirty-five widows were statistically "predicted not to remarry."

77. Kenzer, "The Uncertainty of Life," 113–14. I found his careful research and incisive analysis especially helpful. See the entire article, pp. 112–35.

78. Kenzer, "The Uncertainty of Life," 122–25.

79. Laura Edwards, *Scarlett Doesn't Live Here Anymore: Southern Women in the Civil War Era* (Urbana: University of Illinois Press, 2000), 93–94.

80. Edwards, *Scarlett Doesn't Live Here*, 150–51.

81. Kenzer, "The Uncertainty of Life," 126.

82. Kenzer, "The Uncertainty of Life," 129.

83. Kenzer in "The Uncertainty of Life," 125, found "a near-linear relationship between a woman's age and her likelihood of marrying." According to Nicole Etcheson, who focused on a Midwest county in Indiana before, during, and after the war, federal pensions allowed women to "avoid turning to others for help." See her *A Generation at War: The Civil War Era in a Northern Community* (Lawrence: University Press of Kansas, 2011), 214–15. This is a thoughtful, thorough, and well-crafted community study, but I think this generalization may not apply to working-class widows. Seeming to support Etcheson's contention that widows intentionally rejected their option to re-marry, Judith Giesberg concluded that middle-aged widows in rural Adams County,

326   NOTES TO PAGES 215–218

Pennsylvania, "seem to have preferred to live independently on the land" after the war. See her *Army at Home*, p. 39. Once again, I believe that class is an important factor in the validity of this generalization. The relationship between the choice to live independently and federal pension payments is not discussed.

84. Sally Peeples, 1870 US Federal Census, Guilford, North Carolina.

85. Russell L. Johnson, "'Great Injustice': Social Status and the Distribution of Military Pensions after the Civil War," *Journal of the Gilded Age and Progressive Era* 10 (April 2011): 148.

86. Johnson summarizes this finding on p. 160.

87. Johnson, "Great Injustice," 142, 137–60. The pensions of officers under the 1862 law were close to double or triple that of enlisted men (141, 143–45, 147). In a case study in New Bern, North Carolina, Brandi C. Brimmer has shown that Black working-class women were also disadvantaged by racialized constructions of gender in the federal pension system, especially after 1882, and were often in desperate need of aid. See her "Black Women's Politics, Narratives of Sexual Immorality, and Pension Bureaucracy in Mary Lee's North Carolina Neighborhood," *Journal of Southern History* 80 (November 2014): 827–58.

88. Johnson, "Great Injustice," 156, 158. Megan J. McClintock argues that in their application of the federal pension law of 1862, the Bureau of Pensions superseded state marriage laws by accepting common-law or informal marriage regardless of state statutes. The pension bureau ratified marriages that lacked legal documentation through cohabitation and reputation. The 1882 Pension Act, however, enshrined deference to state statues in adjudicating what conditions determined a legal marriage. "The Impact of the Civil War on Nineteenth-Century Marriages," in *Union Soldiers and the Northern Home Front: Wartime Experiences, Postwar Adjustments*, ed. Paul A. Cimbala and Randall M. Miller (New York: Fordham University Press, 2002), 95–416, esp. 399–400, 411–16.

89. C. W. Spiker to Miss [Emmeline Boley], June 11, 1863, Uncatalogued Miscellaneous Collection, Smithsonian, Archives of American Art.

90. G. E. Hollis to Miss O. A. [Olivia], February 21, 1864, Joseph Espey Papers, UNC.

91. James Reed to Son, May 11, 1834, William Carson Papers, SHSM. "With Sorrow we have to in form you that you brother Calven departed this life after the ilnes of 2 nites and 1 day with a inflamation in the head. . . . all has went on smoothley with us sence you left with the exception of the los of calven so calven is nomore."

92. William Cates to Mother and Brother and Sister, December 19, 1857, H. N. Epps Family Letters, SHSM.

93. Drury Walden [and Stephen Walden who writes the second half of the letter], undated, [but written in the months following the death of his grandchild on July 27, 1833] Roberts Family Papers, LC.

94. M. C. Washburn to Mother, March 20, 1859, Downing-Whinrey, SHSM.

95. J. W. Barksdale and America Barksdale to Cousin, May 14, 1850, Woods-Holman, SHSM.

96. Richard A. Meckel, *Save the Babies: American Public Health Reform and the Prevention of Infant Mortality, 1850–1929* (Baltimore: Johns Hopkins University Press, 1990), 1. Counting deaths only before the age of one, this statistic is staggering.

NOTES TO PAGES 218–221   327

97. Meckel, *Save the Babies*, 1. The dates were July 1, 1987 to June 30, 1988.

98. Mary Cruse to brother and Sister, March 20, 1854, CivWar, MOHS. All the quotations that follow have been transcribed from the same letter into standard English. "I wold have wrten sooner but I have nt ben abel," Mary explained. "O how can I write this morning my hand trembels as I hode this pen my eyse ar dim with terse and my hearte is all moste broken."

99. "O to thinke of this grny it has broken my pease fore ever Caresley had we reach the shorse of this contry than sicknes cieseth holte of my pare children."

100. "O Saly Ann hade my pere children of sickende and died athome I wold tride to of give them up and had them lade at Shanon with oure mother and cisters whare I cold of wente ande nelte over thare litel gaves ande shed tearse fore then."

101. "I can not give them up O my deare children how well I love ed them I broght them here to dye." "This word has know chanse fore me now I have now desir to live my life is onely amysery to me." "You wist to know whare the litel ones wre bered Omy heart wil brake."

102. "Thare namse are swete to me I can note stope with caling them over to yu my dare litel Elisabeth ande jamse and litle rache amda awl lade sufering ate thesame time we did note now wtch wol dye firste."

103. "O Saly an Shed one tere fore me on Monday morning about ten O clck my liteel jamse dirde O then I thought of yu and amanda uncle pap and the gave yearde [grave yard] whare he had to be lade O ithughte I clode note laye him thar alone with strangers in a few ours my deare rache was taken with him O that swete tunge chide how wel i loved her tay ware both layde in thare lit el blak velvet cuverede coffins."

104. "my dere lissa . . . othis affectnet childe how she sufferd with hr thought and joys she was my good childe thate same nighte she dide I nev er can get over the dath of this childe. this desese cesed holte of my deare baby ande tore it from my armes on the blufs of the rive er owas note this harde."

105. "tha are bred ete a cuntry grave yare thare is no curch in that cuntry I never wll close my eyese in pec un tle thay are borne backe ande layde in Shanon Curch yearde." Mary Cruse to Brother and Sister, March 20, 1854, CivWar, MOHS. I think the move she lamented was from Shannon County, Missouri to Weston, Platte County, Missouri.

106. Alonzo died on June 21 and Alle (Mary Alice) on July 11, 1861. US, Find A Grave Index, 1600s to Current.

107. Susan to Wallace Jones, June 10, [1864], Susan Alice Jones Collection, HEH.

108. Susan to Wallace Jones, June 5, [1864], Susan Alice Jones Collection, HEH. She believed her husband's presence would be an antidote to her sorrow. The rose on a broken stem was a symbol of death for nineteenth-century Americans. See Kenneth L. Ames, "Ideologies in Stone: Meanings in Victorian Gravestones," *Journal of Popular Culture* 14 (Spring 1981): 641–56, esp. 648.

109. See 1850 US Federal Census under Susan A. Jones. For population in 1860 see Frazier E. Wilson, *History of Darke Co., Ohio, from Its Earliest Settlement to the Present Time*, vol. 1 (Milford, OH: Hobart Pub. Co., 1914), 586.

110. Ellen [Merrrill] to Mother [Lois R. Davis], January 3, 1858, LWRD, Duke.

328   NOTES TO PAGES 221–223

111. S. J. Kleinberg examines working-class attitudes in Pittsburgh using late nineteenth-century newspapers in "Death and the Working Class," *Journal of Popular Culture* 11 (Summer 1977): 193–209, esp. 198–99.

112. John to Mariah Cotton, August 11, 1862, in *Yours Till Death: The Civil War Letters of John W. Cotton,* ed. Lucille Griffith (University: University of Alabama Press, 1951), 13.

113. John to Mariah Cotton, April 16, 1863, in Griffith, *Yours Till Death,* 61–62; see n. 96.

114. John to Mariah Cotton, April 16, 1863, in Griffith, *Yours Till Death,* 62.

115. Jonathan to Mary Labrant, November 27, 1863, Labrant, HEH. Illinois was home. They later moved to Kansas.

116. Diana Walsh Pasulka, "A Communion of Little Saints: Nineteenth-Century American Child Hagiographies," *Journal of Feminist Studies in Religion* 23 (Fall 2007): 51–67; Jessica F. Roberts, "'The Little Coffin': Anthologies, Conventions and Dead Children," in *Representations of Death in Nineteenth-Century US Writing and Culture,* ed. Lucy Frank (Abingdon: Ashgate, 2007), 141–54; Jalland, *Death in the Victorian Family,* 119–42.

117. Harriet Buck to Eliphalet and Eliza Shattuck, April 1, 1866, Shattuck, MHS.

118. Ambrose Garriot to Brother and Sister, October 5, 1862, Garriott, SHSM.

119. David Vincent, in his survey of 104 British autobiographies, never mentions heaven. He emphasizes the interaction of poverty and debt in his autobiographers' responses to death. See David Vincent, "Love and Death and the Nineteenth-Century Working Class," *Social History* 5 (May 1980): 223–47, esp. 242–45.

120. Unidentifiable correspondent to Caroline Lipscomb, December 18, 1861, Lipscomb, UNC.

121. J. C. Owens to parents, April 26, 1863, Confederate, UNC.

122. Isaac and Sydney Osmond to William and Ann Osmond and family, February 2, 1863, Osmond, MHS.

123. Schantz claims this was true for all Americans (*Awaiting the Heavenly Country,* 61–62).

124. John Shumway to Louisa Shumway, January 1, 1865, Shumway, MHS.

125. John Shumway to Louisa Shumway, January 10, 1865, Shumway, MHS. In this letter, he extolled heaven as a place where he and Louisa would be together for eternity.

126. James Masey to Wife, April 24, 1857, in *The Mind of the Negro: As Reflected in Letters during the Crisis, 1800–1860,* ed. Carter G. Woodson (Washington, DC: Association For the Study of Negro Life and History, 1926; reprint, New York: Dover, 2013), 573–74.

127. A family memory document indicated that the men drew black marbles from a bowl, but I could find no independent verification of this story. As far as we know, they were chosen at random. See Asa Valentine Ladd, Public Member Photos & Scanned Documents Asa Ladd Notes, # 1 Location: Family Tree Maker Records Dean 1944, posted February 14. 2010, Ancestry.com. The US National Cemetery Interment Control Forms, 1928–1962, indicated that Ladd was in Burbidge's regiment at the time of his death. See James E. McGhee, *Guide to Missouri Confederate Units, 1861–1865* (Fayetteville: University of Arkansas Press, 2008), 65, 69, 146–47. He started out in Preston's Battalion Company A. See US Civil War Soldiers, 1861–1865.

NOTES TO PAGES 223-226   329

128. Asa V. Ladd to Wife and Children, October 29, 1864, TP, Asa V. Ladd Papers, SHSM. The punctuation has likely been added at a later date. Family memory documents claim that Amy, Ladd's wife, never received his letter because she had already relocated to Arkansas.

129. Louisa Downing to Louisa Ward, April 12, 1872, Downing-Whinrey, SHSM.

130. Joseph Downing to Mother, January 27, 1871, Downing-Whinrey, SHSM.

131. The centrality of "the promise of family recongregation in heaven" as a spur to conversion in southern revival sermons is discussed in Stephanie McCurry, *Masters of Small Worlds: Yeoman Households, Gender Relations, & Political Culture in the Antebellum South Carolina Low Country* (New York: Oxford University Press, 1995), 174-75.

132. J. M. and A. Pearson to Andrew and Elizabeth Reeves, June 3, 1888, Reeves, UNC.

133. C. Dicken to Mrs. Faney Catenhead, July 23, 1863, in Cadenhead, "Some Confederate Letters," 567-68. He was in Company H, Thirty-Fourth Alabama Infantry Regiment.

134. James T. Moore to Mrs. Cadenhead, July 23, 1863, in Cadenhead, "Some Confederate Letters," 567-68.

135. Christopher Grasso, *Skepticism and American Faith: From the Revolution to the Civil War* (Oxford: Oxford University Press, 2018), 362-63; David W. Rolfs, "'No Nearer Heaven Now but Rather Farther Off': The Religious Compromises and Conflicts of Northern Soldiers," in *The View from the Ground: Experiences of Civil War Soldiers*, ed. Aaron Sheehan-Dean (Lexington: University Press of Kentucky, 2006), 139-40.

136. William J. Gilmore, *Reading Becomes a Necessity of Life: Material and Cultural Life in Rural New England, 1780-1835* (Knoxville: University of Tennessee Press, 1989), 62; Laderman, *The Sacred Remains*, 54-59; Grasso, *Skepticism and American Faith*, 498.

137. Timothy L. Smith, *Revivalism and Social Reform: American Protestantism on the Eve of the Civil War* (New York: Abingdon Press, 1957), 88-89. 91-93. See Kathryn Teresa Long, *The Revival of 1857-58: Interpreting an American Religious Awakening* (New York: Oxford University Press, 1998), 23-25, for an evaluation of Smith's scholarship. Long provides a basic summary of "disparate expressions of evangelicalism" in the first half of the nineteenth century, which she suggests were divided along class lines. Working-class Americans would have participated in the "populist" or "antiformalist" religious tradition most often expressed by Baptists and Methodists. She warns that such categorization should not be treated too inflexibly (6-7); Jama Lazerow, *Religion and the Working Class in Antebellum America* (Washington, DC: Smithsonian Institution Press, 1995), argues for the influence of Protestant religion in antebellum labor protest and reform movements; Steven Woodworth, *While God Is Marching On: The Religious World of Civil War Soldiers* (Lawrence: University Press of Kansas, 2001), emphasizes the similarity of Protestant revivals that swept through both the Union and Confederate armies during the war (246).

138. Thomas Gaither to Molley, [February 1863], Gaither, UNC.

139. Lizzie Fentriss to Sister, August 15, 1865, Bond and Fentriss Family Papers, UNC.

140. Elisabeth Cates to Mother, Brothers and Sisters, "18504," H. N. Epps Family Letters, SHSM.

141. Tillman Valentine to Elizabeth Valentine, April 24, 1864, in Jonathan W. White, Katie Fisher and Elizabeth Wall, eds., "The Civil War Letters of Tillman Valentine,

330   NOTES TO PAGES 226–229

Third US Colored Troops," *Pennsylvania Magazine of History and Biography* 139 (April 2015): 183–86. "[L]et every tear be drye" is a line from the last stanza of a 125-year-old (at the time of Tillman's letters) hymn by Isaac Watts that began "Come ye that love the Lord." It was sung by both Methodists and Baptists in nineteenth-century America. See, for example, *The Baptist Hymn and Tune Book Being "The Plymouth Collection . . ."* (New York: Sheldon, Blakeman & Co., 1858), 199; *Hymns For The Use Of The Methodist Episcopal Church*, rev. ed. (New York; Carlton & Lanahan, 1869), 535.

142. Elizabeth Michaels to John Cope [Jr.], April 9, 1865, John Cope Papers, LC.

143. Isham Upchurch to Winston and Matthew, February 26, 1865, Upchurch, Duke.

144. Isham Upchurch to Brother [his brother-in-law John Beavers], June 1, 1863, Upchurch, Duke. My italics.

145. Ted Ownby, "Patriarchy in the World Where There Is No Parting? Power Relations in the Confederate Heaven," in *Southern Families at War: Loyalty and Conflict in the Civil War South*, ed. Catherine Clinton (New York: Oxford University Press, 2000), 229–44. Romantic was how Ownby characterized the belief in an afterlife of love. He contrasted the romantics with those he called the stoics who closed their letters with "yours until death." He thought this closing reflected the writer's belief that all human connections would end at death. Working-class evidence contradicts this conclusion. The article is insightful but does not separate working- and middle-class perspectives.

146. Lewis Saum found two examples of children singing in the afterlife, as imagined by their mothers. See Saum, "Death in the Popular Mind," pp. 494–95. Also see George L Berry to Sister, March 2, 1862, for an image of children as angels singing in heaven. Civil War Letters Collection, ADL.

147. For a contrasting version of heaven in the English middle-class that combines both family domesticity and godly worship, see Jalland, *Death in the Victorian Family*, p. 283.

148. Karen V. Hansen, *A Very Social Time: Crafting Community in Antebellum New England* (Berkeley: University of California Press, 1994), 151–52.

149. Olive Brown to Abrina Bennett, November 14, 1840, in Dublin, *Farm to Factory*, 68.

150. Jesse McElroy to Sister, April 20, 1867, Bonds Conway Papers, South Caroliniana Library, Digital Collections, http://digital.tcl.sc.edu/cdm/search/collection/bonds.

151. George Beavers to Brother [Isham Upchurch], January 19, 1862, Upchurch, Duke.

152. James Sydney Beavers (1834–1862), U.S. Find A Grave Index, 1600s-Current, Ancestry https://www.findagrave.com/memorial/38958320/james-sidney-beavers?

153. Elias T. Jefferson to Highly Esteemed Ladies [Sara and Lucy Chase], September 11, 1867, Am. Antiquarian Society online. This wish to meet in heaven was repeated by several of the Chase sisters' students. Ted Ownby found that enslaved people were missing from Confederate visions of heaven ("Patriarchy," 237–38).

154. Martha Burgess [and Mary Easterwood] to sister, October 8, 1865, Lipscomb, UNC.

155. Mary to Leonard Caplinger, June 15, 1863, Caplinger, HEH.

156. Sarah Hayter and Elizabeth Coleman to C. J. Hayter, October 9, 1844, in Saum, "Death in the Popular Mind," 493.

NOTES TO PAGES 229–230   331

157. Harriet Buck to Eliza Shattuck, July 26, 1857, Shattuck, MHS.

158. Amy L. Galusha to Brother [Aaron L. Galusha], April 3, 1849, LMGL.

159. Ann Russell Estabrooks to Sister [Ann Osmond], May 29, 1873, Osmond, MHS.

160. J. M. & A. Pearson to Andrew and Elizabeth Reeves, June 3, 1888, Reeves, UNC, is another clear expression of this common belief in an idyllic afterlife.

161. Augustin Echabe and Saioa Perez, "Life-after-Death Beliefs and Self Motivations," *Journal of Social Psychology* 157 (May 2016): 236–46. This is a contemporary study of the relationship among thoughts of death, self-uncertainty, need for control, and life-after-death beliefs.

162. For a richly suggestive modern study on death and self-esteem in the technical jargon of psychology, see Brandon J. Schmeichel et al., "Terror Management Theory and Self-Esteem Revisited: The Roles of Implicit and Explicit Self-Esteem in Mortality Salience Effects," *Journal of Personality and Social Psychology* 96 (May 2009): 1077–87.

163. John Burgess Gaither to Sister Mollie, March 20, 1864, Gaither, UNC.

164. Charles Watson to John Watson, June 14, 1863, Watson, MHS.

165. Of course, not every working-class American believed in an afterlife. See Reuben Lanphear to Eliza Shattuck, January 17, 1864, Shattuck, MHS. "Now my poore boys are gone I have not been up to my place this winter," Reuben lamented the loss of two sons. "I Can not bear to go thare and se whare them poore boys have worked oh my dear Children how can I give them up," he moaned despairingly, "and never se them again." He took no comfort in a heavenly reunion.

166. Phillip Shaw Paludan, "Religion and the American Civil War," in *Religion and the American Civil War*, ed. Randall M. Miller, Harry S. Stout, and Charles Reagan Wilson (New York: Oxford University Press, 1998), 30–31; also Gilmore, *Reading Becomes a Necessity*, 295, 300. After a detailed study of private libraries in parts of rural New England between 1780 and 1830, Gilmore found that families characterized by poverty and a "hardscrabble" existence usually possessed two to four books, one of which was always the Bible and another was likely a hymnal or psalm book. "Hardscrabble families," he noted, "chiefly read works that stressed permanence and eternity." Obviously print culture expanded dramatically in the subsequent decades, but the intertwined themes of permanence and eternity remained paramount in working-class culture.

167. See Colleen McDannell and Bernhard Lang, *Heaven: A History* (New Haven: Yale University Press, 1988), 228–29, 257–75. Schantz in *Awaiting the Heavenly Country* identifies three elements that most antebellum Americans emphasized in their conceptions of heaven. I found that only two were working-class images. The first, beauty and glory, was rarely mentioned in letters. The second, materiality, was a dominant aspect of heaven's appeal to working-class Americans, not just in the reconstitution of the corporeal body but also in the reestablishment of a geographical habitat; the third, which he describes as "loved ones would clasp hands again" was crucial to the working-class belief in an afterlife (39–40).

168. Ann Douglas, "Heaven Our Home: Consolation Literature in the Northern United States, 1830–1880," in *Death in America*, ed. David E. Stannard (Philadelphia: University of Pennsylvania Press, 1975), 55.

332 NOTES TO PAGES 231–235

169. For the middle-class perspective, see McDannell and Lang, *Heaven*, pp. 274–75.

170. For the middle-class view of domesticity in the afterlife, see Douglas, "Heaven Our Home," p. 65.

171. See Faust, "Civil War Soldier," pp. 16–29, for examples of middle-class condolence letters that were self-consciously constructed to affirm the good death of a soldier.

Epilogue

1. Isaiah Francis Wilson to Esther Hawkes, September 15, 1863, Esther Hawks, LC.

2. Wilson identifies his birthplace as "Brantford, C W." He may have been born in Brantford or chose it as the nearest identifiable town to his actual home. Brantford, according to local history, was "secured from the Six Nations Indians, for 5 shillings and was named in 1827." Local white historians identified the first settler as a person of mixed European and First Nation heritage (their term was "half breed,") who built a log cabin in 1805. See Robert Clark et al., *A Glimpse of the Past: A Centennial History of Brantford and Brant County* (Brantford: Brant History Society, 1964), 14, 16. For a popular overview, see "Rivers of Canada—Grand River—Canadian Geographic Education," http://www.cangeoeducation.ca/resources/rivers_of_can ada/grand_river/default.asp. For a brief overview of one Six Nations land dispute, see Graham Darling, "Land Claims and the Six Nations in Caledonia Ontario," Centre for Constitutional Studies, June 18, 2013, University of Alberta, www.constitutional studies.ca/2013/06/land-claims-and-the-six-nations-in-caledonia-ontario/.

3. US Colored Troops, Military Service Record, 1863–1865.

4. 1851 Census of Canada East, Canada West, New Brunswick, and Nova Scotia. The Six Nations of Grand River reserve is the largest by population and next largest by size in Canada.

5. There is a dizzying array of Isaiah Wilsons, and sorting them out proved daunting. Two Black Isaiah Wilsons were born in the United States around the same time as Esther's correspondent, one in Maryland and another in Virginia. Note that the Maryland Wilson fought in another regiment during the Civil War and the Virginia Wilson was five feet, nine inches, and enlisted as a Union navy sailor. See US, African American Civil War Sailor Index, 1861–1865.

6. William B. Hart, "Black 'Go-Betweens' and the Mutability of 'Race,' Status, and Identity on New York's Pre-revolutionary Frontier," in *Contact Points: American Frontiers from the Mohawk Valley to the Mississippi, 1750–1830*, ed. Andrew R. L. Cayton and Fredrika J. Teute (Chapel Hill: University of North Carolina Press, 1998), 96–113; Tiya Miles examines the complex issues of slavery, including kinship, lineage, and marriage, within the Cherokee nation in *Ties That Bind: The Story of an Afro-Cherokee Family in Slavery and Freedom*, 2nd ed. (Oakland: University of California Press, 2015).

7. Isaiah F. Wilson, Civil War Soldiers Records and Profiles; see also Luis F. Emilio, *History of the Fifty-Fourth Regiment of Massachusetts Volunteer Infantry, 1863–1865* (Boston: Boston Book Company, 1894), 368.

NOTES TO PAGES 235-237   333

8. William Cheek and Aimee Lee Cheek, *John Mercer Langston and the Fight for Black Freedom, 1829-1865* (Urbana: University of Illinois Press, 1996).

9. Oberlin Heritage Center blog, September 24, 2014, http://www.oberlinheritagecen ter.org /blog/tag/54th-massachusetts/.

10. Gerald Schwartz, ed., *A Woman Doctor's Civil War: Esther Hill Hawks' Diary* (Columbia: University of South Carolina Press, 1984), 37. Her first soldier-students were members of the First South Carolina Volunteers.

11. Schwartz, *Woman Doctor's Civil War*, 37, 47-54.

12. See http://54th-mass.org/about/roster/. Wilson was not wounded in battle, at least as indicated by his military record. Furthermore, there is no indication on the muster rolls that he was ever sick enough to be hospitalized after the Fort Wagner assault. See US Colored Troops, Military Service Records, 1863-1865.

13. US Colored Troops, Military Service Records, 1863-1865, Muster roll, July to October, 1863, notation in remarks.

14. "Mohawk," *Canadian Encyclopedia* online.

15. Robert Smalls, American Freedmen's Inquiry Commission Interviews, 1863, in *Slave Testimony: Two Centuries of Letters, Speeches, Interviews, and Autobiographies*, ed. John W. Blassingame (Baton Rouge: Louisiana State University 1977), 373-75. Smalls testified that he was a "rigger and Stevedore and not a regular pilot for Charleston harbor," which makes his feat even more remarkable. He explained that "[a] colored man was not allowed to be a pilot," adding, "although I know the waters very thoroughly." While he has been described as a wheelman, his testimony reveals that he had little experience handling a boat until he took over the helm of the *Plantar*.

16. Smalls's exploits have inspired a range of works, from children's books to several novels. One of the first historical monographs was Okon Edet Uya, *From Slavery to Political Service: Robert Smalls, 1839-1915* (New York: Oxford University Press, 1971). Another was Edward Miller Jr.'s, *Gullah Statesman: Robert Smalls from Slavery to Congress, 1839-1915* (Columbia: University of South Carolina Press, 2008).

17. Isaiah Francis Wilson to Esther Hawkes, September 15, 1863, Esther Hawks, LC.

18. Phillip H. Round discusses this Dakota convention in "Indigenous Epistolarity in the Nineteenth Century," in *The Edinburgh Companion to Nineteenth-Century American Letters and Letter-Writing*, ed. Celeste-Marie Bernier, Judie Newman, and Matthew Pethers (Edinburgh: Edinburgh University Press, 2016), 196-207, esp. 201-2. This is one of the most original and important essays in the volume.

19. Round, "Indigenous Epistolarity," 197-98. "In the voluminous archives of the Office of Indian Affairs," Rounds reports, "all regions and tribes are represented by letters." He observes that this Native American correspondence was often signed with name glyphs, for example a Plains pony, which "affirm personal and communal identities quite apart from those recognized by the colonial power structure."

20. Esther and Isaiah were in the same city a few months after the Civil War ended. In July 1865 he was hospitalized for smallpox in Charleston, South Carolina. She was in Charleston that month as well, but probably never knew he was close by. Her attention was oriented toward the freedmen's schools. Her diary mentions a hospital visit only once in July and that was in Summerville, a place that is now a suburb of

334 NOTES TO PAGES 237–238

Charleston. It is unlikely they ever reconnected. See July 24, [1865] entry in Schwartz, *Woman Doctor's Civil War*, 167. Wilson survived and was discharged in October.

21. Library and Archives of Canada, "Census of Canada, 1881" under Origins, www.bac-lac.gc.ca/eng/census/1881/Pages/about-census.aspx#tab3.

22. One Isaiah F. Wilson was born in Canada and was living in 1880 with the Sault Sainte Marie tribe of Chippewa Indians in Michigan. See 1880 US Federal Census. This Wilson looked like a promising, if not precise, match until I grasped that the Chippewa were traditional enemies of the Mohawks. Moreover, this Wilson's parents were both born in Ireland. I located the correct Wilson in the 1881 Canadian census.

23. Isaiah F. Wilson, US, National Homes for Disabled Volunteer Soldiers, 1866–1938. His height in the soldier's home ledger varied by one and a half inches from his military records, but I did not take this to be a significant difference.

24. For a general overview, see Suzanne Julin, "National Home for Disabled Volunteer Soldiers: Assessment of Significance and National Historic Landmark Recommendations," National Park Service History, http://npshistory.com/publications/nhl/special-studies/national-home-disabled-vol-soldiers.pdf. The Hampton branch was not that popular with Black veterans. For a more concise summary, see National Park Service, "History of the National Home for Disabled Volunteer Soldiers," http://www.nps.gov/articles/history-of-disabled-volunteer-soldiers.htm.

25. He is listed in the 1900 US census as Franzes I. Wilson, a transposition of his first and middle names. (This could have been an effort to distinguish himself from other Isaiah Wilsons.) Franzes I. was fifty-eight, living in New Jersey, and married to a woman named Lizzie. These personal characteristics matched the Hampton register. In addition, Franzes I. was identified as an Indian, meaning tribes that descended from Indigenous people in North America, which makes the connection with our letter writer even stronger.

Two anomalies complicate the 1900 US census profile. Wilson's birthplace is described as "East Indies" with a mother born in the "Indies." The East Indies, known as Indonesia today, is a group of islands in the Indian and Pacific Oceans between Asia and Australia. The Indies is referred to as the Caribbean today. It seems at best improbable that a North American Indian, as he is classified in this census, was born in Indonesia to a Caribbean mother and an English father. Perhaps the census enumerator was unclear about what he heard, and quickly translated the information into place-names he could comprehend. The obvious contradiction between Wilson's Indigenous identity and birthplace may have stemmed from this type of miscommunication. Alternatively, he misled another bureaucrat. I believe the census taker was confused. Wilson had no reason to invent an "East Indies" birthplace. He did not officially claim to be born in Michigan until the 1905 New Jersey census. See Franzes I. Wilson, New Jersey, US State Census, 1905.

26. See Mayo Clinic, "Chronic Kidney Disease," https://www.mayoclinic.org/diseases-conditions/chronic-kidney-disease/symptoms-causes/syc-20354521. For an early twentieth-century discussion see J. Rose Bradford, "Nephritis," in *A System of Medicine by Many Writers*, ed. Sir Clifford Allbut and Humphrey Davy Rolleston, 2nd ed., vol. 4 (London: Macmillan, 1908), 585–632.

27. She was twenty-nine years younger than her husband. See Lizzie Wilson, 1900 US Federal Census; Franzes I. Wilson, 1900 US Federal Census; and New Jersey, US State Census, 1905; also Isaiah F. Wilson, US National Homes for Disabled Volunteer Soldiers, 1866–1938.

28. Felicia Luz Carr, "All for Love: Gender, Class, and the Woman's Dime Novel in Nineteenth-Century America" (PhD diss., George Mason University, 2003); Nan Enstad, *Ladies of Labor, Girls of Adventure: Working Women, Popular Culture, and Labor Politics at the Turn of the Twentieth Century* (New York: Columbia University Press, 1999).

Appendix A

1. "The Fear Behind the Failure," *Los Angeles Times*, April 30, 2000, B6; Leo Soltow and Edward Stevens, *The Rise of Literacy and the Common School in the U.S.: A Socioeconomic Analysis to 1870* (Chicago: University of Chicago Press, 1981), 3–4. Their work is an indispensable resource for the study of literacy and education before 1870 in America. The statistical data they provide informs and supports my consideration of working-class literacy.

2. Carl F. Kaestle, "Studying the History of Literacy," in *Literacy in the United States: Readers and Reading since 1880*, ed. Kaestle et al. (New Haven: Yale University Press, 1991), 11–12. The conundrum is that those who made their mark might be able to read proficiently and those who signed their name might not be able to do much else. Nonetheless, the signature as a valid indication of reading ability has been widely defended by historians of literacy. Therefore, it would be foolish to reject this methodology out of hand. See also David A. Gerber, *Authors of Their Lives: The Personal Correspondence of British Immigrants to North America in the Nineteenth Century* (New York: New York University Press, 2006), 80–81.

3. For signature counts on wills and military records, see Kaestle, "Studying the History of Literacy," 11–12. A sensible review of the literature on pre-nineteenth-century female literacy is also found in Kaestle, 20–23. Even in 1860, northern white women had a slightly higher illiteracy rate (2 percent) than men, while in the South the sex differential was 4 percent. The gender gap did not close completely for native-born white women until the late nineteenth century.

4. There is no consensus on what might be a reasonable measure of the ability to write in a large sample. Moreover, the use of signature counts has tended to polarize the categories of literacy and illiteracy, assigning people to one camp or the other on the basis of a measure that is widely believed to indicate reading skills.

5. Steven Rowe, "Writing Modern Selves: Literacy and the French Working Class in the Early Nineteenth Century," *Journal of Social History* 40 (Fall 2006): 55–83. This article is a model of the practice-based study of writing literacy. I learned the term from Rowe. In this approach, written texts are considered not only for their content or for what they demonstrate about a static skill set, but as individual experiences that aggregate over time to create common cultural patterns.

336 NOTES TO PAGES 247–249

6. In the 1840 census, only heads of nonslave families were questioned. In 1850 and 1860 all free individuals over twenty were supposed to be polled. In the 1870 census, individuals ages ten to nineteen were also theoretically included.

7. As quoted in the ninth census, 1870, in Soltow and Stevens, *Rise of Literacy*, 5.

8. Census data have given historians an important tool to broaden the evidence of writing literary. But even with more sophisticated census evidence, demographers have limited access to the attitudes and feelings toward reading and writing of their nineteenth-century subjects. Demography also cannot deal with subtleties in the processes of learning, various stages of writing proficiency, and the relationship between technical skill levels and consciousness.

9. See Soltow and Stevens, *Rise of Literacy*, 153, 50–54, 189–90. Before the 1840 census, other kinds of data must be used to establish literacy rates. Soltow and Stevens rely upon several sources, including the large collection (859 boxes) of US Army enlistment forms, which provide continuous data in a virtually unchanged format from 1799 to 1894. The army enlistee was required to sign a document that attested to his voluntary service and included age, personal characteristics such as height, color of hair and eyes, and occupation.

10. Soltow and Stevens, *Rise of Literacy*, 166–76, 22–24, 159–62.

11. These conclusions are based on data gathered by the US Sanitary Commission between 1862 and 1864 and provided in Soltow and Stevens, *Rise of Literacy*, 116–17, and 52, Table 2.3.

12. Ronald J. Zboray and Mary Saracino Zboray, *Everyday Ideas: Socioliterary Experience among Antebellum New Englanders* (Knoxville: University of Tennessee Press, 2006), xx–xxii and 301 n. 17. They blur class distinctions and mix examples from all classes of New Englanders. It is possible that New England, with the highest literacy rates in the country, merits this treatment. My perspective is that sometimes crucial class distinctions in literary modes of production and reception may be obscured.

13. Soltow and Stevens, *Rise of Literacy*, 116–17.

14. See William J. Collins and Robert A. Margo, "Historical Perspectives on Racial Differences in Schooling in the United States," Working Paper 9770, National Bureau of Economic Research, June 2003, 8, 41, Table 4, computed from the Integrated Public Use Microdata Series IPUMS samples. http://piketty.pse.ens.fr/files/CollinsMargo2003.pdf.

15. Kaestle, "Studying the History of Literacy," 31.

16. Soltow and Stevens, *Rise of Literacy*, 128, 143, 159.

17. Based on 1860 and 1870 census data. See Soltow and Stevens, *Rise of Literacy*, 120, 159. Emphasis is mine.

18. Charles Henry Richardson to Sister [Eunice Stone], September 10, [1862], Richardson, Duke.

19. This conclusion is based on a sample of students from Rochester, New York. See Soltow and Stevens, *Rise of Literacy*, 112.

20. Soltow and Stevens, *Rise of Literacy*, 115–19, 128, 161, 189–91.

21. Soltow and Stevens, *Rise of Literacy*, 24–26, esp. 128–29 and 178, Table 5.11. Children ages eleven to fourteen attended school in slightly higher numbers in cities than in

NOTES TO PAGES 249–252   337

rural areas. This applied to all wealth categories. Rural students were more likely to attend school from ages fifteen to nineteen than their urban peers. Also see pp. 134–35, 144–45, 178–80.

22. Soltow and Stevens, *Rise of Literacy*, 4–5, 100–104, 112.

Appendix B

1. D. Brads to Barwick Roberts, August 10, 1852, Roberts Family Papers, LC. Mary, whom Brads refers to in a familiar way, was most likely his wife. Brads also mentions a woman named Marinda who could be Mary's sister. If so, they are likely the daughters of Stephen Roberts Sr. The recipient, Barwick Roberts, could be one of Mary and Marinda's brothers. See Roberts Family papers for letters and a family genealogy. Because D. Brads did not use his first name and his last is undoubtedly spelled differently in official records, he was hard to trace in census and other formal demographic records. A large segment of the Roberts clan settled in Indiana and Brads references Delphy (or Delphi), which is a town in Indiana. For a sensitive and probing understanding of African-American literacy, see Heather Andrea Williams, *Self-Taught: African American Education in Slavery and Freedom* (Chapel Hill: University of North Carolina Press, 2005).

2. For example, "De rough, rocky road what Moses done travel" was a line from a slave song. See Texas Narratives, Part 2, Prepared by the Federal Writers' Project of the Works Project Progress Administration for the State of Texas in *Slave Narratives: A Folk History of Slavery in the United States from Interviews with Former Slaves*, vol. 16 (Washington, DC: Library of Congress, 1941), 26, https://memory.loc.gov/mss/mesn/162/162.pdf. I first encountered the opening line of this song in Lawrence Levine, *Black Culture and Black Consciousness* (New York: Oxford University Press, 1977), 51.

3. A very popular minstrel song composed by Dan Emmett entitled "Jordan Is a Hard Road to Travel" was performed the year after Brads penned his last line. One commentator, in a short essay, indicates that Emmett may have taken an existing song and substituted some of his own verses. Lyle Lofgren, "Remembering the Old Songs: Jordan is a Hard Road to Travel." https://www.lizlyle.lofgrens.org/RmOlSngs/RTOS-Jordan.html.

   See also Hans Nathan, *Dan Emmett and the Rise of Early Negro Minstrelsy* (Norman: University of Oklahoma Press, 1962), 237–38; Sandra Jean Graham, *Spirituals and the Birth of a Black Entertainment Industry* (Urbana: University of Illinois Press, 2018), chapters 1 and 5.

4. John Fuller to Miss Frances, April 19, 1864, SLFP, Duke.

Index

For the benefit of digital users, indexed terms that span two pages (e.g., 52–53) may, on occasion, appear on only one of those pages.

Figures are indicated by *f* following the page number

abortion, 130, 295nn.81–82
"Absence" (song), 185
adultery, 127–28, 177–78
African Americans
  courtship patterns, 4, 70, 71*f*, 108–10
  interracial marriage and, 103–10
  literacy increases among, 36, 248
  pension program, bias against Civil War
    soldiers in, 326n.87
  photographs of, 19*f*, 60*f*, 71*f*, 127*f*, 144*f*
  poetry and, 176–78, 187–88, 195, 309n.15,
    309nn.19–20, 309–10nn.21–22
  research on letters of, 299n.51
  sharing letters, 39
  slavery and, 4, 188, 236, 248
Ancestry.com, 15
Angelou, Maya, 103, 289n.81
anticipation
  of death, 8, 48, 207
  of marriage within geographical
    location, 53, 82–84
  of reunification in heaven, 227, 230
  of soldiers returning home to
    marry, 82–84
anxiety and fear
  about community ties, 142–43, 299n.50
  of being forgotten, 12–13, 46–48, 49,
    182–84, 186, 187, 198, 273n.154,
    312n.54
  belonging and, 7, 49
  of infidelity, 177–78
  of missing opportunity to marry, 74–76
  poetry to insulate against, 176, 178–
    79, 196
  premature proposals and fear of
    death, 96
  of public humiliation, 94–95

  of ridicule regarding sexual topics, 112–
    13, 116, 176, 290n.4
  writing skills and, 24, 44

Baddeley, Alan D., 308n.2
Barret-Ducrocq, Francoise, 281n.106
Barron, Hal, 274n.4
belonging
  fear of being forgotten and, 12–13, 49
  geographic place and, 6–7, 12–13, 15
  race and ethnicity, 6–7
  sexual humor and, 7
  stable attachments, longing for, 16
bigamy, 162–63
birth control, 129–30, 295nn.81–82
Blauvelt, Martha Tomhave, 280–81n.103
Blewett, Mary, 278n.55, 290n.2, 294n.56
Boag, Peter, 293n.43, 293nn.46–47
Brady, Mathew, 203*f*, 212*f*
breaking up
  during courtship, 66–67, 70–72
  divorce, 123–29, 305n.52, 305n.53
Brimmer, Brandi C., 326n.87
Buckingham, Willis, 319n.120

calendar dates on letters, 27–28,
    265nn.44–45, 266n.47
"Carry me Back to Ole Virginny"
    (Christy Minstrels), 6–7, 59,
    277nn.48–49
Cashin, Joan E., 265n.41
census information
  on literacy, 29–30, 247–48, 266–
    67nn.59–60, 336n.6, 336n.8
  tracing letter origins through, 8–9,
    15, 29–34, 267n.62, 267n.63,
    267–68nn.64–66

340   INDEX

Chasar, Mike, 319n.120
children
  deaths of, 217–22, 327n.108
  rhymes and games, 191, 315n.83,
    315–16nn.85–86
churches, 228. *See also* religion
Civil War
  communal love in letters anticipating
    returning home to marry, 82–84
  condolence letters for widows and
    family, 209–10, 216, 322n.46, 322n.47
  courtship patterns during, 51–53,
    68–69
  emphasis on death in letters, 156–57,
    177, 201–2, 304n.30
  good death and, 209–11, 322n.44,
    322n.46, 322n.47
  graves of unidentified soldiers, 211–
    12, 212*f*
  grief and, 211–13, 323n.57, 323–24n.66,
    324n.70
  homesickness during, 51, 138–39, 140–
    41, 187
  lack of eligible bachelors during, 75–
    76, 77–78
  literacy rates, increase in, 5–6, 28–29,
    34–37, 35*f*
  money sent home by soldiers as symbol
    of affection, 134–35, 138, 141, 171
  mortality rates, 201, 203
  as motivation to write letters, 5–6, 13–14
  number of letters written during, 5,
    260n.17
  pension programs following, 162–63,
    214, 215–16, 324–25nn.71–73,
    326nn.87–88
  photographs, 35*f*, 38*f*, 63*f*, 83*f*, 115*f*,
    136*f*, 144*f*, 174*f*, 203*f*, 212*f*, 234*f*
  Planter boat, surrender to Union
    soldiers, 235–36
  poetry to convey feelings of love, 173,
    177–78, 188–89, 195–96
  poverty of widows following, 214–16
  premature proposals and fear of
    death, 96
  prisoners of war, execution of, 8, 223,
    328n.127
  prostitution and, 296–97n.89

sharing letters as entertainment, 37–39,
  38*f*, 113–16, 271n.102, 291n.11, 292n.18
soldiers' wives, symbols of affection
  from, 133–34, 137, 140, 171
songs and ballads during, 184–87,
  313n.61, 313n.63
as source of income for soldiers, 154
Civil War Pension law (1890), 162–63,
  214, 324–25nn.71–73
class. *See also* middle class; working class
  courtship rituals and, 10–11, 72–73,
    280–81n.103, 281n.106, 281n.107
  death and, 13, 209–10, 222, 230–32
  education and, 43–44
  geographic place and, 50, 274n.7
  heaven and, 230–32, 331n.167
  literacy and, 10, 14, 33–34, 48–49, 269n.79
  military service and, 14
  motivations for letter-writing, 22–23
  pension program, bias against Civil War
    soldiers in, 215–16
  poetry and, 12–13
  privacy and, 12, 39–40, 48, 79, 125, 192,
    273nn.155–56
  prostitution and, 131, 296–97n.89
  romantic vs. nonromantic love and, 11,
    51, 81–82, 85–86, 97, 110, 126, 133,
    283–84n.2
  sex, perceptions of, 125–26, 131–32,
    297n.91
  sexual humor and, 117
closing letters
  nonromantic love and, 137–45, 146,
    298n.21
  with poems, 176
  women signaling interest through, 179
  with "yours until death," 137–38,
    199–202, 231–32, 298n.21, 320n.13,
    330n.145
cognitive processes, 40–43
commitment
  ritual acts of, 70–72, 280–81n.103,
    281n.106
  testing, 96, 97, 102–3, 151, 155–56,
    289n.76
communal attachment and ties
  as antidote to class shame, 48–49
  childrearing and, 154

INDEX 341

churches as gathering places, 228
courtship patterns and, 60–61, 239
death and, 205–6, 219–20, 231, 321n.32
fear of being forgotten, 12–13, 47–48, 49, 182–84, 186, 187, 198, 273n.154, 312n.54
fluid boundary between married couples and community, 146–47, 301n.79
homesickness, 12–13, 23, 51, 138–39, 140–41, 187
letters as proof of, 37, 44–47, 271n.128
marital conflicts and, 7–8, 148, 158–60, 170–71
motivations for letter-writing, 22–23
preserved through letter-writing, 49
support after loss of husbands in Civil War, 213
sustaining after marriage, 133, 142–47
community news, letter writing to share, 39–41, 113, 203, 204–6, 321n.32
courtship, 50–80
breaking up, 66–67, 70–72
choosing individuals, 70–78, 93–110, 239, 280–81n.103
Civil War and, 51–53
class differences in, 10–11, 72–73, 280–81n.103, 281nn.106–07
communal attachment and, 60–61, 239
following decision to marry, 72–73, 93
geographical and racial patterns of, 11, 50–53, 78, 82–84, 108–10, 239, 261n.42, 274n.7, 284n.3
geographic place and pool of eligible mates, 10–11, 53–59, 81–84
group activities and parties, 65–66
intermediaries communicating mutual interest, 10–11, 64–65, 66–70, 79, 86–87, 93, 98–99, 280n.93, 280n.101
narrowing pool of eligible mates, 60–70, 84–93
nonromantic love and, 10–11, 53–59, 72, 81–84, 239, 275n.20
poetry and, 178–81, 185–87, 195–97
ritual acts of commitment, 70–72, 280–81n.103, 281n.106, 281n.107
stages of, 51–52, 74–75, 78, 80

valentine lotteries and, 7, 195–96, 318nn.112–13
women and geographic place, 53–59, 57f, 74, 84

death, 198–232. *See also* heaven; widows and widowers
callousness resulting from Civil War exposure to, 210
of children, 217–22, 327n.108
communal attachment and ties, 205–6, 213, 219–20, 231, 321n.32
condolence letters for widows and family, 209–10, 216–17, 322nn.46–47
deferred funerals and, 221–22
emotional expression and, 231–32
fear of during Civil War, 156–57, 177, 201–2, 304n.30
good death, 13, 206–11, 322n.40, 322nn.46–47
grief and, 211–13, 323n.57, 323–24n.66, 324n.70
infant mortality rates, 218
lack of letters and assumption of, 2
letters preceding, 8, 48, 223
mortality rates, 201, 203
poetry on, 8, 177, 186–87, 198–99, 199f, 225–26, 319–20nn.2–4
premature marriage proposals and fear of, 96
presence in everyday life, 13, 202–4, 230
searching for meaning in, 208
desertion of spouse, 123–29, 293n.52, 294n.56
divorce, 123–29, 305nn.52–53
Dublin, Thomas, 276n.38, 277nn.40–42

education, 14, 34, 41–44, 192, 240, 248–49, 316–17nn.93–97, 336–37n.21. *See also* literacy
Eggleston, Edward, 309n.19
Elder, Angela Esco, 323–24n.66
Elson, Ruth, 273n.158
Emancipation Proclamation, 248
embroidery samplers, 198–99, 199f, 319–20nn.2–4
Emmett, Dan, 337n.3

342 INDEX

emotions. *See also* romantic love; *specific
    emotions*
  communication of, 41–42, 97–98
  courtship testing, 96, 97, 102–3, 289n.76
  death and expressions of, 231–32
  poetry to facilitate expression of, 12–13,
      173–77, 178, 179–80, 183, 196–97,
      310n.31
  reasoning for nonromantic
      engagements, 93–94
  symbols of affection, 133–42
epidemics, 204, 206
ethnicity. *See* race and ethnicity

Fahs, Alice, 307–8n.1
family and friends. *See also* communal
      attachment and ties
  approval of marriages, 60–61, 277n.51
  as intermediaries in courtship, 6–7,
      10–11, 64–65, 66–70, 79, 86–87, 93,
      98–99, 280n.93, 280n.101
  as intermediaries in marital conflicts,
      7–8, 158–60
  jokes about sex with, 116–17, 124–25
  poetry written to, 189–91
  rejection of interracial
      marriages, 103–10
  support for widows during Civil
      War, 214
  trust and shared intimacies between,
      124–25, 158–59
Faust, Drew, 321n.20, 322nn.44–45,
      323n.57, 323n.65
fear. *See* anxiety and fear
Finnegan, Ruth, 314–15n.79
First Eclectic Reader (McGuffey), 192,
      316–17nn.93–97
Fratto, Toni, 320n.4
Frost, Ginger S., 281n.106, 308n.8

"The Galley Slave" (song), 187
gender. *See also* women
  courtship patterns and, 53–59, 57f, 70–
      72, 73–74, 84, 89–91
  desertion and divorce, 163–64
  gender roles as source of conflict, 148–
      57, 152f, 153f, 170–71, 301nn.1–2
  homosexuality and gender
      presentations, 121–22

performance of gender roles as symbol
      of affection, 137–39, 140, 141, 171
  physical appearance and attraction, 59,
      61–62, 73–74, 77, 278n.55, 278n.58
geographic place
  belonging and, 6–7, 12–13, 15
  courtship patterns and, 11, 50–53, 78,
      82–84, 261n.42, 274n.5, 274n.7,
      276n.33, 284n.3
  gender and courtship patterns, 53–59,
      57f, 74, 84, 89–91
  homesickness, 12–13, 23, 51, 138–39,
      140–41, 187
  nonromantic love and choosing mate
      based on, 10–11, 53–59, 81–84
Gerber, David, 264n.25, 271n.128
Giesberg, Judith, 325–26n.83
Gilmore, William J., 264n.33, 331n.166
Gold Rush, 8, 52–53, 275n.20
gossip
  behavior regulation of, 102, 130–31,
      296n.88
  on marital conflicts, 148, 149–50, 157
  narrowing pool of eligible mates and, 61, 70
  privacy and reputations, 90, 95, 130–31,
      296n.88
grief, 211–13, 217–22, 323n.57, 323–
      24n.66, 324n.70, 327n.108
group activities and parties, 65–66

Hansen, Karen, 272n.140, 279n.77, 296n.86
Hayes, Melissa, 293n.40
heaven
  books on, 230, 331n.166
  class differences in conceptions of, 230–
      32, 331n.167
  good death and, 207–8, 322n.40
  personal agency in achievement of,
      224–25, 226–27, 329n.137
  race and ethnicity, 228–29, 330n.153
  reunification with loved ones in, 8, 13,
      199–200, 214, 220, 222–28, 229–30,
      231–32, 322n.44, 329n.131, 330n.145
Henkin, David, 270n.82, 273n.154
Hodes, Martha, 289n.83, 289n.86
Holmes, Amy E., 324–25n.72
home. *See also* geographic place
  hope of coming home after Civil
      War, 155

INDEX 343

money sent home by Civil War soldiers
  as symbol of affection, 134–35, 138,
  141, 171
  soldiers returning home to marry, 82–84
Homer, Winslow, 202*f*
homesickness, 12–13, 23, 51, 138–39,
  140–41, 187
homosexuality, 121–22
hope. *See also* heaven
  of coming home after Civil War, 155
  of finding family lost during Civil War, 211
  in poetry, 180, 311n.32
Howard, Vicki, 288n.62
hurt. *See* marital conflicts; rejection

illness, 204, 206
immigrant letters, 4, 258–59n.14
"The Indian's Entreaty" (song), 187–88,
  313–14n.67
infant mortality rates, 218
infidelity, 127–28, 177–78
interest
  intermediaries to establish, 10–11, 64,
    66, 70, 142
  narrowing pool of eligible mates, 60–
    70, 84–93
  poetry to communicate, 178
  women signaling, 84, 86–87, 179
intimate letters. *See* love letters

jealousy, 96, 97
Johnson, Russell, 326nn.85–88
jokes and humor
  about paternity, 122
  about private letters, 113–16
  about sex, 7, 12, 111, 112, 116–19, 122,
    124–25, 126, 131, 292n.28
  rejection, to aid in, 67–68
  on writing skills, 24–25
"Jordan Is a Hard Road to Travel"
  (Emmett), 337n.3

Kenzer, Robert 324n.71, 325n.77,
  325–26n.83
kindness, 134, 135–36, 170
kissing parties, 65–66

laughter, 25, 43–44, 48, 90, 112–13, 115–
  16. *See also* jokes and humor

The Letter for Home (Homer), 202*f*
letters, researching of
  African Americans, letters of, 299n.51
  archive locations for, 4–5, 14–15
  census information, tracing letter
    origins through, 8–9, 15, 29–34,
    267nn.62–63, 267–68nn.64–66
  collection bias favoring soldiers over
    wives, 213
  photographs, 31*f*, 107*f*, 152*f*, 153*f*, 169*f*
  working class, as source of information
    on, 3–5
letter writing. *See also* closing letters; love
    letters; poetry
  barriers to, 15
  calendar dates, use of, 27–28,
    265nn.44–45, 266n.47
  communal attachment and ties through,
    22–23, 37, 44–47, 49, 271n.128
  condolence letters for widows and
    family, 209–10, 216–17, 322nn.46–47
  death, lack of letters and
    assumption of, 2
  of immigrants, 4, 258–59n.14
  motivations for, 4–6, 13–14,
    22–23, 239
  paper and ink quality and availability,
    24, 36–37
  preceding death, 8, 48, 223
  reciprocity expectations, 44–47,
    271n.128, 272n.140
  rejection, lack of letters and, 46–
    47, 84–85
  to share community news, 39–41, 113,
    203, 204–6, 321n.32
literacy. *See also* spelling mistakes
  African Americans and, 36, 248
  census information on, 29–30, 247–48,
    266–67nn.59–60, 336n.6, 336n.8
  Civil War and increase in, 5–6, 28–29,
    34–37, 35*f*
  class and, 10, 14, 33–34, 48–49, 269n.79
  defined, 247, 335n.2
  education rates and, 249
  grammar and spelling, 9–10
  lack of, 2, 14, 15
  middle-class sense of superiority and, 2,
    14, 33–34, 192, 269n.79
  oral culture and, 251–52

344 INDEX

literacy (*cont.*)
 poetry to convey feelings of love, 173
 rates of, 247–48, 335n.4, 336n.9,
  336n.12
 reading skills and, 26, 28, 247–48,
  264n.33, 265n.41, 265n.43
 women and, 335n.3
 writing as one speaks, 9–10, 26–27, 41,
  264n.33, 265n.41, 265n.43, 266n.47
Long, Kathryn Teresa, 329n.137
longing
 homesickness, 12–13, 23, 51, 138–39,
  140–41, 187
 for stable attachments, 16, 184–
  85, 201–2
loss. *See also* death
 condolence letters for widows and
  family, 209–10, 216–17, 322n.46,
  322n.47
 grief and, 211–13, 323n.57, 323–24n.66,
  324n.70
 marital issues and, 170
love letters. *See also* poetry
 collective, tribal courtship and, 82–84
 poetry in, 78–79, 193, 194f, 308n.8
 sexual desire, expressions of, 12, 111–
  12, 125, 176
 sharing and privacy, 12, 48, 111–16,
  125, 146–47
 from widow to younger man, 29–34,
  31f, 176–77, 215, 267–68nn.62–66,
  309n.14
Lover, Samuel, 180
loyalty
 to community and geographic place, 7,
  11, 44, 53–54, 58–59, 82–84, 120
 sharing letters and, 39
 to spouse vs. community, 142–43, 239
 working-class values and, 140–41, 170

marital conflicts, 148–71
 adultery, 127–28, 177–78
 common arguments, 7–8
 communal ties and, 7–8, 148, 158–
  60, 170–71
 divorce, 123–29, 305nn.52–53
 family and friends as intermediaries in,
  7–8, 158–60

gender roles and, 148–57, 152f, 153f,
  170–71, 301nn.1–2
 gossip on, 148, 149–50, 157
 resolving, 157, 162
 romantic and nonromantic love,
  blending expectations of, 158–62
 scribes as intermediaries in, 167–70,
  307n.85
 testing commitments, 151, 155–56
marriage
 bigamy, 162–63
 birth control and family planning, 129–
  30, 295nn.81–82
 choosing a spouse, 60–64, 93
 Civil War and, 51–53
 common-law marriages and Civil War
  pensions, 326n.88
 communal ties, sustaining, 133, 142–47
 geographic place and courtship
  patterns, 50–53, 274n.5
 intermediaries communicating mutual
  interest in, 10–11, 64–65, 66–70, 79,
  86–87, 93, 98–99, 280n.93, 280n.101
 lack of eligible options for, 75–76
 qualities valued in, 170
 racial homogeneity and, 50, 103–10, 274n.6
 reasoning behind, 93–94
 romantic love and, 81
 stable attachments, longing for, 16
 symbols of affection in, 133–42
 withholding direct expression of love to
  spouse, 137–38, 298n.20
marriage proposals, 73–74, 96, 164, 176–78
Matt. Susan, 257–58n.13,
  261–62n.44, 275n.8
Mays, Ashley Michelle, 322n.47,
  323–24n.66
McClintock, Megan J., 324–25n.72
McGuffey *Reader*, 192, 316–17nn.93–97
middle class
 courtship and, 72–73, 79
 death and, 209–10, 222, 230–31
 education access and, 34, 43–44
 expressions of love, 2, 11
 geographic place and courtship
  patterns, 276n.33
 grief rituals of, 323n.57
 heaven and, 230–31, 331n.167

INDEX   345

literacy and sense of superiority, 2, 14, 33–34, 192, 269n.79
motivation for letter writing, 22
poetry and, 192
privacy and lack of sharing letters, 39–40, 48, 192
romantic love and, 81, 86, 110, 133
sexual experiences and desires expressed in letters, 12, 111–12, 125
valentine poems, 317n.99
migration patterns, 50, 274n.2, 274n.4, 274n.7
misunderstandings, 67–68, 91–93, 155
Myrtle, Frank, 311n.32

Newell, William, 191, 315–16n.86
nonromantic love
closing letters and, 137–45, 146, 298n.21
community support after loss of husbands in Civil War, 213
courtship and, 10–11, 53–59, 72, 81–84, 239, 275n.20
poetry to convey feelings of love, 173–77, 178, 179–80, 181–82, 183, 196–97, 308n.8, 310n.31
reasons for marriage, 93–94
romantic love vs., 11, 51, 81–82, 84–86, 97, 110, 126, 133, 283–84n.2
sharing letters and privacy, 12, 146–47
symbols of affection in, 133–40, 298n.20
violations and testing of courtship patterns, 95–97
widows and widowers, 98–99
Nugent, Christopher M. B., 308n.3

oral vs. written culture
literacy and, 251–52
poetry and, 12, 172, 191, 308nn.2–3, 314–15nn.79–80
remembrance, asking for, 47
writing as one speaks, 9–10, 26–27, 41, 264n.33, 265n.41, 265n.43, 266n.47
Osterud, Nancy Grey, 280–81n.103
Ownby, Ted, 330n.145, 330n.153

paper, quality and availability for letters, 24, 36–37
parents. *See* family and friends

parties, 65–66
paternity, jokes about, 122, 127–28
Peiss, Kathy, 274n.5, 297n.93
pens, 24
photographs
of African Americans, 19*f*, 60*f*, 71*f*, 127*f*, 144*f*
of Civil War soldiers, 35*f*, 63*f*, 83*f*, 115*f*, 136*f*, 144*f*, 174*f*, 203*f*, 212*f*, 234*f*
of working-class people, 21*f*–18*f*, 35*f*, 38*f*, 45*f*, 57*f*, 60*f*, 71*f*, 92*f*, 104*f*, 127*f*, 136*f*, 144*f*, 226*f*
physical attraction, 59, 61–62, 73–74, 77, 278n.55, 278n.58
poetry, 172–97
African Americans and, 176–78, 187–88, 195, 309n.15, 309nn.19–21
Children's rhymes and games, 191, 315n.83, 315–16nn.85–86
in Civil War letters, 173, 177–78, 188–89, 195–96
courtship and, 178–81, 185–87, 195–97
on death, 8, 177, 186–87, 198–99, 199*f*, 225–26, 319–20nn.2–4
to family and friends, 189–91
on fear of being forgotten, 49, 182–84, 186, 187, 312n.54
feelings expressed through, 12–13, 173–77, 178, 179–80, 183, 196–97, 310n.31
folk traditions and, 12, 173, 261n.43
in love letters, 78–79, 193, 194*f*, 308n.8
marriage proposals in, 176–78
middle class and, 192
oral vs. written culture and, 12, 172, 191, 308nn.2–3, 314–15nn.79–80
popularity of, 172–73, 307–8n.1
rejection or ridicule, as intermediary to avoid, 176, 178–79, 196
sexual desire, expressions of, 176
songs and ballads, 172, 184–88, 313n.63, 313–14n.67
valentine poems, 193–95, 194*f*, 310n.26, 317nn.99–100, 318nn.105–6
vernacular, 12–13, 173, 174–76, 179, 181, 182, 191
in working-class education, 192–93, 316–17nn.93–96, 317n.97

346 INDEX

post offices and postage, 35*f*, 36–37, 134–35, 150
poverty, 2–3, 13, 214–16, 255n.3
privacy. *See also* gossip
  engagements and courtships, 94–95
  intermediaries to communicate romantic love, 79
  love letters and, 12, 48, 111–16, 125, 146–47, 273n.157
  middle-class value of, 48, 79, 125
  sharing letters and, 25, 37–40, 38*f*, 48, 111–16, 125, 146–47, 158–59, 264n.32, 271n.102, 291n.11, 292n.18
  working-class marital intimacy and lack of, 146–47
proposals. *See* marriage proposals
prostitution, 55, 119–20, 131, 296–97nn.89–90

Quinn, Edythe Ann, 309n.16

race and ethnicity. *See also* African Americans
  afterlife conceptions and, 228–29, 330n.153
  belonging and, 6–7, 237
  communal love in letters, 82–84
  courtship patterns and, 11, 50–51, 59, 70, 239, 274n.6
  heaven and, 8
  lack of community support and, 29, 238–39
  marriage and racial homogeneity, 50, 103–10, 274n.6
  Mohawk, one of Iroquois six nations, 233–35, 237–38
  pension program, bias against Civil War soldiers in, 326n.87
  romantic love and racial divide, 103–10, 104*f*, 107*f*
  working class and racial prejudice, 105–8
"The Rebel Soldier" (song), 313n.61
rejection
  avoiding, 64, 70–72
  breaking up, 66–67, 70–72
  interracial marriage and, 103–10
  jokes and humor to deal with, 67–68

lack of letters and, 46–47, 84–85
missing opportunity to marry and fear of, 74–77
poetry as safe intermediary to avoid, 176, 178–79, 196
returning to local pool of eligible mates after, 85
religion, 68, 207, 224–25, 228, 298n.20. *See also* heaven
remembrance, asking for, 12–13, 22–23, 47–49, 63–64, 181–84, 187–88, 198–99, 201, 312n.54
reputations, 90, 130–31, 161, 165–66, 296n.88
research on letters. *See* letters, researching of
resignation, 207, 277n.51
romantic love. *See also* love letters
  courtship testing, 102–3, 289n.76
  middle-class emphasis on, 81, 86, 110, 133
  as necessity for marriage, 81
  nonromantic love vs., 11, 51, 81–82, 84–86, 97, 110, 126, 133, 283–84n.2
  racial divide and, 103–10, 104*f*, 107*f*
  sex and, 125
  working-class deviations from nonromantic mate selection, 99–101, 133, 158–59, 201, 239–40, 289n.70
Rothman, Joshua, 274n.6, 290n.95

Salisbury, Laura, 325n.73, 325n.76
samplers, 198–99, 199*f*, 319–20nn.2–4
Schantz, Mark, 321n.26, 322n.44, 331n.167
Schmidt, Leigh, 317n.99, 317n.102
Schwartzberg, Beverly, 255–56n.8, 281–82n.111, 305n.54
Second Eclectic Reader (McGuffey), 192, 316–17nn.95–97
security. *See also* belonging
  communal ties and, 48–49, 112
  group love and courtship, 88
  stable attachments, longing for, 16, 184–85, 201–2
self-awareness, 40–44
self-expression, 41–44
sex
  adultery, 127–28, 177–78

birth control and family planning, 128–30, 295nn.81–82

class differences in perception of, 125–26, 131–32, 297n.91

expressions of desire in letters, 12, 111–12, 125, 176

fear of ridicule regarding sexual topics, 112–13, 116, 176, 290n.4

female employment and sexual misconduct assumptions, 90

homosexuality, 121–22

jokes and humor about, 7, 12, 111, 112, 116–19, 122, 124–25, 126, 131, 292n.28

prostitution and, 55, 119–20, 131, 296–97nn.89–90

women sharing advice on, 111, 128–30, 290n.2, 295nn.81–82, 297n.93

sexual harassment and assault, 7, 122–24, 130

shame

fear of ridicule regarding sexual topics and private letters, 112–13, 116, 176, 290n.4

sexual assault and, 123–24

sexual humor and, 7, 12

women's age and eligibility for marriage, 75–76

writing and spelling skills, 14, 23–26, 44, 48–49, 264n.25

slavery, 4, 188, 236, 248

Smalls, Robert, 236, 333n.15

soldiers. See Civil War

Soltow, Leo, 248, 336n.9

songs and ballads, 172, 184–88, 313n.61, 313n.63, 313–14n.67

Songs and Ballads (Lover), 180

sorrow. See death; grief

"The Southern Soldier Boy" (song), 313n.63

spelling mistakes

as source of shame, 25–26, 48

writing as one speaks, 9–10, 26–27, 251–52, 264n.33, 265n.41, 265n.43, 266n.47

Spencer, C. L., 311n.32

stable attachments, longing for, 16, 184–85, 201–2. See also belonging

Stearns, Peter, 257–58n.13, 273n.160

Stevens, Edward, 248, 336n.9

Stott, Richard, 296n.88

Strode, C. D., 310n.26

Strong, T. W., 193, 318n.106

Talley, Thomas, 176–77, 309n.15

teasing. See jokes and humor

Thompson, E. P., 15

United States Christian Commission, 36–37

valentine lotteries, 7, 195–96, 318nn.112–13

valentine poems, 193–95, 194f, 310n.26, 317nn.99–100, 318nn.105–6

Valentine Writers, 317n.99

Vincent, David, 328n.119

White, Charles T., 277n.48

widows and widowers

Civil War Pension law for, 162–63, 214–16, 324–25nn.71–73, 326nn.87–88

community support after loss of husbands in Civil War, 213

condolence letters for, 209–10, 216, 322nn.46–47

grief and, 211–13, 323–24n.66, 324n.70

nonromantic courtship patterns of, 98–99

poverty following Civil War, 214–16

remarriage of, 214–15, 325n.76, 325–26n.83

Wiley, Bell, 280n.101

Williams, Heather, 289n.94

women. See also gender; widows and widowers

age and eligibility for marriage, 75–76

average age of marriage, 58, 76, 114

Civil War Pension law for, 162–63, 214–16, 324–25nn.71–73, 326nn.87–88

employment and sexual misconduct assumptions, 90

geographic place and courtship patterns, 53–59, 57f, 74, 84, 89–91

literacy rates, 335n.3

physical attraction to men, 59, 61, 73–74, 77, 278n.55

348 INDEX

women (*cont.*)
  prostitution and, 55, 119–20, 131, 296–97nn.89–90
  sexual experiences and advice to one another, 111, 128–30, 290n.2, 295nn.81–82, 297n.93
  sexual harassment and assault, 7, 122–24, 130
  sexual jokes and humor of, 122, 124–25
  signaling interest, 84, 86–87, 179
  symbols of affection in marriage, 133–41, 171
  traits men looked for, 61–64, 135–36, 278n.58, 278n.64, 278n.66
  waiting for men to propose marriage, 73–74
working class. *See also* class, courtship; literacy; nonromantic love; poetry
  community bond and courtship patterns, 50–51, 60–61
  defined, 2
  distrust of progress, 13, 16
  education and, 192–93, 316–17nn.93–97
  in-group marriage expectations for, 51–52

motivation for letter writing, 22–23
photographs of, 21*f*–18*f*, 35*f*, 38*f*, 45*f*, 57*f*, 60*f*, 71*f*, 92*f*, 104*f*, 127*f*, 136*f*, 144*f*, 226*f*
physical attraction and spouse selection, 62, 77
racial prejudice and, 105–8
reciprocity expectations for letters, 47
romantic love and, 99–101, 133, 158–59, 201, 239–40, 289n.70
sharing letters, 12, 25, 37–40, 38*f*, 48, 111–16, 146–47, 158–59, 264n.32, 291n.11, 292n.18
writing instruction. *See* literacy
writing instruments and paper, 24, 36–37
writing skills, shame and, 14, 23–26, 44, 48–49, 264n.25
written vs. oral culture. *See* oral vs. written culture

"yours until death" closings, 137–38, 199–202, 231–32, 298n.21, 320n.13, 330n.145

Zboray, Ronald and Mary, 265n.43, 315n.80